DESTINATION PEKING

Born and currently based in London, Paul French lived and worked in Shanghai for many years. After a career as a widely published analyst and commentator on China he is now a full-time author, focusing on China and Asia in the first half of the twentieth century. He has written a number of books, including a history of foreign correspondents in China and a biography of the legendary Shanghai adman, journalist and adventurer Carl Crow.

His true crime book *Midnight in Peking* was a *New York Times* Bestseller, a BBC Radio 4 Book of the Week, a Mystery Writers' of America Edgar award winner for Best Fact Crime, and a Crime Writers' Association (UK) Dagger award for non-fiction. His Kirkus-starred book *City of Devils: A Shanghai Noir* focuses on the dancehalls, casinos and cabarets of wartime Shanghai. Both *Midnight in Peking* and *City of Devils* are being adapted for film and television.

French is a regular contributor and book reviewer for various publications including the *South China Morning Post, Literary Hub, Financial Times Weekend, Mekong Review,* CNN and *Crime Reads.* He occasionally works in audio drama with productions including *Death at the Airport: The Plot Against Kim Jong-nam* for BBC Radio 4, *Peking Noir* for BBC Radio 3, and the twelve-part Audible Original, *Murders of Old China.*

Praise for *Midnight in Peking*

'A fascinating tale of life and death in a city on the brink of all-out war.'
— *Time*

'He resurrects a period that was filled with glitter as well as evil, but was never, as readers will appreciate, known for being dull.'
— *The Economist*

'The most talked-about read in town this year.'
— *New Yorker*

'A crime story set among sweeping events is reminiscent of Graham Greene, particularly *The Third Man*, while French's terse, tightly-focussed style has rightly been compared to Chandler. *Midnight in Peking* deserves a place alongside both these masters.'
— *The Independent* (UK)

'It is the storytelling flair that marks *Midnight in Peking* so highly above the run-of-the-mill true crime stories: with its false leads and twists, it sucks the reader in like the best fiction.'
— *The Scotsman*

'The shocking true tale, combined with prose you can't drag yourself away from, makes *Midnight in Peking* a work of non-fiction as compulsive as any bestselling crime novel.'
— *Sunday Express* (UK)

'One of the best portraits of between-the-wars China that has yet been written.'
— *Wall Street Journal*

Praise for *City of Devils*

'It's hard to go wrong with dope, decadence, and the demimonde . . . French recounts all this with great energy and brio.'
— Gary Krist, *The New York Times Book Review*

'Wonderfully atmospheric . . . French's two-fisted prose makes this deep noir history unforgettable.'
— *Publishers Weekly* (starred review)

'Nothing lasts forever: In 1930s Shanghai, the no-holds-barred gangster scene was run by an American ex-Navyman and a Jewish man who'd fled Vienna. Their milieu – and its end – comes alive.'
— Carolyn Kellogg, *Los Angeles Times*

'A tale of flash and noir demands a voice to match; fortunately, French combines the skills of a scholar with the soul of Dashiell Hammett.'
— Boris Kachka, *Vulture*

'Move over Weimar: Paul French's *City of Devils*, a history of glam and seedy interwar Shanghai's refugees and criminals, is nostalgic noir at its best.'
— *New York Magazine*

'The story is brought alive by Mr French's Shanghai-noir telling, which echoes Dashiell Hammett and James Ellroy. He grips his reader to the end.'
— *The Economist*

'French's louche and moodily lit recreation of Shanghai is thrillingly done. This atmospheric survey hangs on the zoot-suited shoulders of the two leads. French's story chops and changes between Jack and Joe as they make their wayward ways east until fates and hardscrabble fortunes collide in the dive bars and dancehalls of Shanghai's Blood Alley.'
— Laura Freeman, *The Times* (UK)

'A story with the dark resonance of James Ellroy's novel *L.A. Confidential* and the seedy glamour of Alan Furst's between-the-wars mysteries . . . Reader advisory: By the time you are done with this extraordinary book, you will believe in devils, too.'
— Mary Ann Gwinn, *Newsday*

Also by Paul French

Strangers on the Praia: A story of Refugees and Resistance in
Wartime Macao

Murders of Old China (an Audible Original)

Destination Shanghai: 18 True Stories of Those Who Went…

City of Devils: A Shanghai Noir

Midnight in Peking: How the Murder of a Young Englishwoman
Haunted the Last Days of Old Peking

The Badlands: Decadent Playground of Old Peking

Bloody Saturday: Shanghai's Darkest Day

Supreme Leader: The Making of Kim Jong-un

Betrayal in Paris: How the Treaty of Versailles Led to China's
Long Revolution

The Old Shanghai A-Z

Through the Looking Glass: China's Foreign Journalists
from Opium Wars to Mao

Carl Crow – A Tough Old China Hand: The Life, Times,
and Adventures of an American in Shanghai

North Korea: The Paranoid Peninsula – A Modern History

DESTINATION PEKING

by

Paul French

BLACKSMITH BOOKS

DESTINATION PEKING

ISBN 978-988-79639-6-7
Text and photographs © 2021 Paul French unless otherwise noted

Published by Blacksmith Books
Unit 26, 19/F, Block B, Wah Lok Industrial Centre,
37-41 Shan Mei Street, Fo Tan, Hong Kong
Tel: (+852) 2877 7899
www.blacksmithbooks.com

Edited by James Smith
Printed in Hong Kong

First printing 2021

And once again for A.V.W.

'Biography is the most universally pleasant,
universally profitable of all reading'
– Thomas Carlyle
(and the opening quote to the 1922 edition
of the *China Who's Who Directory*)

Contents

Introduction

'I pride myself that I know the city of Peking rather better than most Europeans, although no one can be wholly familiar with its infinite complexities, or can ever know all the secrets which lie between the blank grey walls of its narrow hutongs.'
                                        – JP Marquand (1937)[1]

Destination Peking is a companion book to my previously published *Destination Shanghai*. It is similar in format – eighteen tales of foreigners who lived their lives, or sojourned briefly, in Peking in the first half of the twentieth century. For some the city would be home for most of their lives, for others perhaps only a temporary visit though one that profoundly affected their lives in some way.

The subjects of this volume, like their contemporaries in *Destination Shanghai*, came from a variety of backgrounds, from the ultra-wealthy such as the Woolworth's heiress Barbara Hutton and her husband the Prince Mdivani of the famous Russian émigré "Marrying Mdivanis", to the very poor such as Mona Monteith, who worked in the city as a prostitute in the first year of the twentieth century. Many had come seeking adventure in the ancient city – writers such as JP Marquand hoped to find amazing tales to tell. Some came as criminals, and others as policemen to catch them. Others identified with China's inter-war causes and ideologies – Americans Ellen Newbold La Motte and Emily Crane Chadbourne found during their sojourn in Peking a cause that would define the rest of their lives as they launched campaigns against the opium trade and opium use; Edgar and Helen Foster Snow discovered Chinese communism; Bill Reusswig and Martha Sawyers left Peking to dedicate their artistic talents to supporting China's war effort against Japan. Shanghai may have been perceived as the great city of opportunity, but Peking could provide too - Olga Fischer carved out a career as an opera singer; the artists Bertha Lum

---

1   JP Marquand, *Thank You, Mr Moto* (London: Fontana, 1937), p.93.

and Isamu Noguchi found inspiration and some commercial success in the shadow of the Forbidden City. Peking, of course, though no longer an imperial city after 1911 or a capital city after 1927, was always a centre of Chinese political machinations – Lev Karakhan journeyed from Moscow to Peking as the first Bolshevik emissary to China; the senior Nazis Eugen and Helma Ott sought to bring their ideology to Asia and Peking.

But, perhaps most of all, it was a city that attracted those enchanted by its beauty, its singular and unique aesthetic enshrined in the lanes and alleyways of the city's numerous hutongs, hidden courtyards, walls, gates and towers. JP Marquand, a long-underrated chronicler of the city in the 1930s, wrote: 'The Hutongs, or alleys, open into irregular squares and taper off again into narrow meanderings. There are no street signs, and nearby the only light comes from occasional corner shrines, dedicated to the Goddess of Mercy, or to the Water God, or to the God of Earth. The walls of the hidden courtyards close about us, making our footsteps echo.'[2]

Foreign visitors and sojourners admired and studied Peking's opera, banquet cuisine, the historic charm and grandeur of its temples, shrines, the *pailou* that arched across the street, ancient stele, and imperial past. Harold Acton and Desmond Parsons, both independently wealthy English aesthetes, lived in beautiful hutong courtyard houses; the young artist Denton Welch (born in Shanghai) spent cold days in the early 1930s antiquing around the Panjiayuan market, while Wallis Spencer, the woman who later become the Duchess of Windsor, hunted fine jade on, of course, Jade Street.[3] The young American travel writer Harry Hervey sought inspiration and story ideas walking atop the Tartar Wall along the edge of the Legation Quarter – observing camel trains approaching the city from beyond the wall while foreign soldiers guarded the embassies within. Arriving on the Trans-Siberian Railway, Robert Byron hunkered down in a peony-strewn hutong courtyard to write of his travels from Palestine to Afghanistan along *The Road to Oxiana*, while the notorious "Hermit of Peking" Sir Edmund Backhouse in his last years penned his fantastical memoirs of the sexual underbelly of the Forbidden City.

Those who made Peking their destination composed the various elements of what was known then as the city's "foreign colony". The first

2   Marquand, *Thank You, Mr Moto*, p.96.
3   Now Baoyu Shijie, which runs parallel to Qianmenwai Avenue.

half of the twentieth century was a tumultuous one for Peking. Mona Monteith arrived at the American Legation negotiating the rubble remaining from the Boxer Uprising and the Siege of the Legations a year before. The preserved bodies of dead soldiers still awaited repatriation. Over the next decades the foreign colony faced the fall of the Qing Dynasty, political upheaval, numerous warlords, the Japanese occupation of the city, and the declaration of the People's Republic of China in 1949.

The Beijing of the first half of the twentieth century was visually and physically very different to today's giant megalopolis of twenty-two million people. Before 1949 the city's population was approximately three million people. Redevelopment and destruction meant a major eradication of the city's physical past. The ancient walls, gates and towers of the city were mostly pulled down – only a handful remain. Roads were widened; the vast soullessness of Tiananmen Square created. Suburbs have sprawled in all directions; ring roads have multiplied. Perhaps the greatest loss of all: the hutongs.

The hutong – the ancient arteries and veins of the city, a unique Peking form of architecture, narrow alleys that once proliferated throughout the city and really defined it for so many residents and visitors. In 1949 there were over three thousand largely pristine hutong. In 1990 the number fell to 2,250 as large-scale demolition commenced. By 2004 just 1,300 remained, with many of those condemned, the ubiquitous character for demolition (*chai*, or 拆) chalked on whole hutong alleys due to be eradicated before the city's showcase Olympics. In 2012 just nine hundred remained; and today? Best estimate is now less than three hundred, with virtually all those remaining being changed significantly by the addition of new and out-of-character buildings, or truncated by demolition.[4]

In the first half of the twentieth century Peking was a city that got dark early, and that generally went to bed early too. For decades there were electric streetlights only within the Legation Quarter. But this in itself made the city special, magical. JP Marquand once again:

---

4   Hard metrics of hutong destruction and preservation are hard to find. These statistics are a mix of the last survey of the Nationalist government in 1949, then People's Republic of China official statistics, and later those of the Shijia Hutong Museum and other heritage NGOs, such as they exist in China.

There is no place in the world as strange as Peking at night, when the darkness covers the city like a veil, and when incongruous and startling sights and sounds come to one out of the black. The gilded, carved façades of shops; the swinging candle lanterns; the figures by the tables in the smoky yellow light of tea houses; the sound of song; the twanging of stringed instruments; the warm strange smell of soy bean oil; all come out of nowhere to touch one elusively, and are gone.[5]

The foreign colony, except for the stateless Russian émigrés and the city's foreign criminal milieu, lived privileged lives. Though foreigners lived across the city they tended to cluster in and around the Legation Quarter, which was a sanctuary from the incredibly cacophonous and chaotic Chinese city outside. This remained so throughout the first half of the twentieth century, even if in their claustrophobic confines they sometimes felt, as Peter Fleming, the intrepid travel journalist (and older brother of James Bond creator Ian), visiting in the 1930s, wrote: 'like fish in an aquarium, going round and round... serene and glassy-eyed.'[6]

Finally, we shouldn't ignore the rivalry between Shanghai and Peking that has existed for nearly two centuries at least. The opposing Chinese cultural outlooks are termed *haipai* vs *jingpai,* the Shanghai style vs the Peking style. Both cities have their respective supporters and detractors both among Chinese people and those foreigners who have pitched up on China's shores over the decades. I genuinely hold great affection for each metropolis, but for different reasons, and find it mildly annoying when someone – Chinese or foreign – elevates one over the other. Many comparisons between the two have been observed over time. *New Yorker* writer Emily Hahn appreciated the Peking evoked in this book, even while she preferred Shanghai: 'Let the aesthetes sigh for their Peking and their dream world. I don't reject Peking... it is a reward for the afterlife. Shanghai is for now, for the living me.'[7] Yet how many sojourners in China, as Harold Acton noted, 'came to spend a fortnight in Peking yet lingered on, for the rest of their lives?'[8]

Paul French – October 2020

5   Marquand, *Thank You, Mr Moto*, pp.94-95.

6   Peter Fleming, *News From Tartary* (London: Jonathan Cape, 1936).

7   Emily Hahn, *China to Me* (New York: Doubleday, Doran & Co., 1944), p.3.

8   Harold Acton, *Peonies and Ponies* (London: Chatto & Windus, 1941), p.7.

A note on names and spellings

Names in this book reflect the spellings commonly used in the first half of the twentieth century. Hence Peking and not Beijing; Nanking and not Nanjing. Where Chinese people were commonly known by Western names to foreign audiences, these are used, rather than the Pinyin romanisations. Additionally, I have used the best-known variations of some Chinese names rather than their more modern variants, such as Sun Yat-sen rather than Sun Zhongshan, and Chiang Kai-shek as opposed to Jiang Jieshi.

Within the text I have used the road names of Peking that were applicable at the time. These are invariably either Wade-Giles (e.g. Chang An Chieh for today's Changan, or Chang'an Jie), or alternative names commonly used by the foreign colony. For instance, the main commercial thoroughfare now known as Wangfujing was usually rendered as Wangfuting between the wars while being generally known by the foreign community as Morrison Street (after the missionary and pioneering Sinologist Robert Morrison, though often confused with the London *Times* correspondent George Morrison who, by chance, lived on the street). Similarly, many roads in the Legation Quarter were also known by European names.

A list of the roads used in the text and their current names, as well as the names of Chinese towns, cities and provinces both before and after 1949 are added as an appendix at the end of the book. The former hutong names have been rendered into English – where they make sense and were known as such – and the current name. For instance: Kuei Chia Chang Hutong was known in English as Armour Factory Alley and is today called Kuijiachang Hutong.

Peking, Peiping and Beijing…

Peking's name has changed many times over the centuries, but this book only concerns the twentieth century. "Peking" is a spelling created by French missionaries of the seventeenth and eighteenth centuries. From 1928 to 1949 the city was officially known as Peiping ("Northern Peace") after Chiang Kai-shek moved the capital to Nanking. Peiping sometimes appears as Beiping. The spelling Beijing was adopted for use within China upon the approval of Hanyu Pinyin on February 11, 1958, during the Fifth Session of the First National People's Congress. As none of the essays in this collection concern the period after February 1958, and as Peiping/Beiping remain somewhat obscure, I have used the name Peking for the city throughout.

The Carl Crow Map of Peiping

The map of Peking (Peiping) used overleaf is from Carl Crow's *Travelers' Handbook for China*. The guidebook was first published in 1913 and swiftly went through several updates and reprints. The first editions of the book were published by the Hwa-Mei Book Concern of Shanghai in China, and the San Francisco News Company in the USA. Later editions with new and revised material were published, up to the final revised edition in 1933, by the famous Kelly & Walsh in Shanghai and Hong Kong, and Dodd, Mead & Company of New York in the USA. This map is obviously from a post-1927 edition given it is titled "Peiping".

The maps in Crow's *Handbook for China* were also updated over the years. We cannot be sure of the cartographer though the most likely candidate appears to be the long-serving art director at his advertising agency Carl Crow Inc. in Shanghai, a Mr Y. Obie.

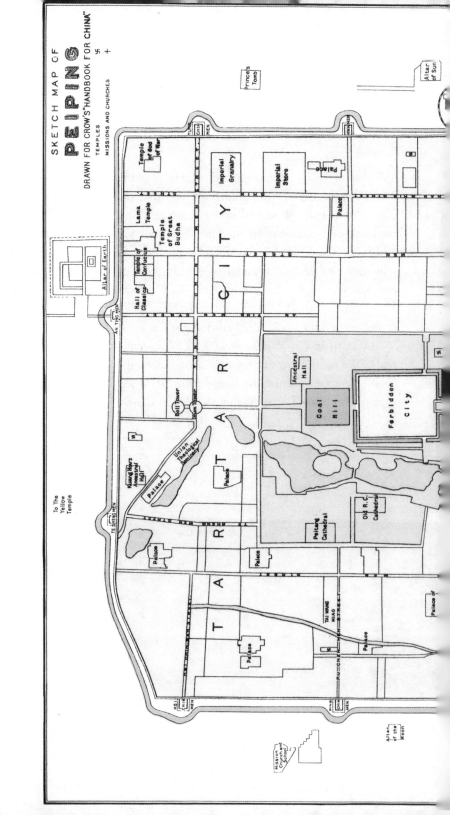

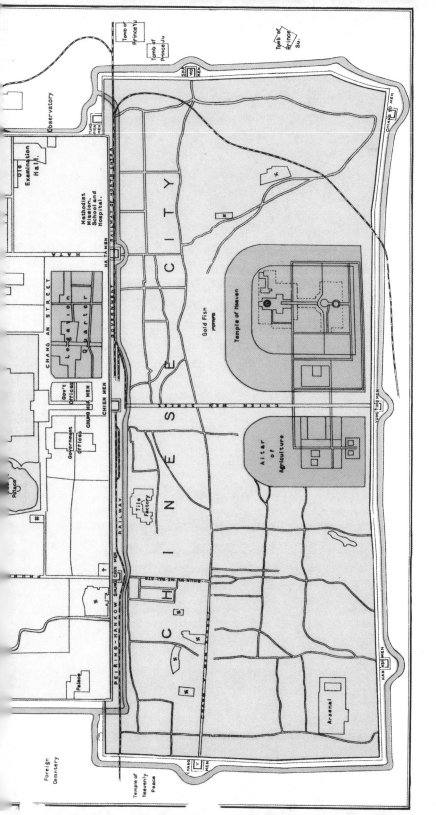

The Rooftop of the Grand Hôtel de Pékin:
Wallis Spencer's Peking World & Those Who Went Up
on the Roof (1924)

The Grand Hotel de Pekin (Pei ching ta fan tien) – Estd: 1920
Chang An Chieh – Peking – Tels: 3151, 3152 & 3153
Cable "Pekinotel" & "Grandhotel" – Facing the Legation Quarter [9]

9   Ed. Alex Ramsay, *The Peking Who's Who* (Tientsin: Tientsin Press, 1922).

Truly a Grand Hôtel

It is fitting to start this collection with an essay about the Grand Hôtel de Pékin. From the moment it opened its doors in 1915 just about everybody who was an established member of the city's foreign colony, as well as anybody sojourning in Peking temporarily, passed through the doors of the Grand Hôtel de Pékin – certainly nearly everybody in this book. That trio of English aesthetes, Harold Acton, Desmond Parsons and Robert Byron, drank cocktails as they watched swallows arc and dive over the Forbidden City. The American socialite and traveller Adelaide Hooker, her new beau the established novelist of Bostonian manners JP Marquand, and the Japanese-American artist Isamu Noguchi all attended tea-dances in the hotel's ballroom. Freelance journalists and left-wing activists Edgar and Helen Foster Snow, aspiring Hollywood screenwriter Harry Hervey, the Prince Mdivani and his new wife the Woolworth's heiress Barbara Hutton, her cousin the playboy Jimmy Donahue, as well as the anti-opium activists Ellen Newbold La Motte and Emily Crane Chadbourne, all stayed in suites at the Grand Hôtel. The first Bolshevik ambassador to China, Lev Karakhan, the Italian fascist Count Gian Galeazzo Ciano, and the senior Nazi party members Eugen and Helma Ott, all attended functions in the hotel. Bertha Lum sold her art from The Camel's Bell shop on the third floor; Olga Fischer-Togo performed

Postcard of the Grand Hôtel de Pékin, 1920

light operetta there at charity concerts to help Chinese flood victims. Even that most notorious recluse Sir Edmund Backhouse visited to see his good friend Henri Vetch, who ran the French Bookshop in the lobby. The Grand Hôtel de Pékin was Grand Central Station, Times Square and Piccadilly Circus all rolled into one; it was the Ritz and the Savoy, the Algonquin and the Waldorf Astoria, Paris's Hôtel de Crillon and the Hôtel Lutetia, the Adlon of Berlin, the Metropol of Moscow – in Peking. In 1915 the Grand Hôtel de Pékin was smarter and more modern than any hotel in Shanghai or Hong Kong. Frank Lloyd Wright's Imperial Hotel in Tokyo, the Peninsula in Kowloon, and Sir Victor Sassoon's Cathay on the Shanghai Bund would all come later.[10] In 1915 the two grandest hotels in all Asia were undoubtedly the Sarkie Brothers' Raffles Hotel in Singapore and the Grand Hôtel de Pékin.

The Grand Hôtel was where, for nearly half a century, the milieu that populates this collection of essays – the foreign colony of Peking – the old timers and China Hands; the tourists and sojourners; the diplomats and journalists; the super-wealthy and those just able to afford the basic *tiffin* all congregated. It was where struggling Russian émigrés spent their last Chinese dollars to eat and drink alongside Americans with Mexican silver dollars to burn. And, of course, it was where the infamous 'Peking gossips' of the Legation Quarter met and whispered poison in each other's ears.[11] Many who came to the Grand Hôtel were famous and regularly appeared on the front pages of newspapers around the world – perhaps most famously the movie star Anna May Wong who drew crowds of film fans to the hotel's doors seeking a glimpse of her. Other guests were not so famous at the time – but one day would eclipse even Hollywood movie stars…

A navy wife checks in

Bessie Wallis Warfield-Spencer knew virtually nobody when she arrived at the Grand Hôtel. She had long dropped the Bessie and was known simply

10   Frank Lloyd Wright's Imperial Hotel replaced the original building designed by Yuzuru Watanabe, which was destroyed in 1922 by fire. The Kadoorie family-owned Peninsula in Hong Kong opened for business in 1928. Sir Victor Sassoon's Cathay Hotel on the Bund was not completed until 1929.
11   Damien de Martel & Léon de Hoyer, *Silhouettes of Peking* (Peking: China Booksellers, 1926), p.6.

as Wallis from a relatively young age. Then the Warfield got lost somewhere along the way, and when she did finally divorce her first husband, the name Spencer too. She remarried and became Wallis Simpson and finally, after another rather mundane and provincial divorce and a spectacular and unprecedented abdication, she became Wallis, Duchess of Windsor. She was to marry a king, acquire a grand title and an enviable jewellery collection, but be forced to live in exile for the rest of her life – in Portugal, Barbados, France. As the world saw it then, forcing a king to abdicate, to choose between her and his crown, a twice-divorced American and his country, between a random love and the duties of his birth right, was a heinous crime. Wallis became "that woman". It was a bitter time that has lingered in the public imagination through prurient rumour, baseless innuendo, countless bad television movies and Penny Dreadful hagiographies by openly declared enemies and supposed friends turned gossips. The cheap tabloid character assassinations regularly continue still in our time.

But that was all later, many years after Wallis's Peking adventure; a sojourn that began on a crisp, cold, star-filled night just before Christmas 1924. A shivering Wallis Spencer arrived late in the cavernous lobby to check in at the Grand Hôtel de Pékin on the city's wide Chang An Chieh, the Avenue of Eternal Peace.

Passport proffered, room key issued, she immediately went to the roof to take in the best possible view of the city. Wallis was to spend the next eight months or so in Peking. She arrived as the abused ex-wife of a drunk and violent American naval officer, Earl Winfield "Win" Spencer Jr. She'd felt compelled to leave him behind in Hong Kong, where he was posted with the US Navy's South China Patrol, after the beatings got too bad and she was hospitalised. Win had showed no particular inclination to stop her going and had promptly sunk back into the bottle. Wallis desperately wanted a divorce and her freedom back.

Wallis wasn't exactly unknowing about the world. She had spent brief amounts of time among the diplomatic crowds of Washington DC and Paris already, as well as some time in Hong Kong, Canton and most recently, after ditching Spencer, a few weeks in the International Settlement of Shanghai. But this sojourn in Peking was to change Wallis fundamentally. She was to emerge from the cocoon of the Baltimore girl married to a disappointed and frustrated naval commander who

Earl Winfield "Win" Spencer Jr.

drank too much and was a little too quick with his fists where women were concerned, into a sophisticated and cosmopolitan woman, fashionable and stylish, able to move in any social circles and command attention in any room, up to and including those of the British monarchy.

It was to be on the rooftop of the Grand Hôtel de Pékin that Wallis Spencer began her journey to become the woman the world would become obsessed with just over a decade later. As she climbed the stairs to the top of the hotel, Wallis was following a well-worn trail already. There were other rooftops – both the Grand Hôtel des Wagons-Lits and the Hotel du Nord opened up their rooftops, though after the Grand Hôtel de Pékin, and neither were ever to be as grand or as popular. The Grand Hôtel's was the Peking rooftop sojourners invariably visited soon after their arrival – to drink cocktails and dance to the band, but also to gaze across the ancient city from just about its highest accessible point.

*

But in the winter of 1924 things looked bleak for Wallis as her freezing cold and long-delayed train, "The International", departed from Tientsin, and finally pulled into Peking at the Chienmen Railway Station. The journey had taken a gruelling thirty-eight hours to cover the barely seventy miles between the two northern Chinese cities thanks to a typhoid outbreak in Tientsin, marauding bandits and skirmishing warlords. One traveller on the train at that time, the American art collector Gertrude Bass Warner, wrote that (even in First Class where Wallis, as a white woman, automatically sat) the seats had no springs, making for a rough ride, especially hard on the spine as the padding was all removed from behind the leather of the seats. The heating was not working thanks to coal shortages, and the train was as cold inside as out. Bass Warner recalled that passengers could see each other's breath as if everyone was constantly smoking, which they were too, only adding to the foggy atmosphere in the carriages where opening a window would have caused a riot.[12] Chinese waiters and porters constantly served weak green tea. There was a plush First-Class dining car serving beer, whisky soda (invariably known as a "*stengah*" in China) and pots of coffee. The dining car had tables for informal games of poker with other passengers, or patience by yourself. The Chinese dining car stewards in their white uniforms ensured nobody's cup ever completely emptied and small dishes of *dianxin* – Chinese snacks – were always refilled. Passengers marvelled at how the stewards were able to keep the dining car clean and maintain the constant supply of these provisions despite the chaos that surrounded them and the train. Soldiers stood on guard on the steel platforms between carriages to prevent bandits boarding the train.

Arriving in Peking Wallis was exhausted and decidedly uncertain about what fate her immediate future held. But she was also excited. This was her first visit to a real Chinese city – Hong Kong had been a British colony, her brief time in Canton was spent entirely cooped up in her hotel room on the foreign enclave of Shameen Island, while the Shanghai International Settlement was of course a treaty port. Peking was really China – camel trains still arrived and departed from the nearby Chienmen Gate; the Forbidden City was close by; Chinese policemen patrolled Chinese streets; Peking was the capital. For sure 1924 was a particularly cold December - snow on the ground, vicious cold winds sweeping down from the Gobi Desert that chilled the alighting passengers to the bone – but the excitement of arriving in Peking was still palpable.

12   Gertrude Bass Warner, *Escape from Peking/Three Japanese Letters*, The Gertrude Bass Warner Papers, University of Oregon Libraries, Special Collections & Digital Archives, Box 10, Folder 10.

To the best of her knowledge Wallis knew just one person in Peking – Colonel Louis Little, the Commander of the Military Guard at the American Legation. Wallis had met Colonel Little before, several years previously, when he was stationed at the American Embassy in Paris. He was a friend of her Baltimore relations. Colonel Little was waiting for the train from Tientsin. He escorted Wallis from the station, through the city's Legation Quarter, past the American Legation, and then the Soviet, before turning left and passing the Japanese and British Legations that faced each other across the street, down to the broad expanse of Chang An Chieh and the Grand Hôtel. It seems that Louis Little, a man with some sway due to being America's most senior military commander in the city in 1924, had secured these rather sumptuous and expensive digs for Wallis. She was by no means a woman of independent means. She had no trust fund or monthly cheque from back home in Baltimore beyond a small inheritance from her grandmother. Her husband, Win, had upon their separation earlier that year agreed to a US$225 a month stipend to be deducted and sent to Wallis from his US Navy pay – what the Navy termed an "allotment".

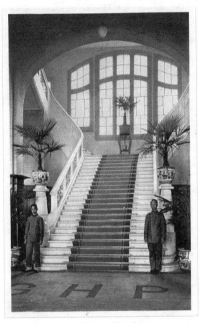

The lobby of the Grand Hôtel in 1920

As well as the financial question of being able to afford to stay at the Grand Hôtel de Pékin, it was also the case that getting a room in the hotel, or indeed any half-decent hotel in Peking, was problematic in December 1924. The Northern Chinese warlord Chang Tso-lin's troops were surrounding Peking ready to take the city by force from rival warlord Feng Yu-Hsiang if he refused to surrender.[13] Chang dubbed himself the "Tiger of Mukden"; Feng was dubbed the "Betrayal General" as,

---

13   The warlords Zhang Zuolin and Feng Yuxiang respectively.

unsurprisingly given his sobriquet, he had betrayed everyone he had ever done a deal with. Peking was effectively under siege by warlord armies.

Into this maelstrom arrived Wallis, met at the station by a Colonel of the US Marines who had high-level access to a suite at the Grand Hôtel. Which begs a question about why a single woman would make this journey at such a perilous time. Wallis wasn't simply coming on holiday. She had brought official American government documents from Shanghai and Tientsin to Peking and, it appears, the US Legation was willing to stand Wallis a short stay at the Grand Hôtel in return for services rendered to the US Government.

And so, despite the cold, the smattering of snow and the late hour, Wallis climbed the staircase to the famous roof and looked out across Peking that December evening for the first time. The hotel was to be her home for the next month, through Christmas 1924 and into the New Year of 1925. She got to know the city's best hotel, and its roof, extremely well.

Up on the roof...

Without doubt in the interwar years the Grand Hôtel de Pékin was the city's oldest and most splendid hotel establishment. Situated just north of the Foreign Legation Quarter and just to the east of the Forbidden City it was perfectly situated at the epicentre of Peking foreign colony life. Its rooftop bar and open-air dancing were the stuff of legend – wealthy sojourners, royalty, celebrities all took suites there, the young blades and beauties flocked to the rooftop tea dances, while Peking's mid-ranking foreign colony dropped their parcels and packages after a hard day's shopping at the department stores, curio shops and jewellers of Morrison Street, and the nearby Tung An Shih Chang, known to the foreign colony as the Morrison Street Bazaar[14]), and took *tiffin* (high tea –

14   Now the Dong An Market. After a fire in 1912 the market was a more permanent structure of steel, glass and iron with skylights, similar to a European *grand magasin*, or arcade. Arlington and Lewisohn in their classic *In Search of Old Peking*, first published in 1935, described the market as 'a kind of covered-in miniature town of its own, crammed with small shops and stalls, where you can buy anything from a cent's worth of melon seeds to the latest in radio sets, and everything at very reasonable prices.' It was demolished around 2008.

or as the famous China Coast pidgin-English poet Shamus A'Rabbit once described it, 'A midday meal of such proportions as to induce sleep'[15]).

The Beaux Arts style seven-storey steel and concrete fireproof hotel had two hundred rooms, all with en-suite bathrooms, flush toilets and steam heating. Each room had a telephone, though in 1924 you could only make calls to other rooms in the hotel and within Peking to the few people with telephones. There was a tearoom for *tiffin* on the ground floor with dancing every night on a sprung wood floor. The hotel had its own orchestra composed originally of mainly Italians, and after 1917 as they appeared in the city in greater numbers, Russian émigré musicians, who performed a programme of light classical music during dinner with the emphasis on waltzes. Later, jazz bands would become a staple. The mirrored ballroom was supposed to imitate the Hall of Mirrors at Versailles. French chefs created dishes that were complemented by the finest and largest wine cellar in China. Autobuses, manned by liveried porters, met all arriving trains at the Chienmen Station to collect passengers and their often-voluminous luggage – Barbara Hutton arrived a decade later in 1934 with fifteen Louis Vuitton trunks.[16] Each train seemed to bring more "*Malalo*" (the name the Chinese gave to tourists from the round-the-world cruise ships who came to town on the train from Tientsin as a side trip to their holiday). The wealthiest *malalo* checked into the Grand Hôtel de Pékin.

15   Shamus A'Rabbit, *Ballads of the East* (Shanghai: AR Hager, 1937), p.52.
16   It should be noted that Hutton was travelling extremely light on that trip – she often travelled with fifty-five trunks, eclipsing Marlene Dietrich's usual twenty-three that shocked the press at the same time. For Hutton, fifteen cases was effectively backpacking!

In the lobby was a branch of the Thomas Cook Travel Agency, American Helen Burton's famous The Camel's Bell store (which also had a showroom on the third floor), and the bookshop of Frenchman Henri Vetch who bought up the libraries of any members of the Peking colony leaving and sold new libraries to any 'griffins' arriving.[17] The lobby also had a number of smaller shops selling antiques, curios, carpets, embroidery, jewellery and jade.

But the rooftop of the Grand Hôtel de Pékin was its most famous attribute. It was reached by one of two American-made Otis elevators, the first to be installed in Peking. The spacious roof garden included a bar, bamboo tables and chairs, a bandstand and a dance floor. During dances a local radio station would often broadcast live. The summer was dedicated to open-air dancing, but visitors went up to the roof year-round for the unparalleled views across what was then a decidedly low-rise city. Only the radio communications mast in the American Legation compound was higher. From the top of the Grand Hôtel one could look out across the Forbidden City, the Legation Quarter and, so it was claimed, on a good day you could see for fifty miles in every direction surrounding the city – out to the Western Hills and beyond.

Anyone who was anyone in foreign Peking visited the roof – certainly visiting wealthy Americans. In 1921 oil magnate John D Rockefeller Jr. looked across eastwards to see the green saddleback roofs and traditional floating swallowtail eaves of the new Peking Union Medical College (PUMC), the city's most modern medical facility and the best in China (outside Shanghai).[18] PUMC had just been built with Rockefeller family money.[19] As a young man between the wars Rockefeller's fellow American Thomas Watson Jr., who was to follow his own millionaire father into the IBM corporation, visited Peking and recalled his visit to the rooftop bar in the company of some English friends, a girl they'd met who was

17   A griffin being the China coast slang for any new arrivals – greenhorns.
18   What Rockefeller didn't know was that these adornments had been added after a suggestion by one of the members of the committee that established the college, a man who was an expert on Chinese architecture and who believed deeply in preserving Peking's traditional skyline, the British diplomat-scholar ETC Werner. See Paul French, *Midnight in Peking* (Beijing: Penguin China, 2012).
19   Mary Brown Bullock, *An American Transplant: The Rockefeller Foundation and Peking Union Medical College* (Berkeley & Los Angeles: University of California Press, 1980).

(immensely shocking to the young men back then) openly living "in sin" with a US Marine stationed at the Legation, a New York debutante, and a French heroin addict. They ordered gin gimlets and sat back to look out over the city at night.[20] The fantastically named Halbert Kellogg Hitchcock was a well-travelled engineer and inventor from Ohio who visited Peking shortly before Wallis arrived in 1923. He took a map of the city up to the roof of the hotel, spread it out and, looking across Peking, tried to identify every point of interest.[21]

The extremely well-travelled Washington DC-born artist Helen Wells Seymour checked into the Grand Hôtel de Pékin in 1924 having experienced much the same as Wallis while travelling up from Shanghai – searchlights on the front and rear of the train, armed guards in every carriage, constant unscheduled stops, fears of bandit attack all the way. Helen was there in the July before Wallis arrived, the rainy season, such as Peking has one. She found it slightly annoying that nobody in the foreign colony dined before 8.30pm and she was constantly hungry in the afternoons and early evenings. On the dry and warm night of Monday July 21, 1924, Helen dined with friends on the roof of the Grand Hôtel de Pékin arriving for the *thé dansant*. She thought the orchestra marvellous and the very notion of dancing under the enormous sky and million stars above Peking thrilling. She noted that many Chinese had come up to the *thé dansant* and that 'there were many lovely Chinese girls dancing.'[22]

In 1933 the Irish playwright George Bernard Shaw arrived at Peking Railway Station on the famous Shanghai Express and immediately took his wife Charlotte to dinner on the roof. Shaw was fascinated by the temple music he could hear on the wind and in a letter recommended Peking to his friend, the composer Edward Elgar, if he wanted to better understand Asian harmonies.[23]

20   Thomas J Watson Jr. & Peter Petre, *Father, Son & Co.: My life at IBM and Beyond* (New York: Bantam, 1990). Incidentally, a 1928 description of a gin gimlet in Peking was, 'gin, and just a spot of lime'.

21   Halbert K Hitchcock, *Trailing the Sun Around the Earth* (New York: GP Putnam's Sons, 1925), p.52.

22   Helen Wells Seymour, *A Japanese Diary* (New Haven, Connecticut: Self Published, 1956), p.136.

23   Letter from Shaw to Elgar, May 30, 1933. Contained in Ed. Dan H Laurence, *Bernard Shaw: Collected Letters, 1926-1950* (London: Max Reinhardt, 1988), pp.341-342.

Soong Ching-ling and George Bernard Shaw, 1933

The Bostonian author JP Marquand checked in in 1934, headed straight to the top floor and also gazed across to the Forbidden City. The view became a fascination for him with repeated visits. He contrasted the quiet and darkness of the Forbidden City with the invasive clanks and screams of the ungreased wheels of the tramcars down below on Chang An Chieh. In 1936 Marquand recreated the rooftop scene, and how easy it was for a newly arrived European or American to slip into Peking foreign colony life, in one of his *Mr Moto* novels (which are far superior to the movie versions): 'The Chinese bar boys were hurrying from table to table with trays weighted with soda bottles and whisky. There was a sound of shaking dice. "Boy," the voices were shouting. "Boy," with the same assurance as the Anglo-Saxon was still the dominant race in the Orient. Several people called to me when I came in. Greenway waved an arm to me. Clough pointed to a chair and I joined them. "Boy," I found myself calling. "Scotch and soda, Boy."'[24]

With darting swallows, the Forbidden City and temple bells on the wind, the Grand Hôtel's roof was always going to be a magnet for the city's community of foreign aesthetes. Around the same time as Marquand was visiting, Harold Acton took his visiting friend, the writer Osbert Sitwell, for cocktails on the roof with others in his aesthete (and largely gay) circle including Desmond Parsons and Acton's first real friends in Peking, the American illustrator Thomas Handforth and Laurence Sickman, an American Sinologist and art historian. Sitwell initially stayed at the Grand Hôtel, requesting a room on the uppermost floor to have the best view possible. The two aesthetes and Acton's friends would spend long evenings looking out over the Forbidden City just after the Chinese New

24   JP Marquand, *Thank You, Mr Moto* (London: Fontana Books, 1937), p.67.

Year in 1934.[25] Sitwell eventually found a courtyard hutong home on Kanyu Hutong (which he translated as Alley of the Sweet Rain[26]) where he worked mornings on his planned book about Brighton and then spent his afternoons exploring the hutongs and temples of the city. [27] Evenings though, if not accompanying Acton to a performance of Peking opera, were often spent back up on the roof of the Grand Hôtel. Sitwell enjoyed Peking, though disliked the occasional dust storms. He described his Peking sojourn in his memoir of his travels in the Far East, *Escape with Me!* [28] Though he only sojourned for a few months and left in the early summer of 1934, Sitwell, like his friend Acton, found Peking a relief from hyper-competitive and busy London. Among his many fond memories of Peking was an encounter with one of the former Imperial Palace eunuchs, a wrinkled and hairless man with a piping voice who enquired of Sitwell: 'Tell me, young man, do you have no group of people (*eunuchs*) like us where you come from?' Sitwell considered the eunuch's question and then replied, 'Yes, indeed we have. We call it Bloomsbury.'[29]

Osbert Sitwell (left); Laurence Sickman

Edgar Snow and his wife Helen moved from Shanghai to Peking in 1933 and stayed in the Grand Hôtel when they first arrived.[30] They were

25   Sitwell recalls his fascination with the Forbidden City in *The Four Continents: Being Discursions on Travel, Art and Life* (London: Macmillan, 1954), pp. 85-91.
26   Now Ganyu Hutong that runs west to east from Wangfujing to Dengshikou subway station.
27   Osbert Sitwell & Margaret Barton, *Brighton* (London: Faber & Faber, 1935).
28   Osbert Sitwell, *Escape with Me! An Oriental Sketch-Book* (London: Macmillan, 1939). *Escape with Me!* is jointly dedicated to Acton and Sickman.
29   John Pearson, *The Sitwells: A Family's Biography* (London: Harcourt Brace Jovanovich, 1978), p.293.
30   Helen Snow, née Foster, and whose writing pseudonym was often Nym Wales.

given the palatial bridal suite and were amazed by the high ceilings and the views across the Forbidden City. It was an immense extravagance for the young couple and they soon moved out and into a series of courtyard houses close by. They then spent some time living in the then rather remote village of Hait'ien (Haidian), near where Edgar was teaching at Yenching University. Wherever they lived in Peking the pair always returned to the Grand Hôtel for drinks and celebrations on the popular Saturday nights – the major night for rooftop dances. Helen spent many hours working in the showroom of Helen Burton's The Camel's Bell as a mannequin for the store's furs, silk gowns and wraps. Edgar would meet her after her modelling sessions and they would head up to the roof for cocktails. After the autumn of 1935, the Snows lived in the sumptuous courtyard house owned by Dr ET Nystrom, a wealthy Swedish geologist. Nystrom was very fond of Helen and would always go to the Saturday night parties on the Grand Hôtel's roof, asking Helen if, after she finished work downstairs, she'd join him. He was obviously a little infatuated with her:

> "Wear your apple-green dress with the court train," he would beg me, and would ask the orchestra for a Viennese waltz as soon as I arrived in the long red-velvet opera cape that was one of Helen Burton's gifts to her local fashion model *(i.e. Helen)*.[31]

Helen loved to dance on the rooftop – an activity Edgar was distinctly less keen on, and so she had to seek out dance partners. However, the number of German and Italian fascists that made the roof their weekend spot rather put her off. Though admitting that the two best dance partners she ever had at the Grand Hôtel were the leading Italian fascist in Peking and a dedicated young Nazi Junker recently posted to China, she felt enough was enough and her dislike of fascism was more important than her love of waltzing.

Edgar Snow was yet to become a well-known name – *Red Star Over China*, the book that would make him, was still a year or two in the future. Anna May Wong arrived in Peking already a celebrity, though a contentious one. The Nationalist government disapproved of her portrayals of Chinese women on screen, but her fans in China were legion

---

31   Helen Foster Snow, *My China Years: A Memoir* (New York: Morrow, 1984), p.149.

Anna May Wong by Carl van Vechten, 1935

and devoted. She had hoped to rent Desmond Parsons's sumptuous Tsui Hua Hutong courtyard home while sojourning in Peking in 1936.[32] But the travel writer Robert Byron, who was housesitting at the time, thought Parsons would be returning from Europe soon and didn't agree to let it to her. So, Wong moved into a suite at the Grand Hôtel where she met a steady stream of reporters eager to interview the Hollywood star on the roof. She also had cocktails and dined there with friends – the Peking-based artist, writer and, later, aide to General Joseph "Vinegar" Stilwell, Frank "Pinky" Dorn, as well as the cameraman HS "Newsreel" Wong, who was working for Hearst Metrotone News and was yet to become internationally famous for his images of a terrified and abandoned baby

32   Now Cui Hua Hutong.

Frank Dorn and Anna May Wong

THE PHILADELPHIA INQUIRER, S

Anna May Wong at Chinese Home

Far from Hollywood, Anna May Wong, Chinese motion picture star, enjoys life in her home at
Peiping, China. The home is famous for its 'Moon Gate' and classic octagonal gates.

Anna May Wong in Peiping, 1936

on the railway tracks in Shanghai the following summer when war came to China.

Also bringing a whiff of Hollywood and fresh from a sojourn in Bali where she stayed with the German artist Walter Spies, the Austrian writer Vicki Baum came in 1936 to see the rooftop and experience the Grand Hôtel de Pékin. She thought that perhaps the Grand Hôtel could be the model for the hotel novel she was planning to set in China in a bid to repeat the success of her 1929 novel *Grand Hotel*, which had taken her to Hollywood when it became an Academy Award-winning movie.[33] Baum was travelling on her Hollywood earnings looking for inspiration. Eventually she opted for Sir Victor Sassoon's more recently opened Cathay Hotel in Shanghai, but she still loved the Grand Hôtel de Pékin.

Wallis moves on…

And it was on the same rooftop that Wallis Spencer, wrapped up warm against the Peking cold, celebrating

33   *Grand Hotel* is of course set in Berlin. Persecuted in Germany as a Jew and having spent time in Los Angeles, Baum wanted to recreate her successful hotel novel in the Far East. Eventually she did in *Hotel Shanghai* (1937 – sometimes alternatively called in English *Shanghai '37* or *Nanking Road*).

the strangest and perhaps loneliest Christmas of her life, had met an old friend, Katherine 'Kitty' Bigelow. It was a completely chance encounter. Wallis had known Kitty back in America when she was also married to a navy airman. That marriage failed and Kitty had gone on to marry a genuine American millionaire, Herman Rogers. Rogers, whose family money was from railway speculation, had a fascination with China. He wanted to write a book about the country, and so had moved the couple to Peking. They lived in high style and had taken a lease on a large and elegant courtyard property on the prestigious Shih-Chia Hutong. As well as being one of the best addresses in the city, Shih-Chia Hutong was not far from the Grand Hôtel, less than a mile east along Chang An Chieh.[34]

Kitty, perhaps a little lonely in a strange city and with her husband working on his book all day, was sympathetic to her old friend's personal circumstances. She immediately invited Wallis to come and stay with her and Herman in their spacious hutong. Wallis's time at the Grand Hôtel de Pékin was running out – the American Legation's largesse had limits; her "allotment" from Win wouldn't stretch to staying any longer in such opulence. Kitty Rogers's kind offer came as a Godsend to Wallis. She packed up and, in January 1925, moved up the road to Kitty and Herman's courtyard home. It wasn't to be the last time she visited the Grand Hôtel de Pékin, but she was no longer a paying guest. Wallis was now a full member of the city's foreign colony – living on a hutong, flagging down rickshaws to the jade markets, attending the race meetings out at Paomachang, taking *tiffin* at the Grand Hôtel. It was to be a glorious six months. She was destined to become one of its most famous legends ever.

By the summer of 1925 Wallis was ready to move on. She'd come to Hong Kong in 1923 as a Navy wife accompanying her husband to his new posting and hoping to restart their unhappy and failing marriage. That hadn't happened. After a brief reconciliation Win Spencer's binge drinking and physical abuse had simply escalated to an impossible level. Wallis had fled to Shanghai in the belief, erroneous as it turned out, that the American Court for China there could grant her a quickie divorce. They couldn't; neither could the Embassy in Peking. Wallis wanted that divorce. There was no going back to Win and no future in remaining

34 Now Shijia Hutong.

married to the man. It was also the case that the political situation in Peking was increasingly chaotic.

Sun Yat-sen had died in March and his funeral cortège passing through the streets of Peking had been the largest since the death of the Empress Dowager Ci Xi in 1909. Without Dr Sun, China's republican revolution appeared rudderless and imperilled. Then the so-called May Thirtieth Movement had led to demonstrations and anger after the Shanghai Municipal Police opened fire on Chinese protesters on May 30, 1925. The shootings sparked international censure and nationwide anti-foreign demonstrations and riots that focussed on Britain and the British. The demonstrations soon spread to Peking. Wallis's rickshaw puller added a Stars and Stripes flag to the back of his vehicle to deter angry protestors from attacking her. It was a real threat. Wallis was in a taxi one day shortly after May 30th when a young protestor attacked the car thinking she was British, smearing his own blood on the windshield. Massive anti-foreign strikes and boycotts broke out in both Hong Kong and Canton, and some merchants in Peking supported them. One day while Wallis was in a curio shop she regularly visited, some protesting students wrote anti-British slogans on her rickshaw in chalk, despite her puller trying to tell them that Wallis was a "'Melican lady". As Wallis exited the shop the students stared at her rather harshly but decided against any more direct action.[35]

It was also the case that Wallis would be twenty-nine years old in June and she felt time and age weighing upon her. She wanted the divorce dealt with and to start life over back in the United States. In her memoirs Wallis wrote simply that, 'in early summer, somewhat in the mood of a female Ulysses, I left for Japan to take a ship to the West Coast.'[36] And so Wallis left Peking and then left China. She took with her a new sense of style that was to define her look in the decades to come – the *Chinois*-inspired dresses, knotwork decorative elements, her trademark chignon hair style. She also took with her quite a few pieces of jade, some Chinese screens, jewellery and various *objets* that stayed with her forever – first at her homes with Ernest Simpson in London, and then at her various homes with the Duke of Windsor through to their final house of exile, 4

35   Wallis, Duchess of Windsor, *The Heart has its Reasons: The Memoirs of the Duchess of Windsor* (London: Michael Joseph, 1956).
36   Ibid.

route du Champ d'Entraînement in Paris's Bois de Boulogne, where she died in 1986.

The time she spent in Peking was Wallis's self-declared 'lotus year'.[37] And her first view of the city was from the roof of the Grand Hôtel de Pékin.

The end of the roof

After the Japanese occupation of Peking in the summer of 1937 the Grand Hôtel's rooftop remained only intermittently open – accessible solely to the Japanese and their permitted hotel guests. However, it was often closed by order of the *Kempeitai* military police who suffered from repeated bouts of "spy mania" and fears of assassination attempts on senior Japanese commanders and collaborationist Chinese leaders. After Pearl Harbor in December 1941 it seemed likely the rooftop would be permanently closed. It was also the case that there were few non-military guests at the hotel and, of course, the city's foreign colony had dwindled to a small fraction of its size just a year or two before.

Still, it did continue in rather reduced circumstances. Laurance "Laurie" Tipton was a formerly Tientsin-based tobacco executive kept under arrest (albeit at Peking's second-best hotel, the Grand Hôtel des Wagons-Lits, rather than an internment camp) during 1942. Billy Christian was a well-known member of the Peking colony who was appointed Chairman of the Relief Committee for Allied Nationals that worked closely with the Swiss Consulate in Peking to represent the interests of British, Americans and other Allied nationals whose diplomatic representatives had had to leave the city. Tipton and Christian were instructed to go to the rooftop of the Grand Hôtel de Pekin in 1942 to meet a Mr Suzuki of the "Japanese Special Police" in Peking. Suzuki was keen to learn English, had plenty of money, access to seemingly limitless bottles of Scotch whisky, and liked to go dancing in what remained of Peking's western-style nightlife.

Amazingly (though this was shortly before full internment for the last Allied nationals remaining in the city) African-American Earl West's band were still playing on the rooftop. Earl Kilgore West had come to China with Earl Whaley's African-American jazz band the Red Hot Syncopators some years before. They had played a lengthy engagement in Shanghai.

37   Ibid.

The Syncopators eventually broke up and split to form several new bands. Earl West, a guitarist, led one group of musicians who all headed north, first to Tientsin's Villa West Lake Hotel, and then to Peking and a contract to play on the rooftop of the Grand Hôtel de Pékin. In Peking, Earl West's band featured both black and white musicians, a Hawaiian-born singer, and a Filipino trumpeter.[38] He was playing the night Tipton and Christian were summoned. Mr Suzuki got drunk that evening and forced Christian and Tipton (at gunpoint) to dance, technically an illegal activity for any Allied national wearing the regulation red armband identifying them as the enemy.

After the war the rooftop re-opened for a short while. Mao is said to have visited it on October 1, 1949 not long after he had just declared the formation of the People's Republic of China in Tiananmen below. But after 1949 it was rarely used. During the Maoist years the hotel was reserved for state guests only – Nikita Khrushchev, Ho Chi Minh, and later Richard Nixon, among them. Since then the hotel has been almost continuously remodelled, refurbished, added to, subtracted from, and now stands amid several new wings on either side that are of no particular architectural or aesthetic merit. False ceilings on the ground floor have rather ruined the impression upon entry and only brides and grooms taking wedding photos seem to use the grand staircase these days. The long corridors still hark back to the enormity of the hotel when it was first built, but the rooms have been repeatedly remodelled with little inspiration.

The rooftop is closed and has been now for several decades. It seems unlikely to ever reopen. Yet once, from 1915 to the dark days of the Japanese occupation, the rooftop of the Grand Hôtel de Pékin was perhaps the most famous location in Peking for both sojourners and the city's foreign colony. It was where so many Peking adventures began.

---

38   Eventually, as also was the case for Laurance Tipton, Earl West and his band were interned at the Weihsien Allied Civilians Internment Camp in Shandong.

Peking's Favourite Bolshevik:
Lev Karakhan (1923)

'The first generation of Soviet spies had been a motley cast of gentleman amateurs, demi-mondain chancers, opportunists and naïve conspirators.' [39]

39   Owen Matthews, *An Impeccable Spy: Richard Sorge, Stalin's Master Agent* (London: Bloomsbury, 2019), p.50.

Before the Kremlin Ball

There is a vivid portrait of the Bolshevik Lev Karakhan in Curzio Malaparte's unfinished manuscript, *The Kremlin Ball*.[40] Malaparte was an Italian of highly contrarian views. According to the novelist and essayist Edmund White he was 'a "mythomane," a compulsive liar who embellishes the truth, not necessarily for gain but out of an irrepressible compulsion.'[41] He was an anti-intellectual and a writer with a memorable turn of phrase. He veered from Mussolini-style Fascism to Maoist-Communism, visited the new Soviet Union as a curious spectator in 1929, was imprisoned by Il Duce for a time, built a modernist masterpiece of a house on Capri, and was a war correspondent with the Axis forces in World War Two.[42] He also wrote poetry and short stories, directed movies, and visited Communist China in 1958 shortly before he died of cancer. Malaparte was born Kurt Erick Suckert of a German father and an Italian mother. His chosen pseudonym was a conscious inversion of Napoleon Bonaparte, adopted for no other reason than just to annoy people. His wartime reportage, contained in two volumes *Kaputt* and *The Skin*, are a revealing look, first at the war through the eyes of the Fascist side of the frontline in Russia, and then of a defeated post-war Italy.[43] But before all of that he first visited the fledgling Soviet Union.

Curzio Malaparte

The Kremlin Ball is quite a remarkable memoir of late 1920s Moscow. However, as with all Malaparte's work the book comes with

40   Finally translated from the Italian by Jenny McPhee – Curzio Malaparte, *The Kremlin Ball (Material for a Novel)* (New York: New York Review of Books Classics, 2018).

41   Edmund White from his introduction to Curzio Malaparte, *Diary of a Foreigner in Paris* (New York: New York Review of Books Classics, 2010).

42   The stunning Casa Malaparte on Punta Massullo, situated dramatically on the eastern side of Capri.

43   *Kaputt* was published in 1944 and *The Skin* in 1949. In English: *Kaputt* (New York: New York Review of Books Classics, 2007); *The Skin* (New York: New York Review of Books Classics, 2013).

a large READER BEWARE neon sign flashing over it – Malaparte often exaggerated, obfuscated, elaborated and unashamedly invented for dramatic and/or personal effect. Yet *The Kremlin Ball* is an almost unique vision of the Soviet capital city in the early years of the Bolshevik Revolution when die-hard communist proletarian heroes still mingled with openly gay commissars, aesthetes in the world of cinema, architecture and art, writers with questionable politics, ballet dancers and bourgeois ambassadors from Europe. They all described attending soirées in beautiful pre-revolutionary legation dining rooms before, wrapped in furs over their silks, they took troikas home in the snow. *The Kremlin Ball* reveals a more cosmopolitan and openly intellectual Moscow shortly before the murder and paranoia of full-blown Stalinism. This is the city prior to when the more puritan Marxist-Leninist ideologues crushed the creativity and bohemian elements of optimistically revolutionary 1917. A Moscow before the midnight knocks on the door by the secret police became the norm and people began disappearing. In memoirs we rarely see this brief interregnum – between the heady, ideologically hopeful days of 1917 and the Terror of Stalinism – portrayed anywhere else.

As Malaparte, himself having just turned thirty at the time, moves through this 1920s communist *demi-monde*, a milieu that already knows its days are numbered as the humourless hardliners rise and the more freethinking begin to fall, Malaparte encounters Lev Karakhan and his prima ballerina partner, Marina Semyonova. They appear immediately, on the first page of the book – *Chapter 1: The Black Prince*. Malaparte is listening to the tango *Ich küsse Ihre Hand* being played when Madame Lunarcharskaya (wearing a rather un-proletarian Schiaparelli dress), the wife of Anatoly Lunarcharsky, the Soviet people's Commissar of Education and Culture, asks: 'I wonder where Lev Karakhan is?'[44] Karakhan, it transpires, is late, because his lover Semyonova is always fashionably late. However, they are forgiven for they are the couple of the moment; the celebrity pair all Moscow society is talking about. Malaparte tells us, 'The men of the communist nobility favoured Semyonova while the women favoured Karakhan.'[45]

---

44   *The Kremlin Ball*, p.11.
45   *The Kremlin Ball*, p.21.

Karakhan's Bolshevik credentials and style (the knee-high leather boots, the Tolstoyan peasant smock, the *pince nez* and the goatee beard[46]) combined with Marina Semyonova's beauty, her white silk dresses and furs, come to symbolize the last days of bohemian revolutionary Moscow for Malaparte. They are the *couple du jour* of *tout suite* Moscow and, Malaparte tells us, 'Karakhan was the handsomest man in the Soviet Union and perhaps, according to Frau Dirksen, the German Ambassador's wife, the best looking man in Europe.'[47] Karakhan, we are told, is not long back from "The East".

Marina Semyonova

A model hero

Lev Mikhailovich Karakhan was indeed a Bolshevik hero. Born in Tiflis (now Tbilisi in Georgia) to an Armenian family in 1889, he joined the Russian Social Democratic Labour Party in 1904 at just fifteen years of age. He then moved to the moderate Mensheviks ("minority"), before becoming a revolutionary Bolshevik ("majority") in May 1917. His ascendancy in the Party was swift. By October, and the revolution, he was a full member of the Revolutionary Military Council. Later, with Leon Trotsky and Adolph Joffe, he acted as secretary to the Soviet delegation to the Brest Litovsk peace talks between the Bolsheviks and the Central European powers that ended Russia's participation in the Great War. Between 1918 and 1920 Karakhan was appointed Deputy People's Commissar for Foreign Affairs. He took an especial interest in China and the Far East. His boss, People's Commissar for Foreign Affairs the goatee-bearded Georgy Vasilyevich Chicherin, was another

---

46   A style that soon went distinctly out of fashion once Stalin's persecution of Trotsky got seriously underway.

47   *The Kremlin Ball*, p.21.

regular on the circuit of the communist aristocracy from the pre-1917, pre-Stalin days described in Malaparte's *The Kremlin Ball*. Chicherin was an intellectual of noble descent and a former Tsarist diplomat turned committed Marxist-Leninist.

Nowadays not many people remember the Karakhan Manifesto, but, in July 1919, it was an important document that rather upset the apple cart of the Great Powers and their "Spheres of Influence" in China. Karakhan formally announced that the new Bolshevik state was relinquishing most of its ("unequal") treaty rights in China that had been formerly held by Imperial Russia. This included voluntarily surrendering all extraterritorial and treaty port rights, including the Russian Concession in Tientsin, as well as Moscow's share of the Boxer Indemnity payments[48] (which would become an issue once again later, as we shall see) and control of the China Eastern Railway (CER).[49]

The so-called Karakhan "Manifesto" or "Declaration", as it was known, was unsurprisingly extremely popular in China with many younger urbanites feeling empowered after the May 4th demonstrations.[50] Indeed, it was a propaganda coup for the new Soviet Union - renouncing Tsarist Russia's involvement in the "unequal treaties", returning sovereign Chinese territory to Chinese control and acting as a close friend of the newly established republic in China all played well to the generally anti-imperialist mood. Karakhan knew that such a move would not only improve Bolshevik-Chinese relations but would hopefully make Marxism-Leninism a more attractive ideology in China, bolstering the emerging domestic communist and left-wing movements, and winning many friends in China for the fledgling Russian Soviet Federative Socialist

---

48   The substantial payments to the foreign countries affected by the Boxer Uprising and extracted by force of treaty. At 28.97 per cent Russia had the highest single share of any of the fourteen nations that extracted an indemnity.

49   The railway line had originally been built by Tsarist Russia under a concession from the severely weakened Qing dynasty. The CER linked Chita with Vladivostok in the Russian Far East and had three branches: the western branch between Harbin and the border town of Manchouli (in Inner Mongolia); the eastern branch between Harbin and the Sino-Russian border at Suifenhe (in Heilongjiang); and the southern branch between Harbin and Peking.

50   The anti-imperialist, cultural and political movement that grew out of student protests in Peking on May 4, 1919 sparked by China's poor treatment by the 'Allies' at the Paris Peace Treaty.

Republic (RSFSR)[51]. This analysis perhaps paints Karakhan's move too cynically – it was also, he believed, the right thing for the new Soviet state to do. Karakhan contrasted his Manifesto with the concomitant ongoing Paris Peace Talks and the Versailles Treaty, which China was to refuse to sign after Shantung was not returned by Japan to China. That had, in part, led to the May 4th 1919 demonstrations by people angry about, among other things, secret treaties and deals done by the European Great Powers during World War One behind China's back while they were supposedly allies.

By contrast the Bolsheviks appeared refreshingly open and honest. Releasing his Manifesto in July, just months after the May demonstrations, Karakhan knew it would find appreciative Chinese ears. While the Bolsheviks certainly did want to advocate for Marxism in China, and officially Marxist doctrine saw the country as an "oppressed nation and peoples", it also allowed the RSFSR to extend its push into Siberia and the Russian Far East, ousting the last remaining White Russian oppositional holdouts, without too much Chinese concern. China would never join with the other allied powers in the so-called Wars of Intervention to overthrow the Bolsheviks.[52] Karakhan hoped the Manifesto would provide a solid Sino-Russian bulwark against Japanese incursion towards Russia's borders, into Mongolia (soon to be a satellite state of the RSFSR) and even further west into contested Sinkiang, which suffered from religious-inspired independence movements and British Great Game shenanigans.

However, six months later Karakhan took back several of the pledges in his Manifesto. The inclusion of the China Eastern Railway had been a mistake, he maintained; it should never have been included in the manifesto. Russian rights over the railway were reaffirmed. Similarly with the Boxer Indemnity monies. Karakhan insisted that the RSFSR would oversee the continuing payments, rather than just scrap them. For a while

51   From 1917 to 1922, the country that came before the Soviet Union was officially known as the Russian Soviet Federative Socialist Republic (RSFSR), which was its own country, as were other Soviet republics at the time.

52   The Wars of Intervention were fought between 1918 and 1925, involving the Bolsheviks vs the White Armies which had the help of many countries including Great Britain, the United States, a number of European nations, Japan and, in 1918, some Chinese forces along the Sino-Russian border. The Karakhan Manifesto played a major part in ensuring the Chinese were to take no further part in the Wars of Intervention.

it seemed as if Karakhan would not follow America's example and stipulate that the indemnity monies be used solely for progressive educational purposes, though eventually he realised that this would have to be the case and announced that the "Soviet portion of the Boxer Indemnity would be allocated to Chinese educational institutions." Despite this climbdown on the original 1919 Manifesto, the general Chinese public's opinion of the new Bolshevik state, Marxism (if not always Leninism), and Lev Karakhan himself, remained overwhelmingly positive, if perhaps not absolute. So naturally there was a lot of interest in China when, in 1923, it was announced that Lev Karakhan was himself coming to Peking, as the first Soviet Ambassador to China.

China Bolsheviks

In April 1923 it was announced that Lev Karakhan had been appointed Soviet Diplomatic Representative to China, based with the northern, or warlord, government in Peking. Russia was split. While sending Karakhan to Peking, the Soviet Union had also decided to financially and politically assist Dr Sun Yat-sen and his rival Southern Government in Canton. They had skilfully, though a little precariously, built relations with China's two opposing governmental factions. The Soviets were making friends and hoping to influence both sides. Moscow sent a team of military men to help

Mikhail Borodin

train an army in Kwantung. In June, five young Soviet officers arrived in Peking for language training, while a veteran Bolshevik, Mikhail Markovich Gruzenberg, soon known to all in China by the alias Borodin, was later despatched to China as the Soviets' principal adviser to Sun Yat-sen. Grigori Naumovich Voytinsky, who had experience in Russia's Far East and with China's earliest organised communists, took over as Moscow's principal adviser to the new Chinese Communist Party, then based in Shanghai. This was Russian Bolshevism's, and the newly formed Communist International's, China "dream team" of so-called *sovetniki* advisers – Karakhan in Peking, Borodin in Canton, and Voytinsky in Shanghai.

The trio knew each other – Borodin, originally from a Jewish family in Belarus, had for a time been appointed by Lenin himself as Soviet Consul in Mexico. Borodin in Mexico City and Karakhan at the Commissariat of Foreign Affairs in Moscow tag-teamed to convince the leftist Mexican government that Russia was its ally in distrusting Mexico's big capitalist neighbour to the north. Revolutionary passions had been inflamed after President Woodrow Wilson allowed the United States Cavalry to pursue the revolutionary general Pancho Villa across the border in 1916. Then, in 1919, Karakhan had tasked Borodin with smuggling seized Tsarist family jewels into the United States, sewn into the lining of a pair of leather suitcases.[53] Voytinsky, born into a Jewish family from Nevel near the Russian border with the Baltic Republics, and Karakhan had regularly discussed the "Eastern question" together, concerning both Bolshevik policies in Siberia and Russia's Far Eastern provinces, the new Chinese Communist Party, as well as the direction of diplomatic relations with China.

In China, Borodin and Voytinsky's roles were essentially semi-secret and somewhat covert. However, Karakhan's diplomatic post was obviously and by necessity more overt as was his primary mission: to secure diplomatic recognition of the Soviet Union from China.

In September 1923 Karakhan was waved off with full Bolshevik pomp as he took the Trans-Siberian Express from Moscow towards Siberia and Lake Baikal. He crossed into China, transferring to the contentious China Eastern Railway, passing through Harbin, Changchun and Mukden before arriving at Peking's main station at Chienmen a full week after pulling out of Moscow's striking Neo-Russian revival-style Yaroslavsky Railway Station.

53   Smuggling jewels was a common task of Comintern agents. Trotsky's former secretary and a Comintern agent, Evgenia Petrovna Shelepina, was suspected of smuggling diamonds in her knickers. The British government noted this due to the fact that she was the girlfriend, and soon to be wife, of the British journalist Arthur Ransome and they had both recently visited China – a story told in my chapter on 'Arthur Ransome and Interpreting the Shanghai Mind' in *Destination Shanghai* (Hong Kong: Blacksmith Books, 2018).

Russian Legation in Peking, 1910

The Soviet Legation

Karakhan went straight to the former Russian Embassy in the heart of Peking's Legation Quarter and, now rather awkwardly given the Wars of Intervention, almost opposite the American Embassy. Quite what state the Russian Legation was in is unclear. After the Bolshevik Revolution the Tsarist ambassador to Peking, Prince Nikolai Kudachev, had been formally dismissed from the post by Moscow. Ignoring any communications from the Bolsheviks, Kudachev, now a stateless "White" Russian émigré, continued to live on in the embassy buildings for a further three years until the Peking (or Northern) government, having been courted assiduously by Karakhan and the Soviet Commissariat of Foreign Affairs, withdrew their recognition and Kudachev was forced to vacate the premises in 1920. No Russian official had lived there for nearly four years; no funds had arrived from Moscow; Kudachev had essentially kept himself, his family and the legation going on charitable donations from Peking's Russian émigré community.

Prince Nikolai Alexandrovitch Kudachev had been reasonably popular with many of the diplomatic community in Peking and the city's foreign colony. He was considered smart enough and a gentleman with, unsurprisingly perhaps for a Tsarist-era diplomat, excellent old-world manners. The prince's sister was less popular – a chain smoker with, according to the author and long-term China sojourner Stella Benson, a 'harsh voice' who dressed appallingly (which may have been due to Kudachev receiving no stipend or wages from Moscow for several years!). He was considered so anti-proletarian (i.e. a complete snob) and vociferously defensive of the old Tsarist regime as to shock even Europeans of a generally quite anti-Bolshevik, anti-socialist, pro-monarchy persuasion.[54]

With the popular Kudachev and his unpopular sister departed, Karakhan took over the embassy. Technically he was now the most senior foreign diplomat in China – he was an Ambassador, whereas all the others were mere Ministers.[55] This automatically made him dean of the diplomatic corps and so always the closest foreign envoy to the senior Chinese leaders. Karakhan may have been a Bolshevik and publicly decried bourgeois manners, but personally he liked a bit of pomp and circumstance and was a stylish man in his dress. On August 9, 1924 Karakhan presented himself to the President of China (at that time the warlord Cao Kun) to deliver his credentials. *Time* magazine wrote that he was 'clad in immaculate evening clothes, shod in shining leather, gloved in white kid, and wearing a glossy silk hat.'[56] He rode in a gilded state coach (presumably a dusted-down relic of the Tsarist Legation days), drawn by six ebony horses and escorted by twenty-four cavalrymen.

Karakhan based himself permanently in Peking from June 1924. Though he was in the northern capital he continued to play both sides and immediately despatched a telegram to Dr. Sun Yat-sen in the south, calling him 'an old friend of the New Russia'. Sun replied offering support and goodwill. This was a slightly odd move by Karakhan as it indicated to the Peking government that Karakhan and, by extension, Moscow's, support was ultimately for Sun and his rival southern government in Canton, though this was probably no surprise to the revolving series of northern warlords who took control of Peking in the 1920s. Sun wrote to Karakhan telling him that if the *Waichiao Pu* (China's Ministry of Foreign

54   See Julia Boyd, *A Dance with the Dragon: The Vanished World of Peking's Foreign Colony* (London: IB Tauris, 2012), pp.135-136.

55   It is slightly confusing but an Ambassador is considered a first class diplomat while the next ranking representative sent abroad is an Envoy Extraordinary and Minister Plenipotentiary (or simply "Minister"), who is considered a diplomatic agent of the second class.

56   *Time*, August 11, 1924.

Affairs at the time) in Peking refused to recognise the Soviet Union then Karakhan should move his embassy south to Canton. Sun also told Karakhan that he had sent his own 'trusted chief of staff and confidential agent' to Moscow 'to discuss ways and means whereby our friends there (*in Moscow*) can assist me in my work in this country (*China*).'[57] That trusted chief of staff and confidential agent's name? Chiang Kai-shek. Karakhan responded by sending Mikhail Borodin to Sun's headquarters.

It was hard for Karakhan to keep abreast of Borodin's progress with Sun, Chiang and the Kuomintang in Canton, and likewise often with Voytinsky's progress in Shanghai. The three highest-ranking communists in China rarely met each other face-to-face; communications were erratic. Karakhan and Borodin were to meet physically in the same place only once a year on average, when Borodin travelled north to Peking, although he wrote almost daily letters to Karakhan. Invariably Borodin and Karakhan only met when circumstances meant Borodin was unable to be close to Sun's side. For instance, in October 1924, a by now seriously ailing Sun Yat-sen travelled to Japan for medical treatment. Borodin took the advantage of Sun's being in hospital to visit Karakhan in Peking.

The Doyen

Borodin would probably have been amazed at Karakhan's progress in Peking. He had managed to establish Chinese recognition of the Soviet Union rapidly in May 1924 and was seen by many in the *Waichiao Pu* as "the doyen" of the Peking diplomatic corps.[58] The Soviet Legation had become a centre for nationalist and radical activity in Peking, helped by the northern warlord Feng Yu Hsiang's conquering of the capital in the spring of 1924 – the so-called "Christian General" had ousted the previous Zhili Clique, invited Sun to Peking, made an alliance with the Kuomintang and expelled the last emperor Puyi from the Forbidden City.[59] Things had turned around to the extent that Sun was able, after his medical treatment in Japan, to travel by train to Peking where he was

---

57   Allen S. Whiting, *Soviet Policies in China, 1917-1924* (New York: Columbia University Press, 1954), p.243.
58   'Usefulness of Old Diplomatic Corps at an End', *The Dayton Daily News*, May 22, 1925.
59   The warlord Feng Yuxiang.

met at the station by Mikhail Borodin (though by now Sun's medical condition was acute and he knew he was dying of liver cancer).

The United Press correspondents covering Peking embassy politics now took the general view that the days of the old Great Powers holding sway in the Legation Quarter were over and that Karakhan was all-powerful.[60] He was said to occupy the best seat of honour whenever the Chinese president held a reception. For the first time, a major power was seemingly on the inside track with the Chinese government, not by gunboat diplomacy, forcing unequal treaties or diplomatic pressure, but through apparent friendliness and support. Karakhan was unafraid to call the British and French 'imperialists' while arguing against the American position (put forward by the former American Ambassador to China, Jacob Gould Schurman) that China would 'evolve' to full national strength. Not 'evolution', replied Karakhan, but 'revolution' is what would return China's national strength.[61]

Such had been his rapid success in playing both sides and winning official recognition for the Soviet Union that, by 1925, Karakhan seems to have felt that his time in Peking was already coming to an end. It was the case that the domestic situation in northern China of endless warlord skirmishes, rival cliques and factional subterfuge tired him. There was little to recommend favouring one warlord over another. The social round of the Legation Quarter was not wholly to his taste… endless balls, lavish dinners and national days, but often with people he considered (quite rightly in many cases) his intellectual and social inferiors and whose politics he often found objectionable (a view obviously reciprocated by many).

Curzio Malaparte, who dubbed him 'The Black Prince' in *The Kremlin Ball*, encountered him as a hero – '…along with Borodin, of the Chinese Communist Revolution and of the Sovietization of Turkestan.'[62] It was clear to Malaparte that, though entranced by the Bolshoi's star ballerina Marina Semyonova and therefore constantly attending soirées in Moscow with her, he wasn't always at his most comfortable at such events, being an undoubtedly loyal and committed Bolshevik.

---

60   'Usefulness of Old Diplomatic Corps at an End'.

61   Quoted in Bert L. Kuhn, 'British Blame Red Influence Among Chinese', *The Honolulu Advertiser*, August 9, 1925.

62   *The Kremlin Ball*, p.22, Turkestan being Xinjiang.

Karakhan appeared to think the interminable internal wranglings of China would never result in anything seriously revolutionary. In 1925 Karakhan spoke with Paul Blanschard, an American Roman Catholic progressive who wrote for *The Nation* and was involved with the League for Industrial Democracy in the USA. Blanschard was touring China and Soviet Russia when they met. Karakhan told him that China was a 'rearguard engagement' in the international workers' struggle.[63]

Sun Yat-sen died in the Rockefeller-funded Peking Union Medical College, PUMC, just off Morrison Street, on March 12, 1925. He was aged just fifty-eight. Karakhan immediately ordered the red flag to be flown at half-mast over the Soviet Embassy and all Soviet installations throughout China.[64] He also ordered a specially made coffin from Moscow, identical to the one Lenin had been laid to rest in barely a year before. Sun Yat-sen's funeral procession through the streets of Peking was held on March 19. Karakhan occupied the prominent place of the chief mourner following behind the surplice choir.

The Black Prince

Lev Karakhan returned home to Moscow in August 1925 the way he had come – heading up through Manchuria on the China Eastern Railway and then back across the vast haul of Siberia on the Trans-Siberian Express.[65] Back in Moscow he once again assumed the post of Deputy People's Commissar for Foreign Affairs under Georgy Chicherin. Karakhan remained closely involved with Russia's China policy and the activities of those colleagues still in China, including Borodin, and his increasingly problematic relations with Sun's "confidential agent" Chiang Kai-shek. Since Sun's death in April 1925 Chiang was now the major

63 *The Peking Leader*, October 23, 1925.

64 According to Dan N. Jacobs, no other nation in China did this until the following day. *Borodin: Stalin's Man in China* (Cambridge, Massachusetts: Harvard University Press, 1981).

65 Some historians have posthumously suggested that Karakhan fled Peking concerned about being assassinated by the warlord Chang Tso-lin (Zhang Zuolin). It's certainly true that Chang would have probably taken great delight in killing a Bolshevik, but he was not to gain full control of Peking until April 1926 so, while Karakhan may have been concerned, it was not an imminent prospect in the summer of 1925.

Old Bolsheviks, from left: Nikolai Bukharin, Ivan Skvortsov-Stepanov & Lev Karakhan, 1927

figure on the right of the Kuomintang, though still in competition with his major rival on the left, Wang Ching-wei.[66] Eventually Karakhan and Borodin decided that Chiang could be handled. It was not their best decision ever.

Malaparte was to encounter Karakhan a few years later in 1929 – 'a tall, athletic man, his head proudly erect atop two broad shoulders... Karakhan, in his language from the Eastern Steppe, means "Black Prince"'. A Bolshevik for sure, but still a rather dandyish one it seems: 'His clothes, his ties, his shoes, his shorts, his gloves, all came from London by diplomatic courier from the Soviet Embassy in St. James's Square.'[67] Malaparte claims Karakhan was an excellent tennis player and that the diplomatic wives would flock to the courts to watch him play. He remembers that Karakhan's 'little speeches, his *bon mots*, his impudent quips' were listened to by all.[68]

After the bohemian days of Malaparte's *Kremlin Ball* Karakhan remained in favour with the new Stalinist regime at first. He married Marina Semyonova, who was the first ever fully Soviet-era trained prima ballerina in Russia and had danced with the Kirov in her hometown of St. Petersburg/Leningrad before Stalin decided she should be transferred to the Bolshoi in Moscow.

Karakhan kept his hand in with Chinese affairs, though perhaps not all his decisions would please Peking (or after 1927, when Chiang Kai-shek relocated the Chinese capital, Nanking). In 1932 Karakhan announced that the Soviet Union would recognise the Japanese annexation of

66   Wang Jing-wei, later to be China's pro-Japanese collaborationist leader in the Second Sino-Japanese War.
67   *The Kremlin Ball*, p.25.
68   *The Kremlin Ball*, p.26.

Manchuria and the newly created puppet state of Manchukuo as well as its capital at Changchun.[69] This was hardly in line with Karakhan's attacks on 'imperialistic' nations in China as Japan's occupation of northern China was a clear land grab by military means. However, perhaps there was a rationale to it, though not a particularly revolutionary one. In 1935 the Japanese-controlled "Manchukuo" state bought the China Eastern Railway from the Soviet Union. Russia sold a railway it didn't build, that was not even on its territory, to an occupying force and pocketed the cash – not a very Bolshevik thing to do. The only other countries to officially recognise Manchukuo were El Salvador, the Dominican Republic, Costa Rica, Italy, Spain, Hungary and Germany. The USSR opened consulates in Harbin and Manchouli while Manchukuo opened consulates in Chita and Blagoveshchensk.

In 1934 Karakhan was appointed Soviet Ambassador to Turkey. Marina was allowed to visit Paris to dance with Serge Lifar at the Paris Opera Ballet. Then, in 1937, Karakhan was recalled to Moscow. On September 20, 1937 he was, as he probably realised was likely to happen, immediately arrested and summarily executed in Stalin's purges with a bullet to the back of the head. Between the start of the Great Purge and the end of 1938 the NKVD (the People's Commissariat for Internal Affairs) arrested 1,548,366 Soviet citizens on charges of counter-revolutionary activity and sabotage. Of these, 681,692 were shot. Of the Comintern's staff of 492, 133 were imprisoned and/or executed – Lev Karakhan among them.[70]

Marina Semyonova was spared, and even awarded a Stalin Prize in 1941. She danced professionally until 1952, then retired and taught at the Bolshoi until she was ninety-six. She died at home in Moscow three days before her 102nd birthday in 2010.

Karakhan died in the so-called Great Purge. Some have claimed that he was shot by Stalin himself.[71] Borodin survived the first stages of the

69   United Press, 'Soviet Russia to Recognize Manchukuo Govt.', *The News-Herald* (Franklin, Pennsylvania), September 22, 1932.

70   Great Purge statistics from Owen Matthews, *An Impeccable Spy: Richard Sorge, Stalin's Master Agent* (London: Bloomsbury, 2019), p.171.

71   I know of no actual historical evidence for this claim. It was made by Henry Taylor (a journalist and, from 1957 to 1961, the US Ambassador to Switzerland) for United Features in 'Stalin Shot Inmates', *Nashua Telegraph* (New Hampshire), March 2, 1972.

purges initially, only to fall afoul of Stalin in 1949 by seeming to overly praise Maoism in China and also for being Jewish, and therefore not trusted in the anti-Semitic purges of the late 1940s. Borodin was arrested and sent to a gulag near Yakutsk, 280 miles south of the Arctic Circle. He died there in 1951. Grigori Voytinsky was luckier. He left China in 1926 to join the Siberian government in Irkutsk. In 1929 he moved to Moscow where he remained closely involved with Chinese and Far Eastern affairs before eventually becoming a professor at Moscow State University. He is now considered one of the fathers of Soviet Sinology. Despite being an old Bolshevik, having travelled abroad and being Jewish, he managed to survive the Great Purges. He died during a surgical operation in 1953. Naturally, there were rumours!

Lev Mikhailovich Karakhan was posthumously rehabilitated in 1956 and described as 'a distinguished leader of the Leninist Diplomatic School'.

Mikhail Markovich Gruzenberg, alias Borodin, was posthumously rehabilitated in 1964.

An "American Girl" in Peking:
Mona Monteith (1901)

American Legation gateway, 1901

'...*the most showy and most stylishly dressed of the occupants of
the branded houses (brothels) of Yokohama, Shanghai and other
Oriental cities are Americans. Some of them are conspicuous
in expensive equipages on the leading thoroughfares. The term
"American girl" in these cities has become synonymous with
immorality.*'[72]

---

72   New York District Attorney James B. Reynolds in the *Chicago Tribune*, February
9, 1909.

You can't catch me…

What scraps of information do we know about Mona Monteith and her China sojourn? What did anyone even at the time really know about Mona anyway? This young American woman travelling in China (and in Japan and Hong Kong too at the very end of the nineteenth century and very start of the twentieth century) only gave away as much as was absolutely necessary for her to survive and keep moving, at times just one step ahead of the law. But even in 1901 it was necessary to reveal a little of your true self if you wanted to obtain a passport, board a ship, check into a lodging house. It all leaves a paper trail, and we can partially follow that trail, along with a few mentions of Mona in the newspapers and the court records of the China Coast, through several years of her evidently eventful life.

Mona's trail leads from the east coast of the United States to Shanghai via stops in Japan and Hong Kong and then onto Peking. She arrived in the city in 1901, then a capital still in the traumatic aftermath of the Boxer Rebellion, the Siege of the Legations, and the riotous looting spree of the "Eight Powers Allied Army".[73] It was an odd place and a strange time for a young, single American woman to turn up. But she did… and her brief sojourn in Peking in the first year of the twentieth century tells us only a little about Mona, but an awful lot about the economy of sin, prostitution and the foreign colony's underbelly in Peking at the time.

But, for me at least, Mona's story started slightly later, in 1907, in the International Settlement of Shanghai, in a shocking announcement from the judge of the United States Court for China, then newly based in the city. Judge Lebbeus Wilfley, the first American judge to preside in Shanghai, accused Mona, and eight other young American women in the city, of being prostitutes. And so, before we rewind to Peking in 1901, let's meet Mona in Shanghai half a dozen years later, by which time she's a China veteran and a firmly established "American Girl".

---

73   The eight powers being Britain, Germany, the United States, France, Tsarist Russia, Japan, Italy and the Austro-Hungarian Empire.

The "American Girls"

In 1906 President Teddy Roosevelt announced from the White House that the United States of America needed its own court of justice in the treaty port of Shanghai, one that could try cases involving errant Americans in China. Britain, France and a host of other nations had long had their own courts in China under the extraterritoriality laws extracted from China after the conclusion of the Opium Wars that basically said that if you were a foreigner in a treaty port then you were subject to the laws of your own country and not China. But America had never set up a court of its own and this partly explained why so many of early Shanghai's illicit casino and bar operators, as well as bordello madams, pimps and prostitutes, were from the United States.

But now Teddy Roosevelt was hopping mad. He'd heard reports that American women were working as prostitutes in Shanghai and other Asian port cities – Tientsin, Singapore, Manila, Yokohama, Hong Kong – and that the term "American Girl" had become commonplace slang for a white prostitute in the Far East. The president felt something had to be done about this slur on America's mothers and daughters. So a court was set up in Shanghai and an American judge, the Honourable Lebbeus Redman Wilfley, then working

Lebbeus Redman Wilfley

in the Philippines (which was, at that time, under American control after the Spanish-American War of 1898), was immediately transferred from his position as America's Attorney-General on the archipelago to the International Settlement of Shanghai. In Manila, Wilfley had been nicknamed the "Convicter", a judge not afraid to regularly hand down often harsh and lengthy sentences to his fellow Americans. As head of the American Court in China, Wilfley got a good salary of US$10,000 per annum and a liberal travel and expenses budget.[74]

---

74   Which would be approximately US$270,000-a-year today.

There was certainly a lot of work for the American Court in Shanghai. American criminals and ne'er-do-wells had been flooding into the city, knowing full well that their country had no effective legal jurisdiction over them. Shanghai was, for American criminals in the know, an actual "Get Out of Jail Free" card – no courts, no judges, no jails. But now they had to face not just an American Court, but American Marshals working alongside the internationally-manned Shanghai Municipal Police. The once not-so-long arm of the law in America had just been significantly extended. The American criminals of Shanghai may have momentarily worried; a few probably did think about moving on to pastures new. But they soon realized that Shanghai's nearly impenetrable maze of extraterritorial legal jurisdictions and enforcement practices would make it almost impossible for the American Court to get convictions, if you were canny and moved quickly enough.

Newly resident in Shanghai, Judge Wilfley tried to deal with the "American Girls", the prostitutes that had so vexated President Roosevelt. In a major publicity coup, he announced to the China Coast newspapers a series of nine names of "American Girls" known to be working either as bordello madams or as prostitutes in notable houses of ill repute in Shanghai.

Called Before the Honourable L.R. Wilfley, Judge of the American Court for China at Shanghai

U.S. People v. Minnie Kingsley, No.16 Soochow Road; Maxine Livingstone, No.53 Kiangse Road; Alice Duncan, No.2 Thibet Road; Dorothy Grant and Zaza van Buren, No.10 Hongkong Road; Emily Moore, No.53 Kiangse Road; Mona Monteith, No.54 Kiangse Road; Alice Sherwood, No.14 Soochow Road; Margaret Kendall, No.10 Hongkong Road[75]

Unfortunately for Wilfley he had reckoned without appreciating how well the American criminal underworld in Shanghai understood the extraterritoriality system. It was to be an embarrassing early failure in Wilfley's attempt to tame wild America on the China Coast. Before the

75   Kiangse Road is now Jiangxi Road; Thibet Road is now Xizhang Road; Hongkong Road is now Xianggang Road; and Soochow Road is now Suzhou South (Nan) Road.

trial all the girls were simply married off to nationals of other countries – Portugal, Ecuador, the Dutch East Indies, Mexico – meaning they took their husbands' nationality and the American Court couldn't touch them. Wilfley, and by extension Roosevelt, looked stupid. Mona Monteith, along with her friends and work colleagues, never even set foot in the American Court and kept right on working just down the road on Shanghai's famous "Line" of foreign brothels on Kiangse Road. And whatever her nationality technically was by this point, Mona Monteith remained an "American Girl".

When Judge Wilfley put Mona's name on his docket in 1907 she was, if we can believe her stated birthdate on her passport, twenty-seven years of age. Young – but Mona had been in China for quite some time already. And while the scandal, furore, and eventually ridiculousness, of the 1907 American Girls trial may have been exciting it was, arguably, not her most thrilling adventure in the country. That was in Peking, in 1901…

Mona comes to Peking

And so rewind half a dozen years from 1907 Shanghai…

When she was just twenty-two, in 1901, Mona had turned up at the impressive embassy of the United States in Peking's Legation Quarter. She was already a well-travelled young woman – shipping records show her on American steamers from the United States' West Coast sailing out to China via Kobe and Yokohama in 1900. Whatever Mona's true occupation and however she made a living she was ultimately a regular citizen of the United States. She requested a new passport.

A normally uneventful and routine process – but consider the surroundings. Peking was still a ravaged city when Mona arrived. Only the year before, the fearsome Boxer rebels had laid siege to the Legations after rampaging across northern China, beheading Christian missionaries and any Chinese who had converted to Jesus. The teetering Manchu dynasty, in its last throes of survival and under the control of the Empress Dowager Ci Xi, had been unable to control the uprising for fear of being overthrown themselves. The beleaguered foreign community had huddled together in a terrified mass and retreated to the hoped-for security of the British Legation. Despite repeated attacks, and having to eat their ponies, the men, women and children were eventually relieved by a hastily assembled

[Edition of July, 1888]

NATIVE

CHINESE NAME 五 成 夫

Fee for Passport, ...$1.00
Fee for Filling Out Application in
  duplicate, ... 0.50
Fee for Administering Oath in
  duplicate, ... 0.50

No. *238*,   ISSUED, *April 9th*, 190 *1*

I, *Miss Mona Monteith*, a native and loyal citizen of the United States, do hereby apply to the Legation of the United States at Peking for a passport for myself and wife and my minor children, as follows:_____, born at_____ on the____ day of_____, 1____, and

_____

In support of the above application, I do solemnly swear that I was born at *New York*, in the State of *N.Y.*, on or about the *8th* day of *Sept.*, 1 *78*; that my father is a *native* citizen of the United States; that I am domiciled in the United States, my permanent residence being at *New York*, in the State of *N.Y.*, where I follow the occupation of_____; that I left the United States on the *23* day of *Dec.*, 19 *00*, and am now temporarily sojourning at *Shanghai*; that I am the bearer of Passport No. ____, issued by_____ on the____ day of_____, 1____; that I intend to return to the United States *soon* with the purpose of residing and performing the duties of citizenship therein; and that I desire the passport for the purpose of traveling in the provinces of *Kiangsu, Chihli, Shantung & Shengking*

OATH OF ALLEGIANCE

Further, I do solemnly swear that I will support and defend the Constitution of the United States against all enemies, foreign and domestic; that I will bear true faith and allegiance to the same; and that I take this obligation freely, without any mental reservation or purpose of evasion: SO HELP ME GOD.

       Mona Monteith

Consulate General of the United States at Shanghai.

Sworn to before me, this *3* day of *April*, 190 *1*.

       John Goodnow
       Consul General.

DESCRIPTION OF APPLICANT

Age: *22* years.
Stature: *5* feet *4½* inches, Eng.
Forehead: *medium*
Eyes: *Dk Blue*
Nose: *medium*

Mouth: *medium*
Chin: *medium*
Hair: *Brown*
Complexion: *fair*
Face: *medium*

IDENTIFICATION

       Shanghai 3/4, 190 *1*

I hereby certify that I know the above-named *Miss Monteith* personally, and know him to be a native-born citizen of the United States, and that the facts stated in his affidavit are true to the best of my knowledge and belief.

       Geo Cowsby
       Shanghai

[Address of witness.]

NOTE.—This form is to be filled out in duplicate, one copy being retained on the files of the Legation and the other forwarded with the quarterly returns to the Department of State. It may be so filled out by the applicant, in which case no fee therefor is chargeable.

international coalition dubbed the Eight Power Allied Army, composed of French, Russian, Italian, Japanese and British-controlled troops from India among others, and including American Marines, some of whom were still camped out in the Forbidden City when Mona arrived. The relief of the Peking Legations had been a dramatic event relayed to an anxious foreign newspaper readership at home.

Legation Quarter graveyard for Boxer Siege dead, 1900

And so now, barely a year after the slaughter and looting, twenty-two-year-old American Girl Mona Monteith walked into the United States Legation, still being rebuilt after the devastation of the Siege, to collect her new passport. A new embassy building was being erected and the road outside – Legation Street – macadamised, though the nearby Jade Canal, better known to the foreign colony at the time as the Imperial Sewer, was still noxious and fetid before being finally covered up some years later.[76] The Senate Committee on Foreign Relations had appropriated US$100,000 for the improvement and repair of the American Legation at Peking in January 1901, approximately US$3 million in 2020 terms.[77]

---

76   The "Jade Canal" bisected the Legation Quarter from north to south along what was called Canal Street. It was eventually covered over and a park erected on top of the old stinking canal. The street, now running from Changan Jie to Qianmen East Street, is called Zhengyi Road. The park remains.

77   *New York Times*, March 2, 1901, p.1.

Most of the last remaining US troops with the Eight Power Allied Army had left China by May 1901, and Company B of the Ninth Infantry were appointed as the Legation Guard. Peking was in many ways still a city effectively under foreign occupation; still tense and the foreign colony nervous. Throughout the first half of 1901 the embalmed bodies of American soldiers killed in Peking were still being transported home. American troops had been occupying the Temple of Agriculture, near the Temple of Heaven, and some barracks at the south gate of the Forbidden City as well as the Legation compound. But bureaucracy is bureaucracy and an out-of-date passport must be renewed, then as now, at your nearest embassy or consulate; and Mona opted for Peking.

Enforcer or collaborator?

Just several days before entering the American Legation in Peking, Mona had stood before United States Consul General John Goodnow in Shanghai. Goodnow asked her to swear that she was Miss Mona Monteith, twenty-two, of New York, New York, born September 8, 1878, a second-generation, native-born American. Someone resident in Shanghai called Wenby then swore that they knew Mona to be an American citizen of good standing. Goodnow and Wenby both signed Mona's passport application form. Then finally Mona herself signed it, solemnly swearing to 'Support and defend the Constitution of the United States against all enemies, foreign or domestic', and that she would 'Bear true faith and allegiance to the same… SO HELP ME GOD'. And with that done, Mona went to Peking with her paperwork and the required $2 fee.

What Consul Goodnow, and the mysterious Wenby, saw before them as they signed Mona's passport application was a young woman of just five feet, four and a half inches in height with blue eyes, brown hair, a fair complexion and, according to the odd categories of the US passport application form in 1901, noted as being "medium" of forehead, "medium" of nose, and "medium" of mouth, chin and face.

The application form also required some other details. "Temporarily Sojourning" at Shanghai was what Mona wrote in the box for the required "reason for being overseas". Then she left the box marked "occupation" tantalisingly empty. She could have found something to put there. Alice Duncan, another of the American Girls later to be targeted by Wilfley, had described herself as a "student"; others preferred "secretary", which was so commonly used by working girls on forms in 1890s Chicago and San Francisco that it had virtually become a byword for prostitute. Even by 1901 the use of the terms "actress" or "dancer" was probably a little too obvious, while French prostitutes invariably described themselves as milliners, dressmakers or manicurists.

JOHN GOODNOW,
Consul General at Shanghai, China.

Perhaps, though, we can assume that Consul John Goodnow was fooled by none of this. Indeed, there is good reason to believe he knew Mona well, perhaps intimately. In 1901 Mona was in the employ of Shanghai's most famous American madam, Barbara Foster, who ran her all-American Girl bordello from luxurious premises at No.52 Kiangse Road – the heart of Shanghai's "Line". Goodnow, so it was strongly rumoured, was a regular client of Foster's. For her part Foster would not have been the spectacularly successful madam she was for many years without cultivating the most powerful American man in Shanghai. Wenby, who is sadly lost to history, we can perhaps assume was a patsy; an American ne'er-do-well, roped in by Barbara Foster as a man with an American passport who could sign a form, thereby helping Mona get her new passport and facilitate Foster's plans for her. Those plans initially meant heading north to Peking to pick up the document.

But before we get back to Peking there is the small matter of what happened to John Goodnow after Mona left town, that may shed some more light on how well he knew Mona. Before the arrival of Judge Wilfley and the official American Court for China, American justice, such as it was before 1906 in Shanghai, was dispensed by the Consul General. Around the turn of the century Goodnow had gone hard after a notorious man best known as "Tientsin Brown". For years the most notorious foreign-run gambling and drinking den in Shanghai was The Alhambra (named after a San Francisco theatre). Brown was the Alhambra's owner and a prime example of the sort of American criminal that flourished in treaty port China in those more lawless times. JH "Tientsin" Brown was a Russian-born, US-naturalised casino and brothel owner of legendary proportions. He had started as the owner of a single small bar in the northern Chinese treaty port of Tientsin, making money on the side semi-legally as an arms procurer for the foreign armies stationed in the city. He parlayed this money into a small fortune through real estate speculation and then a larger fortune by funding the establishment of brothels along the Tientsin British Concession's Dublin Road strip of "bad houses".[78] In 1903, Brown moved down to Shanghai and founded The Alhambra "house of amusement" casino and dive bar.

Goodnow appeared to repeatedly try to close Brown down, but always failed. Still, he looked like an American Consul trying to do the right thing. But Brown very publicly maintained that Goodnow was extorting him with the threat of closure and that he was paying significant sums to the Consul to stay open. Gangster talk perhaps, but gradually people started to believe Brown and not Goodnow, who was eventually himself thrown out of office after an investigation by the State Department in March 1905. The Consul, whose supporters, including the anti-White Slavery campaigner Mrs Archibald Mackirdy, had once described as 'a splendid sample of the best American manhood' who 'struggled hard with the evil at Shanghai and he tried to prevent American Girls coming to live evil lives there', ended his days discredited and disgraced – as an extortionist of The Alhambra where many of the American Girls were known to socialise after "work", and as a patron of Mona's employer Barbara Foster's joint on Kiangse Road.[79] Did Mona, Goodnow and the mysterious Wenby all look at each other and laugh knowingly that day in Goodnow's consulate office in 1901?

Mona on tour

And so Mona arrived in Peking to collect her passport from the American Legation. But she wasn't heading straight back to Shanghai and Kiangse Road. She recorded on her application that she intended to travel. Specifically she intended to visit the provinces of Kiangsu, Shantung, Chihli[80], and elsewhere – all provinces where treaty ports existed with foreign populations and foreign-staffed bordellos too. Did Mona decide

---

78   Now Zhengzhou Dao.

79   Olive Christian Malvery Mackirdy (Mrs Archibald Mackirdy), *The White Slave Market* (London: Stanley Paul, 1912), p.80.

80   Chihli was a northern province of China from the Ming Dynasty until 1911 when it was renamed Zhili Province. In 1928 it was renamed once again as Hebei Province.

to tarry a while in Peking and Tientsin and make some money while having a break from the stuffiness of the small International Settlement? To work for the notorious Tientsin madams, the Polish-born Sanger sisters, or spend some time in Tientsin Brown's old joints for a while? Or did Barbara Foster send her "on tour", swapping girls with other bordellos to ensure a little variety and a change of faces on "The Line" back in Shanghai so as to keep her regular clientele interested and coming back for another peek?

What Mona's tarrying in Peking before moving on to perhaps Tientsin, Tsingtao in Shantung and, probably, Kalgan in Chihli, indicates is that there was clearly a network of brothel owners and madams extending across all the treaty ports of China. Tientsin Brown's American Girl bordellos in Tientsin and elsewhere seem to have been, if not quite as notorious as Shanghai, then arguably even more overt. The US Vice Consul General in Tientsin, Albert Pontius, reported back to Washington DC around this time that the bordellos in Tientsin run by American madams and employing 'American Girls' had become so plentiful and so busy that the situation was becoming 'intolerable'.[81]

Alongside Tientsin Brown's establishments, a pimp by the name of David Adler, believed to be an Austrian, ran what the American authorities termed a 'low hotel' that was full of prostitutes on Tientsin's Taku Road.[82] Adler was described by the American Consul as fat, tough and capable of speaking only two or three words of English. Nathan Kaplun, a Russian Jew who was variously described around this point as either forty-six or sixty years of age (such, one imagines, were the physical effects of his debauched life) ran another 'low hotel' and lived there with a former prostitute. Kaplun ran the All Nations Bar on Tientsin's Peiho (River Hai) waterfront that stayed open till two or three in the morning nightly, had rooms upstairs for prostitutes to work in and was home to all manner of pimps, working girls and gamblers. Meanwhile a pimp named Malakoff, originally from Odessa, ran various low-class brothels across Tientsin. Eventually it was revealed that Kaplun, Adler and Malakoff managed to stay in business as they had all seemingly managed to obtain fraudulent American passports from the corrupt John Goodnow in Shanghai.

---

81   Ellen P. Scully, *Bargaining with the State from Afar: American Citizenship in Treaty Port China, 1844-1942* (New York: Columbia University Press, 2001), p.96.
82   Now Dagu Bei Lu.

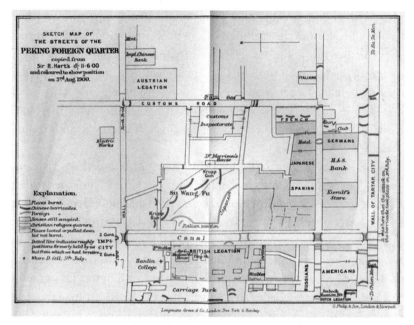

Plan of the Legation Quarter, 1903

And so the American Girl bordello network extended across China – to Weihaiwei and Chefoo and Port Edward in the north (ports of call for the Royal Navy's China Station and the US Navy's Far East Fleet); the treaty ports of Foochow, Amoy and Ningpo; the Manchurian cities of Mukden and Harbin; Dairen on the Liaodong peninsula; even Hailar in remote Inner Mongolia; and of course down south to Canton.

It does seem that women were moved through this network throughout the country for any number of reasons – to introduce new girls into bordellos and keep the punters' interest; if they needed to be moved away from overly amorous or violent customers; or if they needed to get out of town and away from the police and/or courts for a bit.

Peking Vice, 1900

Turn-of-the-century Peking had its own brothel and illicit casino scene with several bordellos staffed by foreign, mostly American, prostitutes catering to the foreign male population alongside those exclusively for the Chinese. They were there before 1900 and long after. In 1935 the Nebraskan journalist LaSelle "Lu" Gilman left his desk in Shanghai to look at Peking's nightlife. Outside the imperial city, beyond Chienmen, it was not overly different to the turn of the century:

Outside Chienmen after dark is a riot and bedlam of sound and color and light: ricksha bells clang, motor horns blare, hawkers squall their wares, from the theaters come a pandemonium of shrill flutes, gongs and drums, dinner-parties in the restaurants are merrily proceeding

The Chienmen Gate Tower following the Boxer Revolt

with the aid of sing-song girls. The narrow streets, as bright as day in the lights of shops, are crammed with humanity of every shade and type - rickshas, hawkers' stands, carts, camels, cyclists, motor-cars, carriages are packed together; soldiers, clerks, artisans, prosperous merchants, wealthy officials, ministers, monks, generals, singing girls, women young and old, rich and poor, virtuous and carefree, and an occasional party of foreigners pass to and fro under the bright shop-banners and across the Bridge of Heaven en route to or from the play-houses, restaurants, shops, pharmacies, bath houses, markets and fairs, gardens, guilds, wineshops and bordellos. Beyond are open tea-stalls, peddlers, chestnut-stands, traveling kitchens - where the poorer folk congregate to buy and sell anything and everything they can lay hands on. The Chinese hedonists have made "outside Chienmen" something never to be forgotten.[83]

American Girls like Mona sometimes arrived on steamers to northern China taking passage from the American west coast via Kobe, Yokohama (a Japanese treaty port at the time with its own foreign-staffed bordellos) or perhaps Manila, then under American control. After some time in

83   LaSelle Gilman, 'Peiping Night-Life Found Outside Chienmen', *China Press*, October 25, 1935.

Tientsin and maybe other northern Chinese towns – perhaps Dairen, Port Arthur, Chefoo – they headed to Peking.

The foreign bordello scene in Peking was reportedly less American-dominated than in Shanghai. French and Belgian women worked alongside their American sisters, though often operating under a claim of American citizenship to avoid the attentions of their own legations. Russian women were active in the prostitution market too. One senior Russian businessman's wife in China was shocked during the Boxer's Siege of the Legations to see a couple of young male diplomats in the Tsar's service escorting several Russian ladies of the night across the barricades and into the Legation Quarter for their own safety in 1900.

Shanghai was a treaty port – effectively foreign-controlled Chinese soil. But Peking was resolutely Chinese and the Qing dynasty's capital city and centre of government. For a long time the Qing government said nothing about the foreign prostitutes working in the city. But eventually, after the Boxer Uprising, and around the time Mona arrived in town, they did finally bring up the subject of the proliferation of foreign-controlled vice in northern China. They claimed that in Peking alone, four foreign-owned casinos and eighteen brothels staffed by both foreign and Chinese prostitutes were operating night and day.[84]

The American Girls continued to be a key group of the foreign underbelly in China up to the First World War. They kept on appearing at American-run bordellos in Shanghai, Peking and across the country's treaty ports. Many of the women we first encountered in 1907, summoned by Judge Wilfley in Shanghai, went on to become madams themselves – the fantastically named Zsa Zsa Van Buren came to run her own substantial bordello.

Zaza Van Buren's great "house," 16 Soo-Chow Road, Shanghai

84   According to the Tsungli Yamen's (Chinese Foreign Bureau) archives and quoted in Eileen P. Scully, 'Prostitution as Privilege: The "American Girl" of Treaty-Port China, 1860-1937, *The International History Review*, Vol.20, No.4, December 1998, p.868.

Others married, often well and happily, and "retired" back to America, to England, to France. A few committed suicide, succumbed to disease and drug overdoses. A couple were murdered by clients. Then the cataclysmic upheaval of the Russian Revolution in October 1917 changed everything. "White" Russian émigrés fled the Bolsheviks through Siberia and into China. They settled as stunned refugees, bedraggled and often totally impoverished. Harbin, Mukden, Dairen, Tientsin and, of course, Shanghai and Peking, acquired large émigré Russian populations. By 1916 the foreign population of China was around 165,000, rising to 245,000 in 1918 and a further jump to 350,000 in 1919. Life was tough and many Russian émigré women with families to support and no real marketable skills or previous work experience had to forget their former lives of leisure and turn to prostitution. Almost immediately the law of supply and demand kicked in with a vengeance. Too many prostitutes, too few clients, and prices fell through the brothel room floor.

Customers didn't have to be economic geniuses to see it in action. The historian Frederic Wakeman, Jr. in his book *Policing Shanghai* noted that a man could keep a Russian mistress for a month on what the average night on the Shanghai "Line" with the American Girls had cost.[85] Very quickly the days of the American Girls were numbered and they disappeared from the scene in Peking as well as in Shanghai and Tientsin.

A final thought on Mona

And here's a final thought about our New Yorker Miss Mona Monteith who claimed to be in her early twenties in 1901 when she arrived in Peking. Was that her real name? Mona Monteith appears only on this passport application, in the records of the American Court for China in Shanghai, and in the Shanghai newspapers reporting her summons before Judge Wilfley in 1906. There are no other records of a Mona Monteith I've been able to find outside of these references – no hospital, marriage, death or other court or newspaper references in Shanghai; no records of Mona arriving or departing any ocean liner from any Chinese port or Hong Kong; nor transiting through Kobe, Yokohama or Honolulu. She

---

85   Frederic Wakeman, Jr., *Policing Shanghai, 1927-1937* (Berkeley: University of California Press, 1996), p.111.

also appears not to have any middle names, unique among the "American Girls" in China I've been able to trace and unusual for the times too. Mona Monteiths are rare – one pops up in 1926 Lincoln, Nebraska, but is far too young to be our Mona as she's just a senior at high school; a "Mona L. Monteith" applies for a marriage licence in Syracuse in 1937, but I think it's the same Mona from Lincoln a decade later getting married. You can't help but wonder: if that was her real name, what eventually happened to Mona after 1907?

Two Aesthetes of Peking:
Desmond Parsons & Robert Byron (1937)

Desmond Parsons (left) & Robert Byron, China

'Peking is a place for cowards who have given up the struggle with the world, and I haven't quite done that.' [86]

86   Robert Byron (Ed. Lucy Butler), *Letters Home* (London: John Murray, 1991).

The Aesthete's Aesthete

Desmond Parsons is a relatively forgotten figure among those European and American aesthetes who made Peking their home between the two world wars. That list includes the Englishmen, Harold Acton, memoirist John Blofeld, and poet William Empson, as well as the Italian diplomat-author Daniele Varè, and the Americans, scholar-aesthete George N. Kates and illustrator Thomas "Tom" Handforth. All remain better remembered today than Parsons. However, in the 1930s Desmond Parsons was revered by the small community of foreign aesthetes in Peking, and generally regarded as the Peking aesthete's aesthete. Tragically Parsons suffered from Hodgkin's lymphoma and his illness forced him to leave Peking in 1937, shortly before the Japanese invasion of the city, to seek treatment in Switzerland. He died there that July aged just twenty-eight. This meant he never wrote a memoir like Blofeld or Kates[87], nor a novel of Peking manners like Acton or Varè[88], nor did he leave a body of scholarly work, as did Empson.[89] Parsons was mourned by his close Peking circle, but largely forgotten everywhere else.

87   The British writer and aesthete John Blofeld lived in Hong Kong and China between 1937 and 1949, after which he moved to Bangkok. He wrote eighteen books, mostly on Taoism and Chinese Buddhism, but is probably best remembered for his Peking memoir *City of Lingering Splendour: A Frank Account of Old Peking's Exotic Pleasures* (London: Hutchison, 1961). George Kates was an American expert on classical Chinese culture and an aesthete who lived in China between 1933 and 1940, settling in Peking from 1935. His best-known work is his memoir of his Peking years and his hutong courtyard house, *The Years That Were Fat: Peking, 1933-1940* (New York: Harper & Bros., 1952). The book includes photographs by another long-time Peking resident, Hedda Hammer Morrison.

88   Acton's *Peonies and Ponies* (London: Chatto & Windus, 1941) and Varè's trilogy set in early twentieth century Peking (in English) *The Maker of Heavenly Trousers* (London: Methuen, 1948); *The Gate of Happy Sparrows* (New York: Doubleday & Doran, 1937); and *The Temple of Costly Experience* (London: Methuen, 1943).

89   Most of Empson's academic output was related to English literature, largely concerned with early and pre-modern works. He was also an advocate of "close reading" and his book (drafted while he was still an undergraduate in the late 1920s) *Seven Types of Ambiguity* (London: Chatto & Windus, 1947) is seen as a key text of the New Criticism school. His book *The Face of the Buddha* was begun in 1931 while Empson was teaching in Tokyo. He then lost the manuscript during World War Two only for it to be rediscovered sixty years later and published by Oxford University Press in 2016.

Desmond Parsons photographed by Robert Byron, Venice, 1933

Desmond Parsons was properly qualified to be an independently wealthy aesthete in Peking in the 1930s, able to dedicate himself solely to his enthusiasms. Born in 1910 the second son of the Fifth Earl of Rosse, his older brother Michael inherited the title, becoming the Sixth Earl of Rosse. This ensured Desmond wasn't burdened with the inheritance of the family estate of Birr Castle in County Offaly, Ireland, but he did get a goodly share of the money.[90] He attended Eton where he had a "passionate friendship" with the future writer and early National Trust champion James Lee-Milne. He was also good friends with Tom Mitford, the only brother of the decidedly more famous sisters. Parsons then studied at

90   Birr Castle is in County Offaly, Ireland. It remains within the Parsons family and is lived in by the Seventh Earl of Rosse, The Rt Hon William Clere Leonard Brendan Parsons, the son of Michael Parsons and therefore the nephew of Desmond.

Oxford and the military academy at Sandhurst, where he proved to be a natural linguist, if not a natural soldier. He came to be regarded as 'one of the most magnetic men of his generation.'[91]

Parsons initially went to China following his friend Harold Acton, another 'magnetic man of his generation'. According to Acton's friends, Parsons was Acton's 'one true love of his life'. Like Acton, Parsons found, in his privileged social position, life a little too easy in London, with too little expected of him. He feared he would become just another 'stereotype, a boring dilettante, content to wander round... looking at old buildings, going to operas and concerts, reading the newest books... so there remains nothing for it but to find me some useful position in China.'[92]

Parsons left Europe at Christmas 1933 and, after travelling in India and South East Asia for a while, settled in Peking in the spring of 1934 renting a courtyard home on Tsui Hua Hutong where, like other aesthetes such as Acton and Kates, he worked hard to recreate the Taoistic courtyards, gardens and traditional room settings.[93] He displayed his carefully curated collections of various Chinese *objets d'art*, including porcelain, fans, scrolls, screens and ceremonial robes. Tsui Hua Hutong was, and what remains of it still is, a quiet hutong. It was a peaceful series of large courtyards with particularly impressive entrance gates running west to east. At the western end of the hutong Parsons had access to the Forbidden City and imperial Peking; at the other, eastern, end he was close to the commercial and shopping thoroughfare of Wangfuting (commonly known as Morrison Street to the foreign colony). Tsui Hua Hutong was just a quarter of an hour's rickshaw ride from Acton's own

91   Quite what is the original source of this oft-mentioned quote is rather obscure. Taken here though from the introduction to Robert Byron, *The Road to Oxiana* (London: The Folio Society, 2000).

92   Parsons to his friend the economist Roy Harrod in James Knox, *Robert Byron* (London: John Murray, 2003), p.348.

93   Now Cui Hua Hutong, which has survived in part. The entire south side of the hutong is gone, though the northern portion of perhaps a dozen formerly intact courtyards remains, but with those courtyards now sub-divided into multiple family dwellings. What remains now runs between Beiheyan Street and Wangfujing. The Wangfujing end of the hutong is somewhat obscured by the constructions of the ominous black cube structure of the National Art Centre and a hotel. Parsons's courtyard in 1935 was numbered No.8.

courtyard home, just across Jingshan Park on the long and narrow Kung Hsien Hutong, at the southern end of the lane, near the home of the famous Chinese opera performer Mei Lan-fang, just to the north of Beihai Park.[94]

Robert Byron, soon to be a long-term guest with Parsons, provided a full and detailed description of No.8 Tsui Hua Hutong:

> The street, like all hutungs *(sic)*, is about 12-15 feet wide – just grey walls of one storey, with trees peeking over the top. The front door is scarlet – and there are large inscriptions over it. No.8 inside is a little court for the rickshaw and the servants' bicycle. Turn left, through a door, into a little vestibule, which is the spirit gateway… turn right again, then to the left once more and you are in the main court. Behind is another whole row of rooms and two more courtyards – in one of which, in a main line with the first spirit gate and the axis of the big room is a tall wooden screen, covered with ducks and lotuses, to impede the spirits from reaching the concubine's quarters. The back court has a big tree in it, and the small court beside it where I first lived a clump of bamboos. Round the walls are various beds which have tree-peonies in them now done up in straw. The great pot in the middle of the main court is filled with lotuses in summer. The whole is of grey brick, bright grey, but the fronts of every pavilion consist of wooden lattices covered with paper. The courts are brick-paved. It all looked very pretty on my birthday *(February 26)* with deep snow on the ground and roofs, all the pavilions lighted up inside and lanterns in the trees – also big round lanterns with red characters on them hanging in the tripods bedside the front door.[95]

Parsons instructed his servants to prepare only Chinese food and embarked on a course in Chinese language while also translating a

94   Now called Gongjian Hutong, Kung Hsien Hutong remains in a relatively decent state of repair, including its many *xiongs* (or adjacent side alleys) running from Dianmen Street, north to south down the side of Beihai Park. It is close to the tourist attraction of Nanluoguxiang Hutong. Gongjian is an interesting hutong as it has a bend in the lane at either end, presumably to afford some additional privacy to the lane as well as prevent it becoming a wind tunnel.

95   Letter from Byron to his sister Anne, February 29, 1936, C/O Tsui Hua Hutong 8, East City, Peiping. *Byron: Letters Home*, p.271-272.

collection of Chinese folk tales from German into English.[96] Acton got him a part-time post at Peking University (aka Beida), even though Acton himself had been sacked over some internal machinations at the university. He also wrote a column for the *Peiping Chronicle* newspaper. The two regularly visited the Chinese theatre together, and fell for the actors though apparently got nowhere with them.[97]

Inspired by the journeys of Sir Aurel Stein, Parsons travelled extensively, including to Dunhuang in China's far western Kansu province, where he photographed the Buddhist murals in the caves there. It was not an easy process as the Chinese, naturally chagrined at Stein's "removal" of many of the cave's contents to the British Museum, now watched the site day and night for looters. Parsons convinced the Chinese authorities he was only interested in taking away photographs and was allowed to shoot a series of images of Dunhuang that were later acquired by Anthony Blunt for the Courtauld Institute in London.[98]

Parsons was the great unrequited love of the English travel writer, journalist and Byzantinist Robert Byron who, having just travelled through Persia and now being in Siberia, thought he might as well continue east to Peking to see the object of his old affections. In October 1935 Byron wrote to Parsons from Novosibirsk: 'At last after all this time I have a hope of seeing you again… I have no idea what I shall do in Peking – I have to write a book on Persia, which is long overdue – I thought I might do that – I can hardly tell you how excited I am… I fear even my intention of spending some time in Peking may seem rather a bore to you… I will try not to disturb the tenor of your life.'[99]

The Road from Oxiana

Byron was five years older than Parsons, but had also passed through both Eton and Oxford, though he had been expelled from the university

96   This translation did appear posthumously as Wolfram Eberhard, *Chinese Fairy Tales and Folk Tales* (London: Kegan Paul, 1937).

97   Knox, *Robert Byron*, p.349.

98   That Anthony Blunt who was a leading British art historian, but who in 1964 was offered immunity from prosecution after confessing to having been a spy for the Soviet Union since his Cambridge University days.

99   Letter from Byron to Parsons, October 5, 1935. Contained in *Byron: Letters Home*, pp.247-248.

for being too hedonistic and rebellious.[100] Byron had found school and college boring and stuffy. He disliked convention, especially politeness, and could be quite hurtful. Asked what in the world he would most like to be he replied, 'To be an incredibly beautiful male prostitute with a sharp sting in my bottom.'[101]

From an early age Byron had travelled widely, writing about his journeys – to Mount Athos in Greece, India, the Soviet Union and Tibet[102]. His journey through Persia and Afghanistan led him to Russia once again and then his decision to carry on east to see Parsons in Peking. Byron left Novosibirsk, headed to

Byron and Acton at Oxford, 1922

Vladivostok and then, by boat, to Seishin in the then-Japanese colony of Korea ('nobody spoke a word of English').[103] He travelled overland to Hsingking ('a bore'), the city now declared the capital of Japanese-occupied Manchukuo (formerly Manchuria). He spent a weekend in Mukden with old friends at the British Consulate ('not so stiff as India')

---

100 At Oxford Byron was a contemporary of Evelyn Waugh and both were members of the Hypocrites Club (motto: 'water is best').

101 Jeremy Treglown, *Romancing: The Life and Work of Henry Green* (London: Random House, 2000), p.31. The novelist Henry Green, whose real name was Henry Yorke, was another contemporary of Byron and Waugh at Oxford.

102 Byron's journey to Greece and Mount Athos led to his books *Europe in the Looking-Glass: Reflections of a Motor Drive from Grimsby to Athens* (London: Routledge, 1926) and *The Station* (London: Duckworth, 1928). His India trip resulted in *An Essay on India* (London: Routledge, 1931) while his visit to the USSR and Tibet led to *First Russia, Then Tibet* (London: Macmillan, 1933).

103 Now Chongjin in North Korea.

before arriving by train in Peking to stay with his old friend in November 1935.[104]

Desmond met him at the Chienmen Railway Station. The two had not seen each other for four years, since a brief meeting in Venice shortly before Byron embarked on his journey to Persia and Parsons was on his way to Peking for the first time. Here on Tsui Hua Hutong, reunited with his old friend, living in the peace and tranquillity of his beautiful courtyard home, Byron could begin work on his travelogue, a work that would become his most enduring, and by far best known, *The Road to Oxiana*.[105] His plan was to complete the book, send it off to his London publishers, and then continue on eastwards to Japan.

*L-R: Desmond Parsons, his mother Lois, sister-in-law Anne
& Harold Acton on Tsui Hua Hutong, 1935*

But there was an ominous cloud on the horizon. Byron's visit coincided with one from Desmond's mother, Frances. Frances was known commonly by her middle name, Lois. She had separated from Desmond's father and so no longer used the honorific Countess of Rosse. She had remarried in 1920, when Desmond was ten, to Yvo Richard Vesey, thus becoming the even more glamorous-sounding Viscountess de Vesci of Abbey Leix. Lois

---

104 These quotes from 'Letter from Byron to his sister Anne, November 30, 1935 C/O British Consulate, Peiping', *Byron: Letters Home*, p.257.
105 *The Road to Oxiana* (London: Jonathan Cape, 1937).

was a formidable woman and had journeyed to Peking to take care of her youngest child. Byron was surprised to see her so far from home but, unbeknown to him, his old friend was sick already with the Hodgkin's lymphoma that would eventually kill him.

The household at Tsui Hua Hutong was in turmoil about what to do. Eventually, it was decided that Parsons should travel within the next few weeks to England for treatment. Parsons himself, unaware of just how sick he was, hoped to return to Peking after a convalescence in Europe and so asked Byron to stay on and look after his courtyard house until his return. Byron agreed.

Grey, grey, grey…

Desmond Parsons had been instantly and deeply enamoured with Peking. He had written to his old Oxford friend and contemporary, the economist Roy Harrod, 'Life here is so pleasant that I do not feel like returning.'[106] His collections of everything from local flora and fauna to photography, his translation work and teaching at Beida, his beloved courtyard home, had all come to mean so much to him. Quite how far his sexual explorations of the city were successful is not clear. Parsons told Byron that he had had mixed success in Peking sampling 'the pleasures of the east'.[107]

But Byron, whilst admiring Parsons in all matters of taste and style and considering him an aesthete's aesthete, doesn't appear to have appreciated Peking quite so much: 'apart from the temples and palaces – all *(Peking)* is grey, the most positive and emphatic grey you ever saw – all the brick is grey – the landscape is as grey as an engraving – the tiles are grey, so is the air.'[108]

This is, of course, for those who know the remaining older districts of Peking and its surviving hutongs, a reasonably accurate description – the bricks and tiling of the hutong alleyways are (or at least were) invariably grey. It is an aesthetic that then, as now, either enchants or appears monotonous to the visitor. To the likes of Acton and Parsons

106 Knox, *Robert Byron*, p.349.

107 Knox, *Robert Byron*, p.347.

108 Letter from Byron to his sister Anne, November 30, 1935 C/O British Consulate, Peiping. *Byron: Letters Home*, p.257

the grey hutongs were a visual Mecca; a treasure trove of gateways and walls behind which were to be found treasures and gems. To Byron this mystique appeared less obvious.

From the start, Byron and Peking seemed not to agree. Byron was distraught at discovering the severity of his old friend's medical condition (Parsons was, after all, not yet thirty years old) and upset by his imminent departure for Europe, while also constantly frustrated by being unable to communicate with the Chinese (not yet speaking any of the language). Almost immediately he came down with a severe bout of flu (the dreaded *"ganmao"* of northern China) and probably a case of exhaustion after his recent travels in Central Asia and the Russian Far East –

Robert Byron

neither of which improved his mood. He spent January 1936 in a state of virtual collapse but managed to rally in February and at last began work on *The Road to Oxiana*. His collection of notebooks from the long trip to Persia and Afghanistan that would form the basis of the book (five or six diaries, a few odd sheets of notes and a batch of typescript) had by this time arrived safely from England, dispatched by his father.

When he had first arrived in November 1935 Byron had embarked, with Parsons when his health permitted, on the usual round of tourist sights. He had enjoyed such routine Peking pleasures as having tweed suits made to order (25 shillings each), as well as an evening suit (£3.15.0 – Byron estimated this to be less than a quarter of the London price for similar) and a number of silk shirts (4/- each), for a fraction of the cost of a Jermyn Street tailor. The two took day trips out of the city, to the Western Hills and the Great Wall. Parsons's courtyard home was palatial, central (technically in the Eastern City District, but close by the Forbidden City), and comprised several interconnected courtyards with bamboo trees providing shade. Byron was housed in a guest pavilion with its own bathroom. Parsons also had other houseguests at the time; his older brother Michael (the Earl of Rosse) and his wife Anne Messel had arrived on their honeymoon, while Lady de Vesci was still in-situ arranging to take Desmond back to Europe.[109] Byron thrilled Michael Parsons by giving him seeds collected in Siberia for his garden at Birr Castle.[110] Harold Acton, who visited daily, was good friends with both Michael and Byron, knowing both from Eton and Oxford. Additionally, he also knew Anne from his school days as they were all only a few years apart. In the two or three weeks Desmond had remaining to him in Peking they all formed a regular party on expeditions.

Byron wrote at a large desk with a green leather top in Parsons's guest pavilion. He had purchased the desk in a local market. He retained a servant (16/- a month) and a head houseboy who spoke English (30/- a month) to attend him. He planned to write for two to three months to finish the manuscript of *The Road to Oxiana*. He was also hoping to perhaps pick up some freelance journalistic work and indeed did manage to, being commissioned to write two articles on Siberia by Ralph Deakin, the Foreign News Editor for the London *Times*. Worried that his communication skills were poor, he enrolled for Chinese lessons, noting the advances in the language made by both Parsons and Acton since their arrival in the city. As a guest of Parsons, Byron had been introduced to many leading British citizens in China including Sir Frederick Leith-Ross, the chief economic adviser to the British government, who happened to be visiting the city for the Leith-Ross Mission in 1935, attempting to persuade China to reform its currency.

Yet after only a few weeks in the city Byron felt distinctly unimpressed by Peking. Writing to his sister Anne (known in the family as Mibble) he declared in November 1935, 'As for Chinese art and the beauty of Peking – I must wait for it to grow on me, or not to do so. But of architecture in the real sense of the word, there is nothing. That I can see straight

109 Michael was Anne's second husband. Anne, the sister of Oliver Messel the theatre sets designer, had married the barrister Ronald Armstrong-Jones in 1925. They divorced in 1934 and she married Michael Parsons a year later. She was the mother of Anthony Armstrong-Jones, 1st Earl of Snowdon and, more famously perhaps, husband of Princess Margaret and therefore brother-in-law to Queen Elizabeth II.
110 While in Peking Michael Parsons had struck up a friendship with China's leading botanist Professor Hu Hsen-Hsu (Hu Xiansu). Over the next thirty years they corresponded, and Hu sent seeds which, along with Byron's from Siberia and others, created the largest and most diverse herbarium in Ireland. The garden's links with China remain today. See Vanessa Martinez, 'The Chinese Roots of Birr Castle Gardens', *The Irish Times*, September 8, 2016.

off. They can build a wall and make it very big – they have an exquisite capacity for space and layout, both large and small – but cubically and intellectually it is all a vacuum.'[111]

This is perhaps a slightly shocking statement from someone living in one of the city's largest and best decorated hutong courtyard homes; one with all the mod-cons added – flush toilets, hot water boilers, an oil heating system, electric lights – although Parsons had retained the wooden lattice and paper windows and not replaced them with glass as many foreigners did when they occupied courtyard houses.

Most who have tried to reconcile Byron's aesthetic eye with his repeated comments about disliking Peking usually suggest that he was feeling sick and depressed at his old friend's ill-health, and so not disposed to liking the city, as well as having just spent time in a more obviously colourful world of lapis lazuli and in Persia and Afghanistan. It is also true that the winter Byron spent in Peking was one of the longest and coldest on record. He did himself admit, 'Perhaps with a *blue* sky and *green* trees the effect is different.'[112]

And, after a few more weeks, his mood did seem to improve. Byron came to admit that the charm of Chinese art was starting to grow on him and he particularly appreciated, as did so many foreign sojourners, the flocks of swallows flying over the city at dawn and sunset with whistles attached to their legs. Ominously he also notes the occasional provocative fly-pasts by the Japanese air force. Indeed, as Christmas approached he seemed to be getting into his stride – the golden roofs of the temples of the Forbidden City impressed him; the crisp and cold climate he felt suited him; he was making progress with the language and liked his teacher, "Mr Jo". Harold Acton arranged a dinner for him with a Manchu prince and princess. He dined with the British Ambassador, Sir Alexander Cadogan and his wife Lady Theodosia.[113] There was plenty still to complain about. Byron (in common with Acton) hated rickshaws and considered buying a pony and trap. He was homesick, bursting into tears when he happened to see some photographs of a Sussex village. He was

111   Letter from Byron to his sister Anne, November 30, 1935 C/O British Consulate, Peiping. *Byron: Letters Home*, p.258.
112   Ibid, p.259.
113   Byron was good friends with the eccentric composer and writer Gerald Tyrwhitt-Wilson, better known as Lord Berners, who had served previously with Cadogan as a diplomat in Constantinople.

suffering from bouts of writer's block and drinking a bit too much, both brought on, he believed, by his worrying about the obviously desperate health of his friend Desmond and his imminent departure.

A cruel diagnosis

Parsons had been suffering from swollen glands in his neck for some time. His condition was finally diagnosed as Hodgkin's lymphoma – a rare and, though his doctors prescribed treatments in Europe, ultimately fatal cancer then. It was an awful diagnosis. Byron and Acton were both distraught. It is certainly the case that, knowing his good friend was dying, Byron's view of Peking was clouded. It had turned all too swiftly from a place of reuniting old friends in a joint adventure in a faraway land, where none had any particular money worries or social concerns, to a place of mourning and imminent loss.

Lady de Vesci was to depart for England with the ailing Desmond that Christmas as his health deteriorated. Byron, it was agreed, would stay on and look after the Tsui Hua Hutong home with a reduced staff in the hope that Desmond would return after his treatment in Europe. Byron agreed to house-sit, but wrote to his younger sister Lucy in depressed tones, 'icy winds make it impossible to go out – the monuments here bore me – my muse is dead – and altogether I wonder why I exist.'[114]

Desmond, his mother, brother and new sister-in-law all departed Peking for Europe on the Trans-Siberian Express shortly before Christmas. Byron had commissioned articles on Russia to write for the *Times* but was despondent and blocked. He retreated from the social life of the foreign colony – refusing invitations to dinner with Acton, and an American woman who invited him to the cinema. He came down with flu again and was confined in the German Hospital on the edge of the Legation Quarter with a temperature of 101°.[115] Byron was sad for his best friend, homesick, feverish, and suffering from painful neuralgia.

Still, he recovered – the fever abated, the neuralgia went away, he finally got his *Times* articles written. He relapsed occasionally – once becoming distraught at a dinner with a British Legation official and smashing

114 Letter from Byron to his sister Anne, January 18, 1936 C/O Tsui Hua Hutong 8, East City, Peiping. *Byron: Letters Home*, p.265.
115 Now the Beijing Hospital on Dongjiaomin Alley.

some glassware. The British Legation Guard were forced to lock him up for the night till Acton could come and retrieve him the next day and, showing the usual pettiness of British officials abroad, pay to replace the smashed glasses. He detested the Chinese New Year Fireworks ('as though Woolwich Arsenal exploded in one's ear every five minutes'[116]). He had to deal with frozen pipes and a burst boiler that upset him immeasurably. Byron remained in Peking till May – now virtually teetotal to stop a recurrence of his tantrum at the Legation. He remained indoors almost constantly, thinking that the long cold Peking winter would never end.

Perhaps Byron should have been able to rely on Acton more. They did go for walks occasionally and dinners, but they weren't overly close in Peking. Acton, like Parsons, had been rather annoyed by Byron's vocal and determined constant dislike of Peking's architecture. To dislike, and indeed to belittle ('cubically and intellectually *[Peking]* is a vacuum') Peking's green saddleback roofs and traditional floating swallowtail eaves, its skyline and the city's geometric symbolism was the ultimate insult to the Peking aesthetes. However, flush with cash

Harold Acton

from his books, journalism and a couple of philanthropic donations from admirers in England, Byron did start collecting Chinese paintings and eventually acquired over forty works.

When together they both dodged the numerous wealthy American heiresses who passed through Peking expecting to be entertained by a witty aesthete or two. Acton was clearly starting to get ideas for his later *roman-à-clef* of Peking expatriate life, *Peonies and Ponies* (1941).[117] Acton

116   Letter from Byron to his sister Anne, January 18, 1936 C/O Tsui Hua Hutong 8, East City, Peiping. *Byron: Letters Home*, p.265.

117   *Peonies and Ponies*, written after Acton left China in 1939, was dedicated 'To Michael and Anne Rosse, whose laughter and whose sympathy refilled my fountain-pen'.

was more forgiving of other visitors and spent time with Virginia Woolf's nephew Julian Bell, the son of Bloomsburyites Clive and Vanessa Bell, who was teaching in Wuhan and visited Peking occasionally. The best Byron could muster concerning Bell was 'a pleasant half-fledged person with a most ridiculous Bloomsbury voice, which reminds one of 1920.'[118]

He continued to work on his travel diaries into the late spring of 1936 and then, finally finished and by now realising that Desmond Parsons was not going to return, he decided to take ship to Japan. Parsons, still determined he would return to Peking, sent money to pay the rent and servants' wages in advance.

Inevitably, just as Byron was about to leave, Peking's social life became a little less incestuous and more interesting – a Lady Fitzherbert arrived on a sojourn, and there were several dinner parties of delicious royal gossip from London; the Austrian writer Vicki Baum ('one of the sweetest faces... hair done like a parakeet... clothes for a Hollywood cocktail party') arrived having just spent time with the louche circle around the artist Walter Spies and the foreign colony of Ubud in Bali. And a genuine movie star, Anna May Wong, also came to town, and, according to Byron, was interested in renting Parsons's courtyard house.[119] After all his complaining he finally wrote, 'It was sad leaving Peking, the house and all my charming servants. I am now wondering and worrying if my book *(The Road to Oxiana)* is as good as I think. Goodbye Darling – I will write again from Tokyo.'[120]

Tokyo and Japan appeared to revive both his spirits and his inquisitiveness about foreign cultures, but he never wholly changed his mind about Peking: 'All my interest in things, which died in the mortal atmosphere of Peking, has revived now.' His companion in Japan, the art historian and specialist in Asian ceramics, Gerald Reitlinger (who was himself a sojourner in Peking for a time), was more convivial in Tokyo than Acton had been in Peking. Together they explored Tokyo and the Nikko National Park. Byron seemed to be back to his old self. Reitlinger

118   Letter from Byron to his sister Anne, January 24, 1936 C/O Tsui Hua Hutong 8, East City, Peiping. *Byron: Letters Home*, p.267.

119   Comments on Fitzherbert, Baum, and Wong – Letter from Byron to his sister Anne, May 17, 1936 C/O Tsui Hua Hutong 8, East City, Peiping. *Byron: Letters Home*, p.276.

120   Letter from Byron to his sister Anne, June 5, 1936 Aboard Ship, Sea of Japan. *Byron: Letters Home*, pp.277-278.

told the novelist Anthony Powell that Byron enjoyed an affair with a Japanese train attendant on the journey. In June, Byron left Japan for San Francisco.

Sad endings

Desmond Parsons never did return to Peking or China. He died of Hodgkin's lymphoma, which many erroneously believed he contracted by drinking unboiled water in China, in Europe on July 4, 1937. Less than a week later Peking fell to the Japanese and was occupied. Parsons's courtyard home was commandeered by the Imperial Japanese Army.

Byron continued to travel after his Peking sojourn, on through Japan and America, even though he was reportedly 'devastated' by Parsons's death. He attended the last Nuremberg Rally with Unity Mitford in 1938. Byron knew Unity through his long-standing friendship with her distinctly less political sister, the novelist Nancy.[121] Byron was anti-Nazi; Unity extremely pro-Nazi and close to Hitler. Her loyalties effectively ended his friendship with Unity and strained his relationship with Nancy.

Then war came and Byron was signed up as a war reporter. On February 24, 1941 he was travelling to Iran on a reporting trip for the London *Times* on the cargo ship *SS Jonathan Holt* when it was torpedoed and sunk by a German U-boat in the Atlantic Ocean with the loss of fifty-one of her fifty-seven crew. Byron, just thirty-five years old, was among the drowned.

When Nancy Mitford heard of his death she wrote that, of all the friends she had lost in the war, it was Robert Byron she missed the most.[122]

---

121 Nancy Mitford (who never visited China) connects all the characters here. She was a lifelong friend of Harold Acton. Indeed, Acton wrote the first biography of Mitford, published just two years after her death, *Nancy Mitford: A Memoir* (London: Hamish Hamilton, 1975). She also knew Michael (the Sixth Earl of Rosse) and Desmond as well as being close to Desmond's slightly older sister and former Bright Young Thing, Lady Mary Bridget Parsons.

122 Nancy Mitford was also extremely good friends with Byron's old Oxford contemporary Evelyn Waugh. When Christopher Sykes published his biographical sketch of Byron in *Four Studies in Loyalty* (London: Collins, 1946) Waugh wrote to Mitford, 'Sykes has written a lot of balls about the late Robert Byron.' Mitford, who usually agreed with Waugh on most matters, appeared to feel differently about the

Apart from a small guide to London – *Imperial Pilgrimage*[123] – *The Road to Oxiana*, written in Desmond Parsons's Peking courtyard, surrounded by the art, ceramics and furniture of the "aesthete's aesthete", was Robert Byron's last, best known and most enduring book.

portrayal and replied that, 'Sykes is having a great success with his life of Robert. I am delighted.' See Waugh to Mitford, November 27, 1946 and Mitford to Waugh, December 12, 1946, in Ed. Charlotte Mosley, *The Letters of Nancy Mitford and Evelyn Waugh* (London: Penguin, 2010), pp.61-64.

123   Robert Byron, *Imperial Pilgrimage* (London: London Transport, 1937).

Peking Takedown – Two Shootouts in Old Peiping: Dewolfe Schatzel & PJ Lawless (1938)

Dewolfe Schatzel, Commander of the US China Marines Mounted Detachment, Peking, 1937

INTERNATIONAL CRIMINAL SHOWDOWN IN
PEIPING
*'THE GUN BATTLE WAS WAGED BESIDE THE HISTORIC
WATER GATE, NEAR THE AMERICAN EMBASSY, INSIDE
THE LEGATION QUARTER'* [124]

---

124 Associated Press wire story, October 26, 1938.

A shot to the heart

Two shootouts in broad daylight, a man left dead in a Chinese courtyard, a daring jewellery store robbery in which a high-security vault was looted by armed men, a bank heist that saw the robbers escape in high-powered cars through the narrow streets – all the work of an international gang of Chinese and foreign criminals run by a Russian émigré "mastermind" who was wanted in at least three cities. These were men who had cheated death by execution, escaped from prisons, and lived in China as outlaws for years. Eventually the gang got taken down by a determined US Marine Provost Marshal and a tough veteran British cop in kill-or-be-killed gun battles. It sounds like Shanghai? It could well have been Shanghai. Old Shanghai's legends were built on such stories of shootouts, international criminals and daring raids. But this was Peking, the city's normally sedate Legation Quarter and the culmination of an unparalleled December 1937 crime wave that swept the city.

On Saturday January 8, 1938 US Marine Corps Second Lieutenant Dewolfe Schatzel, originally from Findlay, Ohio, and a former Commander of the Marines Mounted Detachment, shot and killed Josef Stanishewsky[125], a Polish career criminal living in Peking and described

Mrs. Lamb   Mr. Lamb

125 Alternatively 'Joseph' and alternatively 'Stanishevsky' or 'Staishewsky'.

as 'one of China's most notorious international crooks.'[126] The killing took place at the home of a celebrated American explorer living in the city named Gene Lamb. Stanishewsky and another man, thought to be Russian, had, just days before, rented a wing of Lamb's extensive villa-style home outside the city walls in the Western Hills. Lamb, a well-known figure to readers of American adventure magazines and viewers of cinema documentaries on the Far East, was away on an exploration and only his wife was at home. Schatzel, the Provost Marshal in charge of military policing at the American Legation in Peking, was hunting for a gang of armed robbers thought to include several US Marines. He had received a tip concerning Stanishewsky's whereabouts and indicating the gang was hiding out at the Lamb residence.[127]

Accompanied by a reported fifteen unarmed Chinese policemen, Schatzel arrived at the Lamb house, about 15 miles from the Legation Quarter as the crow flies, early on that Saturday morning hoping to surprise the robbers while they slept. Schatzel knew the men he sought were Russian-Poles, that is to say men who had been born in Poland while it was still part of the Russian Empire. January 7 is the traditional Russian Christmas and was, for the Russian émigré community in Peking, a night of big drinking and long parties. Schatzel figured his chances of finding the men asleep and hungover were pretty good.

The policemen gathered on the veranda of the property and Schatzel rang the bell. A servant answered the door and called to Mrs Lamb that the police were there. Corrine Lamb came out of the kitchen, surprised to see so many uniformed men on her doorstep. Schatzel explained why they were there. She let the men in and pointed out the part of the property where Stanishewsky and the other man lived.

Then jurisdiction took over. Schatzel, as a US Marine Provost Marshal, had been tasked with uncovering any US Marine involvement in the robberies. However, Stanishewsky and his accomplice, as Poles and Russians, were not included in his remit. Therefore, it was only the Chinese police that could legally enter Stanishewsky's rooms. Schatzel

126 'Quick Thinking US Marine Kills Robber', *Honolulu Star-Bulletin*, January 10, 1938, p.4.
127 Schatzel's name appears in records and the newspapers as alternatively 'DeWolf', 'DeWolfe', 'De Wolf' and 'De Wolfe'. He had been appointed the last Commander of the Horse Marine at the Legation in Peking – a job he took even though he couldn't ride a horse at the time (according to Chinamarine.org).

remained outside, back on the veranda where Mr and Mrs Lamb were known to sit drinking cocktails of an evening.[128] The unarmed Chinese policemen entered Stanishewsky's rooms and discovered proceeds from various jewel robberies that had occurred in Peking in late 1937. They knew they had the right place.

Schatzel had moved from the veranda to an interior courtyard adjacent to the rooms rented by Stanishewsky and his accomplice. He stood patiently outside in the courtyard having a smoke, waiting for the local police to apprehend Stanishewsky and the other man. He then heard shouts and the sounds of fighting from inside Stanishewsky's rooms. Moments later the policemen ran from the rooms out into the courtyard 'like rabbits', pursued by a furious Stanishewsky, in his underwear and clearly having been rather abruptly awakened.[129] He was brandishing a pistol which he was waving around. Schatzel maintained, as did other witnesses, that he clearly told Stanishewsky, 'Don't shoot'. Stanishewsky apparently then raised his gun towards the Marine as if to fire. Acting instantly, and as trained, Schatzel withdrew his service revolver from its holster and fired at Stanishewsky. The single bullet hit Stanishewsky just below the heart, killing him instantly.

Stanishewsky lay dead in the Lambs' courtyard. But his accomplice, who Corrine Lamb thought had been at home too, was now nowhere to be seen, presumably having disappeared through a rear entrance when the shooting started and now long gone. A Chinese servant claimed a white man did escape over the back wall of the house into the hills beyond, clad only in underwear, swiftly disappearing from view.

Schatzel searched the dead man and found a long string of pearls reportedly worth C$200,000 (Chinese dollars) in his inside jacket pocket.[130] The Chinese police searched Stanishewsky's rooms and found a number of gold bullion bars, assorted pieces of jewellery and more pearls, which Schatzel described as ranging in size from 'peas to

128 At least according to the US newspaper women's page and society columnist Virginia Safford who visited the couple at their home and described it a little while later in 1939 while on a five-month trip through China and India. 'Virginia Safford', *The Minneapolis Star*, November 20, 1939, p.11.

129 Quote from Dewolfe Schatzel, 'Suspect Marine in Theft', *Intelligencer Journal* (Lancaster, Pennsylvania), January 10, 1938, p.4.

130 'Quick Thinking US Marine Kills Robber', *Honolulu Star-Bulletin*, January 10, 1938, p.4.

hazelnuts'.[131] They also recovered several passports for various countries and in different names. There was no evidence in the Lamb residence of any US Marine involvement in the robberies that had plagued Peking the previous December. But that didn't mean there wasn't any, and Schatzel stayed on the case.

Three days later an American military tribunal at the United States Consulate in the Peking Legation Quarter considered the events of the early morning of Saturday January 8 past. They called the Chinese policemen, they called Corrine Lamb, they called the servants who had been at work that morning. All maintained that Stanishewsky emerged with a gun held high, that Schatzel had no way of retreating from the courtyard swiftly and that he did say to the Polish criminal, 'Don't shoot' before killing him.[132]

It was a fast and unanimous decision by the court. US Marine Corps Second Lieutenant Dewolfe Schatzel, who, before he joined the Marines, had been an Edison Scholar, an award that paid for his education in physics at the Carnegie Institute of Technology in Pittsburgh, had acted in self-defence and was exonerated in the killing of Josef Stanishewsky, a career criminal wanted in Peking as well as in both the International Settlement and French Concession of Shanghai and implicated as a member of an international gang who had carried out a number of jewel and bank robberies in the Legation Quarter in December 1937.

An international gang in Peiping

Dewolfe Schatzel was officially exonerated but that didn't stop the hunt for the gang or questions over US Marine involvement in what was thought to be a ruthless group of international and Chinese robbers operating in Peking. It was an investigation that took place against the backdrop of six months of Japanese occupation of the city since their invasion in July 1937. The old demarcation lines between the generally collaborationist Peking police constables and the more resistance-inclined detective bureau, the foreigners (both civilian, diplomatic and military)

131 'US Marine Kills Fugitive in $500,000 Peiping Theft', *The Philadelphia Inquirer*, January 10, 1938, p.1.
132 'Quick Thinking US Marine Kills Robber', *Honolulu Star-Bulletin*, January 10, 1938, p.4.

living and stationed in the city, and the Japanese occupation authorities (both the Japanese army and the collaborationist government of the pro-Tokyo Chinese puppet mayor Wang Kemin) were unclear, blurred and contentious. The gang, which may well have included a number of Marines that had gone AWOL from the US Legation Guard, was able to exploit these power vacuums and confusion in jurisdictions to their advantage. December 1937 saw a crime spree in Peking unlike any seen before or since.

The entrance to the Legation Quarter

Conditions in Peking in late 1937 were ripe for an upsurge in criminality. The Japanese occupation of the city had come after a move downwards from Manchuria by Imperial Army troops. As they advanced through the countryside to the outskirts of Peking they eventually bedded in at the Marco Polo Bridge (Luguochao), eight miles from the Forbidden City. On the march south they had followed their normal practice of destroying and burning crops, farms and resistant villages. Firstly, this had led to a surge of desperate refugees from the countryside into Peking. This was straining the city's financial and charitable resources, as well as severely testing its rather haphazard welfare system. There was a great deal of tension between Peking's existing population and the new internal migrants, who were seen as competition for business and resources as well as a potentially large and desperate criminal underclass. Secondly, the Japanese encroachment into northern China had led to food shortages in Peking due to extra demand and lost harvests, with looted supplies regularly diverted to the invading Japanese army. Inflation resulted, with prices rising sky-high and the Chinese Nationalist dollar slumping in value. Cash was rapidly becoming worthless – gold, gems, pearls and other commodities and precious items increasingly became the preferred currency. Thirdly, Peking was effectively now an island with travel into and out of the city problematic, train services severely disrupted, and the nascent air services cancelled. In July 1937 the Japanese engineered a 'provocation' near the Marco Polo Bridge and immediately invaded and occupied Peking.

During the occupation the city was, essentially, a large prison under Japanese control. Many of the foreign colony remaining in Peking took to carrying a gun about their person when venturing outside the Legation Quarter. Times were tough; cash in short supply; residents trapped. Along with the three million or so Chinese were the foreign colony. Although no longer a capital city (Chiang Kai-shek had moved the capital to Nanking in 1927), the legations remained as consulates with military protection. In the case of the United States this was the Fourth Marines, though their numbers had been reduced since the downgrading of Peking as the capital, and then again following the Japanese occupation and the need to defend the more profitable (at least for American business) treaty port of Shanghai.

The non-diplomatic foreign population included some business types who were hanging on despite the advice to evacuate and some Old China Hands who felt too old to leave, had nowhere to go anyway, and who (some having been in the city as far back as the Boxer Uprising in 1900) felt the Japanese occupation was just another trial to endure. Then there were the numerous warlord rulers who had come and gone over the 1920s and early 1930s – all had been weathered and Peking had survived. A few determined missionaries and nuns remained too, still trying to save souls or provide charitable nursing care. As well as them there were approximately a thousand "White Russian" stateless émigrés who had been in the city since fleeing the Bolsheviks after 1917, and a small multinational foreign criminal milieu that lived beyond the reach of their national justice systems in 'faraway' Peking and, even under Japanese occupation, felt able to carry on their nefarious activities.

To the law-abiding in both the Chinese and foreign communities of Peking in late 1937 it felt as if the city was descending into utter chaos – the Japanese military patrolling the streets and dispensing arbitrary justice that was especially harsh to the Chinese and occasionally fatal. Martial law was imposed, followed by curfews, inflation threatening to turn into stagflation, food and power shortages, travel restrictions, and the prospect of total war across China as the Japanese swept south down to Shanghai and Nanking. The 'End of Days' atmosphere was compounded by the fact that it was one of Peking's coldest winters on recent record with both coal, dung and firewood in critically short supply.

The city's murder rate spiked with a number of high-profile murders of wealthy Chinese and white foreigners alongside a record number of dead bodies dumped in the streets. The dumped were those dead from hypothermia, unwanted babies, and old people nobody wanted to care for, as well as the mugged and stabbed, and a few overdoses from the Badlands; all mixed together to be collected by the city. It was impossible for the police, subject to Japanese political interference and their numbers severely depleted anyway, to cope or investigate more than a handful of cases.[133]

Into this vacuum stepped what appeared to be a highly organised and experienced international gang of thieves and robbers. From what we can piece together – and it is all to an extent guesswork, gossip, hints in the newspapers and rumour – the gang was a mixture of Chinese and foreigners, all of whom had been in Peking for some time. The Chinese may or may not have been local Pekingese. After the spate of robberies, they appear to have either left the city or simply melted incognito back into the majority population.

The foreigners ranged possibly from recent deserters or serving members of the Fourth Marines to stateless White Russians who had been in the

---

133 There had been several high-profile murders in December in Peking that involved foreigners (an extremely rare occurrence previously). These included the deaths of several Japanese and French nationals that had attracted press attention, and much gossip in the foreign community. These all followed on from the most sensational murder – a year to the day previous to Dewolfe Schatzel's shooting of Stanishewsky – of Pamela Werner on January 7, 1937 – see my book *Midnight in Peking: How the Murder of a Young Englishwoman Haunted the Last Days of Old China* (Beijing, Penguin, 2012).

city since the early or mid-1920s and others, including Stanishewsky and the other Russian-Pole who disappeared, two Germans, and a man referred to only as a 'British-born Jew'.[134]

The gang's crime wave appears to have started in earnest on December 12, when they broke in and robbed a Chinese-owned jewellery store adjacent to the American Consulate at the western end of the Legation Quarter. In fact the building shared a wall with part of the US Marines' compound. The adjoining wall was, on the American side, an empty storeroom. Someone allowed the robbers into the US Legation and then into the storeroom. They broke through the wall, entered the jewellers, cleaned it out, and then calmly walked out of the American legation compound with their swag.

Peking China   Legation Street in Front of the German Legation & French Post Office.

Then, on December 21, the gang staged an audacious raid on a supposedly highly secure warehouse in the Legation Quarter used by several Chinese jewellers and a Chinese bank with branches in the Quarter, as well as on the nearby retail boulevards of Hatamen and Morrison Streets. A heavily armed gang of four men in masks stormed the warehouse, which had once been the vault of the by-then-defunct Russo-Asiatic Bank in Peking. The men quickly overpowered the (equally well-armed) Chinese security guards and tied them up along with the

134 This person, if they ever existed, was never named and only ever mentioned in the Australian newspapers and not in the Chinese or American press. 'Peiping Bank Robber: International Gang Arrested', *The Age* (Melbourne), February 1, 1938, p.9.

warehouse's watchman. They then stole – indeed the papers reported that they 'cleaned out' – the warehouse of gold bullion bars, jewellery, gems and pearls, estimated at a total of C$500,000; some of which, but by no means all, were recovered later at the home of Mr and Mrs Gene Lamb by the Chinese police and Dewolfe Schatzel.

Rumour was that this robbery was the brainchild of the Russian gang leader and that the four masked men were Stanishewsky and his fellow Pole and two AWOL US marines. The gang leader was the man last seen disappearing over the Lambs' back wall. It seems likely that Stanishewsky had rented the rooms from the Lambs specifically for use as a hideout after the robbery. The bound and tied security guards and warehouse watchman were not discovered until hours later the following morning.

The watchman told the Peking police that he thought one of the armed raiders was a US marine. His reason for thinking this is not clear, but the information was reported back to Commandant Colonel John Marston who, still smarting from the last jewel robbery that had utilised his empty storeroom and suspecting the involvement of a serving American soldier in the crime, tasked Dewolfe Schatzel with getting to the bottom of the allegation. Schatzel stayed on the case. Then, on December 27, the gang struck again.

It appears the same gang hit the Bank of Peking, a Chinese-owned bank, two days after Christmas. Reportedly the gang, once again 'led by a Russian, stole £6,500 worth of gold bullion.'[135] The bank was close to the Legation Quarter and used by both Chinese and foreign clients. The gang walked in, masked up, fired shotguns into the ceiling, and told everyone to lie on the floor. Several gang members watched the customers and staff while the others emptied the teller's drawers of cash and then smashed their way into a number of safety deposit boxes, taking more gold and jewellery. They then calmly walked out of the bank where two tan-coloured Ford V8s were waiting to drive the gang away at high speed. It was the most audacious robbery in broad daylight in Peking in living memory and the gang's haul was the largest of any bank robbery in the city's history too.

---

135 'Peiping Bank Robber: International Gang Arrested', *The Age* (Melbourne), February 1, 1938, p.9. £6,500 in 1938 would be worth approximately £440,000 in 2020 money.

The Russian 'Mastermind'

Any number of questions remained about the gang that terrorised Peking in December 1937. Primarily, perhaps, who was the mysterious Russian leader who the newspapers dubbed a 'mastermind'? The Chinese police, as well as the American and British consulates in Peking, all agreed on the answer to that. It was a man they had known about for some time – a man known as Ivanovich Puhalsky.

Puhalsky was named in the newspapers, both in Peking and in Shanghai, where he was known and had a criminal record with the Shanghai Municipal Police in the International Settlement and the *Sûreté* in the French Concession. On January 13, 1938, after the Legation Quarter jewel robberies and the Bank of Peking heist, a week after Schatzel shot Stanishewsky, and a few days after the Provost Marshal was cleared of any wrongdoing, the Shanghai-based American-owned *China Press* newspaper declared that the Shanghai police were on the lookout for Puhalsky. His photograph was circulated, and his known previous haunts were raided.[136]

Where Puhalsky was born and when he came to China is unclear. He is like a character from a pulp novel – one of those people JP Marquand's Mr Moto refers to when he says, in *Mr Moto is So Sorry* (written in 1938), 'There are so many funny people in Asia… So many are here to get away from their police.'[137] Official police records say that Puhalsky had arrived in Harbin, the major Chinese destination for Russian émigrés, in around 1923. In Harbin he met Stanishewsky and other émigrés involved in the White Russian criminal milieu of that city. The Shanghai newspapers, probably receiving information from the Shanghai Municipal Police and/ or the *Sûreté* in Frenchtown, reported that Puhalsky, and Stanishewsky, had previous criminal records and outstanding arrest warrants in Harbin and, before that, in Vladivostok, the last Russian staging post before emigration for most of the White Russian exodus. Though it may have been press hyperbole it was alleged that both men had been previously sentenced to death in Russia but had both managed to escape the

---

136 'Mastermind in Jewel Robbery Known Here: Puhalsky Sought for Half Million Hold Up in Peiping', *The China Press*, January 13, 1938, p.2.
137 JP Marquand, *Mr Moto is So Sorry* (London: Big Ben Books, 1940), p.40.

firing squad or gallows in the chaos of the revolutionary upheavals. Or, alternatively, that they had been lucky and had been pardoned during the mass amnesties that occurred as the Bolsheviks gradually took control of the country and the White Armies needed recruits.

Moving on from Harbin, Puhalsky had come to Peking, reunited with Stanishewsky and other criminals of his acquaintance back in Manchuria, and formed the gang. Certainly it seemed that Puhalsky moved regularly between Peking and Shanghai as he was known to police in both cities. It was also suggested that Dewolfe Schatzel had come close to finding and arresting Puhalsky and that he was indeed the man seen jumping the Lambs' back wall. As far as Schatzel could tell, helped by Mrs Lamb giving a description of the man with Stanishewsky, the other man, now on the run, had been Puhalsky.

The inside men?

With Stanishewsky dead and Puhalsky on the run, Schatzel and the Chinese police continued their hunt for the rest of the gang. The two German members of the gang were arrested some days later by the Chinese police. Eric Herbolt had been a businessman in Harbin but had fallen on hard times and into criminality.

He was found with another German at a rundown hotel on the edge of the Legation Quarter. The second German could not be formally identified as he had destroyed his identification papers before the police arrested him, but he was thought to be one Herman Lazotta (or sometimes 'La Zotta').[138] Dewolfe Schatzel and the Peking police had raided Lazotta's house. As the local cops were arresting him, Lazotta had, as Schatzel put it, 'dropped the dime' on Stanishewsky, and possibly Puhalsky, telling Schatzel to raid Gene Lamb's place.[139] If there ever was a 'British-born Jew' in the gang, he was never found or identified by name.

After the shooting of Stanishewsky, the escape of Puhalsky and the arrests of Herbolt and Lazotta, Dewolfe Schatzel stayed on the case even though Puhalsky was the only known outstanding member of the gang remaining free. But none of these men, dead, in jail, or in the wind,

---

138 And in one newspaper report 'Perman' rather than Herman.
139 As claimed in 'Suspect Marine in Theft', *Intelligencer Journal* (Lancaster, Pennsylvania), January 10, 1938, p.4.

were ultimately his business as the US Provost Marshal. They were all the problem of the Chinese cops. However, Schatzel was convinced a marine was involved and so he stuck with it. And eventually his determination paid a dividend – he did arrest a marine. It was not an AWOL one as suspected, but a serving marine, Private Matthew Mannherz. The marine from Pennsylvania, who had enlisted in 1934, was arrested and held in the US Legation's Marine Guardhouse.

Mannherz was tried for armed robbery and absence without leave by a general court martial. He pleaded not guilty and sternly denied any involvement in the gang. Quite how Schatzel came to arrest Mannherz is unclear, though it was probably the German Herbolt who had tipped him off. Three Chinese – the warehouse watchman and the two security guards from the Russo-Asiatic Bank vault – appeared at the court martial, identified the marine, and testified that Mannherz had been one of the four men who robbed the vault. But problematically the witness statements by the Chinese men didn't seem to matter. Despite the triple identification, and presumably to Schatzel's surprise and consternation, the court martial acquitted Mannherz and he was freed.

That decision by the court martial looked even more problematic when, a few days later, Eric Herbolt was brought into a Chinese civilian court on charges of being one of the four men in the Russo-Asiatic vault heist, as well as the earlier robbery on the Chinese jewellery store adjacent to the marine barracks. Herbolt point blank refused to name Puhalsky as the Russian mastermind behind the gang's heists but did name Mannherz as one of the gang (as he had probably done to Schatzel previously). The Russian gang boss had needed a marine involved as the jewellery shop heist required plans of the marine quarters to see how best to break into the jewellers, and help entering and leaving the legation compound. Consequently, Mannherz had been targeted and recruited. The court martial chose not to reconvene despite this testimony from Herbolt. Mannherz was swiftly rotated out of China on the next boat home. Herbolt and Lazotta were sent to a Peking jail.

It seems clear that the upper echelons of the US Marine Corps and the US diplomatic presence in Peking didn't much like the idea of a young Leatherneck being involved in an international gang of thieves and so they spirited Mannherz away to avoid any embarrassment or besmirching of the Marine Corps's reputation.

And perhaps also worth a thought is that Dewolfe Schatzel seems to have hinted to the Peking police that the Lambs were worth a closer investigation, though he couldn't himself arrest and/or question them as American civilians. The Peking police, it seems, thought that Schatzel might be on to something and brought in both Gene Lamb and his wife Corrine for questioning at the Morrison Street Police Station, home to the Peking Police Eastern Division's detective squad. Their reasoning: Stanishewsky and, probably, Puhalsky, or at least someone else involved in the three December '37 heists, had been living in the Lambs' courtyard home. Indeed, a large amount of the stolen goods from the Legation Quarter jewellery warehouse heist were discovered on their property. It was also the case that in late 1937 Gene Lamb was, as the *China Press* in Shanghai reported, '...in hard-up financial straits.'

Gene Lamb is a rather forgotten character now, but in the 1930s he was, in America at least, a household name. Lamb had been born in 1895 in Minneapolis[140] and, as a young man, entered the US Foreign Service with postings in Nova Scotia and as a vice-consul in Johannesburg. He served with Naval Intelligence during the Great War. Afterwards he decided not to return to the Foreign Service, to what might have been a successful and high-flying diplomatic career, and opted instead to become an explorer. He focussed almost exclusively on Asia and spent much of the next thirty years in China. Lamb was a determined self-publicist and made sure everyone knew about his adventures. Indeed, a major way of financing his trips was through newspaper articles, magazine stories and documentaries shown before the main features at cinemas that all led to high-paying speaking engagements and lecture tours.

Lamb was especially well known for his travels through Mongolia and 'Mohammedan' China (today's Xinjiang and Gansu) where he claimed to have been an adviser to various Muslim warlords. He was also well known for a two-year expedition to northern Tibet under the auspices of the Explorers Club[141], known as the 'Lamb Expedition'. The idea was to collect specimens of flora and fauna, record the voice of Tibet's Grand Lama and finish with a detailed mapping of Lake Kokonor (Qinghai

---

140 Some sources say he was born in Washington DC.
141 An American-based society with the goal of promoting scientific exploration and field study. The club was founded in New York City in 1904 and served as a meeting point for explorers and scientists worldwide.

Lake), China's largest lake that had not previously been mapped in such detail. It was claimed that in 1924 Lamb had been 'the first white man to photograph the Buddha of Tibet.'[142] Lamb claimed to speak three Chinese dialects, Mongolian, Tibetan and some Zulu. His wife Corrine was left alone for quite long periods of time in the 1930s as he travelled back to western China and Mongolia. Lamb made many claims about his 'insider' status in China's republican circles and claimed to be a close acquaintance of Chiang Kai-shek and Soong Mei-ling (Madame Chiang).

Whatever the truth or otherwise of his access to the most senior circles in Nanking, in the 1930s Gene and Corrine were living in Peking and he did some sort of arrangement with the Nationalist Chinese government concerning explorations. But funding in China was scant and the newspapers weren't buying his stories quite so often, while the Japanese invasion of northern China had rather curtailed exploring. He did need money, it seems. Still, if there was any link between the Lambs and Puhalsky's gang it was never proved. The Peking police released the couple a few days later after questioning.

The Lambs returned to America in late 1939. During World War Two, Gene once again worked in Naval Intelligence, though he suffered repeated ill health. Corrine died in 1945. A year later Gene remarried to a woman named Elizabeth. In the summer of 1948 Gene and Elizabeth had moved to Cheyenne, Wyoming, and he was preparing to start a new lecture tour across the United States, if his health could stand it. It could not and he died of heart disease in the Los Angeles General Hospital on August 20, 1948.

With Mannherz acquitted and the Lambs cleared of any involvement in the gang, Dewolfe Schatzel's involvement in the case was over. His commanding officer, Colonel John Marston, ordered him back to regular duties. But the whole business wasn't over for everyone. There was still the matter of the Russian gang boss Puhalsky. And so step forward, the British Chief of Police for the Peking Legation Quarter, PJ Lawless.

142 'Obituary – Gene Lamb', *The Philadelphia Inquirer*, August 21, 1948, p.18. It is not clear if this claim is true as there are earlier photos of candidates for who the paper refers to as 'the Buddha of Tibet': Thubten Choekyi Nyima, the ninth Panchen Lama (1883-1937) was photographed earlier, by several photographers including the Swedish geographer and explorer Sven Hedin, while the Thirteenth Dalai Lama, Thubten Gyatso (1876-1933) was photographed earlier by several people including by the Darjeeling-based photographer M. Sain.

Gunfight at the Water Gate

It's hard to imagine that it was never remarked upon in the late 1930s that the British officer charged with attempting to uphold the fight against the rising tide of crime in the Peking Legation Quarter was a man called 'Lawless'. Peking was not Shanghai – foreigners didn't have treaty port rights and the Peking police policed Peking. But the Legation Quarter was recognised as foreign ground with its own administration, gates and protective force, including a few policemen to deal with any issues that arose among the foreign population. As a foreigner, if you caused trouble, got drunk, got into a fight, swindled someone or murdered them outside the Legation Quarter, you were the Peking police's problem. Disturb the peace and lawfulness of the Quarter and, in 1938 at least, you were PJ Lawless's problem.

Peter Joseph "PJ" Lawless was born in County Wicklow in 1879. His father served in the British Army and the family were moved to Taunton in Somerset when Lawless was in his early teens. In 1893, at just fourteen, he followed his father's footsteps and joined the Somerset Light Infantry with the rank of "Boy" and served till 1913. At thirty-four years old, with a blemish-free twenty-year army career behind him, he took a job as an Inspector in the British Municipal Police in the Tientsin Concession and moved to China. Soon after arriving he must have met his future wife, Louise, the daughter of a Protestant missionary stationed in Tientsin. They were married in Tientsin's All Saints Church in September 1914. Although Lawless had been born a Roman Catholic it was a Church of England ceremony. In the 1930s Lawless left Tientsin to move to Peking as the Legation Quarter's Secretary and Chief of Police – essentially the man who kept order in the diplomatic district.

Lawless was short but stocky. His soft burr, a mix of Wicklow and Somerset accent, belied a no-nonsense attitude. In 1938 PJ Lawless was fifty-nine years old but still maintained a military bearing from his army days. He was known to be efficient, determined, intolerant of laziness and fools, as well as a good soccer player. Lawless was a man who famously didn't bend, saw things through to the end, and didn't forget a criminal's face. Puhalsky's gang had robbed a jeweller, a warehouse and a bank on Lawless's patch. That wouldn't stand and it wouldn't be forgotten.

Puhalsky had been on the run since the January shootout at Gene Lamb's house that left Stanishewsky dead. He'd disappeared but PJ Lawless didn't think he'd gone far. The Japanese had a cordon around Peking and Puhalsky, as a European, couldn't survive long trying to hide out in the countryside. The Chinese police still had a WANTED notice out for Puhalsky and a reward. Lawless reckoned anyone hiding him in the majority-Chinese quarters of Peking would soon sell him out for the money; the same within the Russian émigré community that was mostly poor and desperate. If Puhalsky was still alive, Lawless believed, then he was hiding somewhere in the confines of the Legation Quarter. And so Lawless kept on looking for him. But Puhalsky, wherever he had gone to ground, was well hidden. It was not until nearly ten months later, in October 1938, that Lawless, a copper who famously never forgot a face, finally spotted him and ran him to ground. He'd been right, Puhalsky was still in the Legation Quarter.

PEKING GANG LEADER SHOT

Honolulu Star Bulletin, October 26th, 1938

Lawless tracked Puhalsky down to a hideout within the jurisdiction of the Quarter, at its far western end, near the American Legation's compound, the Peking Railway Station and the massive Chienmen Gate. Puhalsky had been surreptitiously slipping in and out of the Legation Quarter through the city's old Water Gate. In 1938 the old sluice gate was abandoned and disused. It had history though. It had been the gate under the wall of the Tartar City through which British Indian troops had entered the Legation Quarter in August 1900 to break the Siege of the Legations by the Boxers. The sluice gate was five hundred metres away from the British Legation. Lawless, a patient man, finally confronted Puhalsky coming through the gate one day.

Peking's old Water Gate

Peter Lawless forced Puhalsky into a corner and ordered him to surrender. Then several crucial seconds passed. Puhalsky responded by drawing a pistol and firing at Lawless. Fortunately unwounded, Lawless returned fire and hit Puhalsky in his side.[143] Puhalsky, injured, was turned over to the Peking police by Lawless. Still just about alive, Peking's most notorious foreign gang leader of the 1930s was finally under arrest.

Lost records

What happened to Herbolt, Lazotta and Puhalsky is lost to history. Their eventual fate might be tucked away somewhere in an archive, but I can't find it. They were imprisoned in 1938 in a Chinese jail. I do not know which one. It was a confusing and chaotic time. The Japanese were in occupation, and eventually all Allied foreigners, including Peter Lawless, would be interned till the end of the war. The fate of the stateless Russians, like Puhalsky, was unclear. After Pearl Harbour the German-Japanese Axis was cemented – perhaps Herbolt and Lazotta, as Germans, were

---

143 Details of the Lawless-Puhalsky gun battle from 'Peking Gang Leader Shot', *Honolulu Star-Bulletin*, October 26, 1938, p.4.

freed? Perhaps all three were freed? There may have been an amnesty. They may have been repatriated after the war, or they may have died of one of the many diseases that killed prisoners in Chinese jails in wartime conditions. Take your pick. Cholera, typhoid, malaria, tuberculosis, hepatitis, beriberi, gonorrhoea…

Dewolfe and Ida Mae Schatzel on their wedding day, Tientsin, March 1939

Provost Marshal Dewolfe Schatzel got married shortly after his gun battle with Stanishewsky. His university sweetheart Ida Mae came out to China in 1939 and they were married in Tientsin, where Schatzel was then a marine commander.[144] Dewolfe Schatzel remained in the Marine Corps and the couple had three daughters – Susan, Sara and Jane. In the late 1950s he served in Hawaii as Chief of Staff for Fleet Marine Force Pacific and the Schatzels were living in Makalapa. The couple took up golf. In 1960 Schatzel was posted as colonel in charge of the marine barracks on Treasure Island, the US military base in San Francisco Bay. After retiring from the Marine Corps in the late 1960s Dewolfe and Ida settled in Dallas, Texas.

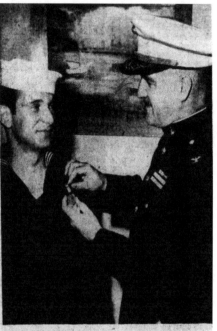

Peter Lawless would be interned by the Japanese in Weihsien Camp in Shandong. In the internment camp Lawless was in charge of the Discipline Committee, adjudicating on matters between inmates. When one inmate was found guilty of stealing from another, or from the camp supplies, Lawless was reputedly harsh on them, forcing them to run laps of the camp in broad daylight so all the other inmates knew who the thief was.[145] After the war

MEDAL FOR HERO—John F. Schiavone (left) of San Leandro receives Navy and Marine-Corps medal for heroism from Marine Col. DeWolf Schatzel in ceremonies in Alameda. Schiavone was cited for leading the rescue of two Marine pilots pinned in the flaming wreckage of a helicopter last year on Okinawa. He lives at 16365 Gordon Way.

Lawless was to testify before the International Military Tribunal for the Far East (IMTFE) regarding Japan's actions in the drug dealing business in China. PJ Lawless died at his home, back in Taunton, Somerset, in 1952. He was seventy-two.

The marine implicated in the Puhalsky Gang's jewellery heists, Private Matthew Mannherz, seems to have rather reinvented himself after Peking. In 1947 an announcement appeared in the newspapers that Miss

---

144 Some sources called his wife Ivy.

145 Greg Leck, *Captives of Empire: The Japanese Internment of Allied Civilians in China, 1941-1945* (Philadelphia: Shandy Press, 2006), p.248.

Josephine Anthony of Frackville, Pennsylvania, had married Mr Matthew Mannherz of Bristol, Pennsylvania, at St. Joseph's Church in Pottsville, PA. The couple seem to have had a fairly prosperous life in Pennsylvania and a son. Josephine died in 1985 in Newton, PA, and Mannherz in 1990 in a Florida retirement home.

Back in 1947 when the local papers reported on Matthew and Josephine's wedding, Mannherz's marine days were not mentioned, nor his possible involvement in a bank robbery and two of the biggest jewellery heists in China's history. However, the bride is noted as wearing a dress of white slipper satin, a tiara of Chantilly lace, a bouquet of white lilies and, as 'a gift from the bridegroom', 'a strand of pearls'. Makes you think, doesn't it?[146]

146 'Miss Josephine Anthony Bride of Bristol Man', *Evening Herald* (Pottsville, Pennsylvania), November 10, 1947, p.5. I should note that it is possible that Mannherz could legitimately claim to have attended the University of Peking as some marines were sent there for language training, though these were normally of a higher rank than Mannherz in 1938 and invariably those who also had some specialist interest in China.

Not the Best Peking Christmas:
Denton Welch (1932)

'I looked out on to the wide streets which had open trenches down the middle. Little clouds of freezing dust flew about, and the low grey-roofed houses seemed like large crouching mice.' [147]

147   Denton Welch's first impressions of Peking in 1932, *Maiden Voyage* (London: Hamish Hamilton, 1943), p.268.

From Shanghai to England to Peking...

When Denton Welch is remembered today it is invariably as a writer and painter. His line illustrations, including those that accompany his (partially fictionalised) autobiography *Maiden Voyage*, were highly praised and his writing considered vivid and individual. Welch was perhaps a little ahead of his time – his 1944 novel, *In Youth is Pleasure*, was considered perverse and unpleasant by some critics at the time. It is a highly sensual novel recalling a bucolic England before the Second World War through the eyes of Orvil, a boy not unlike the younger Denton.[148] Orvil is obsessed with his mortality, having never got over the death of his mother. He is a voyeur and hints at the ambiguity of his sexuality, his overt dislike of boarding schools, and his distant father.

Maurice Denton Welch was born in Shanghai at the Victoria Nursing Home in March 1915. The Victoria had been built by the Shanghai Municipal Council in 1887 to celebrate Queen Victoria's Golden Jubilee. It proudly announced that its twenty-five beds were serviced by 'an efficient English nursing staff.'[149] Denton was the third child after his older brothers Bill and Paul. His mother, Rosalind, was doting and his father, Arthur Welch, a successful China trader. Denton's family was comfortably off and his father a pillar of the Shanghai business community as a director of Wattie & Company, rubber estate managers, with a client list that included Sir Elly Kadoorie. However, he was always to be a remote figure in Denton's life and a man usually referred to, by his son at least, as 'unresponsive'.[150] His mother had a more exciting and adventurous backstory, being a daughter of the late Thomas Bassett of New Bedford, Massachusetts, who had become the captain of a Yangtze steamer and brought his daughters up in China, often aboard his steamers, as Christian Scientists. Denton relished this part of his history – not

148   Denton Welch, *In Youth is Pleasure* (London: Routledge, 1944).

149   *The Directory & Chronicle for China, Japan, Corea, Indo-China, Straits Settlements, Malay States, Siam, Netherlands India, Borneo, the Philippines, and etc.* (Hong Kong: The Hongkong Daily Press Office, 1910), p.840.

150   From the introduction by Michael De-La-Noy to Denton Welch, *I Left My Grandfather's House* (London: Allison & Busby, 1984). The first edition of the book, without De-La-Noy's introduction, was published posthumously after Welch's death in 1958.

least his mother's old family glassware and silver that they kept in their Shanghai home.

Denton and his family regularly travelled backwards and forwards between England and Shanghai, a succession of long ocean voyages he recalled in detail later in *Maiden Voyage*. If opting to remain in China during the summer months then the family holidayed in either the relative mountain cool of Mokanshan, near Hangchow, or the beaches of Weihaiwei, where the family rented a house overlooking Half Moon Bay (Shang Yai Sha Tan). When not with the boys, Arthur and Rosalind were reasonably adventurous for the times and took trips on their own to Java. One year they took young Denton and his brothers to the Diamond Mountains in Japanese-occupied Korea where he marvelled at the frozen lakes and the ground littered with what looked like frozen quartz.[151] The boys saw wild bears in the forest above the family's rented house.[152]

At eight years of age Denton might well have been sent back to England for his education, but his mother, not raised in the English public school tradition, didn't want to part with him at such a young age and so it was agreed he would remain in Shanghai for a few years longer than usual. The family lived in a house 'with long, heavy arched verandahs aflame with Virginia creeper. Inside it was cool and lofty, the floors smelt of polish and the drawing room was scattered with baskets of flowers that friends had sent.'[153] It was a large house with a sizeable garden that included a coach-house for the *mafoo* (groom) and stables that still contained an old carriage.

Denton was initially tutored at a small private school for British children run by a Mrs Paul where, he claimed, he learnt nothing beyond basic spelling. For a time he was sent to England, to family, for reasons he didn't understand initially. All became tragically clear when he returned to Shanghai after the news that his mother had died of nephritis, a kidney disease. Denton and his mother had been very close and he had had no idea of her illness (shades again of *In Youth is Pleasure*). The news naturally devastated him.

151 Now Mount Kumgang in North Korea.
152 Recalled in 'I Can Remember', contained within Denton Welch (Ed. James Methuen-Campbell), *Where Nothing Sleeps: The Complete Short Stories (and Other Related Works), Volume One* (Yorkshire: Tartarus Press, 2005).
153 Ibid.

Eventually, in the autumn of 1929, when he was fourteen, Denton was sent to England once again, this time to Repton School, a private boys' school for the upper classes and with all the stereotypical problems of loneliness and bullying, bad food and cold showers. Looking back on his school days Denton wrote: 'Every morning when I woke up and remembered where I was, I felt something draining out of me, leaving me weak... I knew that I could not stay there.'[154] Indeed he didn't, if *Maiden Voyage* is to be believed, and he ran away from the school at least once. Recalling his own time at the school, the writer Edward Upwood (who was slightly older than Denton) reflected, 'Everyone was homosexual, up to a point, at Repton.'[155] Denton hated the school, though he liked many of his contemporaries there, including Roald Dahl and Denton's best school friend, Geoffrey Lumsden, later a successful actor.[156] Denton spent most of his spare time in Repton's art department. Shortly before his seventeenth birthday he left Repton, glad to finally escape. It was decided that he should return to Shanghai. He was taken to Piccadilly, which was then home to many tailors that specialised in clothes specifically for the tropics and the colonies, to be fitted out in grey flannel and Palm Beach (linen) suits, along with several Panama hats. He was then put aboard a liner to sail home to China via Suez.

In Shanghai, five years after his mother's death, Denton's father had moved from the large family villa on the Avenue Foch[157] in the French Concession to a new modern apartment at Rivers Court on the slightly more suburban Yu Yuen Road[158], an address more suited to a widowed man needing modern conveniences. Rivers Court's modernity was more suited to Denton too, who, though he had spent much of his childhood in Shanghai, and then endured a British public school, had a lifelong horror of dirt, grubbiness and filth. Rivers Court had deep blue carpeting throughout, electric candelabra, and Botticelli reproductions in silver

---

154 Welch, *Maiden Voyage*, p.3.

155 'Hello to Berlin, Boys and Books', *The Daily Telegraph*, May 27, 2004.

156 Lumsden was successful both in the West End and on Broadway. To British television audiences he is best remembered as Captain Square in *Dad's Army*, the pompous commander of the Eastgate platoon of the Home Guard and Captain Mainwaring's sworn enemy.

157 Now Yanan Road.

158 To be precise, Apartment 7A. Rivers Court was at No.753 Yu Yuen Road. Yu Yuen Road is now Yuyuan Road.

frames above fringed and tasselled Knole sofas in the common areas. Denton's father's apartment featured a verandah, Chinese lanterns in the hallway, Persian rugs, a bearskin on the polished wood floor, Korean cabinets, traditional Chinese blackwood stands, American bathroom plumbing, comfy worn leather armchairs, and an open fire.[159] All very *très moderne* Shanghai. Though living alone, his father also maintained a couple of servants. From Rivers Court Denton enjoyed walking into the central districts of the Shanghai Settlement to the east as well as visiting the Chinese villages and graveyards closer to Rivers Court to the west, just beyond the boundaries of the International Settlement.[160]

As a young teenager Denton had developed an interest in Chinese antiques and curios and had become something of a minor collector within the confines of his limited budget. Before his mother had died, she had taken him 'antiquing' while on trips to England, also encouraging him in his interests in drawing, history and architecture. His enthusiasm continued after her death back in China. Through his father Denton became acquainted with a Mr Butler, a porcelain collector, who took him along on collecting trips to Nanking, Kaifeng, and up the Yangtze to Ichang.[161] Back home he explored the antique shops of Shanghai's Bubbling Well Road, Yates Road, Nanking Road and, especially, the curio stores that lined Peking Road.[162] With little studying to do, Denton spent much of the humid summer months by the pool of the Columbia

---

159 Welch, *Maiden Voyage*, pp.122-123.

160 The original building still stands and is now called Jingning Lu. Rivers Court originally accommodated twenty-one families according to the 1936 Shanghai residential listings. They included British, American, German, Danish, Dutch and Greek married couples and their children. Among them were business executives in industry (steel, tobacco, shipping and textiles), finance (stockbroking and commodities trading), professionals (a river pilot and a statistician for the China Customs Service), as well as the manager of the nearby Columbia Country Club, of which many of the residents (including Denton's father) were members. My thanks to Shanghai historian Patrick Cranley for this information.

161 This gentleman could either be Hamilton Butler, a Vice Consul at the United States Consulate in Canton in 1912, or PD Butler, American Consul General at Mukden in 1936.

162 Now Nanjing West Road, Shimen No.1 Road, Nanjing East Road, and Beijing Road respectively.

Country Club.[163] He later made veiled claims that this time was spent exploring the city and, it seems, his sexuality – following a man and spying on him at the Canidrome entertainment complex; going to the St. George's Cabaret with an American marine; daringly inviting a British soldier home to Rivers Court while his father was at work.[164]

Such was Denton Welch's 1932 – a relatively carefree year spent largely exploring Shanghai after the double traumas of the sudden loss of his mother and years of the horrors of the British public school system. But what next for the young man? He knew he would have to decide in the new year. To clear his head, and get some advice from his relatives, Denton's father sent him to Peking to think about his future. He was to spend Christmas 1932 with Uncle Harry and Aunt Dos.

A tailor stitched an old moleskin rug inside Denton's only overcoat to upgrade it from a Shanghai winter coat to a thicker Peking winter coat. Denton boarded the "Blue Express" train for the twenty-seven-hour journey north.

At Uncle Harry's and Aunt Dos's

Though Denton may have known his uncle as Harry and his aunt as Dos, they were usually referred to by the rest of the Peking foreign colony as Sir Harry Halton and Lady Dorothy (hence "Dos") Fox. Harry Fox had come from a relatively humble background as the son of a merchant. He was born in Ealing, West London in 1872, was educated at Dulwich College, and then served as a forty-year veteran of the Chinese Consular and Diplomatic Service.

Sir Harry had initially, as was usual in the China Consular Service, been appointed a lowly Student Interpreter in Peking in August 1890 to perfect his language skills for a couple of years

Sir Harry Halton Fox

---

163 The Columbia Country Club was formerly on Columbia Road (now Panyu Road) and has recently been subjected to a "restoration".

164 The main entrance to the Canidrome sporting and entertainment complex was on Rue Lafayette (now Fuxing Middle Road) and the St. George's Cabaret on Route Doumer (now Donghu Road), both in the French Concession.

before his first posting. In 1893 he had been posted as acting Vice-Consul in Chemulpo.[165] From there he moved slowly up the diplomatic ranks with postings to Cheng-tu and Nankow, as acting Consul at Wenchow, then Samshui, Wuchow, and then Samshui again before, in 1900, being made acting Vice-Consul at Shanghai in 1900 through 1901 (and therefore missing the Boxer troubles in other parts of China and the Siege of the Legations in Peking). In 1902 he was posted once again to Chemulpo; then to Wuchow once more; then to the small and rather insignificant treaty port of Kongmoon before moving to be Consul at Ichang on the Yangtze in 1906.

Fox's career was not exactly glittering – 'plodding' would be a better way of describing it. His day-to-day work in various small treaty ports in southern China and along the Yangtze was about trade and extra-territorial rights. Essential enough perhaps to British interests in China, but dull. Many of these postings – Kongmoon and Samshui in Guangdong (where he got a serious case of malaria and had to be taken to recover in Hong Kong); Ichang in Wuhan; Wuchow in Guangxi, were relatively lonely outposts with small foreign communities largely composed of rather stern and serious missionaries. Paperwork to do, reports to send, local officials to be courted, irate British businessmen to be assuaged, the small budget of the consulate to be stretched as far as possible, and all accounted for down to the last pound, shilling and penny. It helped if you weren't prone to the drink, bouts of loneliness or introspection, and had a supportive wife.

If Harry had a passion then it was the scintillating topic of the control of taxes on goods moving around China, a subject he gave an impassioned speech about to the Royal Central Asian Society in London in 1931, and which was actually broadcast on the BBC. He sat on the committee that returned Weihaiwei to China in 1924 and also on the stunningly boring-sounding (but no doubt very important) International Commission for the Revision of the Chinese Customs Tariff in 1918. Apparently, more revisions were needed and Sir Harry, once again, joined the committee for further revision discussions in 1922. It is easy to see Harry Fox as 'Her Britannic Majesty's Representative' that Somerset Maugham encounters on his travels through China in 1920, recorded in his collection of sketches, *On a Chinese Screen*:

165 Now Incheon in South Korea.

He was a man of less than middle height, with stiff brown hair *en brosse*, a little toothbrush moustache, and glasses through which his blue eyes, looking at you aggressively, were somewhat distorted. There was a defiant perkiness in his appearance which reminded you of the cock-sparrow, and as he asked you to sit down and inquired your business, meanwhile sorting the papers littered on his desk as though you had disturbed him in the midst of important affairs, you had the feeling that he was on the look out for an opportunity to put you in your place. He had cultivated the official manner to perfection.[166]

Maugham was often quite cutting in his descriptions of minor officials, though he does not name his subject or the small treaty port he encountered him in. It probably wasn't Harry Fox, whom Denton described as 'a little man with broad shoulders and large stomach', but it could well have been.[167] Fox was retired by 1920, although Denton did view him as still quite pompous and rather harsh. He had apparently once been quite rude and supercilious to someone at the bar of the Peking Club, an action that had not been forgotten by some of the more staid membership. Legation Quarter Peking could sometimes get quite petty that way. Still, an afternoon's steady drinking and reading of several weeks-old copies of *The Times* was undoubtedly enlivened when the offended member picked Sir Harry up and threw him over the bar into the barman's lap!

Plodding, boring, petty – except that Harry Fox had rather redeemed himself with a good marriage. In 1896, Harry Fox had surprised his colleagues by marrying (or perhaps it was her acceptance of his proposal that led to the surprise?) an interesting woman – Josephine Bassett. Josephine was Rosalind's sister and therefore Denton's maternal aunt. Josephine was also, of course, the daughter of an American Yangtze steamship skipper. The former diplomat PD Coates noted in his study of the men who were the British China consuls that Fox's marriage to Josephine was perfect, considering that his new wife was expected to

166 William Somerset Maugham, *On a Chinese Screen: Sketches of Life in China* (London: Heinemann, 1922), p.57.
167 Welch, *Maiden Voyage*, p.271.

'rough it' at his next posting in Samshui.[168] Sadly, Josephine died in 1900.

Still, Harry Fox pulled off a second marriage to a second interesting woman. In 1905 Harry remarried, to Dorothy Noott (or sometimes Noote) who came from the seaside town of Broadstairs in Kent. While not a Yangtze steamer captain's daughter, Dorothy, whom the family all knew as Dos, was, it seems, keen to travel with Harry to the remote outposts he served in and also keen to stay on in Peking after his retirement. Everyone said that Harry Fox had married well, twice.

Sir Harry finished his formal diplomatic career in 1930 as Commercial Counsellor to the British Consulate in Peking.[169] He was by now a Sir, a Knight Commander of the Most Excellent Order of the British Empire (KBE), and a Companion of the Most Distinguished Order of Saint Michael and Saint George (CMG). Silly British nonsense perhaps, but these things did mean something in the fusty atmosphere of the Legation Quarter's diplomatic circles, especially the British component of them. Sir Harry had also made a good living as a diplomat – minor treaty ports might be dreary postings, but the living costs were lower than in Peking, Nanking or Shanghai, and so Harry and Dos had a nice nest egg on top of his pension and lived in some reported style in the heart of the Legation Quarter. In short, Sir Harry and Lady Dos were well-heeled, veteran China Hands and Legation Quarter notables. 1932 had been a good year for the Foxes too – their only son, Captain PRH Fox, had become engaged to a woman named Enid of whom Harry and Dos heartily approved.

Michael De-la-Noy, one of Welch's biographers, says that Denton recalled Aunt Dos for her 'high dog-collar of pearls', 'scarab rings', and smell of Violettes de Parme. She was always with her loyal maid Mrs. Clutterbuck, who Denton had, as a young man, thought was called 'Clara Butt'. De-la-Noy also says Denton had not liked Dos as a young boy but had grown to like her later.[170] Peking in late December is, of course, freezing, though apparently, when Denton's Shanghai train pulled in to the

---

168 PD Coates, *The China Consuls: British Consular Officers, 1843-1943* (Hong Kong & Oxford: Oxford University Press, 1988).

169 The former Embassy/Legation being technically downgraded to a consulate after the relocation of the Chinese capital to Nanking in 1927.

170 Michael De-la-Noy, *Denton Welch: The Making of a Writer* (London: Viking, 1984).

Chienmen Station she was nevertheless waiting on the platform for him: "A miserable eddy of dust swirled round as we kissed."[171] The drive to the Foxes' Legation Quarter home was no more than five minutes. Denton was shown his rooms and then left to explore Peking at Christmas.

Peking's Legation Quarter

A Legation Quarter Christmas

In Peking's Legation Quarter in the winter of 1932, everyone was reading the new Ann Bridge novel *Peking Picnic*, which was full of Legation Quarter gossip and secret affairs.[172] Bridge was the pseudonym of Mary Ann Dolling Sanders, otherwise known as Lady O'Malley, the author wife of Owen St. Clair O'Malley of the British diplomatic service who had been posted to Peking in 1925 for two years. The novel rather divided opinion between the staid old-school diplomatic community and the younger, racier set. Diplomatic circles were also concerned about the seemingly increasing belligerence from Tokyo towards northern China after the annexation of Manchuria and the announced preparations to create a new Japanese-controlled state of Manchukuo to be headed by the "Last Emperor" Puyi. Still, Peking appeared, despite the encroachment of Japan not that far north, to have been lucky in 1932 – a severe cholera

---

171 Welch, *Maiden Voyage*, p.267.
172 Ann Bridge, *Peking Picnic* (Boston: Little, Brown, 1932).

outbreak was contained south of the Yangtze. Though there was a housing crisis in Peking due to the number of refugees flooding in from the fighting along the Manchurian border, so far the twin problems of food shortages and rampant inflation had not become as severe as predicted by many. And so neither marauding Japanese or warlord troops, nor disease outbreaks, inconvenienced Denton's train ride north from Shanghai.

That same December a Miss Maude May Babcock of the University of Utah, Salt Lake City, was in Peking leading a tour of young ladies to the ancient city. She reported to *The Gazette* of Montreal that she and her young ladies had experienced 'not the slightest difficulty' travelling from Shanghai to Peking by railway, but that European visitors far outnumbered Americans in Peking that winter, indicating to Miss Babcock that Americans were (unnecessarily) more nervous of the news from northern China than their European counterparts. All was calm, according to Miss Babcock, reporting too that the Young Marshal of Mukden, Chang Hsueh-Liang, was occupying quarters at the old Summer Palace next door to several foreigners also resident there, and that they all got on in a most neighbourly fashion.[173]

Despite the cold weather, Christmas was generally considered a quite magical time in Peking. For the foreign colony Christmas shopping was a tradition – Hatamen and Morrison Streets were crowded, as were the stores of the Legation Quarter; Chinese policemen in olive drab uniforms with revolvers were directing the holiday traffic. Charcoal braziers were lit outside shops to provide some sense of comfort and warmth to window shoppers, and fish skin lanterns with candles inside were strung about to allow shoppers to see in the early evening gloom of a Peking December.

For the foreigners who celebrated Christmas, gifts were of course exchanged, and cards sent and received. The holidays ran long, into the New Year (by the Julian calendar), and the Russian Christmas on January 7 according to the Gregorian calendar was also celebrated by many, not just the city's Russian émigré community. There were of course church services – Catholic and Protestant – for those so inclined, while carol services boosted attendance. Some took their Christmas dinner on Christmas Eve and some on Christmas Day, either at home or at one of

173 'Peiping's Charms Intact', *The Gazette* (Montreal, Quebec), December 22, 1932, p.15. The Young Marshal Chang Hsueh-liang (Zhang Xueliang) being the son of the Old Marshal Chang Tso-lin (Zhang Zuolin).

the hotels either within, or close to, the Legation Quarter: the Grand Hôtel de Pékin on Chang An Chieh, the Grand Hotel des Wagons-Lits near the railway station, or (mostly for the more boisterous bachelor contingent) the Hotel du Nord, just outside the Legation Quarter to the east near the Hatamen Gate.

Ice skating was a serious Christmas tradition among the foreign colony in Peking, particularly those of around Denton's age. Ice skates, sweaters, scarfs, caps and gaiters could all be purchased from Lee's General Store on the corner of Hatamen Street and Legation Street. There were several ice rinks including Beihai Lake, and one temporarily erected in the grounds of the French Legation.

Peking Union Medical College in snow

However, the Legation Quarter and the self-obsessed, incestuous world of the Peking diplomatic corps was its own crowded goldfish bowl, and never more so than during the hectic social round of Christmas. The Great Powers – Britain and France, as well as Belgium, Italy, the Netherlands and, by 1932, the United States, were the centre of the social whirl, though the numbers were padded out with diplomats and important personages from elsewhere. Attending a dinner party in the Legation Quarter several years previously, Somerset Maugham recalled the minister from Guatemala, the chargé d'affaires of Montenegro, a Swiss director of the Banque Sino-Argentine, personages from the Hongkong and Shanghai Bank and British-American Tobacco, as well as several Russian princes and princesses (maybe or maybe not real royal personages).[174] Everything was about rank, placement and order – dress, seating arrangements, arrivals and departures, the strength of cocktails poured and the quality and variety of *zakouski* and *hors d'oeuvres* served. French and English always spoken; Chinese never. A world of relative privilege and isolation; self-serving and self-contained. Maugham assumed that they were all utterly bored of each other!

Christmas Lunch

Christmas lunch was always a grand affair at the Fox household. Aunt Dos maintained a blue theme – lacy crackers of blue paper decorated with blue-dyed feathers, spun-sugar baskets full of spun-sugar fruits, blue-dyed linen napkins, cobalt blue glassware, and traditional Chinese blue and white patterned Nankeen china.[175] First off, glistening black Siberian caviar was served by white-liveried Chinese servants on star-shaped pieces of toast topped with circles of hard-boiled egg and miniature gherkins. The *hors d'oeuvres* circulated on silver platters. *Aperitifs* were served.

Denton does not recall the full menu that day. But we can guess at some of its constituents and know that roast turkey was not a viable possibility in Peking. Christmas lunch courses would however be many and, of course, prepared and served by the Chinese staff. Each would be accompanied by an appropriate wine (with orange cordial for the children – Denton was still included on the non-alcoholic side of the table).

---

174 As noted and described by Maugham in his chapter 'Dinner Parties – I: Legation Quarter' in *On a Chinese Screen*, p.28.

175 All this blue is a nice image, but we must be careful. Welch was prone to refer constantly to the colour blue. In his famous self-portrait (now in London's National Portrait Gallery) he is wearing a blue jacket. In *Maiden Voyage* there are countless references to blue – the deep blue of the carpets at Rivers Court; the blue wool of his pyjamas; a picture of the Virgin Mary in Reckitt's blue (a detergent washing fabric brand); his nanny's dark blue suit; his aunt's Nankeen blue cups; dried rose leaves in a blue vase; peacock blue ladies' scarves; blue glass perfume bottles; powder blue jugs; and so on throughout the book.

To start, a Christmas soup in Peking might well be hare, paired with sherry, which old China Hands would pour into the soup rather than drink separately. This would often be followed by "mandarin fish", a deep-fried sweet and sour dish also known as squirrel-shaped mandarin fish, sliced in two and arranged so that the fried fish looks like porcupine quills and blanketed in an orange hue invariably paired with a German hock white wine. The fish course would normally be followed by two entrées – one "white" and one "brown". Often the white entrée would be the ever-popular and traditional *Bouchée a la Reine* (literally the "Queen's morsel"), a *vol-au-vent* filled with either chicken or ham, while the brown entrée was invariably aspic of quails. And then for the real feast...

One meat would not be considered sufficient at Christmas and so, probably, a roast beef would be served (for the Fox household was indeed an English household, even if in Peking) and perhaps some locally shot wild boar and equally local *perdrix farcies* (stuffed partridge) with, naturally, all the vegetable trimmings. The wines, heavy reds by this point, would continue to flow. And then finally perhaps a traditional Christmas pudding or something similar, such as a plum pudding with brandy sauce, and a cold dessert such as meringues – naturally with dessert wines served to accompany. A final cracker pulled and then *digestifs* and cigars (for the men) to finish off.

In between all this food and wine it's hard to imagine there was time to talk, but of course these were diplomats and personages. Politics was discouraged with women at the table, so perhaps horses, hunting and shooting were more acceptable; the news perhaps that the Smithsonian had determined that the Peking Man fossils were the oldest examples of human beings yet found was a subject of interest that year. Everybody feigned to be bored by China – even those like the Foxes who could easily have left and gone home.

After lunch Aunt Dos arranged for Denton to be whisked away by a large lady in a big chauffeured car that honked its horn constantly in the style JP Marquand, a sojourner around the same time as Denton, described as 'a part of the technique of any Chinese chauffeur.'[176] In his memoir he does not recall her name, though she was a fellow antiques lover who took a shine to the young man. He does recall that she 'wore a

---

176 JP Marquand, *Thank You, Mr Moto* (London: Fontana, 1937), p.83.

sort of turban, and had earrings made of rugged lumps of yellow stone.'[177] She had a spray of carnations in the car and stressed her words in unusual places. She took him to see her elaborately decorated Tartar City hutong home filled with blackwood furniture, a collection of bronze statues and bowls in silk-lined cases, and with a pool of carp fish. It was, she said, haunted by the ghost of the mandarin who lived there previously and had hanged himself. She then bundled him back into the chauffeured car and they headed off to see the Temple of Heaven.

When he returned he learnt that unfortunately Sir Harry had suffered a stroke after dinner. This was seemingly of no matter to Aunt Dos and required only a slight rejigging of Christmas Day arrangements. Aunt Dos naturally needed to attend to Sir Harry's medical care and so Denton was despatched for Christmas supper to the Foxes' neighbours, the Randalls. Despite the medical emergency his aunt still had time to check that he had changed correctly into a dinner jacket so as not to appear incorrectly dressed at the neighbours'. He arrived next door, at the table of people he did not know in the slightest, seated between a boy and a girl of roughly his own age.

Even for Denton, who had lived a rather peripatetic life to date – back and forth between England and Shanghai, boarding school, the independence of Rivers Court – this was an odd situation as the two adolescents were alone (with servants obviously): 'Daddy and Mummy have gone out to dinner.'[178] Supper was basically the leftovers from the neighbours' Christmas Day lunch. Supper over, Denton played several games of mah-jong with the Randall children before going back next door to find out about his uncle. Clutterbuck (apparently sitting on her bed reading a Baroness Orczy Scarlet Pimpernel novel) told him that Aunt Dos thought it best if he returned immediately to Shanghai. She then made him a cup of hot chocolate.

Denton Welch left Peking and returned to Shanghai on Boxing Day – the most extraordinary Christmas of his life ending abruptly. Denton never got to see much of Peking beyond glimpses from chauffeured car windows – 'low grey-roofed houses that seemed like large crouching mice.' Almost his entire time was spent within the confines of the Legation Quarter where 'sentries smacked their rifles... smooth lawns flowed

---

177 Welch, *Maiden Voyage*, p.272. They were probably yellow jade.
178 De-La-Noy, *Denton Welch*, p.76.

round clumps of spiky fir trees which half concealed the stout Victorian houses. A wing showed here, an arched verandah there.'[179] Outside the Legation Quarter Denton saw the charcoal braziers outside shops along Hatamen Street, and a line of rather patchy camels with great bald spots on their flanks carrying coal, making slow progress along the street.

Camels in snow at Peking

His nose for antiques did not fail him though. He noted his aunt's 'elaborate Thibetan brass and copper vessels, prayer wheels and sword scabbards studded with coral and turquoise.'[180] She also collected jade trees, a great collecting fad among foreigners in Peking in the 1920s, and Denton much admired her collection.

After that Peking Christmas

Needing to make his own way in the world and find some sort of career, Denton returned to England soon after his aborted Christmas in Peking to study art at Goldsmiths in London. That had been his Christmas decision. Shortly afterwards he was hit by a car while cycling in Surrey and suffered a fractured spine that led to severe pain and complications as well as spinal tuberculosis. It was to leave him a distinctly more sedentary and solitary young man than before the accident. As a writer and painter

179 Welch, *Maiden Voyage*, p.78.
180 Description of the Fox house from *Maiden Voyage*, p.269, "Thibetan" being a variant spelling of Tibetan.

he was championed by both the highly influential Dame Edith Sitwell, and the poet and editor John Lehmann. His literary output found him supporters for his keen attention to aesthetic detail, while he published art criticism in Cyril Connolly's literary magazine *Horizon*. His 1940 self-portrait is today in the collection of the National Portrait Gallery in London. While perhaps it was not so surprising that Sitwell, Lehmann or Connolly would champion him, a less likely admirer was William S. Burroughs who claimed Denton as a major influence and dedicated his 1983 novel *The Place of Dead Roads* to him.

Denton Welch, Dog with Yellow Basket, *circa 1938*

Denton Welch died in 1948 at his home in the hamlet of Crouch, near Sevenoaks in Kent. He was just thirty-three years of age and his death was largely the result of the spinal tuberculosis he suffered after the cycling accident thirteen years previously. His father, Arthur Joseph Welch, had died in 1942 while interned by the Japanese in Shanghai.

Sir Harry and Lady (later Dame) Dos moved back to England after Sir Harry's stroke, settling in a large house called Colismore at Dumpton Gap, on the seafront near Dos's hometown of Broadstairs on the Kent coast. Harry served on a variety of local committees, was involved in the

China Association, and advised the Board of Trade in London on China matters (his fascination with taxes seemingly undimmed). He was also a keen board member of the Alleyn Club for Old Alleynians.[181] Harry died suddenly in October 1936 at sixty-four years of age; Dorothy survived him.

Over the years before his death and then after World War Two it has been Denton Welch's post-China artistic and literary achievements that have been mostly recalled when he is remembered. However, clearly China was never that far from his mind. In both *Maiden Voyage* and several essays in his collected short stories, he returns to his memories of China, both Shanghai and Peking.[182] For the most part, his memories were fond.

181   i.e. people who had attended Dulwich College as pupils.
182   Denton Welch, *Where Nothing Sleeps: The Complete Short Stories and Other Related Works* (Yorkshire: Tartarus Press, 2005).

"Peking is Like Paris":
Isamu Noguchi (1930)

'Peking is like Paris. It's a city of great antiquity... It's a culture that is so embedded in the place that it has a life of its own.' [183]

183   Oral History interview with Isamu Noguchi, conducted 1973, Nov.7-Dec.26, by Paul Cummings, for the Archives of American Art.

"Peking is like Paris"

When Isamu Noguchi arrived in Peking in June 1930 he had not been planning on a trip to China. His original idea had been to travel from Paris to Japan on the Trans-Siberian Express to visit his father, the poet and writer Yonejirō "Yone" Noguchi, who was living in Tokyo. Isamu had only seen Yone intermittently since his father's separation from his mother, the American writer and editor Léonie Gilmour. Despite spending some of his boyhood in Japan, Isamu had returned to America in his teens. While Isamu was preparing to leave for Tokyo in 1929, Yone Noguchi wrote to him expressing his wish that his son did not visit Japan using his family name. Isamu, shocked at this seeming rejection by his father, cancelled his plans to visit Tokyo and instead, at the last minute, rearranged to travel to Peking.

This sudden change of plans by the artist meant that he arrived in Peking having made no advance preparation and with few formal contacts in the city. Basically, he knew nobody. However, those people he did manage to make contact with in Peking were to be highly influential on his art and his emerging Modernist aesthetic.

Without doubt Noguchi's most significant encounter was with the traditional Chinese calligrapher and woodcut artist Chi Pai Shih – a pupil-teacher relationship that was to revolutionise Noguchi's work.[184] He also came into contact with a number of members of the city's foreign colony, either working or sojourning in the city during that time, who were to become equally important to him. While Noguchi's six months spent studying and working with Chi are well recorded, the interactions he had with others in Peking have been somewhat overlooked – but they are worth noting as being influential upon him and his overall artistic outlook.

In 1973, in an interview with the American art historian Paul Cummings for the *Archives of American Art*, Noguchi, looking back on 1930 and his visit to China, observed: 'Peking is like Paris. It's a city of great antiquity, you know, a thousand years. I mean you find the Yuan walls there. It's a culture that is so embedded in the place that it has a life

184   Qi Baishi (1864-1957).

of its own.'[185] This essay seeks to recover some of the 'life' that Noguchi experienced in Peking in 1930 and early 1931 and the network of people he met and interacted with there.

First contact

Isamu Noguchi's major contact in Peking was Sotokichi Katsuizumi, a Japanese national fifteen years older than Noguchi, who was a senior manager with the Peking branch of the Yokohama Specie Bank (Yokohama Shōkin Ginkō), based in impressive headquarters in the heart of the Legation Quarter and close to the Japanese Legation on the Rue Meu. Katsuizumi was international in his outlook and very well-travelled; he had received a Masters in Economics from the University of Michigan in 1922. For a time, when younger, in the earlier 1920s, Katsuizumi had held fairly reactionary views. He had been a Japanese delegate to the 1922 Washington Disarmament Conference, publishing his views of the conference in a book entitled *Critical Observation on the Washington Conference*.[186] Katsuizumi had moved from America to China and joined the Yokohama Specie Bank, effectively Japan's national bank, in Peking as an economist in 1925. He was to remain in the city until 1932.

How exactly Noguchi came to know Katsuizumi is something of a mystery. It is likely that Katsuizumi knew of Isamu's father, Yone, from Tokyo (at least by reputation) and made contact hearing his son was in town. Noguchi based himself in Peking not too far from where Katsuizumi worked in the Legation Quarter. He rented a traditional courtyard property on a hutong which he described as 'splendid living'.[187] The house came complete with a houseboy who spoke French (as did Noguchi, at least somewhat), a cook, a rickshaw boy and their attendant families. The property was at No.18 Great Wool Alley.[188] It was close to the ancient observatory and, being within the boundaries of the old Tartar

185   Oral History interview with Isamu Noguchi, conducted 1973, Nov. 7-Dec. 26, by Paul Cummings, for the Archives of American Art.
186   Sotokichi Katsuizumi, *Critical Observation on the Washington Conference* (Ann Arbor, Michigan, 1922).
187   Isamu Noguchi, *A Sculptor's World* (New York: Harper & Row, 1968).
188   Now Dayangmao Hutong.

Wall, a short walk to the eastern edge of the Legation Quarter.[189] Noguchi recorded taking long strolls through the city with Katsuizumi, dining at Japanese restaurants, and enjoying an occasional soak at a Japanese-style bathhouse with his banker friend. During the day Noguchi began sketching using models sourced by his rickshaw boy, learning Chinese, and took a keen interest in the local habit of attaching flutes to pigeons and releasing them in the air.[190] Crucially, it was through Katsuizumi that Noguchi met Chi Pai Shih. Impressed by the collection of Chi's scrolls that adorned the walls of Katsuizumi's Legation Quarter home, he requested an introduction to the artist. Katsuizumi was happy to oblige.

Katsuizumi had come to know Chi Pai Shih through his friendship with Tanso Ito, another Japanese national resident in Peking. Ito (who was known to Chi Pai Shih by his Chinese name Yiteng) also worked for the Yokohama Specie Bank in Peking. He had worked for the bank previously in Dairen in the 1920s, and was to return to work there again in the 1930s. Ito was a dedicated art lover who had chanced upon the work of Chi and made contact with him, subsequently introducing many of his fellow Japanese in Peking, including Katsuizumi, to the

Letter from Chi to Tanso Ito, 1930s

artist. Both Ito and Katsuizumi, avid collectors and reasonably well-off, were to acquire many works directly from Chi (or from Chi's wife, Chen Chunjun) and form impressive personal collections. Additionally, Chi gave signed and personalised calligraphic scrolls to Ito indicating their close friendship despite the mounting tensions between China and Japan at the time, on the eve of the Japanese annexation of Manchuria in 1931.[191]

Chi was himself a conduit for Noguchi to several other Chinese artists and teachers.

189   Dayangmao Hutong still exists running north-south from Jianguomenwai Street to Beijing Station East Street. This latter street was not there in 1930 and the hutong ran further south into the network of hutongs close to the Fox Tower (Dongbienmen).

190   These incidental details of Noguchi's life in Peking from Hayden Herrera, *Listening to Stone: The Art and Life of Isamu Noguchi* (London: Thames & Hudson, 2015).

191   Chi Pai Shih, Letters to Tanso Ito - http://www.christies.com/lotfinder/paintings/qi-baishi-letters-to-tanso-ito-5515332-details.aspx

Chi Pai Shih (Qi Baishi)

Primary among these was Lin Fengmian, an almost contemporary of Noguchi's, and a pioneer of modern Chinese painting that blended Chinese and Western painting styles. Lin, a native of Kwangtung province, had moved to Europe in 1920 to study painting in France. In 1923, he relocated to Berlin and then, in 1925, returned to China, where he became principal of the Beiping State Vocational Art School. Several years later, in 1928, Lin helped to establish the National Academy of Art, China's first comprehensive art academy (originally based in Hangchow and colloquially known as Guomei[192]), becoming its first

192 The antecedent of the current China Academy of Art.

principal. When the Academy moved to Peking it was Lin who had hired Chi Pai Shih. Lin and Noguchi were attracted to each other, given Lin's European experiences and his advocacy of a more expressionist and modernist approach to painting among Guomei's students and knowing that Noguchi had previously spent his Guggenheim Scholarship assisting the Romanian modernist sculptor Constantin Brâncuși in Paris.

The French connection

Chi's work had long been of interest to a number of European Chinese art aficionados and collectors in the 1920s, as well as the Japanese collectors. Most notable, perhaps, among those foreigners in the city who collected and championed Chi's work, was the Czech artist-turned-dealer Vojtěch Chytil who collected a number of Chi's paintings and calligraphic scrolls during his prolonged sojourn in Peking that are now part of the Chinese collections of the National Gallery of Prague.

Vojtěch Chytil (left); Jean-Pierre Dubosc

Another long-term foreign resident of Peking of interest to Noguchi for his personal collection and knowledge was Jean-Pierre Dubosc. How Noguchi came to know and be in contact with the Frenchman Dubosc is uncertain, though the two may have come to know each other during Noguchi's time in Paris during the 1920s while he was assisting Brâncuşi. Additionally, Dubosc was married to Janine Loo, a painter, sculptor and the daughter of Ching-Tsai ("CT") Loo, the Chinese-born owner of the well-known CT Loo Gallery on the Rue de Courcelles in Paris. Loo had arrived in France around the turn of the century and started commercially dealing Asian art and *objets* under the business name CT Loo et Cie. By around 1910 Loo had expanded into other European countries and the USA (with a gallery on New York's Fifth Avenue). Loo eventually became prosperous enough to found, in 1926, a large antiques and curios emporium, a quite amazing pagoda-inspired structure (though designed by a French architect) adjacent to the Parc Monceau in Paris's well-heeled VIIIth arrondissement.[193] Inside were (and still are) *Chinois* style ceilings, a moon gate and a gallery carved in eighteenth and nineteenth century Indian woods. It is quite possible Noguchi visited Loo's establishment while resident in Paris before leaving for China.

CT Loo was Paris's first major private collector of Asian art, supplying museums in Europe and America and including artefacts and artworks from Japan, Siam (Thailand), Burma and Tibet, as well as China. CT Loo's connections to the Republican government and the cultural elite in China were excellent, helping his business enormously, and he also founded branches of the business in Peking and Shanghai, both to buy and sell.[194] According to Yiyou Wang, who has studied Loo's business, Dubosc was not only CT Loo's son-in-law, but also one of his business partners.[195]

Technically Dubosc was attached as a diplomat to the French Legation in Peking and lived in the city with his family and so perhaps he could not openly admit to having other business interests. Still, he was a well-known and renowned connoisseur of Chinese art as well as an avid collector of Chinese lacquerware and pottery. He wrote extensively on Ming and Qing ceramics and organised exhibitions in China, Europe and America. Dubosc and Janine lived outside the Legation Quarter in a

193 Now the museum Maison de Loo, 48 Rue de Courcelles, 8e, Paris.

194 Geraldine Lenain, *Monsieur Loo: Le roman d'un marchand d'art asiatique* (Paris: Philippe Picquier, 2013).

195 Yiyou Wang, 'The Loouvre from China: A Critical Study of C. T. Loo and the Framing of Chinese Art in the United States, 1915-1950'. A dissertation presented to the faculty of the College of Fine Arts of Ohio University.

large traditional courtyard property in the western part of the city (where few of the foreign colony ventured much) close to Chi Pai Shih's residence and studio on Kuache Hutong (Getting on a Cart Lane).[196] Both Dubosc and Chi had lived in this area since the mid-1920s and presumably knew each other well. Dubosc, through a combination of his own collecting, his diplomatic contacts, and his relationship with the daughter of France's premier Chinese art dealer, was extremely well connected with both Peking's artistic and cultural elite as well as the Republican government. His home was a centre for many visiting or sojourning Europeans visiting Peking interested in Chinese art. As well as his friendship with Noguchi during his time in Peking, Dubosc was to become good friends, slightly later, with Hedda Morrison, the German-Australian photographer who resided in Peking from 1933 to 1946.

Dubosc was an habitué of the antique and curio shops of Peking from where he sourced various treasures for European and American museums, most notably the Guimet Museum in Paris, a specialist collection of Asian art, as well as for CT Loo's dealership business. This meant a lot of buying – CT Loo's customers included the Morgans and Rockefellers, as well as institutions including the Metropolitan Museum of Art in New York and the Museum of Fine Arts, Boston.

Between the two world wars the main art, antique and curio dealers were grouped in several areas along Hatamen Street and Morrison Street with various smaller clusters of dealers throughout the Tartar City and around the pawn shops on the lower part of Chienmen Street. Additionally, occasional bargains were to be found at the Thieves' Market, as well as the various bazaars and temple fairs.[197] However, fakes abounded, and a good eye was required. Hedda Morrison wrote that Dubosc's reputation as a discerning collector was such that Chinese art dealers often came to his house with items on offer.[198] Shortly after the First World War the American sojourner in Peking, Ellen Newbold La Motte, noted these dealers that came to the houses of known collectors would 'bow themselves in with such ingratiation, comments that we

---

196 Now maintained as a museum at No.13 Yu'er Hutong.
197 Otherwise known as the Hsiao Shih, or Small Market.
198 Hedda Morrison (née Hammer), *Travels of a Photographer in China, 1933-1946* (Oxford: Oxford University Press, 1987).

Maison Loo, 48 Rue de Courcelles, 8e arrondissement, Paris, 1930s

couldn't resist, and then stoop over and exhibit such treasures that there's no withstanding them.'[199]

Dubosc was keen, both from an intellectual standpoint and as a sales pitch, to accentuate the relationship between Chinese works of art from the Ming and Qing dynasties and modern European art. In the catalogue for a 1949 exhibition of Ming and Qing dynasty paintings in New York, organised jointly by CT Loo and Dubosc, the Frenchman wrote, 'Vollard, after looking at the landscapes by Wang Yuan-chi remarked, "But I see Cezanne in them."'[200] Here Dubosc was referring to his earlier conversations regarding Chinese art with Ambroise Vollard, regarded as one of the most important dealers in French contemporary art at the beginning of the twentieth century. It can safely be assumed that Isamu Noguchi was keen to hear such cross-cultural references expressed, as he moved between the European and American modern art he had so

199   Ellen Newbold La Motte, *Peking Dust* (New York: The Century Co., 1919).
200   Yiyou Wang, 'The Loouvre from China.'

recently left in Paris, London and New York, and the traditional Chinese styles he was now seeing on a daily basis in Chi Pai Shih's Peking studio.

As an American citizen Isamu Noguchi naturally made contacts within the American community in Peking at the time, sometimes referred to as the city's "American colony". Perhaps primary among those Americans he interacted with was Carl Schuster, approximately the same age as Noguchi. A key element of Noguchi's reason for visiting Peking

Carl Schuster

had been to extend his practice of modernism through a greater understanding of classical Chinese artistic techniques and forms. Schuster was, at the time, in the early stages of becoming America's foremost authority on Chinese folklore and symbolism. Originally from Milwaukee, Wisconsin, Schuster had independent means to fund his scholarship. He had graduated from Harvard in 1930 with an MA and immediately went to Peking as a Harvard-Yenching Institute fellow. There, for three years, he studied Chinese language and art with Baron von Staël-Holstein, a German-Baltic aristocrat from Estonia, "Orientalist", and a scholar of Sanskrit and Tibetan Buddhism. Von Staël-Holstein had studied Oriental languages at Berlin University and had been appointed head of the Deutsche Morgenländische Gesellschaft, the German Orientalist Society. When the Bolshevik Revolution broke out in 1917, he effectively lost his landed estates in Estonia and so decided to remain in Peking, becoming a professor at Peking University and helping establish the Sino-Indian Institute in the city in 1927. Von Staël-Holstein had also worked in helping the Harvard-Yenching Institute to collect books for its library. During 1930 he was moving between Harvard and Peking. It is not firmly known whether Schuster and Noguchi actually met in person (though Noguchi was aware of his work), but they did share a taste for minority folk crafts. Schuster collected examples of folk textile pieces with blue and white cross-stitches from southwestern China. Noguchi also found these traditional Chinese and ethnic minority crafts intriguing.

The 'piratical' Nadine Hwang

Perhaps the most mercurial and fascinating character that Noguchi spent time with socially while in Peking was Nadine Hwang. Hwang is something of a mystery and, while this is partly due to her life not having been fully researched as yet, it may also be due to her own purposeful obfuscation of her background and life for various reasons. For a variety of reasons Noguchi would have felt drawn to Hwang and been comfortable in her company.

Nadine Hwang, 1929

Even Hwang's birth is shrouded in some mystery. It seems she was born in March 1902, making her a contemporary of Noguchi, either in Madrid, Spain (as she later told the Swedish Red Cross) or Chekiang, China as she appears to have told the authorities of Nazi-occupied Paris in 1944. She was, like Noguchi, of mixed race – her father a Qing dynasty diplomat in Spain and her mother Belgian. She was a qualified lawyer and, in the late 1920s, was briefly a lieutenant in the army of the northern Chinese warlord Chang Tso-lin and may also have served his son and successor Chang Hsueh-Liang – respectively the "Old" and the "Young Marshal".[201] Both were effective rulers of Manchuria and

201 Zhang Xueliang and Zhang Zuolin respectively.

much of northern China as well as, intermittently, controlling Peking. The Old Marshal was assassinated by means of a Japanese bomb in 1928 near Mukden. The Young Marshal had studied military techniques in Japan, and was a surprisingly effective successor to his father despite his reputed womanising and opium addiction. He remained powerful until his abortive kidnapping of Nationalist leader Chiang Kai-shek in 1935 which led ultimately to his arrest and the next fifty years spent under house arrest in China and then Taiwan.

It appears that, for about four years, and wearing a male uniform, Nadine Hwang performed some sort of press relations role for the Young Marshal and may well have been brought onto his staff by his adviser, the Australian William Henry "WH" Donald, a.k.a. "Donald of China". It may also have been with the Young Marshal that Hwang adopted a taste for a rather more bohemian lifestyle – she was described as looking 'piratical', regularly performed a swirling swords dance, and shockingly smoked in public![202] Certainly Chang Hsueh-Liang's circle was louche – one of Donald's actions was to send the Young Marshal to Brighton in England for a period to overcome his opium addiction after many years of notoriously drug- and alcohol-fuelled parties.

It is known that Nadine Hwang spent time in Paris at various points from the early 1930s where she was a known *avant gardist* and lived as an open lesbian. In the mid-1930s, after running out of money in France, she became an integral part of the salon and circle around Natalie Barney and was Barney's lover (calling Barney her 'darlingest own'[203]) and part-time chauffeur. Barney's Friday afternoon salons at her apartment at 40 Rue Jacob on the Left Bank had been legendary since before the First World War[204] and while in Paris studying with Brâncuși it is possible Noguchi either attended one of these events or first met Hwang there.[205] Hwang's wide range of interests included her open sexuality, taste for the *avant garde* and modernism and also an interest in the theatre. She organised

202   Judith Thurman, *Secrets of the Flesh: A Life of Colette* (London: Bloomsbury, 2000), p.401.

203   Diana Souhami, *Wild Girls: The Love Life of Natalie Barney and Romaine Brooks* (London: Phoenix, 2004), p.178.

204   And perhaps best recalled in Joan Schenkar, *Truly Wilde: The Story of Dolly Wilde, Oscar's Unusual Niece* (London: Virago, 2000).

205   It does seem that Brâncuși knew Barney even if Noguchi did not formally meet her.

amateur theatricals at Barney's salons along with the French writer, dandy and James Joyce translator, Valery Larbaud, while also rowing publicly with Dolly Wilde (niece of Oscar). Hwang moved in Parisian literary circles too and was close to the journalist and essayist André Germain, who encountered her at one of Barney's salons on the rue Jacob wearing a man's suit and rather fancied her, though was shocked to discover that she was indeed a woman![206]

However Noguchi and Hwang met, they were certainly good friends during his sojourn in Peking and Hwang was able to integrate him into more radical Chinese circles and political discussions. They clearly became close and he described her as 'beautiful'.[207] It has been suggested that Noguchi, via an introduction from Hwang, also met Chang Hsueh-Liang and was offered the post of general in his warlord army.[208] More likely it was Hwang herself who suggested he might like this job – presumably in jest.

Moving on

At the end of January 1931, Noguchi finally decided to move on and travel to Japan. He went to Kobe and then slightly later to Tokyo – where he did eventually meet with his reluctant father – before moving on again to Kyoto, to study ceramics with the well-known potter Uno Jinmatsu for four months, before eventually returning to America in 1932. Though Isamu Noguchi spent only a relatively short time in Peking, most of his contacts stayed considerably longer in the city.

Sotokichi Katsuizumi left Peking in 1932 and returned to Japan. During his China years and afterwards, Katsuizumi became decidedly

---

206   This anecdote about Hwang appears in George Wickes, *The Amazon of Letters: The Life and Loves of Natalie Barney* (London: WH Allen & Co., 1976). Some caution should be exercised regarding Wickes's account of events surrounding Hwang as he misspells her name as "Hoang" and claims she served in the Chinese Communist Army rather than that of the Young Marshal and then, later, the National Republican Guomindang (KMT) Army.

207   Dore Ashton, *Noguchi: East and West* (Berkeley: University of California Press, 1993), p.28.

208   Ibid.

more pacifist in his outlook and wrote a book on parliamentary democracy for Japanese students.[209]

After the outbreak of war in 1937, Jean-Pierre Dubosc and his wife Janine Loo vacated their courtyard house, though their friend Hedda Morrison continued to live there alone and look after it for some years. The Duboscs did briefly return to Peking after the war though they were eventually forced to leave after the Communist takeover in 1949. They subsequently settled in Switzerland.

Carl Schuster left Peking in 1932 to undertake collecting trips in the western and southwestern provinces of China. Then, in 1933, he took his collections to Vienna where he continued his study of art, pursuing a doctoral degree in Art History from the University of Vienna in 1934 with the prominent art historian Dr Josef Strzygowski. Schuster wrote a dissertation entitled 'Chinese Peasant Embroideries'.[210] He worked briefly as assistant curator of Chinese art at the Philadelphia Art Museum, returning to China in 1935 and remaining until 1938, based in Peking again, and undertaking another three trips to southwestern China. During the war he was a cryptanalyst for the US Navy. His collection of Chinese textiles is now housed at Chicago's Field Museum.[211] Much of Schuster's print collection is held at the New York Public Library.[212]

Nadine Hwang worked for the Republican government for some time in the 1930s, moving between Europe and China. As well as remaining a key part of Natalie Barney's by now long-lived salon in Paris (and remaining her on-off lover) and an open lesbian (she once propositioned the writer Colette, who claimed she refused out of loyalty to Barney[213]), she was also close to many key French literary stars. In 1936 she travelled to London on behalf of the Chinese government and, at the instigation of her old friend and mentor WH Donald, lobbied for greater trade links

209   Sotokichi Katsuizumi, *Kaigi no shikata – The Principles of Parliamentary Practice* (Tokyo: Kofukaku, 1934) (in Japanese).

210   For a version of this see, "Some Peasant Embroideries from Western China," *Embroidery Magazine*, September 1935, pp.88-89.

211   Field Museum, Chicago: Schuster Chinese Textile Collection.

212   New York Public Library: Chinese Prints collected by Carl Schuster including a group of Chinese prints, including some important early Buddhist woodcuts and some 250 Chinese popular prints.

213   Judith Thurman, *Secrets of the Flesh*, p.401. Thurman suggests Colette may have been being diplomatic in her memoirs so as not to upset Barney.

between the British Empire (especially Australia) and China. During her time in London she lived with Helena Normanton, the first woman to practise as a barrister in London and the second woman ever to be called to the Bar of England and Wales. Normanton was an outspoken supporter of the Indian National Congress, an ardent feminist, pacifist and French speaker. It then appears Hwang was in Paris for at least part of the Nazi occupation of the city and in May 1944 she was forcibly rounded up by the authorities and transported to Ravensbrück women's concentration camp in northern Germany. She survived the experience and was rescued by the Swedish Red Cross and brought by ship to *Malmö*, Sweden in 1945. She eventually settled in Montevideo.

"Without doubt there is no greater city than Peking"[214]

Ultimately the question is to what degree Isamu Noguchi's relatively brief sojourn in Peking influenced his later work? At this early stage of his career Noguchi was clearly seeking influences and training from a variety of sources, after studying art and sculpture in America and then spending time in Paris with Brâncuși and meeting other modernist artists such as Jules Pascin, Alexander Calder and Arno Breker. While studying in Peking, Noguchi applied Chi Pai Shih's single-stroke calligraphy-influenced brush painting techniques to his own subjects using traditional Chinese calligraphic techniques to find abstraction in the human form. Though adopting the style, Noguchi broke with Chi's more traditional subject matter and drew a sequence of portraits including several nudes (then almost unknown in Chinese brush art) from live models. Noguchi was later to declare that 'all Japanese art has roots in China.'[215]

Though Noguchi's later work, including drawing, ceramics and sculpture, as well as theatre set and furniture design, evinced a variety of influences, he appears to have constantly sought to adhere to Chi Pai Shih's basic principle of balancing the real and unreal that he had learnt working alongside the artist in Peking for those crucial six months. Chi Pai Shih declared, 'The excellence of a painting lies in its being alike, yet unlike. Too much likeness flatters the vulgar taste; too much

214 Isamu Noguchi, *A Sculptor's World* (New York: Harper & Row, 1968).
215 Amy Hau & Heidi Coleman (Editors), *Isamu Noguchi/Qi Baishi/Beijing 1930* (Milan: Five Continents Editions, 2013).

Noguchi, Man Sitting, *1930*

unlikeness deceives the world.'[216] He painted in the Xieyi style, a freehand brushwork or "sketching thoughts" style focussing on expression and painting one's feelings and moods. From Chi, Noguchi was to learn how to use brush stroke to represent the real (i.e. we can recognise the form drawn as human, animal, plant etc.), yet it is not strictly "realistic". This balancing of the real and unreal that he learnt in Peking in 1930 was to be a recurrent theme in Noguchi's work till the end of his life.

216 Howard L. Boorman, *Biographical Dictionary of Republican China (Volume 3)* (New York: Columbia University Press, 1970).

The Last Days of Edmund Backhouse:
Sir Edmund Trelawny Backhouse, 2nd Baronet (1944)

'Take care you don't shortly become a Peking silhouette, one of those peculiar people who avoid Europeans like the plague and isolate themselves in a temple in the Chinese quarter, seeking, alone, the origin of some long forgotten hieroglyphics and, at nights, air their melancholy on the Tartar Wall, which overlooks the yellow roofs of the Imperial City, dreaming of the barbarous and splendid past related in the court annals.' [217]

217   Damien de Martel & Léon de Hoyer, *Silhouettes of Peking* (Peking: China Booksellers, 1926), p.17.

The Last Days

Sir Edmund Trelawny Backhouse (pronounced "back'us"), 2nd Baronet, finally breathed his last in the Hospital St. Michel in Peking on the morning of January 8, 1944. He was seventy years of age, unmarried and had lived in Peking for over forty-five years. He was perhaps the closest embodiment of what the authors Damien de Martel and Léon de Hoyer (the former a French diplomat and the latter a Russian émigré banker) described as 'silhouettes of Peking', those Europeans who consciously avoided the foreign colony, the Legation Quarter and western society in Peking.[218]

In the last months of 1943 Backhouse had suffered with high blood pressure, dizziness, prostate gland enlargement and urinary troubles. He had become irritable with itchy bluish and black patches on his legs indicating poor circulation. He was generally frail and having great difficulty walking more than a few steps. On January 7, 1944 Backhouse's temperature had risen suddenly, alarming his doctors. Early the following morning he died, reportedly without pain and fully conscious. The medical certificate's wording – "SOFTENING OF THE BRAIN" – would undoubtedly have annoyed him immensely as until the end he was still recounting stories from earlier in his life without any evident problems with his memory.

Edmund Backhouse, born a Quaker though never having shown much interest in organised religion until his final years, had converted to Roman Catholicism in 1942. Therefore his memorial service was held at the *Tung Tang* (the East Cathedral, aka St. Joseph's, the Portuguese Church) on Wangfuting, and he was subsequently buried at the Chala Jesuit Roman Catholic Cemetery near the Ping-tze-man (or Fuchengmen) Gate along the Inner City's Western Wall.[219] The next day, a young Chinese man came to the Hospital St. Michel hoping to claim the large diamond Sir Edmund had promised him in his will. Of course, there was no mention

---

218   Damien de Martel & Léon de Hoyer, *Silhouettes of Peking* (Peking: China Booksellers, 1926).

219   Now the Zhalan Cemetery and containing the graves of, among others, the early Jesuits to China Matteo Ricci, John Adam Schall Von Bell and Ferdinand Verbiest. The cemetery was severely damaged by Red Guards during the Cultural Revolution. What is left of the cemetery can be seen at Chegongzhuang Street in Xicheng District.

of the man in Backhouse's last will and testament, no diamond, and the young man refused to explain his connection to the deceased. Backhouse left small legacies to his former Chinese servants, and the remainder of his belongings to his surviving family in England. There was little of any value after his library of thirty thousand books and manuscripts had been shipped to the Bodleian Library in Oxford as a donation. His executor, the Swiss Consul General in Peking, gathered together some well-worn western suits, a winter fur coat, an old Victorian travelling clock, a few books in cheap editions, and a red leather case containing documentation concerning his succession to the baronetcy and its next succession to a nephew following his demise. Backhouse had claimed that several valuable items, including a gold watch and a letter signed by Marie Antoinette, had been stolen. He may or may not have ever owned such a letter.

Backhouse had been born into a wealthy banking family in Darlington, County Durham in northern England. His father had been a director of Barclays Bank while his younger brother was to rise to become Great Britain's First Sea Lord. Edmund was to be the black sheep of the family. By the time of his death it was alleged that he had become an open sympathiser with the Japanese occupation forces of Peking, an avowed fascist, sympathetic to Germany and an Englishman who wished to see Great Britain defeated by the Axis powers. Yet despite the animosity of his later years towards his country, he was commemorated by the Commonwealth War Graves Commission among the list of British civilian war dead in China.

What happened in those last years of Backhouse's life to see him, apparently, go ranting against Britain into his grave?

The Hermit of Peking

The story of Edmund Backhouse is still pretty well known, particularly among those who have read more than a smidgeon of twentieth-century Peking history. Born in 1873, educated at St. George's School, Ascot (where Winston Churchill was a fellow pupil) and Winchester College, he went on to attend Merton College, Oxford. He arrived in Peking on the eve of the twentieth century in 1898. China was not perhaps an obvious interest for the young Backhouse (who was a natural linguist and did study some Chinese at Oxford) who leaned more towards the arts and aestheticism. However, a chief attraction was that Peking was a long way from Oxford where he had run with a rather fast, and largely gay, set, including Lord Alfred Douglas – a friendship that led Backhouse to be on the fringes of the Oscar Wilde scandal and subsequent sensational trial. While at Oxford he accumulated significantly large debts as well as having some sort of breakdown (invariably attributed to either alcohol or drugs, or both) and, having failed to get a degree, he left for China.

Once in Peking Backhouse, just twenty-six, promptly embarked upon his life's career of dissembling, inventing, exaggerating and generally having a high old time interpreting Chinese history and current affairs in the way he thought most likely to attract attention and hopefully make him some money. He fed 'translations' of supposed imperial court documents to the (non-Chinese reading) London *Times* correspondent George Morrison ("Morrison of Peking"), who considered him a genius. He claimed special insider status with the Manchu court, though there's little evidence of his ever gaining anything much more than bathhouse tittle-tattle. However, he certainly was a talented linguist in Russian, Japanese, Manchu, Mongolian and the classical languages. He had excellent French and some Spanish as well as, of course, Mandarin Chinese and the particular Peking dialect of the time.

His books are certainly worth a read, more for their gossipy tone and guarded salaciousness than verifiable factual detail. *China Under the Empress Dowager*, published in 1911, and the follow up, *Annals and Memoirs of the Court of Peking* (1914), were both co-authored with another long-serving China Hand, JOP Bland.[220] The books were taken seriously at the time by most, though we now know that the majority of the "sources" claimed were in fact Backhouse's forgeries. He was a massive collector of documents, both for his own substantial library (which, along with those of George Morrison and ETC Werner, was one of the largest private collections in pre-World War Two Peking[221]) and for donations to Oxford's Bodleian Library. In total he donated over thirty thousand

220   Edmund Backhouse & John Otway Percy Bland, *China Under the Empress Dowager* (London: William Heinemann, 1911); *Annals and Memoirs of the Court of Peking* (Boston & New York: Houghton Mifflin, 1914).
221   Morrison sold off most of his impressive collection to Japanese buyers; Werner's library has been scattered and, over the years, I've found books once part of his collection in Hong Kong University Library, the Shanghai Zikkawei (Xujiahui) Library,

books and manuscripts, including some very rare and valuable items. Backhouse's detractors (of which there are many, most notably the conservative historian Hugh Trevor-Roper) believe he hoped the university would award him a professorship in return for his largesse. But this seems an unlikely, and somewhat boring, career move for Backhouse, who was offered the Chair of Chinese at King's College, London, in 1913 but turned it down.

It has to be said that, like his supposedly insider accounts of the Manchu court, a number of these donations to the Bodleian may not be entirely kosher. Still, Backhouse did make several important contributions to Sinology, including considerably enlarging Sir Walter Hillier's *English-Chinese Dictionary of Peking Colloquial*.[222]

Backhouse dabbled in all manner of business ventures, including a little gun running and armaments smuggling during World War One, supposedly on behalf of the British Legation in Peking (who predictably denied any such association). But none of his schemes ever really amounted to anything. One long-term British resident in Peking described him at this

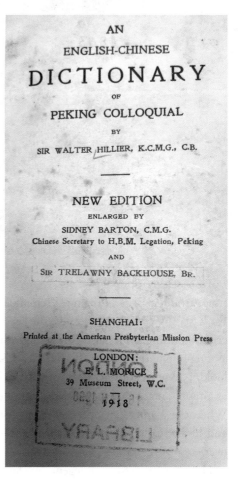

AN
ENGLISH-CHINESE
DICTIONARY
OF
PEKING COLLOQUIAL
BY
SIR WALTER HILLIER, K.C.M.G., C.B.

———

NEW EDITION
ENLARGED BY
SIDNEY BARTON, C.M.G.
Chinese Secretary to H.B.M. Legation, Peking
AND
SIR TRELAWNY BACKHOUSE, BR.

———

SHANGHAI:
Printed at the American Presbyterian Mission Press
LONDON:
E. L. MORICE
39 Museum Street, W.C.
1918

---

as well as on eBay, and in second-hand and antiquarian bookstores as far apart as Seattle, Wales and New York.

222 Walter Hillier, *English-Chinese Dictionary of Peking Colloquial* (Shanghai: Kwang Hsüeh Publishing House, 1933).

Backhouse in 1919

time (around 1917) as 'the most remarkable scoundrel ever known in the Far East.'[223] Certainly he did skirt the law at times, if not act in an outright criminal fashion. He falsely presented himself to the Qing government as a representative first of the American Bank Note Company, who were looking to get a contract to print China's banknotes, and then, secondly, as a representative of the British shipbuilders John Brown & Company. When the planned swindles fell apart, both companies came after him and he had to disappear to Canada for a while until the scandals blew over.

He became a sort of legend in his own time in Peking. Trevor-Roper's biography of him may seem biased to more enlightened modern readers, smacking of old-fashioned homophobia ("deviance" as Trevor-Roper would have it), but the title was an accurate one – the Hermit

223 As described by the American George Sylvester (GS) Hall, an employee of the American Bank Note Company that Backhouse was accused of swindling.

of Peking.[224] Trevor-Roper, later to be made Baron Dacre of Glanton, was drearily upper-middle class and conservative in the worst English way – a conformist, a prude and a man of very fixed ideas. But he was right about Backhouse's withdrawal from virtually all aspects of Peking's foreign social life.

After the early 1920s Backhouse went into self-imposed isolation for relatively long periods. This was partly to avoid angry creditors and further scandals, but also to retreat from the world of the Peking foreign colony, which (with just a few exceptions) he came to despise thoroughly. Sightings of Backhouse, invariably clothed in Chinese robes, with a long white straggly Rasputin-like beard, became the subject of cocktail hour and *tiffin* gossip in the Legation Quarter. He did occasionally wear Chinese robes, though mostly he was spotted about town in rather worn formal black suits of a slightly outdated western cut. Certainly, though, it was his occasional donning of Chinese garb that got him noticed by other foreigners encountering him. One acquaintance described him as sometimes 'wearing a long Chinese gown of dark colour... a black Chinese cap with a large piece of rose-quartz fastened to its front part in the old Chinese fashion. During the hot summer months, he would wear a light-yellow Chinese gown of grass-cloth.'[225]

And he would overtly avoid other members of the city's foreign colony: 'He was said to turn around when, walking on the city wall, he saw a foreigner coming towards him and to cover his face with a handkerchief when passing a foreigner in a rickshaw.'[226] From 1912 onwards he lived outside the Legation Quarter and the nearby busy Hatamen Street, the major concentrations of the foreign colony, at No.19 Shih Fu Ma Ta Chieh, to the west of the Forbidden City.[227] A later generation of

---

224   First published as Hugh Trevor-Roper, *A Hidden Life: The Enigma of Sir Edmund Backhouse* (London: Macmillan, 1976) and then later, and more frequently reprinted, as *Hermit of Peking: The Hidden Life of Sir Edmund Backhouse* (New York: Alfred A. Knopf, 1976).

225   Reinhard Hoeppli, Postscript to *Décadence Mandchoue: The China Memoirs of Sir Edmund Trelawny Backhouse* (Shanghai: Earnshaw Books, 2011).

226   Ibid.

227   Shih Fu Ma Ta Chieh (alternatively Shifuma Dajie) has long since been both redeveloped and renamed as Wenhua Hutong. Around the same time, the New Culture Movement intellectual and early Chinese communist Li Ta-chao (Li Dazhao) lived on the same hutong.

aesthetes – the likes of Harold Acton and Desmond Parsons – would favour these hutongs, but in 1912 there were few, if any, other foreigners living in this area.

Backhouse's reclusiveness and his self-mythologizing makes sorting out the truth from the fiction of his life tricky. While rumours of his homosexuality circulated in the stuffy and prim drawing rooms of the Legation Quarter, Backhouse never spoke of this in his lifetime, though now, in a more enlightened age, we can see he was a gay man and had been since at least his university days. He was often accused of being an opium addict, and one of his best friends was a specialist in treating opium addiction, though he claimed that he had never indulged. Other rumours circulated – that a murder of a Chinese servant (and possibly his lover) at his Shih Fu Ma Ta Chieh home had occurred and been hushed up; that he had translated sensitive documents for the Soviet Legation and that, caught out in 1927 doing this by the Japanese, he was then forced to translate stolen documents for them. With regard to these allegations the historical record is now silent. All are possible, but none are proven.

What does seem clear is that by the mid-1930s, when he was in his sixties, Backhouse was having some money troubles, looking relatively old for his age, and starting to see his health deteriorate. What luxuries he did continue to value included out-of-season strawberries and asparagus as well as decent wine. But times were to get harder still…

War

Following the Japanese occupation of Peking in July 1937 Backhouse was subject to the same restrictions, shortages and effects of inflation as the rest of the foreign colony. After the rumoured murder of his servant Chang Ho-chai, Backhouse left his Shih Fu Ma Ta Chieh house, where he had lived for a quarter of a century, and moved to No.28 Yangjou Hutong, which was not that far away.[228] Yangjou (or "mutton") Hutong was one of Peking's oldest lanes, dating back to the early 1400s, and had, as its name suggests, once been a meat market. Backhouse had a spacious courtyard house where he did entertain those few foreigners he deigned to interact with, such as Henri Vetch, the famous bookseller and publisher with a shop in the Grand Hôtel de Pékin, as well as William Aspland, the

---

228　Yangjou Hutong is now Yangrou Hutong.

English doctor and specialist in opium addiction, James Marjoribanks, a young British diplomat studying Chinese, and a few select others.

But he was only able to stay on Yangjou Hutong for two years. In 1939, when foreigners in Peking living outside the Legation Quarter were ordered to move into the diplomatic enclave, it was unclear what Backhouse would do. There had been some trepidation at the British Legation as to where he would go, given his reclusiveness. In 1900 he had sheltered from the Boxers in the British Embassy compound, but that was a very different Backhouse forty years previously, then having been in China only a couple of years. In 1937 when the Japanese initially occupied the city he had, briefly, registered with the British Legation, stayed with his friend Dr Aspland at the compound, taken his meals in the communal "mess" and, much to the surprise of many, engaged in lively and scholarly conversation with his dinner companions. But this "emergency" only lasted a couple of weeks and Backhouse was soon able to return to Yangjou Hutong.

Since then he had been largely ostracised by official British society in Peking who considered him odd, dodgy, and perhaps even insane in some of his seemingly pro-Japanese utterances. He in turn had consciously avoided all British company and officialdom in China. He was already unwell. Harold Acton, who also lived in the Western City relatively close to Yangjou Hutong on Gongjian Hutong[229], saw Backhouse on the street around this time and described him as 'frail' and (perhaps unsurprisingly, given the Japanese invasion of the city) a 'nervous wreck'.[230] In the end Backhouse opted to move to a German-run boarding house established inside the former compound of the Austro-Hungarian Legation.[231] There Henri Vetch reported him depressed at the news of the death of his brother, Roger, who had died suddenly of a brain tumour.

By the beginning of the winter of 1941 it was clear to most foreigners in China that there would be a probable outbreak of hostilities in Asia

---

229 Which runs from today's Dianmen Street, north to south down the side of Beihai Park.

230 Trevor-Roper, *Hermit of Peking,* p.222.

231 The Austro-Hungarian Empire having collapsed in 1918 had thereby lost its treaty rights in China and forfeited its legation, which became a boarding house with the added attraction of being situated within the Legation Quarter gates.

between America and Britain and the Japanese.[232] It was also the case that the war between Britain and Germany made it impossible for Backhouse to stay in the German-run boarding house. He moved back into the British Legation compound where he seems to have had a single room with a verandah and one servant.

The remaining British and American community in Peking, on stern consular advice, began to pack up and head to the ports of Shanghai or Tientsin where they were then evacuated on to Hong Kong, and from there home to the States or, for the British, to England or Australia. The Japanese onslaught in Southeast Asia was rapid and effective. By Christmas 1941 Pearl Harbor had been bombed, the International Settlement of Shanghai occupied. The defeats kept on coming: HMS *Prince of Wales* and HMS *Repulse* sunk off Singapore; the British Asiatic Fleet retreating to the Indian Ocean; the French Indo-Chinese empire under Japanese control; the Philippines and Hong Kong fallen, and Malaya and Singapore perilously threatened.

Outside his room in the old Austro-Hungarian Legation, Backhouse would have found Peking in 1942 an odd place – occupied by the Japanese and essentially run by their military police, but with the remaining foreign colony still gathering at the Peking Club where Germans and Italians sat at tables close by British and Americans with Russians and French in between.[233] The remaining Allied foreign community, now clustered in the Legation Quarter, by this point included some businessmen prevented by the Japanese from leaving, the so-called "rocking chair fleet" of elderly dowagers (widows of long-time residents of Peking with nowhere else to go), a few collaborators with the Japanese, some hopeless alcoholics and opium addicts, a motley crew of musicians and entertainers who had hung on too long in the city, the stateless Russians and a few Jewish émigrés, the inevitably stubborn missionaries and those like Backhouse who were infirm (by 1941 he was having serious trouble walking).

Red armbands bearing Chinese characters for their respective nationalities were handed out to all Allied nationals to wear, by Japanese

---

232 British tobacco executive and decade long China veteran by 1940 Laurance Tipton asserts that this was the widely held opinion among the members of the foreign colonies of Peking and Tientsin in late 1941. Laurance Tipton, *Chinese Escapade*, (London: Macmillan, 1949), p.12.
233 Tipton, *Chinese Escapade*, p.57.

order. Though at first obviously disliked by many British, Americans and others, they soon became a source of pride and also meant the few remaining functioning Chinese restaurants gave discounts and waiters would surreptitiously give the thumbs up.

As Backhouse's health continued to decline he was finally moved to the St. Michel Hospital in April 1943. There he had a small private room on the ground floor of the building's east wing. The St. Michel was a small Catholic hospital on Legation Street, close by the associated St. Michel Catholic Church[234] and the Vichy-regime-controlled French Legation (under whose auspices the hospital operated). It had just seven Chinese and three European Sisters of Charity working there, overseen by the Reverend Fraisse. Physicians tended to be attending rather than full-time. For a long time from the 1920s Dr Jean Augustin Bussiere was the Medicin-chef assisted by a Dr Bonduel as the Medicin-adjoint.[235]

At the St. Michel Hospital, Backhouse came to know a Swiss doctor called Reinhard (or sometimes in Peking anglicised to "Richard") Hoeppli. Hoeppli, approximately fifty years old at the time, was also a man who was able to move about Peking with greater freedoms than most of the foreign colony due to being the Honorary Swiss Consul. Peking's Swiss colony didn't consist of much more than half a dozen families and some missionaries. However, Hoeppli was also officially charged with handling matters concerning British subjects (and Americans and Dutch) in Peking after the British, Dutch and American consulates were closed and the countries had no direct diplomatic representation in the city.

Hoeppli was a physician who had studied parasitic diseases in Africa after gaining his PhD at Hamburg University in the mid-1920s.[236] From 1930 to 1941 he was the leading parasitologist at the Peking

---

234 Still in operation as a Catholic church as St. Michael's on Dongjiaoming Street.

235 Dr Bussiere was a well-known and highly regarded figure in the Peking foreign colony, having been Yuan Shih-kai's personal physician for a time and was also to be the doctor who cared for ETC Werner's wife Gladys Nina, mother of Pamela Werner, the subject of my book *Midnight in Peking* (Beijing: Penguin China, 2012). He was also a good friend of the veteran French diplomat in China Alexis Leger, better known as a poet by his pen name, Saint-John Perse.

236 Trevor-Roper in his usual dismissive style casts Hoeppli aside as a fraud too, although his work was internationally recognized and cited by many Sinologists, including Joseph Needham. Reinhard Hoeppli, *Parasites and Parasitic Infections in Early Medicine and Science* (Singapore: University of Malaya Press, 1959).

Union Medical College (PUMC), the Rockefeller-funded hospital just off Morrison Street. His research with the Yale-in-China graduate Feng Lan-chou and Chung Huei-lan was important in isolating certain parasites causing diseases in the city as being carried by sandflies living on dogs.[237] The British historians Richard Davenport-Hines and Adam Sisman, who edited the letters of Hugh Trevor-Roper, describe Hoeppli as 'a portly, mischievous bachelor and gourmet, who collected jade.'[238] Hoeppli was spending the 1940s moving between seeing his patients, including Backhouse at the St. Michel, and his temporary one-room Swiss Consulate offices at the nearby Grand Hôtel des Wagons-Lits, close to the Chienmen Railway Station. Until the forced internment of Allied nationals, Hoeppli also worked closely with Billy Christian, a well-known member of the Peking colony and chairman of the Relief Committee for Allied Nationals.

The doctor and the hermit

Hoeppli, who claimed to visit Backhouse daily after his admittance to the St. Michel, was fascinated to meet him and had a particular interest in tales of his sexual adventures and gay life in Peking over the last four decades, including his famous claim to have had sex with the Empress Dowager. Hoeppli became Backhouse's confidant and literary executor. As his physician, Hoeppli leaves no record of what he was able to do to ease any of Backhouse's ailments beyond recalling that he took caffeine in crystallised form and a lot of sleeping pills.

However, Hoeppli did persuade him (perhaps with some financial inducement) to write his memoirs of his early years, including his time at Oxford, as *The Dead Past*[239], and then his more salacious memoirs as *Décadence Mandchoue*, written in 1943. Hoeppli maintained that

237   Published as Feng Lan-Chou, Chung Huei-lan & Reinhard Hoeppli, 'Canine Leishmanasis with Skin Lesions Observed in Peiping', *Chinese Medical Journal*, No.55, 1939, pp.371-382.

238   Eds: Richard Davenport-Hines & Adam Sisman, *One Hundred Letters from Hugh Trevor-Roper* (Oxford: Oxford University Press, 2013).

239   Edmund Trelawny Backhouse (Ed: Reinhard Hoeppli), *The Dead Past* (Scotts Valley, California: CreateSpace Independent Publishing Platform, 2017).

Backhouse's memory was 'prodigious' even going back over fifty years to his school and Oxford days.[240]

Upon his death Backhouse left the two manuscripts to the care of Hoeppli – totalling close to three hundred thousand words – which, once the doctor read them, he found far more 'decadent' than he had originally envisaged! *The Dead Past* recounts Backhouse's encounters with Oscar Wilde, Lord Alfred Douglas, the art critic Walter Pater, the French poets Mallarmé and Paul Verlaine, Aubrey Beardsley, Archibald Philip Primrose (Fifth Earl of Rosebery, First Earl of Midlothian, and a former Prime Minister), and the legendary Spanish courtesan La Belle Otero, most of whom are described as his former lovers.

EDMUND BACKHOUSE . . . the Great Sinologue

For China scholars and those wanting to know more of the Bohemian underbelly of Peking, *Décadence Mandchoue* (so salacious the title had to be in French!) is the title to read. The manuscript remained virtually inaccessible in the Bodleian for decades, though is now available in a very good annotated edition by the China Hand and Backhouse-devotee Derek Sandhaus.[241] *Décadence Mandchoue* certainly doesn't disappoint in a tabloid sense – Cassia Flower and his "elephantine" member; the Duke Lan requiring his regal buttocks to be stingingly whipped till lacerated followed by his apparently endless ejaculations and, of course most famously, Backhouse's claim that he enjoyed a number of trysts with

---

240 Reinhard Hoeppli, Postscript to *Décadence Mandchoue*.

241 Edmund Backhouse (Ed: Derek Sandhaus), *Décadence Mandchoue: The China Memoirs of Sir Edmund Trelawny Backhouse* (Shanghai: Earnshaw Books, 2011). A longer review of *Décadence Mandchoue* and Sandhaus's annotation by myself was published in the *Journal of the Royal Asiatic Society China*, Vol.75, No.1, 2013, pp.306-312.

the (rather aged) Empress Dowager Ci Xi who penetrated him with her enlarged clitoris.[242] The book was not published in China and only read by Reinhard Hoeppli who took the manuscripts out of China with him, edited them and appended a postscript after the war (in Peking in 1946) and a brief biography of Backhouse.

As per Backhouse's will, Hoeppli made just four copies of the manuscript. A typewritten copy was given to Trevor-Roper at Basel Airport in 1973, shortly after Hoeppli's death, with instructions it be deposited in the Bodleian.[243] Another copy arrived by post on the desk of the head librarian at the National Library of Australia in Canberra. The Australian connection came about due to Alastair Morrison, the son of the *Times* correspondent George Morrison ("Morrison of Peking"), and his wife, the photographer Hedda Morrison (née Hammer), who had known Hoeppli during the war (though Alastair had never really known his father who died when he was just five). Also Dr. Lo Hui-min of the Australian National University had compiled Morrison of Peking's letters, including many concerning Backhouse and his work with Morrison.[244]

The last days

Britain had of course declared war on Japan moments after the attack on Pearl Harbor. Backhouse's praise for Japanese civility and talk of "mighty *Großdeutschland*" did look somewhat treacherous in light of all-out war. Allied nationals, including Backhouse, were to be eventually rounded up and taken to the Weihsien Civilian Internment Camp in Shandong. However, Hoeppli persuaded the Japanese occupation authorities that Backhouse was too ill to move and would not survive the three-hundred-and-twenty-five-mile journey.

242 This allegation, that Backhouse was the elderly (though according to him energetic) Empress Dowager's lover, is by far the most difficult to believe. Reinhard Hoeppli did believe it, claiming (in his postscript to *Décadence Mandchoue*) to have been told the tale by his Manchu rickshaw puller several years before he read Backhouse's account in his memoirs. Though, of course, this just indicates perhaps that Backhouse had been telling his salacious tale to all and sundry for years!

243 At least that is the story told by John King Fairbank in *China Watch* (Boston: Harvard University Press, 1987), p.42.

244 Lo Hui-Min (Ed.), *The Correspondence of G.E. Morrison* (Cambridge: Cambridge University Press, 1976).

By late 1943 Backhouse had entered his seventies and was in a state of physical and mental exhaustion; he could barely walk and his hands suffered from constant tremors. France's Vichy regime had installed Roland de Margerie as their consul general in Shanghai. When de Margerie visited the St. Michel on a visit to Peking he found Backhouse, 'very frail, but well cared for.'[245] Still, it was clear the end was near.

Confined to bed in the Hospital St. Michel, Backhouse was probably all too aware that his days were numbered. He had to rely on the Vichy French authorities in China and the Swiss consul Reinhard Hoeppli for support and protection. To have been interned at Weihsien with other Allied nationals (and many of his age, and older, were interned there) would most probably have been a rapid death sentence. He was reliant on a brutal occupying army not overruling Hoeppli; continued French protection; and the Japanese authorities, obviously at war with his own country, not deciding he should be removed.

Trevor-Roper was unforgiving in his assessment of Backhouse's last days. In his final years, he says, Backhouse showed great admiration for the Axis powers, and took a visible delight in their victories over the Allies. His fascist fixation was no product of senility, says Trevor-Roper, as his writings were filled with a longing for the days of European despotism and showed a profound respect for iron-fisted leaders of the Napoleonic mould: 'In his country's darkest hour Backhouse turned coat.'

Was Backhouse a dedicated fascist as Trevor-Roper suggests, just an opportunist, or focussed on his own survival in an occupied city? Japan had invaded and Backhouse didn't want to leave Peking, so he was publicly uncritical of them. Backhouse had long admired the Japanese, though without perhaps fully appreciating the militaristic and aggressive turn the country had taken. He did have old-world views – France, regardless of Vichy, was, to Backhouse, a country of manners and culture; Russia much admired (though Backhouse meant the old imperial Russia rather than the Soviet Union); Germany a country of high culture. It was the

---

245 Trevor-Roper, *Hermit of Peking*, pp.233-234. De Margerie was the son of Pierre de Margerie, a former French minister to China. Roland had lived in Peking as a boy and read Backhouse's *China Under the Empress Dowager*. While Trevor-Roper is keen to vilify Backhouse for his apparent politics, he neglects to mention that Roland de Margerie was the pro-Axis Vichy regime's replacement as *Consul Général de France à Changhai* for the veteran French diplomat and Shanghailander Marcel Baudez, who was not considered loyal enough by Marshal Pétain.

case that Backhouse had rather supported the Japanese annexation of Manchuria largely because he saw it as the start of the possible restoration of the Manchu dynasty he had admired (no great republican, Backhouse!). He was perhaps an old man and out of date, but his opinions that the Japanese were polite and would perhaps help "clean up" China were ones shared by many other Allied nationals at the time, at least until December 1941. Hoeppli does also surmise that Backhouse may have felt his position in the safety of the Hospital St. Michel could be threatened were he critical of the Japanese, French or German authorities.

As to Backhouse's apparent anti-Britishness and pro-Nazi opinions, Hoeppli believed he was being the miscreant he had always been. The Belgian missionary and Chinese linguist Paul Serruys, who met Backhouse at the hospital during the war, recalled that Backhouse made a 'constant attack on the British Government's perfidy, personified in the man W. Churchill whom he had known as a schoolboy in England. They had once had a boxing fight in which Churchill knocked him down saying: someday I'll be prime minister!' It seemed, in Serruys's estimation, 'like the ramblings of an old man.'[246]

Father Paul Serruys

However, it also seems typical of a young man already inclining towards the aesthete, who supported Oscar Wilde and ran with a generally homosexual and Bohemian set in his youth and who would not find a boorish type like Churchill to his tastes, even in their school years.

Hoeppli tells a somewhat different story. While admitting that 'there can be no question that he harboured a strong and lasting resentment against the British and the country of his birth', Hoeppli also notes that Backhouse, while occasionally criticising the English, 'did not like to hear other people attacking them.' Hoeppli believed that Backhouse had long admired traditional high German culture and also felt an ancestral link to the country.[247]

246   Paul Serruys in a letter to David Helliwell (December 1, 1986), quoted in Derek Sandhaus's introduction to the reprint of *Décadence Mandchoue*.
247   On the maternal side, Backhouse's mother was from a Cornish family which traced its history back to Edward the Confessor. On the paternal side there was a link

Finally, as to his conversion to Catholicism, there are also two schools of thought. Backhouse formally converted to Rome in the summer of 1942 and often thereafter signed himself as "Paul" Backhouse. There is some evidence he had been considering a conversion for some time and admired the aesthetics and ceremony of the Catholic church, factors that attracted many English non-Catholics in the inter-war period to convert.[248]

Hoeppli also suggests that by converting, Backhouse may have thought he could access both Catholic-controlled shelter and funds. With German, Austrian, Italian and Vichy French congregants, the Catholic Church in Peking had a somewhat more protected position during the Japanese occupation than other Christian denominations, though it was always watched closely. Backhouse's appointed Father Confessor was Irish (and therefore a neutral), who purportedly hated England and rather admired Germany. Backhouse may have agreed with him simply to keep the peace and his bed. Hoeppli reports that close to the end Backhouse dismissed the priest and considered him 'pestering'.[249] Serruys, although religious himself and Catholic, believed that at the St. Michel, Backhouse was technically under house arrest at the chapter house of the Jesuits in Peking.

It probably did help to be a Catholic when he finally moved to the Catholic-run hospital. Politics, ideologies or religious beliefs never seem to have played any importance to a devout sensualist and aesthete such as Edmund Backhouse. When he realised his death was imminent, he arguably renounced his religion – 'I wish they *(the priests)* would leave me alone.' Though, according to Hoeppli at least, Backhouse did receive the sacrament – 'if they don't help me, they will at least do no harm.'[250]

Rather than having any dedicated support for fascism or overt religious beliefs, Hoeppli saw Backhouse as an eccentric, commenting, 'When one lives apart from others, especially when one shows strange habits, as a rule rumours, mainly of an unfavourable kind, develop.'[251] Hoeppli completes his postscript to the author of *Décadence Mandchoue* thus:

---

with Germany dating from the eighteenth century.

248   Evelyn Waugh, Graham Greene, Malcolm Muggeridge, Compton Mackenzie, GK Chesterton, the war poet David Jones, etc.

249   Reinhard Hoeppli, Postscript to *Décadence Mandchoue*.

250   Ibid.

251   Ibid.

Sir Edmund with all his shortcomings was most extraordinary and perhaps never revealed his personality completely... REQUIESCAT IN PACE! [252]

Postscript

Dr Reinhard Hoeppli remained involved in parasitology, moving to the then-British colony of Singapore in the 1950s (where he was also, and rather long-windedly, for a time the Honorary Swiss Consul at Singapore for the Federation of Malaya, Sarawak, North Borneo and Brunei) before returning to Africa where he was involved in tropical medicine in Liberia in the 1960s.

Décadence Mandchoue sat in the restricted vaults of the National Library of Australia in Canberra and the Bodleian in Oxford, dismissed by Hugh Trevor-Roper as a 'pornographic novelette'. It was finally published in an unabridged and annotated version in 2011. To judge from the Amazon reviews the jury is still very much out on Sir Edmund – 'insightful gossip of the final years of the Qing Dynasty' to 'shameless gay erotica.'

The rows over Backhouse continue. I'll give the last word to Derek Sandhaus, who spent many years obsessing over *Décadence Mandchoue*. Whatever his faults, Sir Edmund 'knew Peking and its people better than just about any of his foreign contemporaries. His final work *(Décadence Mandchoue)* is a eulogy for the *(Qing)* dynasty, an erotic love letter to a bygone era. Even if it were completely fabricated, and I do not personally believe that it was, it would still be an engaging and often hilarious historical fiction by a well-informed linguistic genius.'[253]

---

252 REST IN PEACE. Reinhard Hoeppli, Postscript to *Décadence Mandchoue*.
253 Backhouse, *Décadence Mandchoue*.

Finding Love and Mr Moto in Peking:
JP Marquand & Adelaide Hooker (1935)

'Nearly anything's proper in Peking. No one will be surprised.' [254]

254 JP Marquand, *Ming Yellow* (Boston: Little, Brown, 1935).

We need a hero....

In 1933 one of America's largest-circulation weekly newspapers, the *Saturday Evening Post*, had a big problem. Earl Derr Biggers, one of the *Evening Post's* best-loved serial fiction writers, had died suddenly. And with his death so his creation, the phenomenally popular Hawaiian-Chinese detective Charlie Chan, died too. The paper needed to replace Biggers and Chan, and they wanted another character with an Asian angle. Charlie Chan had been a big hit for the *Evening Post* while *Collier's* magazine was still finding success running Sax Rohmer's Fu Manchu stories, and excerpts of John Taintor Foote's 1926 novel *Number One Boy* (an 'American romance with Oriental mysticism'[255]) had been a very successful serialisation. American readers, the *Evening Post* believed, wanted yet more of the same or similar. A new Asian character was required.

JP Marquand

John Phillips (JP) Marquand had graduated from Harvard and then served as a lieutenant in the US Field Artillery in World War One. He worked as a cub reporter on the *Boston Transcript*, wrote copy for the *New York Tribune*, and then for the ad agency J Walter Thompson. But it was to be in writing stories that he found his *métier*. In the early 1930s Marquand emerged as a successful author of indubitably shallow but highly polished "slick fiction" for the *Saturday Evening Post*, as well as aspiring to be a serious novelist of New England manners and society. He had achieved some literary success on the East Coast, and his first novel had been published in the large-circulation *Ladies' Home Journal*. The editors of the *Evening Post* decided Marquand would be their new star writer to replace Biggers and in order to help him come up with the required Asian character in 1934, they sent him to China and Japan, a trip that would change his life in a myriad of ways.

These days JP Marquand, and the character he created after his trip to the Far East, the Japanese secret policeman Mr Moto, are largely forgotten.

---

255 John Taintor Foote, *Number One Boy* (New York: Appleton, 1926).

Nobody much reads Marquand's serious fiction now either. The six Mr Moto books aren't seriously reprinted, though they're easy enough to pick up second-hand. The movie adaptations with Peter Lorre as Moto are hardly shown these days and are, of course, problematic, being replete with racial stereotypes and Lorre in yellowface. They started in the mid-1930s and so always battled a rapidly changing perception of Japan and the Japanese in America. The Hollywood B-movies have rather sullied the reputation of the novels which, though containing some stereotypical caricatures, are also well crafted and contain accurate descriptions of China and Japan at the time, particularly of 1930s Peking. It's a shame that Marquand's Mr Moto has become lost, and in many cases, reviled, because there was more to him than people think – and he was, in many ways, a direct product of the author's 1934 China sojourn.

A first trip

The *Saturday Evening Post* financed a ten-week trip to Japan, Korea and China. It was to be a sojourn that would lead to Marquand having a long-term fascination with northern China, and to offer new directions for his writing. The trip to Peking was also to provide him with an escape from a failing twelve-year marriage to his wife Christine, and a way of ducking an ongoing, but collapsing, affair with the satirist Helen Howe. In China he was to find a new romance and, as his biographer Philip Hamburger of the *New Yorker* – who spent many hours observing and interviewing the author – learnt, found a country he loved and always wished to return to:

> I was sent to China in 1934 by the *Saturday Evening Post* with
> instructions to do a series of stories with authentic Oriental
> background. Naturally, I did a great deal of poking around in Chinese
> cities and finally wandered to Japan. There I was constantly shadowed
> by a polite little Japanese detective. Suddenly, it dawned on me that he
> was just the protagonist I was looking for – and while my shadow did
> his duty very conscientiously.[256]

256 Philip Hamburger, *JP Marquand, Esquire: A Portrait in the Form of a Novel* (Boston: Houghton Mifflin, 1952).

Later Marquand told a probably apocryphal anecdote of his time in Tokyo, but one which was regularly used in his publisher's marketing of the Moto books – 'I was constantly followed by Japanese detectives who used to search my baggage very clumsily almost every night. They all looked and talked exactly like Mr Moto.'[257]

Mr Moto, the shrewd, the polite, the efficient sleuth was born.

To Peking in search of inspiration

But first Peking. Marquand left for China in 1934, sailing across the Atlantic and then via Suez from Europe. He travelled through Japan and Korea, up into Japanese-occupied Manchuria, visiting Mukden and Hsinking. Disappointingly Marquand had found Japan a strange parody of America – the western clothes and the stilted jazz of Tokyo's Imperial Hotel did not impress him. Korea was authentic, but a depressing colony under Japan's yoke. Likewise, Manchuria was under Japanese tutelage and similarly depressing. Mukden was, it seemed to Marquand, effectively a Russian city that appeared to him as 'a cross between Nebraska and the moon'.[258] In Hsinking he recorded nothing else of his time except that he visited a sordid Japanese-run opium den. Feeling uninspired and underwhelmed by the East, Marquand eventually arrived in Peking in early April. His mood changed because he was immediately impressed, writing to Helen Howe, 'I just got here this morning, but that is long enough to realize, even for a cynic like myself, that Peking is the most beautiful and delightful city in the world...'[259] Like any other sojourner on the corporate tab he checked into the Grand Hôtel de Pékin.

Marquand, with a hired rickshaw puller ($2.50 weekly), set out to explore the city. He stopped at his bank and then the US Legation in the Legation Quarter before he visited the Forbidden City. For Marquand the ancient imperial citadel was love at first sight. He rapidly developed an obsession with the old imperial quarters. He later recalled, 'I remember

257 Marquand told and retold this story repeatedly when marketing his Moto books. This formulation comes from the jacket cover of *Last Laugh Mr Moto* (London, Tom Stacey Reprints, 1972).

258 Quoted in Millicent Bell, *Marquand: An American Life* (Boston: Little, Brown & Company, 1979), p.213. Bell is quoting from Marquand's letters to Helen Howe and his Asian notebooks that are now part of the Boston University Marquand Collection.

259 Ibid.

the first time that I had set eyes on Peking streets, and recalled that baffling impression of utter unfamiliarity, that lack of any basis for comparison with my own world, which every scene had presented.'[260]

The Forbidden City in 1934 was decidedly less packed with tourists than nowadays and Marquand could wander freely from one almost deserted courtyard to another for the price of a few pennies' entry fee. The Forbidden City was not fully restored at the time and Marquand marvelled at the peeling paint and split wood beams, the occasional yellow roof tile that had slipped and broken on the ground amid the weeds growing up between the paving stones. From there his rickshaw conveyed him to the Temple of Heaven and then to the Eastern City and all the smells of Peking that repelled the Legation Quarter set but attracted the more aesthetically-inclined sojourners.

The coal carts pulled by men with ropes across their backs, the distinctive odour of the "honey wagons" collecting human waste for fertilizer, the camel trains at the Chienmen Gate – Marquand ticked off all the top 'aesthete' sights of Peking. But it was the Forbidden City that called to him most – he was to return again and again over the next few weeks. He made friends with other sojourners of a similar frame of mind. George N. Kates, who had come to Peking in 1933 to 'immerse' himself in the old city, and Bud Ekins, the United Press correspondent in Peking, were early acquaintances.[261] Later he took a liking to Walter Bosshard, a Swiss photographer and explorer of Central Asia. Marquand was always cognisant that he needed material for whatever planned character took shape. With Bosshard he ventured out to the town of Kalgan, the gateway trading town to Inner Mongolia, and a hard-scrabble place of Chinese, Russians and all manner of other traders, adventurers and bandits. He was starting to find inspiration.

Then with Kates, and Alan Priest, the curator of Chinese art from New York's Metropolitan Museum, Marquand visited China's coal capital of Taiyuan to see Wutai Shan, the famous five peaks, each topped by a Buddhist temple. Lucy Calhoun, the widow of a former American ambassador to China and the sister of Harriet Monroe, the well-known

260 Marquand is speaking through his character Tom Nelson in his second Mr Moto novel, *Thank You, Mr Moto*, though these seem so clearly the author's own impressions of Peking.
261 For more on Kates see the chapter, *The Peiping World of Peonies and Ponies*.

Chicago poet and editor of the journal *Poetry*, also joined the trip – a fortuitous meeting for Marquand as it would later prove. But Marquand didn't distinguish himself well on the expedition – drinking too much, and annoyingly flirting with some of the younger women in the party. Kates recalled one night that ended 'with smashed glasses and an overturned table.' Rather embarrassed, Marquand returned briefly to Peking before getting the train to Shanghai and the boat back to America.

Ming Yellow and Moto

Most likely written on the boat home and then rapidly serialised in the *Saturday Evening Post* in December 1934, *Ming Yellow* is a rather slight novel in many respects and one rarely read today.[262] After serialisation it was published as a book the following March. *Ming Yellow* feels as if Marquand is still writing in the "slick fiction" style he was, at the time, best known for, and is not quite ready to dive headlong into the more sensational and populist pulp genre. Obviously, the *Evening Post* was keen to recover some of its investment in their new "star writer", but it's a pretty derivative work.

As far as can be divined, Marquand felt he could and should write a stand-alone China novel before starting on the first Mr Moto. *Ming Yellow* concerns a foreign journalist with the Composite Press Service, Rodney Jones – an American who, after eighteen months in Peking, is tired of the goldfish bowl of the city's foreign colony and reporting on the internecine chaos of China's northern warlords (not unlike Marquand's new acquaintance Bud Ekins). He encounters the beautiful and wealthy Mel Newall visiting Peking with her millionaire industrialist father, who is also a collector of extremely rare Ming yellow porcelain. The Newalls are accompanied by their obsequious factotum, Paul Steuben. Also in the mix is a western-educated Chinese called Philip Liu, who claims to have contacts in China's hinterland who have a stash of Ming yellow pottery for sale. An expedition ensues – cut-throat bandits, bug-infested country inns, plenty of betrayal and, naturally, Rodney and Mel fall in love.

Ming Yellow is standard melodrama, decidedly B-movie in tone and, given the wealth of novels and pulps featuring treasure hunting in the

262 JP Marquand, *Ming Yellow* (Boston: Little, Brown, 1935).

face of bandits in China at the time, not overly original.[263] Annoyingly *Ming Yellow* is full of cod Chinese aphorisms that carry on over into the Moto books and obviously take their cue from the earlier Charlie Chan stories. However, at the start of the book we do get a sense of the author himself in Peking, dining at the Grand Hôtel de Pékin, visiting courtyard homes, and hearing bandit tales from the more adventurous likes of Ekins and Bosshard. At times – really the best times in the novel – it is clear Marquand is writing and describing the Peking surroundings he had come to know:

> The sun was shining through the leaves of the old tree so that the shadows and the sunlight made a pattern on the flagstones; and the flagstones were powdered with that yellow-reddish dust. The sun brought out the yellow, like the yellow glaze on tile, causing the color to dominate the red of the open door. He knew that the same color was moving in Mr. Newall's mind – Yellow – Ming Yellow.[264]

Marquand is also aware of the peculiarities of Peking air so familiar to anyone living in the city then (or now for that matter) – tinged with dust and often sharp with cold:

> It often seemed to Rodney Jones that old residents of that amazing city *(Peking)* blamed everything which was inexplicable upon the air they breathed. They blamed the air of North China for their nervousness and irritability; they excused excessive drinking and mild chicanery, and men for running off with the wives of other men, because of the wind which blew across Peking from the greatest solitudes on earth. Sometimes it was laden with fine yellow dust; again it was so clear and pure that the sunlight refined it into crystal

---

263 *Ming Yellow* has a little of John Buchan's Richard Hannay novels about it, a touch of Francis Van Wyck Mason's Captain Hugh North of G-2 Military Intelligence series, and shades of Somerset Maugham's *Ashenden,* as well as the many imitators that followed them all. Four of Buchan's Hannay books – *The 39 Steps* (1915), *Greenmantle* (1916), *Mr. Standfast* (1919), and *The Three Hostages* (1924) – had been published at the time; so had seven of Van Wyck Mason's Hugh North books, including his major Far Eastern-set adventure, *The Shanghai Bund Murders* (1933); while Somerset Maugham's *Ashenden* spy stories had first appeared in 1927.

264 Marquand, *Ming Yellow.*

white. There was a mysterious stillness sometimes in that limpid air, as though the remoteness of the Gobi Desert and the Mongolian plateau had not entirely left it.[265]

A return to Peking and falling in love

Having delivered *Ming Yellow* to the voracious *Evening Post*, Marquand settled down to write the first Mr Moto. In *Your Turn Mr Moto*[266], Marquand returned to his 1934 sojourn, and though Japanese, his hero's journey duplicates the author's own arrival in China – though with considerably more melodrama.

Marquand took all the knowledge he had soaked up in China, the conversations in Lucy Calhoun's salon, those trips with George Kates, Bud Ekins and Walter Bosshard, and put it all into his first Mr Moto novel, *Your Turn Mr Moto,* published in 1935 and written shortly after his visit to China and Japan. Like all the pre-war Motos, the plot hinges on Japanese machinations against China. The story concerns a washed-up and alcoholic US air ace from the Great War, Casey Lee, stranded in Tokyo. In return for the chance to fly again, Lee accepts Mr Moto's seemingly innocuous offer of travelling to Shanghai. It is of course a ruse and Casey is caught up in an espionage plot that involves him with a White Russian femme fatale, Sonya Koroloff, and the head of US Naval Intelligence in Shanghai, Commander James Driscoll. Those who think the book is anything like the Lorre movies will be surprised to find that within the first fifty pages Marquand deals with the Japanese occupation of Manchuria, the fallout in Asia of World War One, deteriorating US-Japanese relations, the rapid militarisation of Japan, the desperate plight of the White Russians in China and their continued quest to overthrow the Soviet Union and reclaim Russia for the Tsar. None of these are issues you'll find discussed in much depth by Peter Lorre dressed as a clown and uttering some trite truism. Marquand's Moto is far more menacing, leaving us in no doubt that beneath his surface politeness he is determined and ruthless. Before we get to the end of the fast-paced novel of just 150

---

265 Marquand, *Ming Yellow.*
266 The original *Saturday Evening Post* serial was titled *No Hero.* The subsequent hardback book of the story was called by the same name, though the mass circulation paperback was titled *Your Turn Mr Moto* and, in Britain, *Mr Moto Takes a Hand.*

or so pages we have had disquisitions on the specific place of Shanghai in the Chinese economy, the plight of the White Russians and the history of the city of Harbin, the role of warlords in northern China, the relative strengths and weaknesses of the Japanese versus the American navies, and the advantages and disadvantages of Shanghai's dancehalls over those elsewhere.

Marquand managed to convince the *Evening Post* that more Moto would require more Peking. They fell for it. And so Marquand returned to the city in 1935. This time he knew people, and had met Lucy Calhoun the previous year in Taiyuan. Before leaving the United States, Marquand arranged lodgings at her boarding house. "Aunt Lucy" was the unofficial First Lady of the Legation Quarter by virtue of her longevity in Peking and being the widow of a very popular American ambassador.

Lucy Monroe Calhoun had been born in 1865, the younger sister of Harriet Monroe who become one of America's best-known female poets. The Monroe sisters were both talented, thanks in large part to having access to their father's extensive library. Lucy became a successful art critic, freelancing at various Chicago newspapers. She then married William Calhoun, a good friend of President McKinley, who was appointed US minister to China, where the couple witnessed – from America's embassy in the Legation Quarter – the fall of the Qing Dynasty and the creation of the first Chinese Republic. However, shortly after leaving China, William Calhoun suffered a stroke and died in 1916. Widowed, Lucy signed on as a nurse in France in the First World War. In the 1920s she returned to Peking, establishing her hutong home as a boarding house, in fact a highly desirable boutique hotel for acquaintances, and a salon for all manner of interesting people living in, or passing through, the city. She also collected art, furniture and curios. Lucy Calhoun remained in Peking until the Japanese occupation of the city in 1937.

Calhoun's large courtyard house was the perfect place for Marquand to stay during his second sojourn to the city. A restored ancient temple on Matajen Hutong, close by his beloved Forbidden City, the ground-floor rooms were roofed with herring-bone patterns of grey tiles. The furniture comprised a tasteful mix of Chinese lacquerware and hardwoods mixed with comfortable western sofas and throws. The garden courtyards were all paved and the flower beds expertly tended. It was a complete sanctuary in which Marquand could work in peace and quiet until the cocktail

Above and opposite: Aunt Lucy's place

hour, when he would always find someone interesting who had come to stay with, or call upon, Aunt Lucy.

In his second Mr Moto book, *Thank You, Mr Moto*, written while staying at Aunt Lucy's, Marquand gives what is no doubt a vivid description of her hutong home:

> It was one of the most beautiful rooms that I have seen in any country. There was not a trace of Europe in that room. Pillars of camphor wood supported carved roof beams. The trim around the door and windows was sandal-wood, carved into a design of herons and lotus flowers. Poetry scrolls were hanging on the walls in bold black Chinese characters... Stiff-backed chairs and tables of black and gold lacquer stood along the walls...[267]

And it was here, over cocktails at Aunt Lucy's, that he met two of the remarkable trio of Hooker sisters who were also staying. For a writer of novels of New England manners, the Hooker sisters of Greenwich, Connecticut were interesting – direct descendants of Thomas Hooker, the Puritan colonial leader, who founded the Colony of Connecticut. The

267   JP Marquand, *Thank You, Mr Moto* (London: Fontana, 1937), p.98.

eldest of the Hooker sisters, Blanchette, had married John D. Rockefeller III.[268]

Marquand first fell into conversation with Helen Hooker. Helen was heading the long way round from America to London to marry Ernie O'Malley, an Irish revolutionary and writer. O'Malley had been a commander in the Irish Republican Army in the War of Independence and then the subsequent Civil War. He had suffered injuries, gone on hunger strike at Mountjoy Prison, was finally released and then went on tour, raising funds for the new Irish Republic. He was also a keen writer and visited the Bohemian haunts of New York where he had met Helen, wealthy (the Hookers owned the sizeable Hooker Chemical Company) but also Bohemian, in 1933. The couple had fallen in love and did indeed marry in September 1935 at Marylebone Registry Office in London. At around the same time, Marquand had finally divorced Christine while between Peking sojourns.

Adelaide, Helen's sister, was remaining in Peking for a while longer. And it was Adelaide that Marquand was immediately attracted to. They

268 John D. Rockefeller himself had a long fascination with East Asia and Japan. He founded the Institute of Pacific Relations in Japan and, later, was to be close to Douglas MacArthur in post-war Japan. He was also the founder of the Asia Society and a reconstituted Japan Society in the United States.

got off to a slightly confused start –
Adelaide thought he was English. He
was actually often mistaken for such.
Philip Hamburger notes the 'singularly
cultivated inflections of the man's
voice.'[269] However, they took to each
other. Helen moved on to London
and Adelaide and Marquand began
exploring the city together. Adelaide
was a graduate of Vassar and University
of Rochester and had spent several years
in Germany studying singing with the
German operatic soprano and voice
coach Lilli Lehmann. She was also an
occasional music critic for the American
newspapers and had spent time in the
Soviet Union as a reporter where she
was both pursued by the police and
contracted tuberculosis.

Marquand was fascinated with the
street life of Peking – soothsayers, sword
swallowers, men with dancing mice,
fortune-tellers, letter writers – and
Adelaide soon shared his fascination.

Adelaide Hooker, 1931

The couple announced their
engagement in April 1937. Marquand
discovered that the newspaper- and book-reading public, as well as
Hollywood, loved Moto and wanted more. His career (the success of
Moto allowed him to also refocus on his less pulpy novel writing) and his
personal life were set, thanks to his sojourns in Peking.

What can we say, Mr Moto?

Marquand's second Moto book, *Thank You, Mr Moto* (published in
1937), sees him flesh out the Moto character and describe the Peking he
had experienced on his second visit. Set against the gradual surrounding

269 Hamburger, *JP Marquand Esquire*, p.4.

of the city and encroachment into it by the Japanese, the story is, once again, not primarily about Mr Moto but rather about Tom Nelson, an American aesthete seeking to immerse himself in old Peking and keep a distance from the frivolous foreign expat community. However, partly due to his acquaintance with beautiful young sojourner Eleanor Joyce who has come to the Orient seeking "experiences", he becomes involved in a sinister murder. Mr Moto appears at various points working in the background, and is even more sinister now (his gold teeth are emphasised, his smile and phrasing even more ingratiating).

Marquand's Peking in *Thank You, Mr Moto* is one of hutong backstreets with foreigners residing in considerable luxury. The community includes those with long-term China knowledge and appreciation as well as the more frivolous on the grand tour. They mix at parties, servants are plentiful, rickshaws are at the ready, the Legation Quarter offers sanctuary not far away. A familiar romanticising of the city, perhaps, but not necessarily an inaccurate portrait of its foreign denizens and sojourners in 1937. If there are passages redolent of the memoirs of aesthetes like Kates, John Blofeld or Harold Acton, then it is because he did, briefly, inhabit their world of hutongs, courtyards and salons and shared their aesthetic delight of Peking. There are also shades of Vincent Starrett's *Murder in Peking*, a best-seller when published in 1946. Starrett did visit Peking (and spent time with ETC Werner) and had probably read both Marquand and Acton.

In the third book of the series, written in 1938, *Mr Moto is So Sorry*, Marquand once again returns to a China he knows – Mukden, Japanese-occupied Manchuria, elements of the Peking Man discovery of the time, and Mongolian expeditions.[270] Then times changed and *Last Laugh Mr Moto*, which appeared in 1942, just after America had declared war on Japan, takes place in the Caribbean.

Historically it has been the Peter Lorre movies that have killed Mr Moto. The movies were a massive dumbing-down of the novels, to a far greater extent than even the numerous film versions of Earl Biggers'

---

270   JP Marquand, *Mr Moto is So Sorry* (London: Big Ben Books, 1940). The Peking Man homo erectus fossils, estimated at approximately 750,000 years old, were excavated at Choukoutien, near Peking, between 1929 and 1937. Mongolian expeditions were popular in the inter-war period, not least those undertaken by the American Roy Chapman Andrews.

Charlie Chan character. Mr Moto has suffered from a number of problems. Firstly of course we no longer accept yellowface and Lorre's buck-toothed, comedic Mr Moto is ridiculous to a modern audience. Secondly, the Second World War happened, and American notions of Japan changed. In Marquand's far more subtle novels Moto is never a front-and-centre character, but rather the *eminence grise* in the background, attempting to manipulate people and events. He is suave and sophisticated, far more so than the bumbling character Lorre depicts: 'Mr. Moto was a small man, delicate, almost fragile. ... He was dressed formally in a morning coat and striped trousers. His black hair was carefully brushed in the Prussian style. He was smiling, showing a row of shiny gold-filled teeth, and as he smiled he drew in his breath with a polite, soft sibilant sound.'[271]

Marquand's Moto is always impeccably tailored, if perhaps in slightly outdated fashions; he does not have buck teeth; his English is excellent, but with a slightly over-elaborate politeness; he does not personally resort to violence or physical intimidation; he works for the Japanese secret police, believes in his emperor and in the manifest destiny of Japan to control China. Lorre's Moto was moved to become the central character in the movies; he routinely wears ridiculous disguises and engages in a bit of haphazard judo; he works for the International Police; and doesn't espouse any of the Japanese nationalistic rhetoric of the time.

While there is some argument, it appears that Marquand never had any involvement in the scripts for the films, though they added to his bank balance. He wrote half a dozen novels featuring Moto, five written before Pearl Harbor. Marquand then 'interned Moto for the duration', returning to him only once, after a fifteen-year gap, in 1957, where Moto makes a brief appearance in *Stopover: Tokyo,* working for the American post-war occupation authorities.[272] Marquand was resistant but the *Saturday Evening Post* offered him $5,000 to travel to Japan and a rather decent advance of $75,000.

---

271 Marquand, *Your Turn Mr Moto.*
272 Also variously known as *Right You Are, Mr Moto* or *The Last of Mr Moto* and originally serialised in the *Saturday Evening Post* as *Rendezvous in Tokyo.* By coincidence, the artist hired to do the cover for the American first edition of *Stopover in Tokyo* was Martha Sawyers, though I don't believe she and Marquand ever met, at least not in Peking. For more see chapter 17, 'The Woman Who Created the Wartime Image of China in America'.

The Moto books feature the political dilemmas Marquand had encountered on his 1934 and 1935 trips. He includes detailed discussions on deteriorating Sino-Japanese and Japanese-American relations and the shifting world situation. Marquand's Moto is a menacing figure representing a Japan that is feigning friendship with America while, in reality, is in the midst of attacking China and emerging to potentially threaten the United States. Marquand's novelistic take on the mid-to-late 1930s is informed and ultimately, for us with hindsight, correct. Moto is a master strategist of the espionage game, a manipulator of his pawns of all nationalities, yet he fades into the background, is lost in the crowd – an Asian George Smiley in some respects. Readers ought to have worried about Mr Moto and his bosses and his beliefs. Where Marquand's books sought to warn American readers of the deteriorating situation in the Far East and the rise of Japan, the Hollywood movies portrayed a cooperation that didn't exist and fostered a lampooning version of Japanese Intelligence that would, within a few years, be no laughing matter for those who found themselves facing the real-life Mr Motos of the *Kempeitai*.

After Moto

Moto was fun but he haunted Marquand, and meanwhile there were people in literary Manhattan who thought his attempts at higher literature were repetitive and pointless and that he would have done better to stick with Mr Moto.[273] But Marquand was a highly successful author by the early 1950s. One or another of his books had been constantly on the best-seller lists since the mid-1930s, his books were dramatized and performed on Broadway and turned into successful movies by Hollywood. It was estimated in 1953 that he had sold 1,542,547 copies of his books in cheap editions bought by the American reading masses, plus a further 2,291,293 copies through America's powerful book clubs.

Marquand was to become rich both through his serious novels and his Motos. Through his marriage to Adelaide, he became linked to the Rockefeller family. Marquand had two children from his first marriage and a further three with Adelaide. The couple maintained homes in scenic Newburyport, Massachusetts and in the Caribbean. Shortly after

273 Hamburger, p.8.

Marquand published his final Moto novel in the late 1950s, he and Adelaide divorced. JP Marquand died in 1960 aged sixty-six. Adelaide died in 1963, aged sixty.

Though he maintained his love for Peking throughout his life, Marquand was never grateful to Mr Moto. Even when Moto made an appearance in *Stopover Tokyo*, which was Marquand's penultimate novel[274], he disparaged his creation. Still, the public loved *Stopover Tokyo*, which was marketed largely on the hook of the appearance of Mr Moto. The *Saturday Evening Post* serialisation boosted the paper's circulation temporarily[275]; it was a best-seller; the *New York Times* called it 'superlative'.[276] Hollywood rapidly turned it into a B-movie with Robert Wagner and a young Joan Collins.[277] Yet Marquand had little good to say about his creation:

Adelaide Hooker in 1937;
JP Marquand in 1960

> Mr Moto was my literary disgrace. I
> wrote about him to get shoes for the
> baby. I don't say I didn't have a pleasant
> time writing about him and he returned
> in *Stopover Tokyo* but I don't think
> I'll ever meet him again. Moto was

274   His last novel was the popular, but not generally well-reviewed, *Women and Thomas Harrow* (Boston: Little Brown, 1958).

275   Serialised in the *Post* from 24 November 1956 to 12 January 1957 under the title 'Rendezvous in Tokyo'.

276   Harvey Breit, 'In and Out of Books', *New York Times*, February 17, 1957.

277   *Stopover: Tokyo* (Twentieth Century Fox, 1957) is a reasonably decent film noir that is rarely shown now. Most of its appeal derives from the fact that it was largely shot on location in Kyoto, though the middle-aged Mr Moto of the novel is entirely absent from the movie.

an entirely different piece of writing from a so-called serious novel. He really became famous when they took him up in the movies. In book form he has never really sold well – never more than 5,000 to 6,000 copies. I can't say why people remember him, except they must remember the serials and pictures.[278]

Marquand's later life carried many remembrances of his time in China: a wooden statue of the Goddess of Mercy, Kwan Yin, at the apartment on New York's East Sixty-Seventh Street; and in the retreat he maintained at his ancestral home on Kent's Island in the Chesapeake Bay were numerous small Oriental *tchotkes* from his travels, a shelf of books on China, and more concerning his deep and long-lived belief in *feng shui*.

278   Lewis Nichols, 'The World of John P Marquand', *New York Times*, August 3, 1958.

Nazi Parties in Peking:
Eugen, Helma & the Nazis of Occupied Peking (1943)

'My position here is extremely delicate. I would not care to make any statement without the authorization of the American authorities.'
– Major General Eugen Ott, speaking from Peking shortly after his detention by American forces in 1946 [279]

279 Victor Keen, 'Nazis' Ambassador to Japan in Tokyo on Secret US Job', *Daily News* (New York), February 10, 1946, p.20.

A Wartime Exile

In 1943 the small community of dedicated German Nazis, along with a few sympathisers and fellow travellers from the Axis nations who were living in Peking, were joined by a new couple – the Otts. The arrival of the Otts into what was effectively an embarrassing exile for the remainder of the war shone a light on the lives of the Nazis resident in Japanese-occupied Peking, their organisation, sympathisers and their activities in the city.

The Otts, arguably, immediately went straight to the top of the Nazi social hierarchy in Peking. Eugen Ott was a Great War hero, a former high-ranking officer in the Reichswehr (German army) of the Weimar period, and latterly a former Nazi ambassador to Tokyo. His wife, Helma Bodewig Ott, was considered to come from a good Munich family, was socially well connected, and attractive in a rather imposing way. Their family residence in Peking was assigned to them by order of the Japanese prime minister, Hideki Tojo himself.

However, there was a cloud over the couple: a major black mark that the local leaders of the *Schutzstaffel* (SS) in Peking – Charlie Schmidt and Adelbert Schulze – as well as others in the small German colony in the city had heard rumours and gossip about. Eugen Ott was in disgrace. He had been summarily removed from his post in Tokyo after being completely fooled and taken in by the Soviet Union's most successful spy in Asia, Richard Sorge. And, scandalously, Sorge had also been Helma's lover for years; a relationship Eugen not only knew of, but apparently had quietly accepted.

In disgrace or not, Eugen Ott was a senior figure in the Nazi Party in Asia and one of the earliest party members. His removal from Tokyo to Peking greatly interested Allied intelligence trying to work out what the machinations in the Nazi's Far East command structure meant. Until the Otts arrived in Peking in 1943 the city's Nazi community had not been closely examined. The main wings of the Nazi command in the Far East were in Tokyo (the city the Otts had just been banished from), Shanghai (where the majority of the Nazi espionage operations in the region were concentrated), and the puppet capital of Nanking (the Nazis had recognised Wang Jing-wei's regime, formally the Reorganized National

Government of the Republic of China, as the legitimate government of China) where the Nazis maintained diplomatic representation.

Peking had largely been a backwater for Nazi activity in Asia. The controversial arrival of the Otts shone a light on the city.

Loyal but duped

Eugen Ott was a career military man. Born in 1889 he had served with distinction on the Eastern Front in World War One and, afterwards, had remained in the Reichswehr. His wife Helma had been born in 1894 to a family of lawyers. She had first been married during World War One to a communist-leaning Frankfurt architect called Ernst May, who became a respected town planner there after the war, and who also worked on housing developments and town planning in Soviet Russia. Though later Helma denied any communist affiliations it seems that she was, for a brief time, active (at least socially) on the political Left in Munich during the creation of the short-lived Bavarian Soviet Republic in 1919. However, the marriage didn't last and the couple separated.[280] Helma was divorced and living in Munich when she met Reichswehr officer Eugen Ott. They married in 1921, her brief flirtation with communism apparently over. Helma became first an army wife and then a woman married to a key figure in the Nazi power structure.

Ott had a key role as a major liaison between Hitler, leading Nazis and the senior military leadership. He was the adjutant to General Kurt von Schleicher, the last Weimar chancellor of Germany, a rival of Hitler's who was murdered by the SS during the Night of the Long Knives in the summer of 1934. Ott survived, but his position was precarious due to his previous association with von Schleicher. It was said that a position was being found for him in Bavaria but Helma suggested her husband be sent to Manchuria to observe the new Japanese-occupied territory of Manchukuo, before moving to Tokyo as Nazi Germany's ambassador

---

280 May was to draw up blueprints for the planned industrial city of Magnitogorsk near Chelyabinsk, largely inspired by his earlier visits to Britain's garden cities, but his ideas were never realised. His contract expired in 1933 after he was severely criticised by loyalists to Stalin. He left for British East Africa (now Kenya). May did design some impressive buildings in Mombasa but left the country during the Mau-Mau Uprising and returned to Germany. He died in 1970. For more on Magnitogorsk see Stephen Kotkin's *Steeltown, USSR* (Berkeley, California: University of California Press, 1992).

Eugen & Helma Ott in Tokyo, 1938

to Japan. Helma's rationale was that the reprisal purges might not have stopped with the Night of the Long Knives and so the further away Eugen was from the internal arguments in Berlin the better. And so that is what happened – shortly after von Schleicher's death the Otts departed Germany for Manchuria and then Tokyo.

The Otts arrived in Tokyo to quite a fanfare and a press eager to snap the couple.[281] Ott had retained some strong contacts and good connections back in Berlin and was able to secure both funds and permission to build a substantial new ambassadorial residence on the grounds of the embassy itself. Shortly after his arrival Ott met the Russian agent Richard Sorge, who had moved his base from Shanghai to Tokyo. Ott completely fell for Sorge's cover story of being a German with specialist knowledge of East Asia. The two became firm friends and confidants. Sorge became an adviser to Ott on matters East Asian and shared his extensive library of texts on Japan with Ott. Simultaneously Helma embarked on an affair with the dashing, and seemingly quite reckless, Sorge.

Sorge's most recent biographer, Owen Matthews, speculates that the Otts' marriage was 'loveless' and that Eugen didn't object to the affair, even referring to Sorge as '*der unwilderstehliche*' – the irresistible one. It certainly seems to have been a sexual relationship though and, even though the two were approximately the same age, Helma reportedly

---

281 It is unclear whether the Otts were accompanied by their children. It seems that for at least part of their time in Japan their son Helmuth (born 1923) remained at school in Germany.

mothered Sorge quite intensely for a while – redecorating his bachelor flat, hanging new curtains. While Helma clearly seems to have felt something for Sorge, his courting of her may have been no more than him trying to find a new source of information on German intentions in East Asia for his masters in Moscow. Asked by a fellow Soviet spy about Helma, Sorge is said to have replied, 'Oh, don't talk to me of that woman. But what do you want me to do? We need her.'[282] The affair ultimately ended, but Sorge's friendship with Eugen Ott continued. When Sorge's treachery was revealed in 1941, despite Ott's disbelief, his position as ambassador became untenable.

Overnight Eugen Ott turned from a star Nazi diplomat at the court of Germany's major ally to an embarrassment. At first Ott had offered to return to Berlin and even volunteered to fight on the front lines. His offer was refused, and Ott was kept on the German Foreign Office payroll, retaining his rank, title and salary for over a year after Sorge's arrest. The new German ambassador to Japan, Heinrich Georg Stahmer, arrived in Japan on January 28, 1943, but Ott continued to maintain his residence

Richard Sorge in Tokyo, 1940

at the German Embassy, not only keeping the home and refusing to move out, but also continuing to act as if he were still the official ambassador. Ott made a tour of the southern islands of Japan and continued having conferences with high-level Japanese officials even though he no longer had any official title.

All this put the new ambassador in a difficult position. Unlike Ott with his army background, Stahmer was a professional diplomat and had long overseen Japanese relations at the German Foreign Ministry in Berlin. He had previously been a close aide to Foreign Minister Joachim von Ribbentrop and acted as a German special envoy to Japan. His last

282 Owen Matthews, *An Impeccable Spy: Richard Sorge, Stalin's Master Agent* (London: Bloomsbury, 2019), p.134.

post before being reassigned to Tokyo had been as ambassador to the pro-Japanese puppet government of Wang Jing-wei in Nanking since 1940.

Prior to the Sorge revelations, Nazi Germany's representation in Asia included Ott in Tokyo, Stahmer in Japanese-occupied China, and Ernst Wendler, Germany's wartime ambassador in the nominally neutral, but often Japanese-leaning, Thai capital of Bangkok. This had been the triumvirate of Nazi diplomatic power in the region. The move of Stahmer to Tokyo was a clear sign that Ott (who, prior to his posting to Tokyo, had no knowledge of Japan or Japanese whatsoever) was dismissed. Stahmer eventually managed to reclaim the embassy residence from Ott and remained the German ambassador in Tokyo till the end of the war.

And so quietly, so it was often said at the time, Ott was 'transferred to the German Consulate in Peking' for the remainder of World War Two. However, it seems that in reality, Ott was sent into exile to Peking – a city of little official or strategic importance in the war. Ott performed no official function at any German consulate in China and spent the rest of the war years in Peking as a private citizen under the protection of the Japanese occupation forces.

What finally seems to have persuaded Ott to accept his fate and move from Japan to China was the provision of a sizeable residence in Peking for him and his family by no lesser a personage than the Japanese prime minister.[283] To the foreign media the Nazis spun the move as a diplomatic reshuffling – hence the many articles claiming Ott had a position at the German consulate in the city – to avoid allegations of the Otts being sent into "exile".[284] However, this was exactly how Josef Meisinger, the hardcore Nazi chief of the Gestapo at the German embassy in Tokyo (and who spent much of the war in Shanghai), described it to the American newspapers when he gave interviews to the Associated Press after being arrested in Tokyo in 1945.[285] It was 'exile'.

---

283 As suggested in '701.6294/5–3146. Letter to the Political Adviser in Japan (George Atcheson Jr) to the Secretary of State (James F Byrnes). Confidential, No.441, Tokyo, May 31, 1946 (Received June 25, 1946)', *Foreign Relations of the United States, 1946, The Far East, Volume VIII* (Washington DC: United States Government Printing Office, 1971).

284 Though this did not stop the US newspapers referring to his move to Peking as such.

285 'Japan was an Uncertain Ally Until Dec. 7, 1941, Nazi Says', *The Journal Herald* (Dayton, Ohio), September 10, 1945, p.14.

The Otts of Peking

In December 1943 it was reported in *The San Francisco Examiner* that former Nazi ambassador Eugen Ott was 'living quietly in Peking.'[286] The paper suggested that he had once again requested permission to try and return to Berlin on a "blockade runner" (the ships that tried to outrun the Allied cordons back to Europe from Asia). It seems Berlin dismissed his request and ordered him to remain in Peking. If he hadn't fully realised it before, Ott must then have known that he was in exile for the duration. If it was any comfort to him he must also have realised that if the revelations about his friendship, and his wife's affair, with Sorge had come out when he was in Berlin, they would both undoubtedly have been executed.

Eugen Ott would not have been hard to spot in 1943 Peking had you come across him. He was six feet four inches tall (1.93m), barrel-chested, weighing in at an apparent eighteen stone (250lbs), and with a face covered in sabre scars from frequent duels as a younger man. Looking at pictures of Ott it is hard not to agree with the description of him provided by Clark Lee, the Associated Press's Manila correspondent in 1941, who had encountered Ott in Tokyo and Shanghai over the years immediately before the war: 'He had many of the mannerisms of a Hollywood-version Prussian officer.'[287] *The Times* of London had described him less dramatically, but similarly, as 'bluff, courteous, efficient, and a model soldier.'[288]

He would have been even easier to recognise if he was accompanied by his wife. Helma herself was striking at well over six feet tall – the Japanese nicknamed her *matsu no ki* – the pine tree.[289] Helma was always elegantly dressed (favouring evening dresses pretty much round the clock due to her height) and wore her prematurely snow-white hair undyed. She reportedly did not wear make-up and had an aversion to painting her fingernails. In a picture taken in Tokyo in April 1938, shortly after Ott had presented his ambassadorial credentials to the Emperor in the

286 'Japs Fail to Make Nazi-Soviet Peace', *The San Francisco Examiner*, December 5, 1943, p.20.

287 Clark Lee, 'Nazis Playing Major Role in Directing Japan War Efforts', *Honolulu Star-Bulletin*, December 23, 1941, p.6.

288 'Nazi Intrigue in Japan', *The* (London) *Times*, November 13, 1940, p.5.

289 Matthews, *An Impeccable Spy,* p.134.

Phoenix Hall of the Imperial Palace, it appears that Helma is even taller than her husband, even though Eugen seems to be standing on a step, indicating she may have been as tall as two metres.

Helma Ott at a reception at the German Embassy, Tokyo, 1938

Helma was described by any number of acquaintances over the years as a highly intelligent and independent woman. In both Tokyo and Peking, she defied convention by weeding her own garden wearing a large "coolie" hat! – sending shockwaves through the expatriate community in Tokyo who would not think of performing such menial tasks. This surprise at not hiring a gardener like everyone else was compounded by Helma's frequent weeding at night by torchlight due to her insomnia. However, she was also often referred to as haughty, aloof and imperious. Helma herself acknowledged this assessment but blamed it on what she considered her shyness. She had reputedly been bored in Tokyo – hence quite a lot of drinking, and the affairs with Sorge and (allegedly) other men in the city's German community. Japanese-occupied Peking in 1943 was not going to improve matters. The German community in Tokyo had numbered about two thousand and Helma had been the ambassador's wife. The German community in Peking in 1943 numbered a few dozen, many not of Helma's social class or intelligence at all, and she was effectively in disgrace.[290]

---

290   Many of the descriptions of Eugen and Helma Ott come from a long profile of them both, and Richard Sorge, in 'Portrait of a Spy', *Der Spiegel*, June 27, 1951. Many

Quite how relations were between Helma and Eugen in Peking is hard to decipher. The betrayal of Sorge, now revealed as a spy, added to the anger he must have felt (though never seems to have expressed) towards Sorge and Helma for their affair. Ott had been betrayed by both a friend and a wife. Additionally, Helma had long been rumoured to be a little "pink".[291] If there was any trace of her earlier flirtation with communism then it was in a certain dislike of convention. There had been raised eyebrows among the Japanese and Tokyo diplomatic corps when Helma had been seen to shrug her shoulders impatiently when Ott, in his role as German ambassador, bowed to a Japanese Shinto shrine.

It does seem true that Helma was a snob and very conscious of social rank and the deference that should be paid by those she perceived as the Otts' social inferiors on the diplomatic and military ranking scale. She was known to be quite rude and socially cutting to anyone not taking the issue of rank seriously enough. Again, how would their sojourn in Peking, as ostensibly private citizens, affect this after all her time in the social spotlight as the wife of an ambassador?

Eugen and Helma's marriage didn't appear to have had much going for it in Tokyo. He was said by some to be hen-pecked; he certainly didn't seem bothered about her affairs. So how was it going to weather the limited social opportunities, severely curtailed nightlife, and the claustrophobic remnants of Peking's pre-war Axis-leaning foreign colony? If the Otts' marriage really had been totally loveless by the time they'd arrived in Tokyo, nearly a decade previously, affections were unlikely to be rekindled in Peking.

Peking's Nazi social set

What the newly arrived Otts did have to fall back on in Peking was the social life of the senior ranks of the Imperial Japanese Army occupation force and the small Axis community in the city, composed largely of Germans and Italians, the official representatives and remaining supporters of collaborationist Vichy France, as well as a few citizens of

---

of those interviewed for the piece knew the Otts in both Tokyo and Peking.

291   At least according to wartime Japanese socialite Mitsutaro Akira, quoted in Matt Wilce, 'Journalist, Gymnast, Schoolboy, Spy', *The Ambassador* (the magazine of the American School in Japan), Fall, December 14, 2017.

'neutral' nations – Swiss, Spanish, Portuguese and some Latin American countries. There were several Irish priests and also a few German religious Sisters working as nurses in a couple of small hospitals in the Legation Quarter, including a woman named Gertrude Spaeth, who provided medical services to the Axis community. Additionally, one or two missionaries had stayed on, along with a few businessmen, and several widows of German businessmen who ran boarding houses and had been in China too long to consider returning home. Peking's Gestapo leaders lodged for a time with the German widow of a Chinese doctor in her house in the Eastern City.

Livening things up slightly, perhaps, there were also a few German men who had been expelled from the United States for pro-Nazi activities. They had taken ships from the American west coast (the Atlantic crossing being impossible by 1940) to Japan, hoping to get from there to the Trans-Siberian Railway in China, across Siberia to Moscow, and eventually back to Germany. However, with the end of the Nazi-Soviet Pact and the German invasion of the Soviet Union in June 1941, they had become trapped in Peking. Many of these so-called "Bundt Germans" had American wives and spent much of their time in Peking trying, largely hopelessly given that there was no American diplomatic presence in the city after December 1941, to regain their US citizenship.[292] As their money ran out so they came increasingly to rely on the German consulate. There was also a small group of Chinese who socialised with the Axis nationals. Although Japanese-occupied and military-controlled, much of Peking's day-to-day life was being regulated by the "North China Political Council", the local form of Wang Jing-wei's puppet regime, headed by the collaborationist politician Wang Kemin who did mix with senior Nazi officials in the city.

Until the Ott's arrival, the most senior-ranking Nazi in Peking had been Charlie (or sometimes Charley) Schmidt, chief of the Gestapo in the city. After Schmidt was his number two, and eventual successor to the top Gestapo job in Peking, Adelbert Schulze. Both men headed the *Geheime Staatspolizei für Nord China und Mongolei*, the Gestapo Branch

---

292 So-called as most of the men were members of the German American Bund, a pro-Nazi organization established in 1936. The spelling "Bundt" was used, perhaps, to differentiate from "bund" (derived from a Hindi word for a raised embankment) then in common use in China – e.g. the Shanghai bund, Hankow bund etc.

for North China and Mongolia, throughout the war years and were Heinrich Himmler's men in Peking. Schulze seems to have assumed the leadership from Schmidt sometime in early 1945, shortly before the German surrender in Europe.

Charlie Schmidt remains something of a mystery. It seems he started out in Shanghai as a Nazi operative and was later sent to Peking to become the North China Gestapo boss. Schmidt may have been involved in the German military assistance mission to Chiang Kai-shek in the 1930s under Alexander von Falkenhausen. That mission worked with the Chinese Nationalist army and defence industry until 1938 when it was forced to withdraw from China under Japanese pressure.[293] It is also possible that Schmidt also worked for, or with, the Wehrmacht Field Marshal Walter von Reichenau, who specialised in the German army's political relations and went to China in 1934 to handle the political and diplomatic aspects of von Falkenhausen's military mission.[294]

In Peking Schmidt's major task was to look for possible traitors, spies and anti-Nazis among the Axis community. For instance, the pioneering German scholar of Chinese furniture Gustav Ecke had been friends with

293 Though there was, at this time, no formal "Axis" co-operation pact beyond the more general Anti-Comintern Pact of 1936. That would come later with the Agreement for Cultural Co-operation between Tokyo and Berlin in November 1939. The formation of the "Axis Powers" occurred with the Tripartite Pact of September 1940. Naturally after the summer of 1937 Germany's aid to Chiang Kai-shek's army was problematic for German-Japanese relations.

294 Both von Falkenhausen and von Reichenau were hardcore Nazis. The former returned to Europe to head the military government of Belgium during the Nazi occupation. However, he came to despise Hitler and was sympathetic to the plots to assassinate him. For this he was arrested and sent to Dachau. In 1951 von Falkenhausen was tried in Brussels for his part in the deportations of Belgian Jews during the occupation. However, some prominent Belgians argued that von Falkenhausen had taken steps to mitigate the transportation. Consequently, he got a prison sentence rather than the death penalty. Among von Falkenhausen's defenders was the Chinese-Belgian Tsien Siou-Ling (Qian Xiuling), who had known the German from his China days. She claimed he had spared many Belgian prisoners. For his part von Reichenau had issued the notorious "Severity Order" which encouraged German soldiers to murder Jewish civilians on the Eastern Front. He was known to have been present at many atrocities including, perhaps, Babi Yar (the area was certainly under his command at the time). Von Reichenau suffered a stroke in 1942 and then the plane taking him to hospital crash-landed. He died shortly afterwards of a combination of the stroke and severe head injuries sustained during the plane crash.

other notable aesthetes such as Laurence Sickman, George Kates and his fellow German, the photographer Hedda Morrison. An anti-fascist, he ensconced himself in the library of the city's Fu Jen Catholic University cataloguing examples of classic Chinese hardwood furniture and seems to have avoided Schmidt's attentions.[295]

However, Schmidt was extremely suspicious of the thirty-year-old Mongolist Walther Heissig, who he suspected of being a double agent. Austrian-born Heissig had arrived in Peking in 1941 after studying Sinology, Chinese, Mongolian and ethnography in Berlin and Vienna. He aimed to continue his research on Inner Mongolian traditions and religions at Fu Jen alongside Gustav Ecke.[296] There appears to be no real evidence of any extreme political views (either left or right), or espionage leanings, on Heissig's part, and he seems to have spent most of the war years in Peking largely secluded in various Lama temples around the city. It's not clear why Schmidt suspected Heissig, except for a vague reference that possible treachery may have been suggested to the Gestapo chief by an intelligence officer of Vichy France in Peking at the time. It was also the case, after the war, in the early State Department employee loyalty investigations in Washington DC in 1950 (that presaged McCarthyism) that the American Mongolist Owen Lattimore was questioned about Heissig, and admitted to having met him once, 'for about half an hour in Peking', and that Heissig had offered Lattimore his valuable library of texts on Mongolia.[297] It's also worth remembering the general Nazi distrust of Sinology and Sinologists – the Nazis persecuted the French

---

295   Ecke's work on Chinese domestic furniture was published by Henri Vetch in 1944. In 1945 Ecke married the artist and scholar Betty Tseng Yu-Ho. Four years later the couple moved to Hawaii, where Ecke served as the curator of Chinese art at the Honolulu Academy of Arts and as professor of Asian art at the University of Hawaii until the mid-1960s.

296   In 1949, amidst the repression of Catholic institutions in Peking, the departments of Fu Jen were merged into the city's other universities. Fu Jen was re-established in 1961 in Taiwan.

297   'State Department Employee Loyalty Investigation: Hearings Before a Subcommittee of the Committee on Foreign Relations, United States Senate, Eighty-First Congress, Second Session, Pursuant to S. Res. 231, a Resolution to Investigate Whether There are Employees in the State Department Disloyal to the United States, Part Two', (Washington DC: US Government Printing Office, 1950), pp.1884-1887.

Sinologists Paul Pelliot and Henri Maspero, with the latter dying in Buchenwald.[298] Also teaching at Fu Jen while Heissig was there was the older German Sinologist Dr Walter Fuchs, who had worked as a curator at the Berliner Museum für Völkerkunde (Berlin Museum of Ethnology) before moving to China in 1926 to teach, first in Mukden, and then at Fu Jen. He spent much of the war years at Fu Jen and Peking's Deutschland-Institut. Fuchs had joined the Nazi Party in 1937. Perhaps the Deutschland-Institut sounded innocent enough but it was an organisation that was deeply committed to furthering Nazi war aims in China. In 1941 the Institut was involved in discussions about forming a 'North China Autonomous Government' that would structure Peking and northern China along similar lines to those used to create Manchukuo after the Japanese occupation. Fuchs was reported to be using the Institut and the idea of a 'North China Autonomous Government' to cement Axis relations in China and thwart American aims of limiting Japanese expansion. America, so the Associated Press reported, believed that the Deutschland-Institut was 'spending vast sums of money entertaining political and other important Chinese in the city *(Peking)*.'[299]

Fuchs lived in a large courtyard house on a hutong and was surrounded by a marvellous collection of maps, *objets d'art* and Chinese curios. Among the well-known private libraries in Peking – including those of Edmund Backhouse, ETC Werner, and George Morrison – Fuchs's was the only one to survive the war, although its owner had to leave China without taking it with him and only found out later that it had survived intact.[300] In 1944 senior Gestapo agents in Shanghai travelled north to Peking in an

---

298   It is an interesting question as to why the Nazis appear to have been so anti-Sinology. I do not have a clear-cut answer, I'm afraid, but have speculated somewhat on my blog. See 'The Nazi Distrust of Sinology', Chinarhyming.com – http://www.chinarhyming.com/2008/12/02/the-nazis-distrust-of-sinology/

299   'Japs Approve Moves in China', *The Times Herald* (Port Huron, Michigan), September 11, 1941, p.22.

300   Morrison sold most of his library to Japanese buyers, Backhouse donated most of his to the Bodleian at Oxford, while Werner's was broken up and turns up in various libraries and collections (as well as occasionally on eBay) intermittently. Fuchs was unaware his Peking library had survived the war intact and was told of this only later when he was back in Germany by the German Sinologist Martin Gimm who, after the war, taught at the University of Taipei.

attempt to strengthen Gestapo activities in the city. Fuchs was appointed a "watchman" for them, overseeing the German community in northern portions of the city and at Fu Jen University.[301]

It seems that the Gestapo in Shanghai were not overly impressed with Schmidt. As well as roping in Fuchs to become more involved in Nazi activities in the city, they also started the move to promote Schulze to replace the apparently under-performing Schmidt, effectively sidelining the Gestapo Branch for North China and Mongolia.

Adelbert E. Schulze had long been Schmidt's number two in command in Peking. Schulze had been born in Colombo, Ceylon (Sri Lanka) around 1897. His father was chairman of the *Deutscher Verein*, or German Club, in Colombo and ran a 'well known' business representing international insurance companies in Ceylon, which closed with his death in 1910.[302] Schulze tried his hand in various business ventures, most of which seem to have failed, encouraging him to move on from Colombo. By the time he arrived in Peking in the 1940s he was already a China veteran. Schulze was definitely living in Harbin around 1930 after a firm he was involved in running back in Colombo had apparently failed and he'd had to skip town swiftly ahead of his creditors. He was German, but had a Russian wife, and reputedly spoke Russian fluently. As early as 1931 he had assumed the role of *Ortsgruppenleiter*, or group leader, of the Nazi Party in Japanese-occupied Manchuria. He was, by all accounts, ruthless in rooting out any Germans in Manchuria not fully supportive of the Nazi Party.

Moving to Peking he had, if anything, become even more ruthless in his determination to purge any Germans not considered pro-Nazi enough. In 1942 he apparently sent a list of suspect Germans in his area to regional Gestapo boss Meisinger, who was basing himself in Shanghai at the time. Meisinger, through his contacts with the Japanese military police, the *Kempeitai*, in Manchuria had many of those named by Schulze

---

301 Details of the Gestapo's contacts with Fuchs in Peking from Shanghai-OSS-Int-1. Doc. 5-149-8, Box 50. CIA Library, Special Collection, Nazi War Crimes Disclosure Act, Huber, Franz Paul, Doc. 519b7f9a993294098d513439.

302 Schulze's father was apparently 'well known' in Colombo and chairman of the *Deutscher Verein* according to Arnold Wright (Ed.), *Twentieth Century Impression of Ceylon: Its History, People, Commerce, Industries and Resources* (London: Lloyd's Greater Britain Publishing Company, 1907) & J. Ferguson (Ed.), *The Ceylon Handbook & Directory*, (Colombo: Ceylon, 1891).

arrested and tortured.[303] Meisinger rewarded Schulze by promoting him to the post of *Geheime Staatspolizei für Nord China und Mongolei*.

Other senior Nazis visited Peking occasionally. Stahmer's successor as German ambassador to the puppet court of Wang Jing-wei in Nanking and Shanghai, SS-Oberführer Dr Ernst Woermann, passed through Peking from time to time. Woermann had been born in Dresden in 1888 and was a Doctor of Medical Jurisprudence. As a diplomat he had served in Paris and Vienna after the First World War before becoming German Consul in Liege, Belgium. He had joined the Nazi Party in 1937 and the SS a year later. He had reported favourably on the work of the *Einsatzgruppen*, the Nazi's mobile killing units, in Russia after the German invasion of the USSR and was actively aware of the deportation and murder of Jews in Auschwitz, as well as the forced deportation of Jews from the Netherlands, Belgium and France. Shortly before being sent to China, he was involved in

Ernst Woermann aboard a German U-Boat to China, 1943

organising the round-ups of Jews in Bulgaria, Hungary and Denmark.

Though based in Nanking, Woermann apparently passed through Peking often, usually en route to Tokyo for talks with Japanese foreign minister Mamoru Shigemitsu. Woermann was the senior German diplomat in China, and also possibly the German of highest social rank, the Woermanns being an old and aristocratic Hanseatic family. Woermann was perhaps the only German in Peking whom Helma Ott considered to be of her own superior social rank, though the black mark against Ott after the Sorge debacle in Tokyo probably meant Woermann kept his distance from the couple.

---

303 Schulze's actions in Manchuria contained in 'Counterintelligence War Room, London Questionnaire for Colonel Meisinger (Item 11a) on agent "Boris"', in Christopher Andrew & Jeremy Noakes, *Intelligence and International Relations, 1900-1945* (Liverpool: Liverpool University Press, 1987), f/n.76, p.187.

Josef Meisinger, based between Tokyo and Shanghai (and often travelling from one to the other by submarine), also visited Peking a few times. He was, like Ott, effectively in political exile from Berlin. An early acolyte of Himmler, he had originally been brought to Berlin to launch a campaign to root out homosexuals and abortionists. This had, in part, led to the downfall of Hitler's one-time close ally Ernst Röhm. Meisinger had then been sent to Eastern Europe, away from Berlin. However, even Reinhard Heydrich, a key architect of the Holocaust, had become appalled at Meisinger's brutality against Jews and other Poles while deputy commander of the notorious *Einsatzgruppe* IV in Poland. His time there had earned him the nickname the "Butcher of Warsaw". The fact that Meisinger knew both Heydrich and Himmler meant that he narrowly avoided a court martial, and his friends had him spirited out of Europe by U-boat to Tokyo in 1941. Meisinger and Woermann were the German officials in China most compromised with the Holocaust back in Europe. Meisinger was occasionally accompanied by his assistant and translator Karl "Fred" Hamel, a fluent Japanese speaker.

A time of boredom

So what did the Otts do in Peking? Good Nazis like Schmidt and Schulze kept their distance; so too did diplomats like Woermann. Helma had her gardening; Eugen was apparently quite a good and keen chess player, but who did he find to play with? It seems to have been a time of boredom mostly.

So many questions remain about their lives at this time. Did Helma continue to indulge in affairs? What of their children? We're sadly, but unsurprisingly, lacking in Axis memoirs of China during World War Two. The press corps was virtually non-existent, pro-Axis where it did exist, and still highly censored. When the American occupation forces in Japan questioned the likes of Meisinger and Hamel after the war, in Tokyo, daily life was not very high on the agenda as the Allies sought to round up the last missing Nazis of East Asia. Just how cordial relations were between the Nazi community, the Japanese occupiers and the Chinese puppet administration is hard to gauge, but they do not seem to have been especially close.

Though more privileged than most, even the Otts and the other senior Nazis in Peking during the occupation suffered from shortages. Money was short and a common complaint was that transfers from Berlin were consistently late, erratic and invariably less than expected. What to spend it on anyway? Vodka took the place of whisky and gin; dinner parties were reduced from the traditional five to three courses; petrol was severely rationed. Like senior Japanese and collaborationist Chinese leaders in Peking, the city's Nazis had commandeered cars. However, Mercedes had never paid much attention to the Chinese market and so, ironically, leading Nazi and *Kempeitai* officials drove around the city in all-American, leather-upholstered Buicks, Cadillacs and Packards.

Tiananmen, 1945

The Japanese occupation of Northern China and Peking ended on August 17, 1945, with the surrender of the Japanese military in the city to Chinese Nationalist forces from Chungking at a ceremony in the Forbidden City. Peking reverted to Chinese Nationalist control; remaining Japanese troops were confined to barracks pending repatriation. The Nazi defeat in Europe had of course happened back in May.

American GIs arrived in Peking. Allied nationals who had been interned at Weihsien and other civilian camps began returning. Claire Taschdjian (née Hirschberg) was from a Berlin-Jewish family that had moved to China in 1934 before settling in Peking in 1938 and remaining throughout the war. In 1944 she married Edgar Taschdjian, an Austrian-born Armenian with an Italian passport. She later recalled the Peking of 1945 with US soldiers having access to unbelievable luxuries such as Spam, processed cheese, sugar, Chesterfield cigarettes and, to everyone's amazement, Milky Way chocolate bars. The GIs in Peking had their own bakery and often discarded their army rations as worthless, meaning the foreign colony snapped up their powdered Nescafé, oily tins of canned butter, and the powdered grape juice (super-high in vitamins) that the soldiers dubbed "battery acid" but tasted great to Pekingers after the austerity of the occupation years. A large black market sprung up on Chang An Chieh as well as a massive flea market on the old polo grounds between the Legation Quarter and Hatamen Street, close to the old Badlands district that partially reopened many of its bars and brothels to service the Americans with dancehalls featuring Russian émigré taxi-dancers who charged $1 for three dances (a steep discount on Shanghai prices at the time!) and which didn't close until three or four in the morning. Stalls hawked unwanted K-rations and army surplus. Japanese families, about to be sent home, sold off all manner of lacquerware, china and curios at rock-bottom prices.[304] By the summer of 1946 all Japanese military and civilian personnel in Peking had been repatriated.

One task for the Americans in Peking was to find and arrest any Nazis still at large in the city. The US occupation authorities in Tokyo after August 1945 had pretty complete records of active Nazis across Asia and began to round them up. But it took a while. China's Nazis – in Harbin, Canton and Shanghai, as well as Peking – went underground to evade capture, though all were caught within two years. More senior Nazis and Axis officials in Peking handed themselves in voluntarily to the Americans and the Chinese Nationalist authorities.

What became of the old Nazis of Peking?

Ernst Woermann was tried at the "Wilhelmstrasse" Ministries Trial by the American Military Tribunal. He was found guilty of persecution of the

---

304 Claire Taschdjian mixes her memoirs with a mystery story set in Peking in *The Peking Man is Missing* (New York: Felony & Mayhem, 2008), p.176.

Jews, massacres of civilian populations and plotting for war.[305] On April 11, 1949 he was sentenced to seven years in prison. On December 12, the sentence was lowered to just five years. However, he did even less jail time. He was released from prison in 1950 or 1951. Woermann died in 1979 in Heidelberg, aged ninety-one years old.

Ernst Woermann in the dock and on trial, 1949

Josef Meisinger, who spoke good English, turned himself in to the US Counter-Intelligence Corps in Yokohama in September 1945 and gave them twenty boxes of cigars he'd hoarded (and, less willingly, a substantial amount of gold bars and currency). In prison in Japan he was watched closely by American guards as he threatened to attempt suicide. He was taken from there to Frankfurt and then to Washington DC to be questioned by American and British war crimes investigators specifically on the construction of the Warsaw Ghetto. In 1946 he was extradited to Poland and put on trial. He was sentenced to death and then executed in Warsaw's Mokotów Prison in March 1947.

Meisinger's assistant and translator, Karl Hamel, was arrested in Tokyo by the Americans after the war too. He appears to have cooperated enthusiastically with his interrogators in describing the Nazi wartime power structure in Japan and East Asia. He was repatriated to Germany in 1947. Hamel was last reported free and working for BASF in Ludwigshafen after the war.[306]

There was much confusion after the war's end and many of the former Nazi Party operatives in northern China did receive some shelter from the Nationalist government. Some, including Schmidt and Schulze, were being shielded by the Ministry of Defence. This greatly annoyed

305 '7 High Nazis Convicted for Deaths of 6,000,000', *The Boston Globe*, April 12, 1949, p.3.
306 John W.M. Chapman, *Ultranationalism in German-Japanese Relations, 1930-1945* (Folkestone, Kent: Global Oriental, 2011), p.27.

Meisinger in his cell – Tokyo, 1945

the American Nazi-hunters looking for them to be deported. In August 1947 Schulze was reported as being 'missing' but was rumoured to be 'shielded by Chinese gendarmes' in Peking. It also seemed that Walter Fuchs was not to be handed over, along with Herman Lorenzen, who been a Nazi Party member in Peking; Paul Wilm, a German agricultural expert who pioneered the introduction of mineral fertiliser in China; and, most mysteriously, Ludwig Ziegler, a sausage manufacturer with ties to the Chinese army.[307]

Fuchs was eventually returned to Germany where, in 1949 and after some investigations of his activities in Peking, he eventually got a teaching post at the University of Hamburg before being formally cleared of any war crimes and eventually going on to teach at universities in Berlin and Cologne, where he died in 1979.

Ott was still reported in the newspapers as being at large in Peking in September 1945.[308] Soon after, though, he and Helma voluntarily surrendered to US forces. Eugen Ott died on January 23, 1977 aged eighty-seven in Tutzing, Upper Bavaria, in what was then referred to as

307 'Former Gestapo Chief in North China Vanishes', *St. Louis Post-Dispatch*, August 27, 1947, p.11.
308 'Japan was an Uncertain Ally Until Dec. 7, 1941, Nazi Says', *The Journal Herald* (Dayton, Ohio), September 10, 1945, p.14.

"West" Germany. What became of Helma after the war is not entirely clear, though she was still corresponding with former Germans who had been in Asia during the war in the mid-1960s. One tantalising rumour says she left Peking and went to the Soviet Union, raising the intriguing notion that she may have never quite left her communist past behind and had, indeed, always been supplying information to Moscow, and that her love affair with Sorge was their version of a dead letter drop. This could also mean that perhaps it was not Richard Sorge who was the greatest Soviet spy in Asia, but rather his lover, trusted senior Nazi, and the German ambassador's wife, Helma Ott. The truth, or otherwise, of that may well lie deeply buried in a Russian archive.

China became something of a dumping ground for problematic Nazis from the 1930s and continued to be so in World War Two. Men like Ott and Meisinger were sent to the Far East the way problematic Bolsheviks were sent to Siberia. There was little for them to do there – Meisinger engaged in some espionage and tried to persuade the Japanese occupation authorities in Shanghai to hand the city's Jewish refugees over to him to be murdered, but was refused. Wang Jing-wei's government was never taken very seriously by either Tokyo or Berlin. Peking was a largely forgotten city during World War Two and the Otts a largely forgotten couple within it.

The Peiping World of Peonies and Ponies:
Harold Acton (1941)

*'Peking's such loads of fun. Jugglers, fortune-tellers, acrobats,
puppet-shows, temple tiffins, treasure hunts and Paomachang
picnics – not to speak of costume jamborees, galas and fancy-dress
affairs – always something original! Home-made natural fun, not
imported or artificially manufactured as in Shanghai. And there's
always a delicious spice of the unexpected.'* [309]

309 The indomitable Mrs Mascot explaining why Peking is the Chinese city for her
in the opening scene of Harold Acton's *Peonies and Ponies* (London: Chatto & Windus,
1941), p.9.

Sorting out the Peonies from the Ponies

Harold Acton's comic novel *Peonies and Ponies*, though published in 1941, describes life in Peking shortly before the Japanese occupation of the late 1930s, and thoroughly skewers the pretensions of the city's foreign colony. In the novel Acton is easily the equal of the now better-remembered authors of novels of manners: Evelyn Waugh, Nancy Mitford or Christopher Isherwood. The publisher, poet, heiress and activist Nancy Cunard recalled Acton as 'swift, gay and full of sparkling, malicious shafts and arrows when occasion demanded,' but also as 'a man of real culture, the excellent linguist, the beautiful lecturer with an exact technique.'[310] The literary critic Allan Johnson writes that Acton was 'the undisputed tastemaker of the "Brideshead Generation", but he is a writer now more talked about than read.'[311] Johnson and other literary critics attribute Acton's marginalisation partly to his sojourn and his fascination with China that ultimately rather removed him from London society and set him apart from those who remained in the mainstream of English literary society.

In his autobiography, *Memoirs of an Aesthete*, written only half a dozen years or so after his Peking comedy of manners, Acton claims that the characters in *Peonies and Ponies* were '...amalgams of actual people: whose characters are not? Had I drawn them straight from life, not only would the book have been libellous, it would have been dismissed as pure, or impure, grotesquerie.'[312] So *Peonies and Ponies* is clearly a *roman à clef*, a novel in which real people or events appear with invented names. However, Acton declined to specifically name those real people, opting not to "out" those denizens of 1930s Peking whom he had chosen as models for his characters. At the time of the publication of *Peonies and Ponies*, and subsequently *Memoirs of an Aesthete* (1948), and even later in his second volume of memoirs, *More Memoirs of an Aesthete* (1970), many of these people were still very much alive. Acton, caustic and

---

310   Nancy Cunard (Ed. Hugh D. Ford), *These Were the Hours: Memories of My Hours Press* (Carbondale: Southern Illinois University Press, 1969), p.161.

311   Allan Johnson, *Masculine Identity in Modernist Literature* (London: Palgrave Macmillan, 2017), p.124.

312   Harold Acton, *Memoirs of an Aesthete* (London: Methuen & Co Ltd, 1948).

bitchy as he could be, was in full possession of both good manners and an understanding of England's strict libel laws.

Now of course these people, and Acton himself, are all long dead. So perhaps we can run through the cast list of old Pekingers who found themselves immortalised in the pages of *Peonies and Ponies*. Acton did create composite characters and so for many there is not one single character original but rather a number. Indeed, when we start to pick apart the possible influences Acton incorporated in his characters, *Peonies and Ponies* becomes a veritable *Who's Who* of the Peking foreign colony in the 1930s.

Bright Young Things in Peiping

Acton was a Bright Young Thing. He went up to Oxford in 1923 to read Modern Greats where he famously recited passages of *The Wasteland* through a megaphone from the balcony of his rooms at Christ Church. He co-founded the *avant garde* magazine *The Oxford Broom,* published a collection of poems and was a member of the Railway Club, whose

members dined in black tie aboard the Penzance to Aberdeen express, cramming in the courses between Oxford and Leicester. Among those who were to become noted Bright Young Things were Michael Parsons, Sixth Earl of Rosse, whose brother Desmond was later to be Acton's closest friend in Peking. As we are considering whom Acton may have had in mind as role models for his characters in *Peonies and Ponies* it is worth noting that he himself was one of the composite elements that made up the character of Anthony Blanche in Evelyn Waugh's own *roman à clef, Brideshead Revisited*[313], published a few years after *Peonies and Ponies*.

Acton by Thomas Handforth, 1933

313 Evelyn Waugh, *Brideshead Revisited* (London: Chapman & Hall, 1945).

Waugh himself wrote, 'There is an aesthetic bugger who sometimes turns up in my novels under various names *[meaning Blanche]* – that was 2/3 *[the poet and journalist]* Brian Howard and 1/3 Harold Acton. People think it was all Harold, who is a much sweeter and saner man *[than Howard]*".[314]

In the late 1920s Acton moved to Paris, had his portrait painted by the Russian émigré Pavel Tchelitcheff (or Tchelitchev), wrote more poems, was Best Man at Evelyn Waugh's marriage to Evelyn Gardner (hence their nicknames of He-Evelyn and She-Evelyn) and published a novel, *Humdrum*, that received almost universally bad reviews.[315] He moved to Florence and worked on yet more poems (published by Nancy Cunard's Hours Press as a favour rather than strictly on their merit) and also published his rather better received

Thomas Handforth, 1936

history, *The Last of the Medici* (though the prim Home Office in London complained about the book's scandalous contents).[316]

In his obituary of Acton the book critic, poet and contemporary of Acton, Alan Pryce-Jones, wrote that life in Florence with its trivial social round weighed heavily upon Acton as he was in reality a hard worker and a careful scholar.[317] It was to escape this triviality that, in 1932, Acton travelled to Peking. When he first arrived, Acton shared a courtyard house with Thomas Handforth – the American illustrator in Peking on a Guggenheim scholarship – on Ganyu Hutong, part of a pleasant cluster of alleyways close to Morrison Street and the Grand Hôtel de Pékin. It was a popular area with new sojourners, being a traditional hutong,

314 Evelyn Waugh, Mark Amory (ed.), *The Letters of Evelyn Waugh* (London: Weidenfeld and Nicholson, 1980). Waugh also dedicated his second novel to Acton "in homage and affection" – *Decline and Fall* (London: Chapman & Hall, 1928).

315 Harold Acton, *Humdrum* (London, Harcourt, Brace & Company, 1929).

316 Harold Acton, *The Last of the Medici*, privately printed for subscribers by Florence: G Orioli, Lungarno Corsini, 1930.

317 Alan Pryce-Jones, 'Obituary: Sir Harold Acton', *The Independent*, February 28, 1994.

but also close to those things more familiar.[318] Handforth's home was a nightly salon for artistically inclined members of the foreign colony and some Chinese to discuss art, and Acton made many of his initial acquaintances on Ganyu Hutong.[319]

Eventually Acton came to know the city well enough to find his own courtyard home, on the other side of the Forbidden City from Ganyu Hutong, across Jingshan Park on the long and narrow Kung Hsien Hutong: at the southern end of the lane, just to the north of Beihai Park.[320] He enrolled in Chinese lessons and developed a deep interest in Chinese literature, drama and poetry. Quite why he chose China, and specifically Peking, is not altogether clear. It was true he had yet to find any real success or recognition as either a poet or novelist. Conventional London society viewed him with some disapproval for his extrovert nature and he was gay. Life in Peking, with its more tolerant attitudes (at least for foreigners), was appealing as well as perhaps liberating. Acton himself claimed that a well-timed gift from an American uncle of five thousand dollars enabled him to act on a dream first engendered in him by a Chinese cook he had employed in London:

318 Handforth had apparently taken over the lease on the Ganyu Hutong property from Harry Hussey, a Canadian architect trained in Chicago, who had supervised the construction of the Peking Union Medical College (PUMC) and settled in Peking in 1928. He talks of the hutong in *Harry Hussey, My Pleasures and Palaces: An Informal Memoir of Forty Years in Modern China* (New York: Doubleday, 1968).

319 Thomas Schofield Handforth could well have been a chapter in this collection. Born in Tacoma, Washington, Handforth was a contemporary of Acton, Parsons and many of the other aesthetes, being born in 1897. He had served in World War One as an anatomical illustrator with the US Army's Sanitary Corps. He then studied at the École des Beaux-Arts in Paris. As an illustrator his most famous work (lesser known now but very well known before World War Two) was *Mei Li* (1938), an illustrated story of a young Chinese girl escaping over Chinese New Year to explore a walled city. It won the Caldecott Medal for children's literature in 1939. His interest in Asian art was apparently sparked by seeing Hokusai's work as a young man. David Emil Mungello says Handforth was 'apparently homosexual' in his book *Western Queers in China: Flight to the Land of Oz* (New York: Rowman & Littlefield, 2012), p.94. When he died in Los Angeles in 1948 at just fifty-one, he was attempting to get back to Peking to retrieve the two printing presses he had sealed behind a wall of his Ganyu Hutong home during the Japanese occupation. Handforth is one good friend of Acton's who does not appear to be caricatured in *Peonies and Ponies*.

320 Now Gongjian Hutong.

Acton on a snowy Kung Hsien Hutong

Unconsciously he *(the Chinese cook)* had watered a seed long dormant within me: an innate love of China beyond rational analysis and an instinct that I had some vocation there. Until I went to China my life could not be integrated and I knew it.[321]

Acton's seven years in China were prolific ones in terms of his output. He taught English literature at Peking National University[322] and published a large number of articles – on China's literary scene, on poetry, the rise of the vernacular Chinese novel, the country's resistance to Japanese aggression, and Peking Opera – for a diverse range of publications including Harriet Monroe's *Poetry*[323] in America and John Lehmann's *Penguin New Writing* in

---

321 Acton quoted in, *James Knox, Robert Byron: A Biography* (London: John Murray, 2003), p.348.

322 Now Peking University (PKU, or Beida).

323 See particularly the special "China Edition", *Poetry*, April 1935, Vol.XLVI, Issue 1. Acton's contribution to the issue is an editorial commenting on contemporary Chinese poetry.

England.[324] He also published respected translations of the Qing-dynasty historical drama *Peach Blossom Fan* and the collection *Modern Chinese Poetry* [325], both in collaboration with Chen Shih-hsiang, a Chinese literary scholar, and *Famous Chinese Plays* in collaboration with LC Arlington.[326] After leaving China, Acton would go on to translate *Glue and Lacquer,* a tale selected from the seventeenth-century vernacular writer Feng Menglong's *Tales to Rouse the World*, with a preface by the Bloomsbury-based Sinologist Arthur Waley and illustrations by the English artist Eric Gill.[327] Acton became the influential centre of the circle of British, and some American, Japanese and continental European, aesthetes living in China at the time.[328] It was during this period, and in this milieu, that he began to think about a comic novel detailing the lives of Peking's foreign colony, *Peonies and Ponies.*

The main characters of the foreign colony:

Mrs Mascot – Sheila Mascot is in many ways the main character of the novel and Acton's heroine of sorts (at least as the great survivor of the ebb and flow of the foreign colony's incestuous gossip machine) – *'I am Peking... at least so many people have told me so that I've come to believe it. I've a moral certainty that I was Chinese in a former incarnation.'* Mrs Mascot has aspirations to a life of glamour and of being THE expatriate society hostess of Peking, though she has competition and is forced by circumstances to make a living (her husband, a rather badly fallen

324 Acton's two major articles for Lehmann being: 'Small Talk in China', *Penguin New Writing*, No.15, October-December, 1942 and 'A Monopolist', *Penguin New Writing*, No.22, 1944.

325 *Modern Chinese Poetry*, translated by Harold Acton & Chen Shih-hsiang (London: Duckworth, 1936).

326 Harold Acton & LC Arlington, *Famous Chinese Plays* (Peiping: Henri Vetch, 1937). Vetch's French bookstore was in the lobby of the Grand Hôtel de Pékin. For more on Arlington see Chapter 18, *Drinks with the Foster Snows of Kuei Chia Chang Hutong.*

327 Harold Acton & Lee Yi-Hsieh, *Gold and Lacquer: Four Cautionary Tales* (Waltham St Lawrence, UK: Golden Cockerel Press, 1941).

328 For more on this see Chapter 4, *The Peking Aesthete's Aesthete – Desmond Parsons & Robert Byron* (1937).

missionary, has deserted her after losing his faith). This necessitates her having *'many strings to her bow'*:

> *It was a hard life, forever trying to foist things on people who did not want them, summoning all the powers of suggestion and auto-suggestion, tactfully persuading Mrs X that the entire colour-scheme of her Park Avenue drawing-room would be nil if she failed to invest in some rare specimen of Ming cloisonné, and Mrs Y that she had found the only jade pendant in the whole wide world for her individual bust. And between the coming and going of globe-trotters she was busy breeding Tibetan lion-dogs, supervising a beauty-salon, a lending library, and an Olde Albion Tea Shoppe. Beside these activities, she was president of the Ladies' Inner Circle for the Appreciation of Hopei Crafts and Arts. Oh it was a hard life, and she had only herself to blame if she often tottered on the brink of a nervous breakdown, but she faced it manfully, determined to convert everything into terms of riotous fun.*

Mrs Mascot embodies many of the tropes of the Peking of the time – her penchant for collecting antiques, for breeding Tibetan lion-dogs, and for cultivating educated Chinese friends, as well as the foreigners of the Sinological and diplomatic circles. As many of the foreign colony did at the time, Mrs Mascot rents a disused temple in the Western Hills. She hopes that her decorating style is *'more Chinesy'* than other foreigners (though Acton indicates that her taste was a little more *Chu Chin Chow* than genuine).[329] She is also the proprietor of The Whoopee Hop cabaret. She is certainly a composite character and there are quite a few contenders for her makeup.

In their book *The China Collectors: America's Century Long Hunt for Asian Art Treasures,* authors Karl E. Meyer and Shareen Blair Brysac suggest that Lucy Calhoun may have been a model for Mrs Mascot.[330] It's a strong possibility. Calhoun was a very well-known figure in inter-war Peking. She was born Lucy Monroe in Chicago in 1865 and was the older

---

329 The long-running musical comedy with a Chinese setting and actors in Yellowface that was a hit on London's West End stage during World War One, running for five years and 2,238 performances. *Chu Chin Chow* also had some success in America and Australia.

330 Karl E. Meyer & Shareen Blair Brysac, *The China Collectors: America's Century Long Hunt for Asian Art Treasures* (New York: St Martin's Press, 2015), p.247.

sister of Harriet Monroe, Acton's aforementioned friend, poet, fan of things Chinese, and founder of *Poetry* magazine to which Acton contributed. The Monroe family was educated, bookish and fashion-conscious, but not very well off. Lucy married William J. Calhoun in 1904. Howard Taft appointed Calhoun America's ambassador to China and the couple arrived in Peking in 1909. Calhoun served till 1913, seeing China move from the crumbling Qing Dynasty to the new republic and the first years of Yuan

Lucy & Ambassador William J. Calhoun on the steps of their residence, American Legation, 1911

Shih-kai's doomed attempt to restore a monarchy with himself at its head. The Calhouns returned to Chicago in 1913 and William became a sought-after 'China Hand' by American businesses looking to get into the Chinese market. In 1916 he had a stroke and died. At fifty-one Lucy became a widow.

At first Lucy went to France to serve as a wartime nurse. But then she decided to return to Peking, to turn her beautiful hutong home, a former temple close to the Forbidden City, into a small hotel for sojourners wanting to spend some time in the city. She became generally regarded as the unofficial "First Lady" of the Peking diplomatic corps. Mrs Mascot has a similar background to Lucy Calhoun – well bred, but not independently wealthy. She's about the same age; inhabits a courtyard house where she plays host to visitors; and is knowledgeable about the city and Chinese antiques and curios. Lucy Calhoun was perhaps a little more educated than we are led to believe of Mrs Mascot, and certainly less vulgar and obvious, though Mrs Mascot's vulgarity is partly what makes her so amusing and ultimately lovable.[331]

Lucy was a member of the "Purple Cows" Legation Quarter dining club, 1913

Old Peking historian Julia Boyd believes Helen Burton to be the main inspiration for Mrs Mascot and she's undoubtedly right that Burton must have been in Acton's mind.[332] Burton ran The Camel's Bell curio store in the Grand Hôtel de Pékin, hosted a popular salon, organised temple picnics, was the go-to source for *'Chinesy'* items, jade and furs for visiting tourists and, like Mrs Mascot, had adopted six young Chinese girls (gossipy Poppy Trumper suggests Mrs Mascot's adoptees are probably her ex-husband's illegitimate offspring, while it later transpires that they are the escaped concubines of a warlord). Towards the end of *Peonies and Ponies* Mrs Mascot opens The Chow Club, where guests will don Chinese garb and visit a Chinese restaurant. Burton was known for her entertaining too. For those without any suitable Chinese garments

331   For more on Calhoun see chapter 9, 'JP Marquand and Adelaide Hooker – Finding Love and Mr Moto in Peiping'.
332   Julia Boyd, *A Dance with the Dragon: The Vanished World of Peking's Foreign Colony* (London: IB Taurus, 2012), p.183.

Mascot has started a unisex costume salon, and again Helen Burton did sell Chinese apparel.

Another contender for the composite that eventually ended up as Mrs Mascot is the American society hostess Bernardine Szold-Fritz, a relatively close acquaintance of Acton's in London and Paris (where she had been a reporter for the *Chicago Evening Post* and the *New York Daily News*). Acton was to meet her again in Shanghai during a hot summer in the mid-1930s. Szold-Fritz was determined to 'see everything, taste everything, smell everything in this steaming oven.'[333] She had been born in Peoria, Illinois and later married the successful and wealthy Shanghai stockbroker Chester Fritz. In the mid-1930s she maintained a mixed European-Chinese salon of intellectuals in Shanghai (that included the likes of *New Yorker* correspondent Emily Hahn and Sir Victor Sassoon), established the International Art Theater in Shanghai, and took Acton to a garden party hosted by a son of the prominent Qing politician, General Li Hung-chang.[334] Szold-Fritz was, like Mrs Mascot, keen to attract any passing celebrities to her Shanghai salon and confessed to Acton that she was excited at the prospect of potential visits from Jean Cocteau and the Mexican artist Miguel Covarrubias.[335] In 1939 she and her husband left Shanghai and settled in Los Angeles, where she established her "Hollywood salon", bringing together leading literary and artistic personalities of the era, many of whom were American expatriates she had met during her European and Chinese sojourns.

There might also be some elements of the poet, novelist and hotel manager's wife Margaret Mackprang Mackay. Margaret Mackprang was American and moved to China to become the wife of Alex Mackay, born in Peking of a north China-based Scottish family of long standing. At the time they met, Mackay was managing the Imperial Hotel in Tientsin. They later moved to Peking. In Peking and Tientsin Margaret discovered a love of poetry and was reasonably prolific in turning out works that were picked up by the American newspapers for their charming portrayal of Peking, though it would be a stretch to describe them as anything

333 Acton, *Memoirs of an Aesthete*, p.286.
334 Li Hongzhang.
335 Cocteau never made it to Shanghai; Covarrubias did. For more on his visit see Part 2, Chapter 3, 'Miguel Covarrubias' in Paul Bevan, *A Modern Miscellany: Shanghai Cartoon Artists, Shao Xunmei's Circle and the Travels of Jack Chen, 1926-1938* (Leiden: Brill, 2018).

more than passable.[336] The Mackays were social, though Margaret, at least from what we can divine from her autobiography, was not nearly so pompous as Mrs Mascot.[337]

Mackprang Mackay's 1939 novel *Lady With Jade* is an interesting take on the foreign colony, though little read or ever republished these days.[338] The story is set around 1930 and centres on an American, Moira Chisholm, who separates from her husband and stays on in Peking, a city to which she has become deeply attached. Flora is sybaritic, an aesthete with a passion for beauty and Chinese style. She opens a curio shop, selling old brocades and jewellery, antiques and local crafts. She is successful, the shop does very well and she becomes something of a celebrity among the foreign colony. But slowly she withdraws into her collections. She refuses marriage twice, then finally does fall in love only to renounce the marriage at the last minute. She decides that no man, no partner can ever be a satisfactory substitute for the immaculate, classic perfection of the jades and *objets d'art* to which she has given her life, and which she now just wishes to retain for herself and not part with. Acton did know Mackprang Mackay, at least a little and certainly by reputation. They both contributed to the 1935 special China edition of *Poetry*.[339]

Allan Johnson suggests Mrs Mascot is 'Something in the vein of Elsa Maxwell', the American gossip columnist and professional hostess.[340] Certainly the plump, exuberant and ever-optimistic Maxwell has something of the Mrs Mascot about her, though Maxwell never ventured to China. She carefully, as people might say today, "curated" her party guests and largely established her own worth through her *soirée* attendees. Acton had attended at least a couple of Maxwell's parties in Venice in the 1920s, and wrote of her what could be a character sketch for Mrs Mascot, noting that she was 'an acute psychologist of the idle rich. She prescribed strenuous action: Keep them hopping! Persuade them that they are living

336   For more on Mackprang Mackay see Paul French, 'The China Poetry of Margaret Mackprang Mackay, 1934-1938', *Royal Asiatic Society China Journal*, Vol.79, No.1, 2019, pp.174-184.

337   Margaret Mackprang Mackay, *I Live in a Suitcase* (New York: John Day, 1953).

338   Margaret Mackprang Mackay, *Lady With Jade* (New York: John Day, 1939).

339   *Poetry*, April 1935, Volume XLVI, Issue 1.

340   Johnson, *Masculine Identity in Modernist Literature,* p.127.

at top speed; turn them into bloodhounds; let them satisfy their cravings for exhibitionism!'[341]

Finally, some (including Allan Johnson) have suggested elements of Mrs Mascot could have come from the prototype "Holy Roller" Aimee Semple McPherson, the Canadian-American Pentecostal evangelist and media celebrity. McPherson was very much in the news at the time and was also sent up as Mrs Melrose Ape by Evelyn Waugh in his novel *Vile Bodies* (1930). "Sister Aimee" first visited China in 1908 on a Pentecostal evangelistic tour which turned into a disaster – Aimee contracted

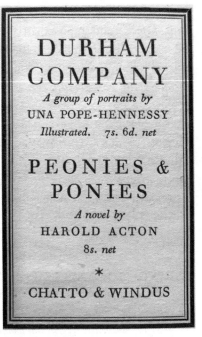

malaria; her preacher husband Robert got both malaria and dysentery. Robert died in Hong Kong and shortly afterwards Aimee, a nineteen-year-old widow, gave birth to their daughter in the British colony. She did return to China later, in the late 1920s, and had a mission station in Shanghai, but never actually sojourned in Peking.

Philip Flower – As with Mrs Mascot, Acton's main male character is a composite and arguably has many elements of Acton himself. Flower is an aesthete, a '*Confucianist*', a hutong dweller with fifteen years' experience of China who feels drawn to the Chinese language and culture. '*He felt about Peking intensely, as certain poets have felt about their mistresses... he felt as if he were married to Peking, and this marriage was to be an inexhaustible adventure*'. His hobbies are Peking opera and ancient poetry; shopping for goldfish at the Lung Fu temple and seeking out tranquil rock gardens. He craves the company of Chinese able to engage in smart intellectual conversation, though considers himself too unsociable for the foreign colony and yet too British for Chinese intellectual society. He shies

---

341 Sam Staggs, *Inventing Elsa Maxwell: How an Irrepressible Nobody Conquered High Society, Hollywood, the Press and the World* (New York: St Martin's Press, 2012), p.147.

away from talk of *'amahs, Number One boys, squeezes, mafoos, losses and gains of "face"'*, and shuns expatriate society.[342] He has few western friends, though does like to confide in the modernist artist Elvira MacGibbon. So sure is Philip in his love of Peking that he has *'already purchased his own burial-ground in a secluded corner of the Western Hills.'*

Flower is not quite Acton in Peking, but certainly he must have drawn on elements of his own experiences and feelings about the more frivolous elements of the foreign colony. He is also a throwback to a slightly earlier era of Peking aesthetes who openly yearned for a return to more imperial times, such as the French naval officer and novelist Pierre Loti, or, somewhat later, the Italian diplomat-memoirist Daniele Varè[343]:

> *Sufficient to know and be profoundly grateful, to realise that he was as far as it was possible to be from post-war politics and the general jumpiness of Europe while comfortably within the orbit of its dubious civilisation, imbibing serenity from the geometrical quietude of China's ancient capital. And everything about him still remained supernatural, brought grist for pantheistic reverie and wonder.*

But of course there were any number of other British and American aesthetes in his circle for Acton to draw upon. We can certainly see elements of Acton's good friends Desmond Parsons (who has his own chapter in this collection of course), as well as perhaps George N. Kates and John Blofeld. Kates, an American, lived, or in his own words 'immersed' himself, in Peking for seven years almost concurrently with Acton, between 1933 and 1940. Like Acton he lived close to the old imperial centre of Peking in a traditional courtyard house. Moving in, Kates proudly declared that he had 'no electric light, no wooden floors, no heating apparatus except several cast iron stoves and no plumbing did I ever install'[344]. His memoir of that time, *The Years That Were Fat*, is one of the best of the period and reveals Kates as a true aesthete in the

---

342   Squeeze being the money the servants made between the price paid at the store for goods and the bill officially presented to their employer – generally accepted within reason; a *mafoo* being a stable groom (though also slang for a pimp!).

343   Obviously, I'm thinking here of Pierre Loti's *The Last Days of Peking* (1902) and Daniele Varè's novels *The Maker of Heavenly Trousers*, *The Gate of Happy Sparrows*, and *The Temple of Costly Experience* (all 1937).

344   Meyer & Blair Brysac, *The China Collectors*, p.116.

Philip Flowers style, focusing almost solely on developing and deepening his admiration for the Chinese sense of harmony and proportion in all things. *The Years That Were Fat* wasn't published until 1952, though Acton must have known Kates in Peking.[345]

John Blofeld was English and an aesthete and lived in a succession of courtyard houses, though Blofeld was not as long a sojourner in Peking as Kates or Acton. After a time in Hong Kong, Blofeld obtained a teaching position at the Hebei Academy of Industry in Tientsin in 1935, with a teaching schedule that allowed him to spend three nights a week in Peking. He returned briefly to England in the summer of 1937 and so missed the Japanese occupation of the city. He did return to Hong Kong and China later, married a Chinese woman and travelled extensively in Asia, eventually settling in Bangkok. His memoir of Peking – *City of Lingering Splendour: A Frank Account of Old Peking's Exotic Pleasures*[346] – could easily have been written by Philip Flowers. It wasn't published until 1961 and Acton and Blofeld do not appear to have been acquainted, at least to any extent I can divine.

Secondary characters of the foreign colony:

Lancelot Thistleby – *'another novelist in search of local colour'* visiting Peking. Thistleby is the author of a best-selling Orientalist novel, *Yashmak*, and is working on a new novel, *The Thirteenth Concubine*, to be set in Bali (his planned destination after Peking) though he changes the location to China. Thistleby is initially uninspired by Peking – too grey, the tea *'an infusion of bird-seed'*, and not nearly enough genuflecting by the foreign colony to the great visiting author for his liking. Struggling to complete his Peking novel he can get no further than *'In the Jade Canal the frogs were croaking, croaking...'* until he realises that he loves Mrs Mascot and is inspired to finish the book. It is finally dedicated: *'To Peking – To Sheila Mascot'*. Thistleby is last seen beginning his next novel, *The Jade Thumbring*.

345 George N. Kates, *The Years That Were Fat: Peking, 1933-1940* (New York: Harper & Brothers, 1952).

346 John Blofeld, *City of Lingering Splendour: A Frank Account of Old Peking's Exotic Pleasures* (London: Hutchison, 1961).

Perhaps at the forefront of Acton's mind when creating Thistleby was the Canadian-born American writer and journalist Vincent Starrett, author of *The Private Life of Sherlock Holmes*. As well as being a prominent mystery writer, Starrett was also somewhat of a "China Hand" and visited Peking several times in the 1930s where he built up a large circle of friends. Some years ago I purchased a copy of Starrett's *The Private Life of Sherlock Holmes,* thinking it sounded interesting and being vaguely aware that he had spent some time in China.[347] The copy that arrived was not a 1934 first edition, but was an early edition from the mid-1930s and, quite by chance, was signed by Starrett and dedicated to the retired British diplomat and Sinologist ETC Werner with many thanks for Werner's kindness in showing him some of Peking during his sojourn. I had a year or so before just published my own book, *Midnight in Peking*, the true story of the unsolved murder of Pamela Werner, the only daughter of ETC Werner.

In 1935 Starrett, and his companion Rachel "Ray" Latimer (Starrett was separated from his first wife at the time and awaiting a divorce), spent about eighteen months in Peking, living in a rented hutong courtyard house with fourteen rooms and nine servants near the Forbidden City.[348] Their home was so close, Starrett wrote, '...that I could see the Forbidden City's fabulous red roofs from my bedroom window.' The half-moon gate entrance, their own rickshaw, the red tiled roof, were all details that would feed into his mystery novel *Murder in Peking,* which,

Vincent Starrett in his rented Peking courtyard home, 1935

347 The stories are fun pastiches of Conan Doyle, claiming to be the investigations Dr Watson never had time to write up.

348 Starrett was a well-paid writer and book reviewer at the time but this luxury lifestyle was mostly thanks to the exchange rates between the weak Chinese dollar and the strong American dollar in the 1930s.

according to an interview Starrett gave to *Book Bulletin* in 1950, was written largely during his sojourn in the city (though wasn't finally published until 1946).[349] Starrett was keen to stay on in Peking – living openly with Ray was socially problematic in Chicago but decidedly less so in Peking. However, they were forced to leave by the Japanese invasion in 1937. In his autobiography, *Born in a Bookshop,* Starrett recalled, 'My stay in China was at an end. Overhead – flying daily over my Chinese residence, now surmounted by an American flag – were Jap planes in war formation; daily the streets of the Legation Quarter resounded to the marching feet of the soldiers of Japan, the first step in the game of intimidation that preceded the invasion.'[350]

After World War Two Starrett finally published *Murder in Peking,* which has a cast of characters who easily overlap with the world of *Peonies and Ponies.* This may indeed be because many of them are based on the same people. He dedicates the book to no less than nineteen of his old Peking friends, including the man who many considered the inspiration for the amateur detective character in the novel, Charles John Hope-Johnstone. This is not in itself a great piece of detective work as, while appearing somewhat similar in character to Hope-Johnstone, Starrett names him Hope Johnson!

Elvira MacGibbon – a French-Canadian artist recently relocated from Paris (*'where she experimented with all the "isms"'*), Elvira is living in a restored Peking mansion in the Tartar City, working *'in sober Soviet overalls'* as a sculptor (in wood or stone) on a work entitled "Frustration". She considers herself *'the only ultra-Modern in Peking'.* Elvira competes with Mrs Mascot for the title of top foreign colony hostess with her "At Homes" when *'anybody who was anybody'* in the foreign colony drops by to visit her Chinese garden close to Morrison Street. However, she really yearns to create a salon for the *'New China'* to congregate in and talk of modern ideas, though most Chinese recoil from her overt independence. She works to gramophone recordings of the Balinese gamelan and declares that *'there is too little passion in Peking'.* She is proudly childless, separated from her husband, professes to despise those in the foreign colony who

349 Vincent Starrett, *Murder in Peking* (New York: Lantern Press, 1946).

350 Vincent Starrett, *Born in a Bookshop: Chapters from the Chicago Renascence* (Norman, Oklahoma: University of Oklahoma Press, 1965).

never leave the Legation Quarter and detests those who mock modern art.

The main model for MacGibbon would seem to be the American artist sojourning in Peking at the time, Bertha Lum. This collection has an essay about Lum, 'The Artist and the Madonna of China', which I won't repeat here. Lum's portrait of the Madonna is perhaps close to Elvira's sculptures of Diana of the Ephesians, though Lum may not have been quite the 'ultra-Modern' that MacGibbon is (and she also did have several children), and her look was different – Lum, at this time, was invariably photographed in a kimono Bohemian-style rather than overalls.

Lucile Swan

But perhaps we can also consider the American sculptor Lucile Swan as part of Elvira MacGibbon's composite character. Swan had studied at the Art Institute of Chicago and then married the painter Jerome Blum just before the Great War. They travelled together to Corsica, Cuba, Japan and Tahiti before a sojourn in China. They later divorced and, in 1929, Swan returned to Peking where she opened a sculpture studio. During the first week of her sojourn in Peking she attended a dinner party given by Dr Amadeus Grabau (who was teaching at PKU), known as "the father of Chinese geology". At the party she met and fell in love (indeed began a lifelong infatuation) with the Jesuit priest, palaeontologist and Sinologist Teilhard de Chardin (who was considered very handsome by many women in Peking, including Helen Foster Snow, wife of Edgar "*Red Star Over China*" Snow). But Lucile was unable to shift Teilhard from his priestly vows of celibacy, though he did hire her to create the famous clay reconstruction of "Peking Man's" skull, which had been unearthed on a dig near Peking that he had been involved in.[351] Swan herself became

---

351 Peking Man, *homo erectus pekinensis*, was discovered in the 1920s during excavations at Choukoutien, near Peking. Swan and de Chardin corresponded until his death in 1955 – see, Eds. Mary Gilbert & Thomas King, *Letters of Teilhard de Chardin and Lucile Swan* (Chicago: University of Chicago Press, 2005).

well known for her clay figurines of children, Chinese jugglers, sword dancers and other Chinese characters that caught her eye as she wandered through Peking.

Cedric and Veronica Aspergill – British diplomat Cedric is considered the *'Don Juan of the Diplomatic Corps'*, and lusts after the young Chinese women (*'Oriental hussies'*, as Veronica would term them) he meets at Elvira MacGibbon's at-homes. He is rather bored of his wife Veronica. The feeling is mutual and Veronica pines *'for those Bloomsbury parties where one sat on the floor and discussed Soviet films to the accompaniment of the latest "swing" records.'* Stuck with each other, they opt consciously to behave like *'the couples in Noel Coward's plays'* and aspire to become Peking's premier Bright Young Couple. The horror of Legation Quarter society and their shared desire to leave the city – *'Oh for the friendly aroma of a tube-station'* – keeps them tenuously together.

Cedric dresses in a vaguely Bohemian manner, *'corduroy trousers, open necked lemon shirts'* and later a *'Basque beret and bright suede brogues'* redolent of artistic Chelsea. Veronica spends all day in her mauve lamé pyjamas. The more stiff-backed Captain Gulley considers Cedric a *'slacker'*, though Mrs Mascot rather defers to him in matters of taste, considering him to be *'the sole representative of London's Bright Young People in Peking.'* The snobby Trumper family consider the Aspergills *'rank outsiders'*. It is the Aspergills who openly declare that they prefer *'peonies to ponies'*, that is to say, the aesthetes of Peking to the foreign society symbolised by the members of the Paomachang Race Club. Cedric is musical and working on a series of *études* for the piano that take their inspiration from Peking street hawker cries, along with one piece entitled "Pagoda Glimpsed Through Ginkgo Trees". Cedric and Veronica claim a love of Chinese culture, such as the opera, though Veronica notes that *'One can't stand too much of it… gives one the collywobbles.'*

It seems most likely that the major component of Cedric is Colin Tradescant Crowe, who had been born in Yokohama the son of a British diplomat and followed his father, after Oxford, into the Foreign Office. Crowe was at the British Consulate in Peking between 1936 and 1938, during Acton's own sojourn.[352] He was a popular figure at the consulate

---

352 The capital having been moved to Nanking in 1927, the embassy was subsequently downgraded to a consulate.

that was, at that time, run by the overtly misogynistic and racist Consul General Nicholas Fitzmaurice. The almost universally disliked Fitzmaurice was fortunately moved down the ranks in late 1937 to a post of little importance, at the (by then) rather forgotten backwater treaty port of Amoy. By turn Crowe moved upwards to the consulate in Shanghai in 1938 until 1940. While in Peking Crowe met and married Eleanor Lum in 1938, known to her family and friends as "Peter", the daughter of Bertha Lum (see Elvira MacGibbon above). Peter herself was something of a Sinologist and highly independent. She went on explorations in search of Nestorian Christian remains in Inner Mongolia in 1936 and was later to write books about China.[353] By virtue of marrying Colin, she became Lady Crowe.

Another possible composite for Cedric is Simon Harcourt-Smith, who served eleven years in the British foreign service in China and in the Foreign Office's Far Eastern Department. He was an early friend of Acton's in Peking. In 1942, a year after *Peonies and Ponies* came out, Harcourt-Smith published *Fire in the Pacific*.[354] The book was slightly redundant at time of publication – i.e. just after Pearl Harbor – as it warned of the dangers of not firmly backing China as an ally and of not paying sufficient attention to the aggression of Japanese militarism. Acton knew Harcourt-Smith, a keen amateur horologist as well as a diplomat, and the two had visited Shanghai together in 1933. In his memoirs Acton recalls the Harcourt-Smiths were, like the Aspergills, 'pining for Europe: they were enervated by the dry climate, depressed by their colleagues, and bored by the society I have described in *Peonies and Ponies*.'[355] Towards the end of Acton's novel, Veronica finally has enough of Cedric and elopes to Mongolia with Captain Gulley. In real life Harcourt-Smith and his wife Rosamund remained married after their own Peking sojourn, both becoming historical novelists.

Heliogabalus[356] – the beloved dog of Cedric and Veronica and most probably based on Helen Foster Snow's equally beloved white Kansu

353 For instance, Eleanor Bettina Peter Lum Crowe, *The Purple Barrier: The Story of the Great Wall of China* (London: Robert Hale, 1960); *My Own Pair of Wings* (San Francisco: Chinese Materials Center, 1981).

354 Simon Harcourt-Smith, *Fire in the Pacific* (London: Alfred A. Knopf, 1942).

355 Acton, *Memoirs of an Aesthete*, p.286.

356 After Heliogabalus, the Roman emperor from 218 to 222.

greyhound, which she named "Gobi". That dog had been a gift to Helen from the Swedish explorer Sven Hedin.

Poppy Trumper – wife of the very English Archie Trumper, a *'martinet'* and generally disliked. The Trumpers consider themselves *'the pukka representatives of Peking's Old Residents'*. And, as such, they maintain a highly Anglo lifestyle – their rented temple in the Western Hills is decorated *'to produce an illusion of their Surrey nest'*. Poppy is rather judgemental of anyone slightly Bohemian, or not observing strict Legation Quarter etiquette, such as the Aspergills – *'Peking has manners, Mrs Aspergill, even if Mayfair hasn't'* (the Aspergills by turn consider Poppy *'suburban'*). Despite her high opinion of herself, Poppy is not beyond trying to sell visiting tourists a jade trinket or two, or of being a gossip (even suggesting Philip Flowers has a *'male seraglio'*).

Quite frankly there were simply too many English women with the attitudes of Poppy Trumper to consider a single one of them as the role model. Poppy is simply the British Legation Quarter wife incarnate.

Captain Gulley – the former Scottish military man wonders why anyone chooses to live in a hutong when *'quite decent European houses of solid masonry are to be had in Peking for the asking?'* He is an amateur Mongolist and *'tinkering'* at a book about Emperor Qianlong's military campaigns that will never be finished. He suspects women like Elvira MacGibbon and Mrs Mascot of *'secret vices'*. Despite being officially an *'Old Resident'*, Gulley sees little charm in Peking, maintains an opinion of the Chinese that is *'quite Gilbert and Sullivan'*, and claims that his heart remains in Peebles. He is secretly lonely and would like a companion, possibly Elvira MacGibbon whose independent ways and artiness rather intrigue him.

Gulley does not appear to be based on any particular old Peking characters and the city was not generally considered a great place for retired military men. Most likely Gulley is more of a type encompassing elements of those military sorts and explorers who passed through Peking in the 1930s. Candidates include Sven Hedin, who led the Sino-Swedish Expedition to Mongolia in the early 1930s and whose time in Peking overlapped with Acton[357]; Peter Fleming, who went overland from

357 The book of Hedin's that Acton would probably have known best was Sven Hedin, *The Silk Road* (London: George Routledge & Sons, 1938).

Peking to Kashgar and on to British India in the mid-1930s, famously writing about it, as well as being humorously described as 'terrifically ex-military' by WH Auden and Christopher Isherwood who encountered him in China[358]; and the British diplomat-explorer Eric Teichman, who also skirted Mongolia *en route* to Sinkiang in the mid-1930s. Hedin, of course, was Swedish rather than Scottish (and later flirted with the Nazis), and Fleming perhaps a bit too young and aristocratic (he was also the Squire of Nettlebed in Oxfordshire) to be Gulley. It is perhaps the now little-remembered Teichman who best fits the profile of Captain Gulley.[359]

Rosa Hawkweed – There are a number of likely contenders for the main inspiration for Rosa Hawkweed, '*the portmanteau-like person... whose luscious romances about life in Ningpo were remarkable inasmuch as the authoress had never been within a hundred miles*

Sir Eric Teichman at the Paomachang Autumn Races, 1932

of the milieu she had chosen... and sprinkled so liberally with passional, in lieu of mere local, colour.' Rosa is considered rather a bore by the foreign colony for both her novels and her ostentatious cigarette holders, but she is listened to avidly for her "Far Cathay" tales by visiting tourists. Her best-known novel of Peking is *Gangplanks to Buddha-land*.

Three obvious inspirations for Rosa are Ann Bridge, Nora Waln and Stella Benson. Bridge probably remains the better known of the three as her two China novels, *Peking Picnic* (1932) and *The Ginger Griffin* (1934), are reasonably regularly reprinted. Bridge was the pseudonym of Mary Ann Dolling Sanders, Lady O'Malley, born to an Anglo-American family that subsequently lost their fortune. She married a diplomat, Owen St.

---

358 Fleming's China adventures are contained in *One's Company: A Journey to China: A Journey from Peking to Kashmir* (London: Jonathan Cape, 1934) and *News From Tartary* (London: Scribners, 1936). Fleming is hilariously sent up in WH Auden & Christopher Isherwood's *Journey to a War* (New York: Random House, 1939).

359 Teichman wrote up his travels in Eric Teichman, *Journey to Turkistan* (London: Hodder & Stoughton, 1937).

Clair O'Malley, in 1913, though it was not a happy union. O'Malley was posted to Peking in 1925 and Bridge stayed for two years. *Peking Picnic*, her first novel, was very successful, setting her on a life-long career as a writer. The novel is set among the Legation Quarter diplomatic set. The follow-up, *The Ginger Griffin*, tells the tale of a young English woman who comes to Peking to live with her diplomatic uncle and embarks on a love affair. Both books were reasonably light but thoroughly enjoyable fare, and were read closely by the foreign colony for gossip. Rosa Hawkweed maintains that she has two loves – Peking and Menton, on the French Riviera. For Bridge her two loves were, at one point at least, Peking and, for all her life, the Swiss Alps.

Nora Waln was from a Pennsylvania Quaker family that had a long-standing business arrangement with the Lin trading family of Hopei province. This excited Nora's interest in China and she went to stay with the Lins in 1920, eventually writing a novelised account of the family and its various travails, *House of Exile*.[360] While in China, Nora married an Englishman working for the Chinese Post Office. The couple left China to live in Germany in 1934.

Shropshire-born Stella Benson took a job with a mission school and hospital in China in 1920. There she met James (Shaemus) O'Gorman Anderson, an Anglo-Irish officer in the Chinese Maritime Customs Service. They married in London a year later when James was home on furlough. The Andersons returned to live and work in China and, for the next decade, Stella followed her husband through a variety of often quite remote postings across the country – Chungking at the head of the Yangtze; Mengzi on the Yunnan-Burma border; Nanning and Pakhoi in southern China; the remote border between China and Korea, as well as some time in Hong Kong. In 1930 she published *The Far-Away Bride*, the story of the Malinins, a White Russian émigré family in Japan who are poor but generally happy, easygoing and affectionate to each other despite their constant bickering.[361]

However, it's also worth considering the less commonly remembered Elizabeth Cooper, the author of *My Lady of the Chinese Courtyard*, as

---

360 Nora Waln, *The House of Exile* (Boston: Little, Brown, 1933).
361 Stella Benson, *The Far-Away Bride* (New York: Harper & Brothers, 1930).

a possible composite for Rosa Hawkweed.[362] Cooper's *epistolary* novel is sometimes described as a 'forgotten classic' and it does have its fans, while it also goes some way to evoking the life of a Chinese upper-class woman through a series of letters. Cooper herself was from Iowa, born in 1877, and was an inveterate traveller her whole life. She spent a decade in China, in Shanghai mostly, with a husband in the American diplomatic service.

Doctor Hector Pilchard – Pilchard is an elderly, but lively, Sinologist and the author of *Fecundity Symbols* who often lectures to visitors on *Peking: Past and Present*. However, he enjoys The Whoopee Hop and has a taste for more erotic fiction. He mistakenly believes that Rosa Hawkweed was the author of one of his favourite novels, *Nipples of Nippon*.

The aforementioned British diplomat-scholar ETC Werner is a possible candidate for the composite and certainly may have been in the back of Acton's mind. Acton did cross paths with Werner, but never got to know him well. However, it is unlikely Werner ever perused a copy of *Nipples of Nippon*, or similar.

A better candidate is the eccentric fringe member of the Bloomsbury Group, the aforementioned Charles John Hope-Johnstone. Born in 1883, Hope-Johnstone initially worked as a tutor to the children of the bohemian artist Augustus John, edited *The Gramophone* magazine with the novelist Compton Mackenzie, served in the First World War, was the editor of *The Burlington Magazine* after the war (until he was sacked by Roger Fry), was a keen amateur photographer, and got married and then divorced in short order. Hope-Johnstone was a good friend of the Hispanist Gerald Brenan. Just before the outbreak of the Great War they decided to walk from England to China. They got as far as Bosnia, pushing their belongings in an old pram – one and a half thousand miles from London! – before running out of money. In 1939 Hope-Johnstone accepted a lecturing position at Peking University. He stayed until the 1940s and managed to find work as a private mathematics tutor to the children of the remaining foreign colony.

But given Pilchard's fondness for socialising with the younger set and enjoyment of giving a speech, a far more likely candidate is Lewis Charles

---

362 Elizabeth Cooper, *My Lady of the Chinese Courtyard* (New York: Frederick A. Stokes, 1914). I am indebted to Dr Frances Wood for introducing me to Cooper.

"LC" Arlington, who seems the better match. Acton knew him well and they had collaborated on a translation together.[363] Arlington was really the China veteran's China veteran. By the time of his death in 1942, or thereabouts, he had been in China seventy years! A Californian by birth, Arlington had arrived in China in the 1880s to accept a post with the Qing Imperial Navy. He saw the fall of that dynasty, the rise of the republic, the warlord era, and the Japanese invasion, all while working for the Chinese customs and then the postal service. He retired in the 1920s and wrote about China pretty much full time. He became good friends with a young man at the British Legation, William Lewisohn, and together they compiled the classic guidebook to Peking, *In Search of Old Peking*, published by Henri Vetch from his bookshop at the Grand Hôtel de Pékin.[364] Arlington was a man Acton knew well, and *In Search of Old Peking* was a key text of his sojourn. That he would base the character of Hector Pilchard on him is both a tribute and, one likes to think, something that (had they been able to meet again before Arlington's death in Hong Kong) would have been a shared joke.

Freddie Follicle – the scurrilous editor of the *Peiping Star Bulletin* who runs reports on all the social events of the foreign colony and is eyed with both desperation and suspicion by Mrs Mascot and others looking for column inches, though all too aware that Freddie can be rather cutting of their pretensions.

The most likely model for Freddie Follicle is Sheldon Ridge, the editor of the *Peiping Chronicle*, which had been started in the early 1930s as the *Peking Chronicle*. The *Chronicle* was far from the best newspaper ever produced in China and Ridge not the best editor by any stretch of the imagination. However, many foreigners, including Acton, found it amusing and read it avidly. To save costs, most of the journalists hired by Ridge were Chinese with less than fluent English, while the paper was typeset by printers who knew no English at all. Famously, when two skaters fell through the ice on a Peking lake, the *Chronicle* reported: 'They eyed ice angrily for some time before leaving in disgruntle' while

363   Acton & LC Arlington, *Famous Chinese Plays* (Peiping: Henri Vetch, 1937).
364   LC Arlington & William Lewisohn, *In Search of Old Peking* (Peiping: Henri Vetch, 1935).

a famous *Peiping Chronicle* headline declared 'PRINCESS ELIZABETH TO BECOME MOTHER OF HER OWN CHILD'.

Ridge had been brought in to make improvements to the *Chronicle*, but he couldn't do much with the limited resources, though he was supposedly highly knowledgeable about both China and Mongolia. Despite his business plan to revive the *Chronicle's* fortunes, the paper's owners favoured a more tabloid approach. Ridge eventually closed the paper after serious threats to his life from pro-Japanese forces who objected to his criticism of Tokyo's actions in China.

The Chinese characters in Peonies and Ponies:

Alice Tu (Tu Yi) – a young Chinese girl just returned from Paris where she had met Elvira MacGibbon and become somewhat obsessed with her. Alice loves France and has acquired a certain Parisian attitude. She now teaches French at a Peking university. Alice Tu is a barely disguised Alice Ying, one of Acton's colleagues at PKU. Ying had moved to Peking from Shanghai, where she had been a protégé of the aforementioned Bernardine Szold-Fritz. In his memoirs Acton describes Alice Ying as 'a plump little Shanghai plover with pretty dimples, who could patter French, German and English with the same cute fluency.' Acton also notes that like Alice Tu in *Peonies and Ponies*, Alice Ying spoke French with a pronounced Parisian accent.[365]

While Alice Tu's Francophile past was most probably inspired by Alice Ying, her style (Elvira MacGibbon considers her '*chic*') was probably inspired by Rose Feng, a young Chinese woman Acton met early in his China sojourn. Rose went to many of the mixed soirées in the Legation Quarter and was also fluent in French. Acton describes her as having '*scintillating eyes, full red lips, a tiny nose prettily curved, a pink rose-petal complexion, rippling black hair cut short and figure slim but not over slim, with hands and arms that gave one an itch to sculpt.*'[366] Acton claims she enjoyed flirting with European men and that many in the Peking diplomatic corps were in love with her.

---

365 Acton, *Memoirs of an Aesthete*, p.331.
366 Ibid, p.279.

Feng Chung-han – described as a *'poet with a future'*, inspired by the Bengali poet much admired in China at the time, Rabindranath Tagore. He is also Alice Tu's suitor, despite being somewhat priggish and formal. The most prominent modernist poet, who definitely met Tagore and worked as his interpreter during one of his China visits, was Hsu (Xu) Zhimo. Like Feng, Xu was a modern poet interested in freeing Chinese poetry from its classical shackles yet remained quite traditional himself. Xu liked the English Romantics and the French Symbolists but disliked America after spending time at Columbia University. Despite an arranged marriage in 1915, Xu indulged in numerous love affairs, many with women writers close to the Crescent Moon Society he founded. He was also rumoured to have had affairs with both the writer Pearl Buck and the left-wing journalist Agnes Smedley though was rather priggish in feigning revulsion at these rumours. Xu died on a flight from Nanking to Peking in 1931 when his plane crashed in Shandong. Acton arrived in China shortly after Xu's death and so the two never met, though of course Acton was acutely aware of his poetry and reputation.

Dr Li Ssu – an attendant at Elvira MacGibbon's salon and a man who learned English from missionaries and is an active Rotarian. He is a philosopher, though Acton describes him as a *'Chinese Vicar of Bray'* [367] – *'he strove to be all things to East and all things to West'*. He criticises Chinese traditions such as foot binding though maintains that his own wife's '"lily hooks" had never been unbound.' A publicly vocal enemy of Confucius, he surreptitiously studies the Confucian classics. He is overly keen to impress the foreign colony he secretly despises.

Dr Chang "HH" Hsin-hai, another of Acton's PKU colleagues, is the likely model for Dr Li. He taught English and had a broad outlook but was, so Acton says, really of the eighteenth century. Chang was Shanghainese and had studied English literature at both Johns Hopkins and Harvard. He was also political and served as one of China's delegates to the Washington Naval Conference in 1921.[368] Throughout Chang's

---

367 The English satirical description of someone who fundamentally changes their principles and opinions as external requirements change around them.

368 A very important conference for China which, though not a great naval power, did manage to get Japan to return Shandong to Chinese control, an aim not achieved at the Paris Peace Conference in 1919 and therefore leading to China not being a signatory to the Versailles Treaty.

Mei Lan-fang as Fairy Scattering Flowers, 1930s

career he alternated between representing the Chinese government and being a professor of English.

Ruby Yuan – a clearly lesbian and cross-dressing Chinese army officer who smokes in public and is attached to a rather debauched warlord's headquarters as a liaison officer. The tall, athletic and Americanised Ruby loves jazz, dancing and The Whoopee Hop. The character seems clearly based on the now little-remembered Nadine Hwang (sometimes Huang), who was mixed-race and (at least slightly later in Paris) openly lesbian and often dressed in men's clothes. Nadine had served in a Chinese warlord's army in the 1920s in a role not dissimilar to that of a liaison officer. Born in Madrid, she was the daughter of a senior Qing diplomat and a Belgian mother, was of above average height and her figure meant she easily got work as a mannequin for several couturiers while living in Paris in the 1930s.[369]

Yang Pao-chin – the object of Philip Flowers's affections, Yang is a male opera singer who plays female roles. He has excellent teeth but annoys Flowers (who favours Chinese dress) by preferring to wear *'brilliantly coloured blazers and checked plus fours'*, wanting to reject tradition and embrace the modern. Yang finds Philip Flowers's protestation that *'My body is foreign but my soul is Chinese'* incredulous, though wishes to retain a foreign friend and patron.

It would be difficult not to see shades of the most famous Peking opera star of the time, Mei Lan-fang, in the character of Yang Pao-chin, although Yang is not internationally famous and the character does refer to Mei Lan-fang's success in America. Acton spent most of his Peking sojourn living on a hutong close to Mei's major Peking residence. During their time exploring Peking together, Acton and his good friend Desmond Parsons regularly visited the local opera and befriended many young aspiring performers not unlike Yang Pao-chin.

*

369 To avoid repetition I point readers to the previous chapter on Isamu Noguchi's sojourn in the city, 'Peking is Like Paris', which contains a longer description of Nadine Hwang.

Peonies and Ponies remains a seriously under-read classic of writing on inter-war China, Peking, and especially the pompousness, silliness and oddities of the city's foreign colony. Perhaps knowing the real cast of characters that inspired Acton is a helpful way into the novel for those that have yet to read it? Perhaps, knowing these people, it is a good excuse to reread it? Either way, Harold Acton's great comic *roman à clef* of late 1930s Peking remains under-appreciated as a fantastic recreation of a specific time and place.

Who was the Real Olga?
Olga Fischer-Togo (1922)

FISCHER TOGO, Olga, Opera and concert singer. *Address:* 6 Kwei Chia Chang. Born at Vienna. *Nationality,* Austrian. Studied Vienna Conservatory, afterwards in Milan under Maestro Aversa. Made debut as "Nedda" in Pagliacci. Assumed art name of Tôgo after Russo-Japanese War. Did war work in Siberia and Japan. *Decoration:* Red Cross of Austria.

'The concert given at the Peking Institute of Fine Arts on Tuesday night by Miss Olga Fischer-Togo, assisted by Maestro Gennaro Brigida and his orchestra, proved to be one of real artistic merit. Many people attended.' [370]

The Peking art of reinvention

Olga Fischer-Togo was once the best-known European opera singer in Peking and across Asia. She performed to packed houses and appreciative audiences in Tokyo, Yokohama, Kobe, Mukden, Harbin, Tientsin and Shanghai in the first two decades of the twentieth century. Her performances were invariably well attended, and she always sold out any recital in her home base of Peking where she lived throughout most of the 1920s and 1930s. Olga Fischer-Togo not only sold a lot of tickets but also raised large sums for charity through her guest appearances – flood and famine relief, orphanages, hospitals… she seems to have always been willing to show up, sing and call upon people to donate to worthy causes. In 1922 she wrote a book about her adventures on the Trans-Siberian Railway travelling through Russia, encountering stern Soviet border guards and getting into some sort of contretemps over her transit visa that nearly saw her end up in a Bolshevik jail. Her locally produced book sold well in Henri Vetch's French Bookstore in the lobby of the Grand Hôtel de Pékin – the bookshop every Peking foreign colony library depended on. She was a celebrity.

Olga lived for many years in a large courtyard property on a shady hutong near the Tartar Wall in the Eastern City. She was one of the few European women to receive her own separate directory listing in the 1922 *Who's Who of China*.[371] Now, though, Olga Fischer-Togo is entirely forgotten. She is rarely, if ever, mentioned in memoirs, opera histories or studies of old Peking. Indeed, I have never been able to locate a single photograph of her in my researches.

But this is perhaps not surprising because Olga Fischer-Togo was not keen to leave too much of a trail. She enjoyed her notoriety, her celebrity, but it seems nobody got too close to her. To my knowledge she did not marry, had no long-term partner and never had children. So you see, only what Olga Fischer-Togo wanted us to know about her is available: her carefully crafted public image, and her own oft-told and self-mythologised Peking back story. It was a story of prodigious classical musical talent and refined old-world taste, served up with a large helping

---

371 Important as there was only a *Who's Who of China* in 1922 and it never became an annual publication.

of *ancien régime* Europe – Italian opera and Austro-Hungarian nobility – combined with exciting adventures in war-torn China and Japan. And then there is what appears to be the real back story of Olga Fischer-Togo; a somewhat different tale of Manhattan bars and cabarets, boardwalks, immigrants and the old country, and of sojourning entertainers far from home.

Olga Fischer-Togo is a wonderful example of that all-too-common member of the foreign colony of Peking in the first half of the twentieth century – the almost completely self-invented characters who made new lives and reputations for themselves, free of all the baggage of their pasts, their crimes and misdemeanours. Olga Fischer-Togo was far from the worst example – the law wasn't looking for her! Her story was entertaining rather than deceitful or malicious. But she's still an invention. And, in fact, her real back story was arguably more interesting than her invented one.

First, let's hear Olga's own preferred version of her life….

"Togo"

Kuei Chia Chang, or Armour Factory Alley in English, is a short and charming hutong that keeps reappearing in my research. It is not surprising, perhaps, as it was a residential hutong consistently popular with foreigners in Peking in the first half of the twentieth century. Situated in the Eastern Tartar City, today's Dongcheng District, the hutong was close by the Tartar Wall alongside an old, long silted up, tributary of the Grand Canal. The hutong afforded easy access to the Legation Quarter to the west, as well as the shopping, dining and socialising districts around Hatamen and Morrison Streets to the north. When I began writing about foreign correspondents in China between the wars, Kuei Chia Chang appeared as the home of Edgar Snow and his wife Helen Foster Snow in 1936. When I began researching my book *Midnight in Peking*, Kuei Chia Chang jumped out again, this time as the home of the former diplomat and Sinologist ETC Werner, and his murdered daughter Pamela, in 1937. Then I came across Olga Fischer-Togo.

Olga was one of the hutong's longest and, at the time, best known residents. In 1922 Miss Olga Fischer-Togo was recorded as living at No.6 Kuei Chia Chang. When Olga first moved onto the hutong it was, like most of the Tartar City hutongs (even those, such as Kuei Chia Chang, with sizeable foreign populations), quite basic in many ways. One novel of Peking's foreign colony written around the same time notes:

> They all got into rickshaws and quickly crossed the Legation Quarter. Reaching the Tartar City, they passed through the dark hutungs *(sic)* where the wheels of their vehicles sunk into the mud and branches of huge trees overhanging the gutters brushed against their faces. The streets were empty; only solitary hawkers passed occasionally, swaying as they went, carrying baskets suspended from bamboo poles, and crying their wares before the closed doors. Here and there, very high up, above the roofs, red lanterns, the sign of bath houses, shone through the night like eyes of fire.[372]

Peking was a town that, particularly in the winter months, got dark early and went to bed early. It was so quiet that from Kuei Chia Chang you could hear the early morning hours rung on the clock bell at the Hongkong and Shanghai Bank on Legation Street, and the sound of the train whistles over a mile away arriving at the Chienmen Station from Tientsin and Shanghai.

In her potted biography in the 1922 edition of the *Who's Who of China*, essentially a directory of the most important and notable foreigners living in China at the time, Olga claimed to be Austrian by birth. She was a soprano singer who had been appearing in concerts and light operas across Japan and northern China since before the First World War. We don't know as much about Miss Olga Fischer-Togo as we should but one character trait we can be sure of is that she was a strong, independent woman – single, successful, reasonably well-off.

So here's what we know based on what she told *Who's Who* and the newspapers in Peking. Olga Fischer was born in Vienna in 1875, in the capital of the Austro-Hungarian Empire. She was one of twelve brothers and sisters. She studied music at the Vienna Conservatory, and then at the Milan Conservatory. She made her stage debut in Milan as Nedda in an early production of Ruggero Leoncavallo's *Pagliacci*, a role most famously played by Dame Nellie Melba in London several years previously. Olga

---

372   Damien de Martel & Léon de Hoyer, *Silhouettes of Peking* (Peking: China Booksellers, 1926), pp.45-46.

suggested that her family had spent some years in the United States at the start of the twentieth century, but that she considered herself Austrian.

Then, somehow, Olga Fischer claimed to have become involved in the Russo-Japanese War (1904-1905) as a nurse, where two things happened. Firstly, she was awarded the Austrian Red Cross (a medal usually given for services to nursing in wartime), and secondly, she adopted the stage name "Togo," apparently in order to improve her profile and garner some name recognition with Japanese opera audiences. Certainly, from about 1912, she began appearing frequently in recitals in Tokyo and other Japanese cities. She was described in the English-language press in Tokyo as a 'well-known' opera singer.[373] By 1913, she seems to have made the journey to China and began appearing at concerts in northern China and Peking. She made her debut in Shanghai in 1914. Olga does appear to have lived in Japan for a time and then to have resided in Tientsin for a while. In Tientsin she was recorded as the Secretary of the German Women's Association for the treaty port.

Olga continued to appear regularly across China with a break during the years of World War One when, one imagines, her Austro-Hungarian heritage might have been problematic to audiences composed mostly of the Allied nations (which included Japan). Indeed Olga, apparently then living in the Austro-Hungarian Concession in Tientsin, appealed to the Joint Distribution Committee (JDC), the largest international Jewish humanitarian organisation, for relief.[374]

Soon after the Armistice, in 1919, it appears that Olga moved full-time to Peking from Tientsin. She is recorded as being back performing at the Peking Institute of Fine Arts, where she was accompanied by Maestro Gennaro Brigida and his orchestra.[375] At the same time as performing it appears that she was teaching – being listed as an 'instructor' at the Peking School of Music from at least the fall term of 1920 and claiming to be a graduate of the Milan Conservatory.[376] In Peking, as in Tientsin and Japan, she seemed largely to move in German circles. Olga was good friends with Joseph Schedel, a well-known German pharmacist in Peking

373 *Japan Times and Mail*, March 30, 1913.

374 Letter from Miss Olga Fischer-Togo, Austrian Bund, Tientsin to Mr Jacob Schiff, February 25, 1917, American-Jewish Joint Distribution Committee Archives, Item ID: 5811 NY AR191418/3/4/75.

375 *Millard's Review of the Far East*, December 6, 1919, Vol.XI, No.1.

376 *The Music Magazine & Musical Courier,* Vol.80, 1920, p.30.

who had also lived for a time in Japan. According to Schedel, the pair had originally got to know each other before the First World War in Tokyo when Olga was living by the beach at Higashihama (or East Beach to the foreigners in Japan), near Yokohama.[377] Their friendship continued after the war when they met again and were both living in Peking.

Still, quite how Olga Fischer came to the Far East is never quite explained. Nor how she ended up as a nurse in the Russo-Japanese War (and for which side?[378]). The best guess is that Olga Fischer's initial trips to the Far East were to visit one of her older brothers, Emil, who had lived in China continuously since 1900. Emil Sigmund Fischer had been born in 1866 in Vienna. He first came to China in 1894, visiting Shanghai and Tientsin. He then took a post as an import and export banker in the northern treaty port.[379] He had married and lived with his wife Viola until her death in 1932, always resident in Tientsin. Around 1930, in his mid-sixties, Emil retired but decided to stay on in China. In his spare time he was also a widely travelled man (claiming to have visited every country in the world except Australia), and a prolific author of guides, often published under his adopted Chinese name "Fei-shi".[380] He started submitting travel articles to *Collier's Weekly* magazine in America around 1900.[381] His books included *Through the Silk and Tea Districts of Kiang-nan and Chekiang; Overland via the Trans-Siberian Railway; Guide to Peking: Environs Near and Far; The Present Outlook in Manchuria; Travels in China, 1894-1940*, and others, as well as travel journalism for a

---

377 *Markus Holzammer, Der Apotheker Joseph Schedel: Tagebücher Aus Japan (1886-1899) und China (1909-1921)* (Wiesbaden: Franz Steiner Verlag Wiesbaden GmbH, 2003), p.201 (in German).

378 This is unclear if, indeed, it is true that she was a nurse. The Austro-Hungarian Empire declared itself neutral in the Russo-Japanese War. It seems unlikely Olga would have been a nurse for Tsarist Russia or for Japan. It is possible she was with a charitable relief organisation, but I can find no trace of her in the war, or of her having actually received any medals from Austria.

379 It is somewhat unclear who Emil worked for, as some sources say Deutsche Bank and others Fischer & Co., listed as an import-export company. It is of course possible, given that 'side hustles' were as popular then as now, that he performed both functions.

380 *Times Union* (Brooklyn), November 8, 1936, p.12.

381 The first I can find is 'A Journey from Shanghai to the Tea Country by Pig Boat', *Collier's Weekly*, August 1900, and an interview with Li Hung Chang (Li Hongzhang) in a 1901 edition.

wide variety of magazines.[382] Emil was certainly a well-known and highly respected member of Tientsin society. Olga appears to have lived at his residence in Tientsin when she arrived until she moved to Peking and Kuei Chia Chang around 1920.

Olga seems never to have married and appears to have lived alone in some style on Kuei Chia Chang. She was clearly earning a decent independent living as a soprano in 1922 China. And her celebrity was to ratchet up a further notch the following year when she published a relatively sensational book (at least within the goldfish bowl of the Peking foreign colony), *My Trip from China, via Siberia to Europe: Including Experiences in a Siberian Prison*. As with many of her brother Emil's books (and *The Peking Who's Who*), Fischer-Togo's book was published by the Tientsin Press.[383]

Olga had recently attempted to travel from China back to Europe via the Trans-Siberian Railway, seemingly to attend some concerts. Indeed she claimed to be the 'first non-Russian foreign woman who since the Great War has travelled unaccompanied from China to Europe via Siberia.'[384] It was a tumultuous time to make the journey – in 1922 the Russian Civil War was still waging between the Bolsheviks and the last remnants of the White armies. In Russia it seems she had encountered numerous problems with over-zealous Bolshevik commissars, various officials demanding bribes, and brief periods of incarceration and quarantine due to the global influenza pandemic – the so-called Spanish Flu – and other outbreaks of cholera and typhoid across Russia.

Just getting out of China was a chore – a Japanese steamer from Tientsin to Dairen, then a train to Mukden and another overcrowded train to Changchun, change to the China Eastern Railway for the Russian-gauge train to Harbin (dining car service cancelled!), a night at the Hotel Moderne (a den of thieves apparently), a train to the Sino-Russian border

382 *Through the Silk and Tea Districts of Kiang-nan and* Chekiang (New York: Journal of the American Geographical Society of New York, 1900); *Overland via the Trans-Siberian Railway* (Tientsin: Tientsin Press, 1908); *Guide to Peking: Environs Near and Far* (Tientsin: Tientsin Press, 1924); *The Present Outlook in Manchuria* (Tientsin: Tientsin Press, 1935); *Travels in China, 1894-1940* (Tientsin: Tientsin Press, 1941).
383 *My Trip from China, via Siberia to Europe: Including Experiences in a Siberian Prison* (Tientsin: Tientsin Press, 1923). The Tientsin Press was the book and atlas publishing arm of *The Tientsin and Peking Times* newspaper.
384 *My Trip from China, via Siberia to Europe*, p.3.

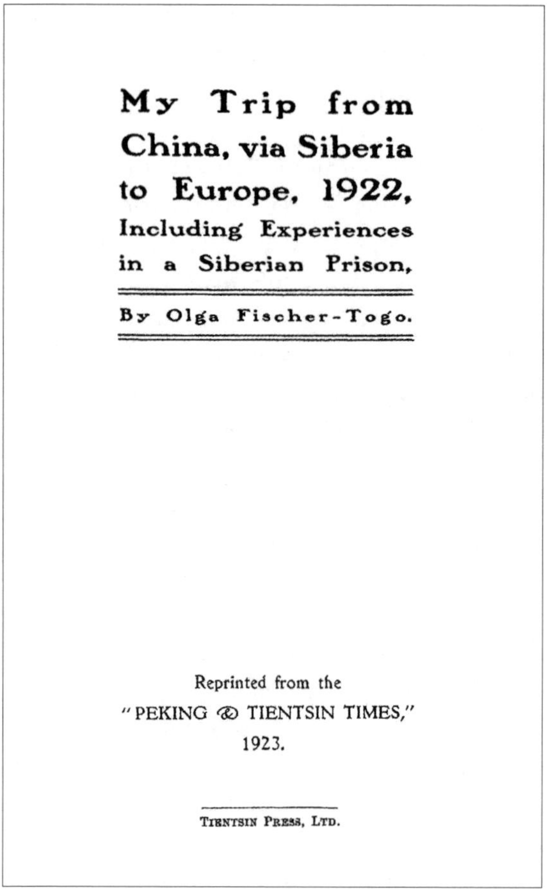

My Trip from
China, via Siberia
to Europe, 1922,
Including Experiences
in a Siberian Prison,

By Olga Fischer-Togo.

Reprinted from the
"PEKING & TIENTSIN TIMES,"
1923.

TIENTSIN PRESS, LTD.

at Manchouli, then another train across the border to Chita (still held by the White forces and overrun with flies at the time), before a final dash to make the Trans-Siberian Railway heading into 'Communist Russia' and destined ultimately for Moscow. There does indeed appear to have been some mix-up over visas and currency in Novo Nikolaevsk (Novosibirsk) and Olga was briefly put in a prison cell while things got worked out. Actually, she was fed and given blankets and told all the local hotels were full and this was the only space they had, and she didn't have to share with any local ne'er-do-wells. The next day she was on her way.

The tone of the book is rather huffy, as though disease, revolution, the aftermath of war, rapacious officials and police commissioners, and starving beggars were all specifically targeting Miss Olga Fischer-Togo, soprano, of Peking to make her life hell. She sprinkled liberal amounts of Lysol over her hotel rooms and train carriages to ward away bugs and bacteria and constantly clutched a handkerchief soaked in *eau de cologne.* However, despite her travails she made it to Europe, met old friends in Berlin, attended operas and concerts and then returned to Kuei Chia Chang Hutong in Peking with her completed manuscript in her valise.

But...

But, is any of this true? Some of it perhaps, even maybe most of it. Olga, it seems, doesn't always outright lie, but there's an exaggeration here, a discrepancy there. There is certainly another story of Olga Fischer's life and this tale starts with a man called Louis Fischer, a slightly younger brother of Olga and Emil.

Louis, described around the turn of the century as a 'businessman from Cincinnati', was born in 1880 in Austria. In September 1900 Louis married a woman called Barbara, the daughter of John Reisenweber, an

John Reisenweber

ex-Alderman of New York City. But just four months later, in February 1901, Barbara died suddenly and unexpectedly in the couple's new home in Cincinnati.[385] Rather quickly, Louis married Barbara's older sister Emma in 1902. Louis appears to have worked previously in a hotel in Utica, New York State, and so was well-suited to go and work in his father-in-law's business. As well as his involvement in New York politics (and a friendship with President Warren G. Harding), Louis's father-in-law had started Reisenweber's Restaurant and Hotel on Manhattan's Broadway and 58th Street – Columbus Circle. It seems that sometime after

Barbara's death and his remarriage to Emma, John Reisenweber brought Louis into the business to run Reisenweber's. Louis then brought his brother Julius Fischer in as treasurer of the company.

---

385 'Mrs. Barbara R. Fischer', *New York Tribune*, February 19, 1901, p.4.

Reisenweber's, 1905

In the early decades of the twentieth century Reisenweber's was a top nightspot in Manhattan. Louis, officially the president of the Reisenweber's company, really put the business on a modern footing with dinner-dance tickets and, in 1913, became known as the man who invented the concept of the cover charge, so popular was Reisenweber's. He was a committee member of the New York City Hotel Men's Association and well known about town. Reisenweber's had been initially established at its location by Columbus Circle in 1856 as a pre-Civil War roadhouse and was pioneering from the start. Looking back on Reisenweber's in the 1920s, the *Brooklyn Times Union* newspaper noted that 'Dancing and modern cabaret first saw light at this institution.'[386] A Los Angeles newspaper commented that Reisenweber's was the first New York establishment to sign a jazz orchestra as its resident band.[387] Exaggeration perhaps, but it was a large beer-cellar type place that, at its height, could seat five thousand diners at

386　*Times Union* (Brooklyn), August 13, 1925, p.3.
387　*Los Angeles Evening Express*, December 24, 1928, p.20. The band was Sophie Tucker and the Five Kings of Syncopation.

a time. [388] The actors George Raft and Rudolph Valentino are thought to have started out at Reisenweber's as humble taxi-dancers.

Reisenweber and Fischer expanded to New York's Coney Island in 1909 with a Reisenweber's Restaurant and Casino on Ocean Parkway, next to the New Brighton Theatre, a vaudeville house. Nearby was a space for historical re-enactments that attracted large crowds and where Pawnee Bill's Wild West Show pitched their tent for a while. Louis then bought the Shelburne Hotel, close by on Brighton Beach, in 1914 and moved into its best suite permanently. Louis featured in the New York newspapers as a regular guest and host of charitable events there until he sold it in 1925.

Reisenweber's Restaurant and Casino, Brighton Beach

But the passing of the Volstead Act and Prohibition in 1920 killed the beer-hall trade. For a while, Louis tried to run the business in a slimmed-down fashion – two rooms, the "Paradise" and the "Crystal". But without alcohol, Reisenweber's couldn't even fill these two rooms and folded. Louis was no gangster looking to run a speakeasy, and so he left the cabaret business. United Cigar Stores took over most of the building. In 1925 Louis sold the Shelburne and retired. He had done well out of the business and lived with his second wife Emma in the prestigious Essex House, the 1931 art-deco apartment building on

388 Reisenweber does seem to have been the first New York restaurateur to introduce a combined dinner and show ticket as well as a dance floor for patrons and the, at the time, infamous and much disliked notion of a 25-cent cover charge, though it may not have been the first venue in New York to have a house jazz band.

Central Park South, overlooking the Park. Louis couldn't quite keep out of the catering business and opened an inn at Bear Mountain Park in the Hudson Valley. In February 1941 Emma died; Louis followed her that October. The *Brooklyn Daily Eagle* noted: 'He leaves a brother, Emil Fischer, of Tientsin, China, and three sisters, Mrs William Prager, Ida Fischer and Olga Fischer...'[389] The three sisters and Emil shared Louis's estate between them.

The truth lies somewhere in between

So, what do we know about Louis that tells us anything about Olga? Well, whether there were a dozen Fischer siblings as she had claimed is unclear, but certainly Olga (born 1875) had two sisters (Ida and the woman named only as Mrs Prager, living with her husband in Kansas), as well as her brothers Emil (born 1866), Julius (born 1867) and Louis (born 1880). All appear to have been born in Vienna into a Jewish family and to have come to New York as immigrants in 1892 (when Olga was sixteen or seventeen) and been granted American citizenship.

By the mid-to-late 1890s the Fischers were, to all intents and purposes, a fairly typical New York immigrant family. Emil graduated from New York University where he must have developed an interest in the Far East as he immediately enrolled in Chinese classes at Columbia. Louis and Julius moved around a bit (to Cincinnati and a few other US cities) and then worked together for Reisenweber's in Manhattan. Ida appears to have been involved in musical entertainment in the city in some way and certainly sang occasionally at the Shelburne Hotel.

As regards Olga's nursing experience during the Russo-Japanese War, it is possible, though at twenty-nine Olga might have been considered slightly old for a wartime nurse (even if we could divine why she was there as an American citizen of Austrian birth?). Emil was already living in China, so it is not impossible she was passing through Japan on the route out of the west coast of North America to China. The pharmacist Schedel's diaries do indicate Olga was sojourning in Yokohama at the time.

---

389 'Louis Fischer, 61, Restaurateur; Operated Noted Reisenweber's', *Brooklyn Daily Eagle*, October 27, 1941, p.9.

More, it is a question of how Olga saw her nationality. In Yokohama, before World War One, she was seen by Dr Schedel as part of the German community in Greater Tokyo. In Tientsin it was the German Women's Association she became involved with, not one of the many active American societies and clubs she could have engaged with in the treaty port. During World War One she was living in the Austro-Hungarian Concession and suffering some deprivation. At this point she does appear to have recognised her US citizenship, contacting the Joint Distribution Committee in 1916 and 1917 by writing directly to Jacob Schiff, the German-born naturalised American head of the Jewish relief organisation.[390]

Yet in her 1922 *Who's Who of China* entry she declares her nationality only as Austrian. Was it all, like the "Togo" she added to her name apparently after the Russo-Japanese War, just advertising? A partially invented legend to improve business? Did Austrian sopranos who claimed to have trained in Italy get more work, or were they assumed more cultured than Americans?[391] Even during World War One, when being German or Austrian meant being ostracised by many in the foreign colony, she did not shout about her American citizenship. However, in print she wrote in English and not German. Ultimately, whatever organisations she chose to become involved with and however she chose to describe herself, we do know that she maintained her US passport all those years. So, was it all just a disguise, a preferred Olga to the real one?

The Fischer family do seem to have maintained contact despite distance. It seems Olga and Emil saw each other regularly and shared the same publisher in Tientsin. There were various grandchildren in America; lots of nieces and nephews as the years passed. Certainly in 1923, 1928 and then again in 1936, when Emil visited New York, he stayed with Louis and Emma. Louis and Julius worked together, until Julius died of a stroke in 1929. Ida and her sister, Mrs Prager, appeared at

390 Letter from Miss Olga Fischer-Togo, Austrian Bund, Tientsin to Mr Jacob Schiff, February 25, 1917, American-Jewish Joint Distribution Committee Archives, Item ID: 5811 NY AR191418/3/4/75. See also: Letter from Secretary, Joint Distribution Committee to Miss Olga Fischer-Togo, Austrian Bund, Tientsin, April 19, 1917, American-Jewish Joint Distribution Committee Archives, Item ID: 5811 NY AR191418/3/4/75. Both references provided to me courtesy of Mátyás Mervay.

391 Though I have found no hard evidence, it is quite possible that Olga could have studied in Italy in her early teens.

various family get-togethers at the Shelburne Hotel. Though the family were Jewish, apart from Olga's wartime appeal to the American-Jewish Joint Distribution Committee, I can find no signs that their religion was especially important to them or played any meaningful role in their lives or reason to leave Vienna for New York.

It seems Louis did undertake at least one journey to Asia in 1929, probably just after Julius's death. However, although we know Olga did visit Europe, passing through Italy and England, it is unclear whether she ever returned to the United States until after Louis's death and indeed until just before World War Two.

The land of reinvention

Peking was full of foreigners who reinvented themselves. This volume is full of them too, though usually in the case of Peking, fairly benign reinventions – life away from the restrictions of their home lives and family expectations, after divorces, and occasionally a step or two ahead of the law. In his comic novel of Peking expatriate manners, *Peonies and Ponies,* Harold Acton satirised those who sought to be seen as higher class, smarter or more exciting by being in Peking. And it may have been that simple with Olga. She created a more intriguing, exotic past for herself – Austria, Italy, Japan; the stage, wartime service, a more elegant and sophisticated *Mittel European* family background. Olga sought to appear more Bohemian, more cosmopolitan than the New York of Manhattan beerhalls and the gaudy Brighton Beach boardwalk. Olga was by all accounts a highly talented soprano. She clearly loved to sing, to perform.

In Peking Olga did what she could do, what anyone moving to the city might do, in the first half of the twentieth century – she reinvented herself as Madam Olga Fischer-Togo of Austria. Yet, by the late 1930s, she and her brother Emil were being recognised as US citizens again. The best explanation for this is that they had long had dual nationality. Being Viennese born after World War One their Austro-Hungarian citizenship transferred to the new state of Austria. However, being Jewish, they were stripped of this citizenship by the Nazis after the Anschluss in 1938. Though Olga may have always been proud to be Viennese and Austrian and downplayed, or just ignored, her immigration to New York, it seems Austria did not want anything to do with the Jewish Fischers.

In Japanese-occupied China, as American citizens, Emil and Olga found themselves liable for internment as enemy aliens. Olga narrowly managed to avoid internment by having left China shortly before Pearl Harbor. Emil remained in China. He was interned after being reportedly badly beaten by the Japanese some years earlier.[392] In December 1938 Emil was assaulted by Japanese soldiers on the borders of the British Concession after complaining of their treatment of a French friend. Emil survived internment and managed to somehow secure an early release. He returned to his home in Tientsin. Emil died several months before the end of the war and the Japanese occupation of China, in March 1945. He was aged seventy-nine.

Olga died in the United States in 1968 aged eighty-eight.

---

392 'Japanese Troops Beat US Citizen', *Honolulu Advertiser*, January 2, 1939, p.1.

The Artist and the Madonna of China:
Bertha Lum (1930)

PEKING PAPAL DELEGATE BUYS MADONNA BY IOWA

Mrs. Bertha Lum (left), American artist whose painting of the Madonna (right) has been purchased for the private chapel of apostolic delegate to China.

'In Bertha Lum's remarkable life and work, West and East merged.' [393]

393 Mary Evans O'Keefe Gravalos, *Bertha Lum* (Washington DC: Smithsonian Institute, 1991), p.32.

The perfect work

In January 1930 the newspapers reported that the Vatican's Papal Delegate to China had purchased a piece of art to decorate his private chapel in Peking. His Excellency and Apostolic Representative Archbishop Celso Benigno Luigi Costantini claimed to have searched for several years before settling on the perfect work for his chapel. He claimed to have viewed hundreds of paintings by both Chinese and foreign artists. In the end he settled on a portrait of the Madonna by an American artist resident in Peking, Bertha Lum. Archbishop Costantini determined that the portrait was 'neither occidental nor oriental, but rather a composite face.' Art critics he had consulted told him that 'the soft blues and greens and the dark and pale yellows would harmonize splendidly with the decorations of worship in the Archbishop's various edifices of worship.'[394] Costantini liked Lum's portrait of the Madonna so much that he commissioned copies to be hung in every Catholic church in China.[395] Overnight Bertha Lum, an artist from Iowa then residing in Peking, became the best-known artist working in China.

Archbishop Costantini

In 1930 the purchase of an original work of art by the Papal Delegate to China was big news. The headquarters of the Vatican's Delegation to China had only just relocated to Peking in 1925. Before that it had been in Hankow since its original establishment in 1922, with Costantini appointed as the first apostolic delegate to China. Since then some Chinese Catholics had petitioned for the delegation to be moved to Peking. Costantini had convened the first Chinese National Council in 1924, which took place

394 Both quotes: 'Peking Papal Delegate Buys Madonna By Iowan' (Associated Press), *Kingsport Times*, January 19, 1930, p.5.

395 I should note that while newspaper reports of the period indicate that Costantini viewed many paintings before deciding on Lum's, Mary Evans O'Keefe Gravalos claims that he commissioned the portrait from her. This version does make some sense, given that none of Lum's other work is religious in theme. O'Keefe Gravalos, *Bertha Lum*, p.27.

in the Siccawei Cathedral in Shanghai.[396] In 1928 Pope Pius XI in the Vatican had addressed a message of support to Chiang Kai-shek (himself having officially converted from Buddhism to Methodism in 1927 when he married Soong Mei-ling[397]), and all Chinese Catholics, calling for the peaceful political unification of China and effectively endorsing Chiang's great Northern Expedition to bring the country together and suppress the northern warlords.

By 1930, of course, Peking was no longer the capital of China. However, Chinese Catholics argued that the delegation (effectively Rome's embassy in China) should always be in the city which was 'not only the first city of the land, but also the home of the earliest apostles of the gospel *(in China)*.' Technically neither of these statements was true – in 1930 Nanking was the capital and first city and, while it is possible the first converts to Christianity in China were in Yuan-dynasty Peking (or, to be precise, Khanbaliq then), other places can claim the honour too, including Xian, as well as a host of locations in southern China.

Anyway, the Papal Delegation did relocate and took over a Chinese temple in Peking as its headquarters. What was previously the Chinese ancestors' shrine became a Christian altar, though the stone tablets venerating the dead, as per ancient Chinese rites, were left standing around the edge of the space. The Grand Hall, which had originally been reserved solely for welcoming members of the Manchu imperial family to the temple, became the pontifical audience chamber adorned with a large portrait of the current pope, the bespectacled Pius XI, an Italian pope who had overseen the creation of the Vatican as an independent state. Archbishop Costantini though still had a lot of empty wall space to cover. Bertha Lum's Madonna was to be his primary acquisition. Lum became a major story out of China in the American newspapers which included pictures of her and her painting. But who was she?

396   St. Ignatius Cathedral, also known as the Xujiahui Cathedral.

397   It is often said that Chiang's conversion to Christianity and Methodism was merely to please the Methodist Soong family. However, one of his biographers, Jay Taylor, suggests that Chiang's diaries indicate that his Christian faith was actually strong, as well as sincere, and that he felt that Christianity reinforced Confucian moral teachings. Jay Taylor, *The Generalissimo: Chiang Kai-shek and the Struggle for Modern China* (Boston, Massachusetts: Belknap Press of the Harvard University Press, 2009).

China's most famous foreign artist

Bertha Lum was born in 1869 as Bertha Boynton Bull in Tipton, the county seat of Cedar County, Iowa. Her father was a lawyer and her mother a schoolteacher. She had a sister and two brothers. She was a carefree girl whose flame-red hair and emerald-green eyes were constantly admired and remarked upon. Both her parents were keen amateur painters and they encouraged a certain Bohemianism in their daughter. Bertha moved to Duluth in 1890 and declared herself to be an artist. Only five years later, in 1895, did she get around to enrolling in the Frank Holme

The Pagoda, *Bertha Lum, 1909*

School of Illustration in Chicago, as well as taking classes at the Art Institute of Chicago. Later Bertha studied stained glass with Anne Weston, a friend of the master of the American art nouveau stained glass movement, Louis Comfort Tiffany, and the woman who designed the stained glass for the White City at the Columbia Exposition in Chicago in 1893.

The Expo of 1893 was crucial for Bertha's artistic development. She attended the exhibition of Japanese prints and woodblock cuts held as part of the fair and was captivated and immensely impressed by what she saw. Bertha began to study American artist and art critic Arthur Wesley Dow's seminal 1899 book *Composition*, which specifically praised Japanese woodcuts. From there she discovered the work of Ernest Fenollosa, the American historian of Japanese art who was teaching at Tokyo's Imperial University and had helped found the Tokyo School of Fine Arts.[398] She also closely read the writings of another American *Japaniste* Lafcadio Hearn, whose deep study of Japanese culture and society, especially the country's legends and ghost stories, were highly influential on her.

In 1903 Bertha married Burt Lum, a successful Minneapolis lawyer, and they spent their seven-week honeymoon primarily in Japan. It seems certain the trip was Bertha's deepest wish and Burt was happy to please her and tag along. Once in Tokyo she sought out a printmaker to teach her the *ukiyo-e* technique. *Ukiyo-e*, or "pictures of the floating world," were a style of Japanese painting and woodblock prints that originally depicted Tokyo's pleasure districts during the Edo Period (seventeenth to nineteenth centuries). They featured images of female beauties; *kabuki* actors and *sumo* wrestlers; scenes from history and traditional folk tales; landscapes; flora and fauna; and erotica. In a Tokyo art shop Bertha found a set of traditional Japanese woodcutting tools with which she experimented once the newly-weds returned to their new family home in Minneapolis.

But clearly Japan was more than just a passing interest for Bertha. In 1907 she returned once again for a prolonged fourteen-week sojourn. Through contacts at Tokyo's Imperial Art School she was introduced to the Yokohama block cutter Igami Bonkutsu.[399] Bertha worked in his studio for two months, learning how to cut woodblocks. Through Bonkutsu she met the printer Nishimura Kamakichi and studied in his studio for a further four weeks. Kamakichi allowed her to spend the month observing his young apprentices colouring in prints.

Once again Lum returned to Minneapolis and family life, though she kept experimenting with her woodcuts and stained glass. Burt's law practice continued to be successful and, in 1911, she decided to take her two young daughters, Catherine Balliet Lum and Eleanor Bettina "Peter" Lum, to Tokyo for six months over the winter. Though Bertha had

398   Arthur Wesley Dow, *Composition: A Series of Exercises in Art Structure for the Use of Students and Teachers* (Garden City, New York: Doubleday, Page & Co., 1899). Dow was also Professor of Fine Arts in Teachers College, Columbia University New York City, and had formerly been an instructor in art at the Pratt Institute in New York.
399   A Japanese master carver (1875-1933).

Passing Crowds, *Bertha Lum, 1922*

diligently learnt how to both carve and print she decided that for speed, and because it was also traditional, she would hire carvers and printers and work collaboratively. This naturally did produce a larger body of work more rapidly than she could hope to achieve working alone. In 1912 Bertha was the only foreign artist to appear in the Tenth Annual Art Exhibition in Tokyo.

Then it was back once more to America. Burt's practice had moved and so now they settled in California with homes in San Francisco and Los Angeles (where the Lums were reputedly Hollywood neighbours of Rudolph Valentino). The Lums lived for the best part of a decade in California. As well as woodcuts and block printing Bertha began diversifying into producing screens, which sold well to the Hollywood movie industry cognoscenti.

However, it appears that her marriage to Burt was in trouble. In 1922 Bertha decided to relocate to China on a more permanent basis. She took her children Catherine and Eleanor ("Peter") with her on the voyage via Tokyo and Weihaiwei. On her first sojourn in Peking she stayed for two years, returning to America in 1924 hoping to rekindle her marriage. But time apart from Burt had not improved things, and in 1927 she moved back to China. The couple divorced a year later. Bertha's studio in Peking was now a fresh start, and in more ways than just her personal life. Most of Bertha's original collection of woodcuts and block prints had been left in storage in Tokyo after she had returned to America. Her entire archive of years of work since 1911 was destroyed in the Great Kanto Earthquake of 1923 that devastated Tokyo.

After Bertha's divorce from Burt it seems she started using the surname "Lumn", adding an "n", at least professionally when she signed her artwork, although her children continued to be called Lum as before.

A Peking studio

Bertha's daughter Peter later wrote that, though her mother had visited Tokyo many times, she decided to settle in Peking because she wanted to learn more about Chinese woodblock printing.[400] By the time Bertha established her permanent studio in Peking in the mid-1920s she had already exhibited widely. She had displayed her work at the San Francisco International Exposition in 1915, as well as in galleries in New York, Washington DC, Minneapolis, Chicago, London, Paris, The Hague and, according to one American newspaper, 'various cities of the Orient.'

Woodcuts with Asian themes were popular with western galleries and the art-buying public at the time, so Bertha was in some demand. Her contemporaries, and competitors, included several other female artists with Asian connections. Lilian May Miller, a painter, woodblock printer and poet, had been born in Japan to American diplomat parents. Her work focused on representations of Japan and Korea. Another contemporary was Helen Hyde, an American

Lilian May Miller, 1918

etcher and engraver. Hyde had been introduced to *Japonisme* by the great French collector of Japanese art, Félix Régamey, who had spent time in China and Japan in the 1870s and had himself been an artist.[401] Hyde

400   Peter Lum, *Peking: 1950-1953* (London: Robert Hale, 1958), p.16.
401   Perhaps Régamey's best-known work inspired by China is *The Chinese Imperial Marriage at Pekin* (1872), which I believe is now in a private collection.

had gone on to study painting with the elderly master painter of the Kano School, Kano Tomonobu, who had spent time in France studying European painting, taught at the University of Tokyo and worked closely with Ernest Fenollosa.[402] Hyde had also sketched Chinese children in San Francisco's Chinatown before moving to settle in Japan with several brief sojourns in China. Certainly, her colour woodcuts are somewhat similar in inspiration and style to Lum's.

Several British women also worked in similar fields. Elizabeth Keith was Scottish. In her late twenties she travelled to China, Japan and Korea, and decided to settle for a decade in Tokyo. Her work, which often emphasised traditional Japanese and Korean costume and textiles, sold well in New York and London in the 1920s and 1930s. Similarly, the English artist Katharine Jowett produced many block prints of Chinese landscapes around Peking. Jowett, the daughter of a Wesleyan Methodist minister, was a generation younger than Lum or Helen Hyde (both born in the late 1860s while Jowett was born in 1890). Jowett had come to China in her early twenties, following a young Methodist missionary she thought she was in love with. It turned out she wasn't, but she stayed in Peking all the same. Instead, she married Hardy Jowett, a long-time member of the British community in Peking, an Old China Hand, Wesleyan Methodist, and former officer with the Chinese Labour Corps in World War One. Jowett's prints sold well between the wars in China among the foreign colony. She was not as prolific in her output as Lum, Hyde, Keith or Miller, and perhaps the relative scarcity of her work served to ultimately increase its value. Chairman Mao is said to have had a set of Jowett's prints in his study at Zhongnanhai in the 1950s, though where he acquired them from is something of a mystery. Were they already there and he liked and left them? Did he bring them with him? Did he ever even pay them any attention at all?

Bertha's first Peking studio in 1922 had been close to the Forbidden City in a courtyard house on a hutong that had once belonged to Prince Tzu, a son of the Daoguang Emperor. It was ideally situated to observe the last remaining symbols of imperial ceremony allowed in the new republic. Bertha's daughter Peter remembered standing outside the studio and watching a procession of much pomp pass by – it was the wedding

---

402 The Kano school of painting was the dominant style of painting from the late fifteenth century until the Meiji Period (i.e. 1868).

ceremony of the last emperor, Puyi.[403]

When Bertha returned to Peking in 1927 from California, she again settled close to the Forbidden City, establishing a new hutong studio. Although her work sold well in New York, California and London (and certainly gave her a helpful income), her most immediate and loyal market was Peking's foreign colony and sojourners passing through. She was good friends with Helen Burton, the American proprietor of The Camel's Bell store in the lobby of the Grand Hôtel de Pékin, who prominently displayed her work. She also knew the owners of many of the various art and curio stores, such as the Golden Dragon, that clustered in the lobby of Peking's other luxury hotel over in the Legation Quarter, the Grand Hotel des Wagons-Lits.

Bertha always lived near the Forbidden City though she was a constant visitor (as were so many of the foreign colony in the interwar years) to the Western Hills and the many, often dilapidated, temples. Temple weekends were all the rage. Helen Burton had one – the Temple of Flowering Fragrance – that she entertained at most weekends in the spring and summer. It was

China Boy, *Bertha Lum, 1904*

403 Wanrong, posthumously known as the Empress Xiaokemin, married Puyi on November 30, 1922. Wanrong died in prison at the age of thirty-nine in June 1946 from the effects of malnutrition and opium withdrawal.

considered one of the best invitations in town. Bertha also, with her children, took excursions to Mongolia.

And it was here in this studio near the Forbidden City that Bertha crafted her Madonna that, in 1930, caught the eye of His Excellency and Apostolic Representative Archbishop Celso Benigno Luigi Costantini. News that Costantini had purchased her portrait for his office made the newspapers back in America. Bertha was pictured, in her studio in Peking, in a kimono with short bobbed hair. It was perhaps the peak of her career in China, led to several commissions and

Peking Dust, *Bertha Lum, 1924*

boosted the price of her work at The Camel's Bell.

As for Bertha and her Madonna?

Bertha's reputation in Peking remained high throughout the 1930s. She was now in her sixties. In 1933 or thereabouts the Qing diplomat's daughter and former lady-in-waiting to Dowager Empress Ci Xi, Princess Der Ling, decided to write her memoirs, *Imperial Incense*, focussing on her time at the imperial court with Cixi. She commissioned Bertha to produce half a dozen colour illustrations (and some black and white woodblock-style prints) to accompany the book.[404]

The Japanese invasion of Peking in the summer of 1937 meant it was time to leave. It was also the case that Bertha's eyesight was beginning to deteriorate. She was now nearly seventy. Peter had married an English diplomat, Colin Crowe, and moved to Shanghai, from where she was to be evacuated from China in 1940. Bertha's other daughter Catherine

404 Princess Der Ling, *Imperial Incense* (New York: Dodd, Mead & Co., 1933).

married a Shanghai-born Italian, Antonio "Tony" Riva, who was very well known in the foreign colony and involved in the aeronautical business.

Bertha returned to the United States for the duration of the war, returning after the liberation of Peking and living with Catherine and Antonio, though no longer working. After 1949 things became increasingly difficult. Shortly before the communists took over the city Bertha had written to Peter reporting that they 'had no light and no water.' When the communists actually entered Peking she wrote that they seemed 'honest and efficient' and that life was continuing pretty much as usual.[405] But things weren't normal – in 1951 Antonio Riva, along with several other foreigners living in Peking, were accused of plotting to assassinate Chairman Mao and other senior communist leaders by bombing the viewing platform in Tiananmen Square during the 1950 National Day Parade. Although it appears there was no actual plot, Riva and a Japanese citizen, Ruichi Yamaguchi, were executed by firing squad.

Bertha, now entering her eighties, was living with Catherine who was naturally distraught. Her other daughter Peter was also back in China and living at the British Embassy with her husband who was the newly appointed Head of Chancery. Bertha was able to spend her days at the embassy though was not permitted to sleep there by order of the Kung An Chu public security bureau.[406] The heating at Catherine's house was cut off and Bertha was cold there. Peter wrote that her mother was now 'a very old lady, bewildered by the strange things that are happening in her once beloved Peking, and simply cannot understand why she is not allowed to spend even one night with us.'[407]

In 1953 Bertha eventually left China permanently with Catherine to settle in Genoa, Italy. She died in February 1954. Today Bertha Lum is rarely remembered. Prints and woodblocks come up for sale occasionally and sell for somewhere in the region of only US$500-US$600.

And her Madonna? Its final fate is unknown to me. However, the fate of the Holy See in China continued to intertwine with Bertha's life. The Holy See had compromised itself with the Nationalist government before the Sino-Japanese War by appointing Bishop Auguste Ernest

405 Lum, *Peking: 1950-1953*, p.17.
406 Gong An Ju, or the Public Security Bureau (PSB).
407 Lum, *Peking: 1950-1953*, p.39.

Pierre Gaspais as the 'Vatican's Representative *ad tempus* of the Holy See and of the Catholic Missions of Manchukuo to the Government of Manchukuo'. While the Vatican did not officially establish diplomatic relations with Japanese-occupied Manchuria, this step still annoyed Nanking as an effective recognition by Rome.[408] When the communists came to power in 1949, relations soured even further between the Vatican and Peking. The Riva trial, his execution and a life sentence handed to Tarcisio Martina, the regional apostolic prefect, led to the cessation of formal diplomatic relations between the People's Republic of China and the Holy See in 1951 and the Vatican's expulsion from China.[409]

So, was *The Madonna* still in China or had Archbishop Celso Costantini taken it with him when he left China to return to Rome in 1933? In 1953, Costantini was made a cardinal by Pius XII. He died in 1958. His beatification process to possible sainthood is currently ongoing and appears to be strongly supported within the church. Lum's Madonna does not appear in the catalogue of the Vatican Museums nor of the National Museum of China. To the best of my knowledge, Bertha Lum's *Madonna* is a lost work of art. Unless anyone knows differently?

---

408 The Vatican did not formally establish diplomatic recognition and ties with the Japanese puppet state of Manchukuo. However, this is widely believed to have happened due to an incorrect reference to such a recognition in Bernardo Bertolucci's 1987 movie *The Last Emperor*.

409 Martina was expelled from China in 1955 and died in Verona, Italy in 1961.

The Heiress, the Prince and White Russia in Peking: Barbara Hutton & Prince Mdivani (1934)

'Money alone can't bring you happiness, but money alone has not brought me unhappiness. I won't say my previous husbands thought only of my money, but it had a certain fascination for them.'
— Barbara Hutton

A whirlwind romance

By the time the heiress Barbara Hutton arrived in Peking in 1934 she was one of the most gossiped-about women in the world. Fabulously wealthy, newly married to the émigré Georgian Prince Mdivani and touring the world in style on an extended honeymoon. But though the world's newspapers carried almost daily updates on the heiress and the prince, they never seemed to have stopped and asked themselves: what were the couple really doing in Peking? It had been a whirlwind year…

In March 1934, the wonderfully named American newspaper columnist Oscar Odd ("OO") McIntyre tried to list the things that made the city of New York "New York-ish". It was a very Damon Runyon-ish sort of list and included –

Coffee drinkers at Lindy's
Flea circuses
Dawn stay-outs at Reuben's
The Arnold Rothstein murder
The *New Yorker* magazine
Pinkish cocktails
Bowery breadlines
Paul Whiteman's band
The ushers at the Roxy…

And… 'Barbara Hutton's romance'.[410]

That same month the American newspapers were assiduously following the love life of the fabulously wealthy Woolworth retail empire heiress and "Million Dollar Baby" Barbara Hutton, the only news story that seemed able to compete with the continuing drama of the Great Depression. Indeed, Barbara Hutton's romantic antics appeared to be, along with Hollywood movies and the three-ringed circus, a major way of escaping the drabness of the Depression. In what seemed to be a whirlwind romance, "Babe" (a nickname Hutton always hated) had just married

410   OO McIntyre's 'New York Day By Day' column was syndicated widely but this version from the *Miami Daily News*, March 11, 1934.

Prince Alexis "Alec" Mdivani, the second-youngest of a once-wealthy and prominent Georgian family. Mdivani's father had been a former *aide-de-camp* to Tsar Nicholas II of Russia. The family had been forced to flee the Bolsheviks and live in exile as White Russian émigrés.

Mdivani claimed to be a prince, though it was a contestable claim – princes, counts, countesses, dukes and duchesses fleeing the Bolsheviks were ten-a-penny and their provenance invariably dubious. Hutton though really was one of the wealthiest women in the world, dubbed the "poor little rich girl" after the Noël Coward song, and the "five-and-ten-cent-store-heiress" after the Bing Crosby hit.[411] She was not yet twenty-three.

Prince Mdivani was not quite thirty. He was the most famous of the clan the American press dubbed the "marrying Mdivanis", who all strove quite deliberately and determinedly to make good matches essentially as a family business. Alexis's older sister Nina had married a Stanford professor. His eldest brother Serge had married the actress Pola Negri, and then, with a degree of callousness quite unmatched, calmly divorced her when she lost her fortune in the 1929 Wall Street Crash. Serge then married the opera singer Mary McCormic. The second-eldest Mdivani brother, David, had married the actress Mae Murray, bankrupted her, and then begun an affair with the French cabaret star Arletty in Paris. Alexis's younger sister Isabelle Roussadana (or "Roussie" to the family) married the Spanish painter Josep Maria Sert. Alexis himself had married the heiress Louise Astor van Alen, a member of the super-rich Astor clan, in 1931, but the relationship had not gone well. Then the prince met the five-and-ten-cent-store heiress sunbathing in Biarritz.

It seems that, though an Astor, Louise was not quite rich enough for Mdivani tastes. Alexis's sister Roussie actively sought to break up the couple and encouraged Alexis to trade up to the wealthier Hutton. She engineered it so that Alexis could seduce Hutton (who was a good and close friend of Louise's) and then marry the heiress, figuring this would greatly increase the combined Mdivani family wealth. Hutton, Astor van Alen and the Mdivanis were all part of a constantly moving high-society party that had eventually pitched up in San Sebastian, Spain. There Roussie

411   Coward wrote *Poor Little Rich Girl* for his 1925 musical revue *On With the Dance.* Crosby had a hit with *I Found a Million Dollar Baby (in a Five and Ten Cent Store)* in 1931, though it had been previously sung by Fanny Brice and others.

arranged for Louise and her family to catch Alexis in the act of seducing Hutton in a guest cottage at the estate where they were all staying. If not quite *in flagrante delicto*, it was apparently quite close. Though the stuff of farcical B-movies, Roussie's plan actually worked. The couple were caught getting up to something naughty in the cottage. Hutton fled to Paris, distraught and embarrassed. Louise separated from Alexis after getting a "quickie divorce" in The Hague. Then, after Roussie had pretty much blackmailed Hutton by saying she would tell the newspapers she was a woman of easy virtue, Barbara agreed to marry Alexis.

Their engagement was announced from Bangkok in the Kingdom of Siam, where Barbara had gone to avoid publicity. Indeed, she intended to marry Mdivani in Bangkok. Hutton had previously visited the Dutch East Indies island of Bali. The island was all the rage then as a tropical paradise and she followed in the footsteps of Charlie Chaplin, Noël Coward, the Austrian author Vicki Baum (who was also for a time a Peking sojourner), the dance specialist Beryl de Zoete and others.[412] Staying in the artist village of Ubud, she had fallen violently in love with the German painter and Bali enthusiast Walter Spies. It was made clear to Barbara that an affair was not possible, as Spies was openly gay, but they became good friends. Spies then accompanied her to Cambodia to see Angkor Wat. So taken was the heiress with Bali that she commissioned Spies to build her a bungalow with a swimming pool on a lot next door to his house in Ubud. However, by the time it was finished, Hutton had long moved on, both geographically and mentally. Still, Spies was (when compared to Europe or the United States) relatively close by on Bali and he agreed to be Mdivani's best man at the Bangkok wedding, though they'd never met. It transpired however that Hutton was still underage in terms of consent. Her guardians were never going to approve such a flagrantly money-grabbing match and so the whole thing was called off, leaving Spies to get the steamer back to Bali and the Mdivanis to work out a new plan.

All that was required was for Barbara to not change her mind about the prince until she reached the age of twenty-one. She achieved both these

---

412 As well as a ballet dancer, dance historian and choreographer, Beryl de Zoete was also the translator of Italo Svevo and Alberto Moravia into English, as well as the wife of the British Library's top Orientalist and translator Arthur Waley (who famously never travelled to either China or anywhere else in Asia).

things and the couple were married on June 22, 1933, in the St. Alexander Nevsky Russian Orthodox Church in Paris. Though not completely happy with the match, Barbara's father provided a US$1 million dowry. It was reported that Alexis was given a US$250,000 marriage settlement and awarded a US$50,000 a year allowance, neither being too shabby in 1933 money.[413] This was reportedly a better deal than he had had from the Astors when he married Louise. The prince and the heiress then boarded an ocean liner to Manhattan to celebrate with a party for eight hundred guests at the Ritz-Carlton Hotel.

Why Hutton married "His Highness Prince" Mdivani is not totally clear. The Russian émigré historian Lev Lyubimov called it the "Mdivani spell".[414] Alexis was certainly considered handsome with thick black hair, a determined stride, a tennis player's physique, and expensively capped teeth. Hutton caused a minor storm in the American media by stating that 'His expertise in wise spending and in gaining access to the choicest circles is one of the reasons why I married him.'[415] This was interpreted by most as being a snub to American men and East Coast high society fops, while others, higher up the social scale on both sides of the Atlantic, rather raised their eyebrows given that many saw the Mdivanis as basically fraudulent and opportunistic Russian émigrés, and not genuine Russian émigré high society at all.

Perhaps now, with hindsight, we can better understand Hutton and her disastrous choices in men throughout her life. Her mother committed suicide (over the pain of mastoiditis, said some; over her husband's constant philandering, said others) when she was just five years old. Their "family home" was an apartment in the Plaza Hotel in Manhattan. After her mother's death Hutton's father moved the family to Los Angeles where he largely ignored his young daughter. After five years she was sent to live with various cousins. At just five years old, inheriting one third of the total Woolworth fortune, she became one of America's wealthiest people and a constant fixture of speculation and gossip in the newspapers. Her

413   'Princess Mdivani', *New York Daily News*, June 17, 1934, p.20.

414   Mdivani's title is in quotation marks as it is not clear he had any genuine entitlement to it! Lyubimov (himself a Russian émigré and journalist after 1917 who opted to return to the USSR after World War Two) quoted in Rusudan Daushvili, 'Alexis Mdivani: "The Charming Prince"', *Georgian Journal*, December 11, 2014.

415   C David Heymann, *Poor Little Rich Girl: The Life and Legend of Barbara Hutton* (New York: Arrow Books, 1991), p.99.

views and experiences of people, especially men, were perhaps not the most normal or well-balanced.

Slipping into Peking

The newly-wed Mdivanis' trip to the Far East in early 1934 was billed in most of the newspapers as a year-long round-the-world honeymoon, though it actually began seven months after their Paris wedding. Alexis was already in Japan and Barbara sailed there to meet him. Mdivani had already visited India and Saigon. The couple reunited in Yokohama and travelled together to Tokyo. With Barbara was her young cousin James "Jimmy" Donahue, already an emerging playboy and something of a court jester to New York's wealthy elite. He was himself a regular fixture

Mdivanis Visiting In Peiping After Reunion At Tokyo

—*Associated Press Photo*

BAIKO   PRINCESS MDIVANI   PRINCE MDIVANI

on the society and gossip pages, rumoured to be bisexual.[416] Jimmy, the son of Barbara's mother's sister, and only three years older than Hutton, was her favourite relation and they got along well. He had also inherited a decent-sized portion of the Woolworth estate and was independently wealthy.

Reuniting in Japan, the celebrity Mdivanis were photographed by the Associated Press in Tokyo chatting with Baiko, a noted *onnagata* (female impersonator) in the Kabuki theatre.[417] Hutton was now referred to as the "Princess Mdivani" almost as often as the Woolworth Heiress.

The Mdivanis arrived in Peking by train from Tientsin on February 8, 1934. Their arrival had not been pre-announced or promoted. The China coast newspapers had no idea that the newly-weds were coming to town. And so, at first, it seemed that their visit to China might pass unnoticed, something that would have been impossible in the United States or Europe. But a lone Japanese newspaperman had decided to linger at the Peking Railway Station that chilly day. He realised who the couple were and, sensing a story, quickly asked Barbara Hutton the first question that came to mind – if she planned to invest any of her millions in China? The answer, if any, was unreported.[418]

But it was recorded that the prince looked dapper in a dark suit and overcoat with a trilby hat, while Hutton was swathed entirely in black fur – coat, stole, hat. They were accompanied by Jimmy, six servants and fifteen monogrammed Louis Vuitton luggage trunks, having travelled in a private coach, and were collected at the station by a fleet of chauffeured cars – this was how the Mdivani-Huttons travelled thinking they would

---

416   We should note here, as this is a book about Peking sojourners, that it was widely believed that somewhat later, after World War Two, Donahue had an affair with a woman also well known as a sojourner in pre-war Peking, Wallis Spencer, by then having moved on to become Wallis Simpson and, at the time of her supposed liaison with Donahue, the Duchess of Windsor.

417   Onoe Baiko VII, born Sizo Terashima (1915-1995), was Japan's leading post-war *onnagata* and designated a Living National Treasure in 1968. The skill was traditionally passed from father to son. Baiko was the illegitimate heir of Kikugoro VI, who adopted him to preserve the family heritage. Baiko first performed at the age of six, becoming a household name after appearing on television after the war.

418   'Mdivanis Arrive in China's Old Capital', *Jefferson City Post-Tribune* (Missouri), February 9, 1934, p.9.

attract no attention.[419] No official announcement of arrival, perhaps, but an entourage that was rather hard to miss if you happened to be at the Peking Railway Station.

Now, alert to their presence in the city, all the local newspaper correspondents and stringers trailed Hutton and Mdivani around Peking sensing a payday. A mischievous rumour had started that Hutton was pregnant. She wasn't, and vehemently denied it, though speculation remained rife anyway. However, it was true that the couple planned to stay in Peking for several weeks and were, by mid-February, living in Peking's most exclusive hotel, '...accepting few invitations to social affairs... and shunning publicity.'[420]

They established themselves at the Grand Hôtel de Pékin with a suite of rooms, according to the Associated Press, settling 'in the bridal suite and ten additional rooms at a daily cost of two hundred gold dollars.'[421] Quite good digs! They spent money in style – Hutton had a long white ermine cape made by Helen Burton's The Camel's Bell store in the Grand Hôtel's lobby at some considerable cost, even with the favourable exchange rate to the American dollar.[422]

But why were the couple in Peking at all? And why had they come as incognito as an heiress, an exiled prince, a playboy and their enormous retinue could? Among those most excited about their arrival were members of Peking's White Russian émigré community and particularly its Georgian component. Men in supposedly pre-Bolshevik Georgian Army uniforms, claiming to be exiled Georgian nobles and senior Tsarist military officers, arrived regularly in the lobby of the Grand Hôtel de Pékin, many stating that they had served with, or known, Alexis's father, General Zakhari Mdivani. Bouquets of roses were left at reception for the princess.

While the prince ensconced himself in all-day meetings with the Russian and Georgian exiles, Barbara toured Peking. Like so many

---

419   And indeed this was low-key for Barbara Hutton who mostly travelled with at least fifty trunks.

420   'Barbara Hutton Not Expecting Child', *The Boston Globe*, February 17, 1934, p.2.

421   'Mdivanis in Shanghai', *The Salt Lake Tribune*, March 3, 1934, p.19.

422   Hutton did not care to have the stoats' delicate bellies used in the cape and so they were set aside. Helen Foster Snow claimed she grabbed them to make herself a short ermine cape for just the cost of the labour required – $20. Helen Foster Snow, *My China Years* (London: Harrap, 1984), p.86.

ARRIVE IN CHINA—Princess Barbara Hutton Mdivani and her Georgian noble husband as they arrived at Peiping. The pair is on a world tour and will remain in China for some time, having arrived there from Japan. (Associated Press.)

other wealthy, and not so wealthy, European and American sojourners before her, Hutton fell in love with Chinese antiques and curios. She met Princess Rong Ling, known in English as Nellie and partly raised in France where her father had been the Qing dynasty's ambassador, and was partly advised by her on some purchases. Rong Ling, it seems, put Hutton into contact with 'impecunious courtiers' selling off looted items from the Forbidden City and elsewhere.[423] Hutton also pursued an interest in jade that she had cultivated as a young girl when she had met the owner of the exclusive San Francisco home furnishings and home décor store Gump's, which specialised in exotic rugs, porcelains, silks, bronzes and jades sourced from China and Japan. Every year the store's proprietor, Alfred Livingston Gump, himself a fan of all things Oriental, sent his buyers to Japan and China with orders to bring back plenty of

---

423 See Karl E. Meyer & Shareen Blair Brysac, *The China Collectors: America's Century-Long Hunt for Asian Art Treasures* (New York: St Martin's Press, 2015), p.246.

rugs, ceramics, textiles, statues and jades to sell to California's millionaires. Gump's customers had included the French actress Sarah Bernhardt and the American president, Franklin Delano Roosevelt.

White Russian machinations

If anyone asked what Mdivani was up to in China it was all just a romantic and pleasant honeymoon. Cousin Jimmy was simply tagging along as a friend of the couple, close relation of Barbara, and shopping companion. However, the reality was rather different. Jimmy had been added to the Hutton-Mdivani entourage to keep Barbara company while Alexis disappeared with the succession of shadowy Russian men who turned up at their hotels in Tokyo, Tientsin, Peking and, after Peking, Shanghai. Mdivani was meeting with the leaders of various White Russian émigré groups across Asia – first the small communities in British India and French Indo-China, and then the larger groups in Japan and China. These were controversial meetings, and therefore closed and secret.

Of course, China had become a home in exile to many thousands of Russian émigrés – those who would become collectively known as the "White Russians" – after the Bolshevik Revolution. The exact number of émigrés is unknown – somewhere between 800,000 and two million. Many went north and left Russia through the Baltic States and Finland, eventually destined for western Europe, and perhaps on to America. Others reached the Black Sea ports and boarded ships to Turkey and Constantinople (today's Istanbul). A third group, numbering around 250,000 men, women and children, went east between 1918 and 1922, crossing the Sino-Russian or Sino-Mongolian borders into Manchuria and down into northern and eastern China. Others went as far as you could go on Russian soil across a frozen Lake Baikal to Vladivostok and then on rusting, crowded and leaky tramp steamers to Japan, Korea and back into China. Safe, but now in exile in Harbin, Tientsin, Dalian, Shanghai and Peking, the émigrés were stateless, displaced and largely impoverished, far from their spiritual home, and politically disorganised.

It's been said that 'The Far East was the Wild West of the Russian diaspora. Some émigrés found an El Dorado there; others stumbled into their graves.'[424] Certainly White Russian politics in China was a chaotic mix of ideas and dreams, passions and pragmatisms. Some older exiles stayed loyal to their former political allegiances – Social Democrats, Mensheviks, Constitutional Democratic "Kadets", even the odd anarchist or two. Most, though, including many of the former Tsarist soldiers and officers in exile, gravitated towards extreme anti-communist movements that invariably combined a hatred of Bolshevism, Stalin and the USSR with older Russian hatreds such as anti-Semitism. A combined hatred of Jews and communists blended with a desire to restore the monarchy moulded into a peculiar variety of White Russian fascism. Within these organisations were myriad variations who advocated the return of the Romanov Royal Family, or the ascendancy of other royal aspirants; the primacy of the Russian Orthodox Church; Siberian, Baltic, Crimean, Ukrainian independence; or a total reconstitution of the Russian Empire. And there were others who believed that democracy would eventually come to Russia, that the greater threat to their Motherland came from militaristic Japan, Nazi Germany, the appeasement-leaning Western Europeans, and that there should be a reconciliation with Stalin to preserve the Russian state as a unitary whole. Some apparent pragmatists hedged their bets – applying for Soviet passports but remaining in exile for the time being to see how things played out (the so-called "radishes" – Red on the outside, White on the inside).

The only two things that were crystal clear in the mid-1930s émigré community were that Stalin was solidly in power in the Kremlin, and that the legion of Russian émigré factions possessed a unique ability to fight each other rather than any common enemy. While the majority of émigré organisations globally opposed the Soviet government in Moscow, there was another dimension to the thinking of the Chinese-based émigrés – namely the massively contentious issue of whether or not to recognise the Japanese-annexed territory of Manchuria. Occupied in 1932 and renamed Manchukuo, the territory was staunchly anti-Soviet. However, any formal White Russian acceptance of Manchukuo was bound to enrage the Chinese Nationalist government in Nanking and perhaps lead to problems for the Russian émigrés in China and their precarious status.

---

424 John J. Stephan, *The Russian Fascists: Tragedy and Farce in Exile 1925-1945* (London: Hamish Hamilton, 1978), p.31.

And, in 1934, recognition was a possibility and a serious debate. Large numbers of Russian émigrés lived in Manchukuo by default – Harbin, Dairen, Hsinking and elsewhere right across from the Korean border and Gulf of Pechili to the Russian and Mongolian borders.[425] If Japan were to continue its expansionist policies by invading the resources-rich Soviet Far East from Manchukuo, which side would the White Russians support? A certain number of China-based groups were sympathetic to Japan, reasoning Tokyo might be able to defeat the Red Army and overthrow the Communist government in Moscow. Some of the exiled Russian groups were openly embracing fascistic and militaristic ideologies and forging alliances with both the Nazis and the Japanese militarists. According to Mdivani, other groups of émigré Russians would 'side with the Reds' to defend Russia, regardless of politics, against any and all invaders. Mdivani estimated émigré opinion to be divided approximately fifty-fifty.[426] He also knew that the divisions among the Russian émigré groups were being stoked by Soviet *agents provocateurs* who constantly meddled and tried to influence émigré politics.

It was clear that a generally respected figure was needed who might be able to bring consensus to a White Russian émigré community described as 'congenitally fractious'.[427] There was increasing extremism and polarisation among the émigré movements – there had been demonstrations, counterdemonstrations and a few punch-ups between factions. Proto-potential and invariably self-styled leaders were emerging – too many to count. Men such as Grigory Mikhaylovich Semyonov (or Semenov), a Cossack from the Transbaikal in Russia's Far East who had settled in Nagasaki, Japan before moving to Harbin. He then spent some time in America before returning to China once again, living in Tientsin and taking a Japanese government pension. He had forged close relations with Tokyo's intelligence services in China, working for the puppet Manchukuo Emperor Puyi (the "Last Emperor") in Manchukuo's capital Hsinking. Or Konstantin Vladimirovich Rodzaevsky who founded a Russian Fascist Party in Manchuria, an organisation that was arguably more obsessed with supposed Jewish conspiracies than Stalin's occupation

---

425   Now the Bohai Gulf.
426   John B. Powell, 'From Across the Sea', *Chicago Tribune*, April 22, 1934, p.16.
427   Stephan, *The Russian Fascists,* p.45.

of the Kremlin. After the Japanese occupation of Manchuria, Rodzaevsky and his party were to be especially favoured by Tokyo.

The Prince & Princess Mdivani, 1934

But Prince Mdivani, though often mocked in the western newspapers, was seen by most White Russians as one of the most high-profile Russian émigrés worldwide, from a well-respected and heavily decorated military family that supposedly had had close ties to the last Tsar. He it was who might be able to first assess which way the majority of the Chinese and Japanese White Russian movement was leaning, and then what the implications of these alliances were. Whether Mdivani was chosen for this role by some émigré group in the major centres of White Russian politics in Paris or New York is not clear. He may have simply assumed the role of rapporteur himself. Either way, this was the primary reason Prince Mdivani had brought his young bride Barbara Hutton on a "honeymoon" to China and to Peking. Mdivani may have been generally presented by the European and American press as a frivolous playboy, marrying heiresses and travelling the world in style but, within the White

Russian world, he was seen as potentially the figure that émigré groups could rally around and forge a common position.

It never happened though. Semyonov was largely impotent, fêted by the Japanese but bereft of followers. Rodzaevsky and the Russian Fascist Party collaborated with the Japanese authorities, but mostly in kidnappings, extortion and drug trafficking. They became sanctioned gangsters. In Peking, as well as in Shanghai and Tientsin, one-man-band hucksters and fraudsters, as well as criminal gangs ostensibly claiming to be patriotic Russians, proliferated. There could be no great coming together. Mdivani could do nothing and so left Peking for a brief stop in Shanghai and then a boat to Europe. By the outbreak of war in China, the White Russian groups had mostly collapsed, without funds or members. Many ended up collaborating with, and controlled by, the Japanese.

After China

As for Barbara Hutton and Prince Alexis Mdivani's marriage, there wasn't much left after China either. By May 1934 the newspapers were reporting that Hutton was in a nursing home in London, probably with acute depression, while Mdivani was noted to be out on the town hosting parties at the famous Ivy Restaurant and dancing at Quaglino's. It seemed the marriage was on the rocks already. The newspapers asked quite bluntly if Hutton was 'Tired of Being a Princess?'[428]

It seemed so. In June 1934 it was announced that Hutton would tour continental Europe while "Prince" Mdivani remained in London, mostly intending to play polo. Hutton claimed to still be ill and was hiding out with her father in the Dorchester Hotel on Park Lane. The newspapers claimed her problem was not necessarily medical, but rather was Mdivani, "the million dollar stomach ache."[429] The rift grew until they finally divorced in Reno, Nevada, in March 1935 after just twenty-two months of marriage. Prince Mdivani retained a quite substantial post-divorce cash settlement.

428   A widely syndicated article, but this version, 'Tired of Being a Princess?', from *Corsicana Semi-Weekly Light* (Texas), June 1, 1934, p.11.

429   The "million dollar stomach ache" line was used by many commentators and journalists. This reference from 'Their Rift is Ended', *New York Daily News*, June 4, 1934, p.3.

Jimmy Donahue back in Manhattan after Peking with actress Dorothy Dilley, 1934

Barely six months later, in August 1935, it was reported that Prince Mdivani had died instantly in a car accident on the Spanish border near Perpignan in France. A female companion in the car, the twenty-three-year-old German Baroness Maud Thyssen, was badly injured.

By the time she was informed of Mdivani's death Hutton had already remarried the British-born American entrepreneur and racing car driver Count Kurt Haugwitz-Reventlow, with whom she was to have her only child, a son named Lance. That marriage lasted a few years, followed by an affair with the aviation millionaire Howard Hughes (while he was simultaneously engaged to Katharine Hepburn). In 1942 Hutton married the Hollywood star Cary Grant. When that marriage also failed she moved back to Europe and, in 1948, married Igor Troubetzkoy, a race car driver and another White Russian émigré "prince". When he sued Hutton for divorce, she reportedly attempted suicide. Her next marriage was to the Dominican diplomat, and playboy, Porfirio Rubirosa. The journalist and author Phyllis Battelle famously noted that 'The bride, for her fifth wedding, wore black and carried a scotch-and-soda.'[430] The couple stayed together till 1959 despite Rubirosa's continuing and well-known affair with the Hungarian actress Zsa Zsa Gabor. Hutton then married the German tennis star Baron Gottfried von Cramm who was also killed in a car crash, and finally, while living in Tangier, she wed Prince Pierre Raymond Doan Vinh na Champassak, whose family were royalty in French Indo-China. Her last marriage survived just two years.

From 1966 Hutton lived alone and isolated, distraught after her only son Lance was killed in an aeroplane crash in 1972. Taxes, profligate husbands, her own generosity, and some bad investments, had all severely depleted her fortune. Hutton's final years were spent in Los Angeles in a suite at the Beverly Wilshire Hotel where she died in 1976, aged sixty-six. Some reports said that at the time of her death she was down to her last US$3,500 cash.

And all those Peking baubles?

Still, it seems Hutton never lost her taste for Chinese curios and antiques, many of which she acquired in Peking during her 1934 sojourn, occupying herself with shopping while the prince held court at the Grand Hôtel de Pékin. At her second wedding, to Count Kurt Haugwitz-Reventlow, the Princess Rong Ling was a prominent wedding guest and still advising the heiress on purchases. Hutton's huge jewellery collection included several jade pieces bought in Peking in 1934, and more jade purchased later via dealers. Though her final estate contained very little cash money, her jewellery collection was virtually intact.

Since 1985 various items have come up for sale and some items appearing at auction appear to date to her brief Peking sojourn. In 1988 a fine carved jade bracelet was sold at auction at Sotheby's Hong Kong for HK$7.4 million. Other fine pieces have surfaced via the Mdivani family – in 1988 a jadeite bead necklace by Cartier from the estate of Princess Nina Mdivani was auctioned in Geneva and then appeared for sale again in Hong Kong in 1994. It transpired that Barbara had given the necklace to her childhood friend Louise van Alen, Alexis's first wife, who later

430   Phyllis Battelle, 'Dazed Babs Hutton, Latin Lover Wed', *The Times* (Shreveport, Louisiana), December 31, 1953, p.19.

passed it on to Nina Mdivani. In 1994 it sold for double its previous hammer price, achieving an astonishing US$4.2 million; a worldwide record sum for a piece of jadeite jewellery at the time.[431]

It seems that while Barbara Hutton's taste in men was never very good, her judgement in Chinese jade, discovered while she was sojourning briefly in Peking, was far, far better.

431 Approximately US$730 million in 2020 terms. Jadeite is the rarer, more valuable, form of jade.

Two American Ladies in Peking:
Ellen Newbold La Motte & Emily Crane Chadbourne
(1919)

MISS ELLEN N. LAMOTTE.

"I think when war is over I shall ask Miss La M. to go with me to the interior of China and hire a houseboat." [432]

432 Letter from Emily Crane Chadbourne to Gertrude Stein, August 4, 1915. In Cynthia Wachtell's introductory biography of Ellen La Motte, *The Backwash of War: An Extraordinary American Nurse in World War I* (Baltimore: Johns Hopkins University Press, 2019), p.71.

Sojourners with a cause

Ellen Newbold La Motte and Emily Crane Chadbourne sojourned in Peking as friends and companions for brief periods of time during and in the aftermath of World War One. They never stayed for very long and they never sought to seriously interact or ingratiate themselves with the foreign colony to any significant extent. Crane, a very wealthy woman, largely concerned herself with acquiring and collecting Chinese arts and crafts, most of which were later donated to American museums and institutions. Ellen La Motte at first used her time in Peking to process her emotions after having been a nurse on the frontlines in Europe. Then, together, they found a cause, one that would stay with them for a lifetime and across three continents – the campaign against opium.

Once they found their cause, the anti-opium campaign took them around the globe – to the League of Nations in Geneva, New York City, London and various world cities. They were among the primary campaigners against the opium trafficking trade, they were not afraid to lay the blame for its continuance at the door of national governments and they were vociferous and prolific in their outpourings against it. This was to be a lifelong cause for La Motte and a journey that began back in 1915 in war-torn Europe with a dream of visiting China some more peaceful day.

Winter and war

In the bitterly cold January of 1915, two American women who had remained in Paris after the outbreak of war were seriously considering the notion of enlisting in the war effort in some way. They discussed the possibility of driving ambulances in Belgium, or perhaps signing up as nurses on the Serbian Front.[433] Ellen Newbold La Motte, who was a Johns Hopkins-trained nurse, did join up and headed to the Front,

---

433 La Motte eventually served in France though the Serbian Front was a very popular destination with the more adventurous type of middle-class women looking to help, even though it was a rather little-known campaign back in Britain and America. In *Brideshead Revisited* Evelyn Waugh has Charles Ryder's dead mother referred to as having served there – 'She went to Serbia with the Red Cross in World War I and was killed there.'

despite her lifelong fear of guns. Emily Crane Chadbourne did not. Having been witness to their many long and often passionate debates around supporting the war effort, their friend Gertrude Stein, then living in Paris, writing and acquiring works of art, would write a "little novelette" story, as she described it (actually a quite experimental piece of writing), about Ellen and Emily's respective decisions titled *How Could They Marry Her.*[434]

La Motte joined the American Ambulance Service and served in a French field hospital in Belgium. What she saw of the supposedly "Great" war disgusted her and was to affect her deeply. She kept a diary, released extracts from it in the *Atlantic Monthly,* and later turned those extracts into a book, *The Backwash of War* (1916). La Motte's graphically realistic depictions of the horrors of the Front were too much for many readers, particularly those in her native America, then in 1917 only just tentatively entering the war. *The Backwash of War* was largely suppressed ('through fear of the effect that it would have upon

Ellen La Motte serving in Belgium, 1915

civilian morale'[435]), and not republished again until 1934. In her story *How Could They Marry Her* Gertrude Stein had employed surreal voice-montage techniques in order to maintain a distance from the awful battlefield carnage. La Motte, by contrast, adopted harsh realism and unelaborate prose to convey the carnage of the trenches:

> Rochard died today. He had gas-gangrene. His thigh, from knee to buttock, was torn out by a piece of German shell. It was an interesting

434 *How Could They Marry Her* (1915), contained in Gertrude Stein, *Reflection on the Atomic Bomb: Volume I of the Previously Uncollected Writings of Gertrude Stein*, edited by Robert Bartlett Haas (Los Angeles: Black Sparrow Press, 1974).
435 'Skygac's Column', *The Toiler* (Cleveland, Ohio), March 26, 1920, p.2.

case, because the infection had developed so quickly. The Médicin Chef took a curette, a little scoop, and scooped away the dead flesh, the dead muscles, the dead nerves, the dead blood-vessels. The piece of shell in his skull had made one eye blind. There had been a haemorrhage into the eyeball, which was all red and sunken, and the eyelid would not close over it, so the red eye stared and stared into space.[436]

Some reviewers compared her to another young American writer who had volunteered to drive ambulances in the war, Ernest Hemingway.[437]

La Motte's friend, Emily Crane Chadbourne, reunited with her once Ellen had completed her war service. Together they decided to fulfil their long-held idea of travelling to the Far East, specifically to China, and to sojourn for a time in Peking. It was an idea they had discussed back in Paris before the start of the war but that had never come to fruition. Together in Peking the pair began to process the atrocities of the Great War and come to appreciate the high-handed imperial attitudes of the "Great Powers" towards weakened early Republican China. As they began to explore the city's culture and arts, they came to see opium as the greatest post-war scourge on China. In opium they were to find their joint lifelong cause and launched themselves into a long career campaigning against the trade.

Ellen and Emily

Ellen Newbold La Motte was born in Louisville, Kentucky in 1873. Her parents were the locally well-known Ferdinand Fairfax La Motte, a wealthy businessman, and his wife Ellen (whose maiden name was Newbold). She attended the fashionable Miss Rebecca Powell's School in Arlington, Virginia. For a while in her teenage years, and while her father was suffering from some business troubles, Ellen was sent to live with a friend of the family, the Wilmington, Delaware industrialist Alfred Du Pont. She then studied at the Johns Hopkins Training School for Nurses

436   Ellen Newbold La Motte, *The Backwash of War: The Human Wreckage of the Battlefield as Witnessed by an American Hospital Nurse* (New York: GP Putnam's, 1916), p.49.
437   By John H. Johnston, *English Poetry of the First World War* (Princeton: Princeton University Press, 1964), p.78.

(where she appears to have first met her fellow student Gertrude Stein) and, after graduating in 1902, became a nurse in a Baltimore tuberculosis hospital. After some years nursing she decided to travel. With financial assistance from a relative, Ellen went to live in Paris in 1913 where she published her first book, the textbook *The Tuberculosis Nurse, Her Function and her Qualifications.*[438] It was in Paris that she met Emily Chadbourne and once again Gertrude Stein, who had been living in the French capital since 1903. Stein was a well-known "out" lesbian.

Mrs. Emily Crane Chadbourne.

Emily, shortly after she left America for Europe, 1908

Born in Chicago, Emily Rockwell Crane was the daughter of the multimillionaire Richard Teller "Old Iron Man" Crane and Mary Prentice Crane. The family fortune derived from their Chicago plumbing and bathroom equipment business. Emily was raised in privilege and her parents were major patrons of the arts in the city. Emily married Thomas Chadbourne in November 1896 in Chicago, but the marriage was a disaster. Chadbourne fell hopelessly in love with his dentist's wife. Emily charged him with desertion in 1905 and subsequently left for Europe to escape the inevitable gossip and tabloid newspaper speculation. Thomas was not, it seems, a gallant man and, having eloped with the dentist's wife, asserted that it was Emily who had deserted him! It was terribly embarrassing for Emily, but her sizeable stipend of Crane family money meant she was free to indulge her passion for buying and collecting art across the Atlantic, away from the Chicago

438   The book was extremely well-regarded in the medical community at the time. Ellen Newbold La Motte, RN, *The Tuberculosis Nurse, Her Function and her Qualifications* (New York: GP Putnam's, 1915).

society gossips. In 1914 it was reported in the American newspapers that she might be remarrying, this time to Baron de Vaux of Normandy. The marriage never seems to have happened – it appears the Baron, previously married himself, was unable to obtain a divorce nor dispensation from the Pope. That appears to have been the end of men for Emily.

In Paris she met Stein and La Motte. From the moment they met it seems Ellen and Emily became a couple and are always thereafter described as 'best friends', 'confidantes' or 'close companions.' Ellen never married while Emily never remarried. They lived together effectively as a couple for the rest of their lives.

Lamotte—"Peking Dust," 1919. This is alsa a pleasant book to read concerning manners and customs in Peking. It is written by a woman.

A not overly helpful review of Peking Dust in an American newspaper, 1920

Amid the dust of Peking

While Ellen had been nursing in Belgium, Emily had been living in London, in a Tudor house near Park Lane, hosting fund-raising piano concerts for the war effort. By early 1916 Ellen and Emily had reunited, left France, and returned to the United States to visit relatives and friends in Chicago. From the west coast they set sail for the Far East in 1916. They reached China by late summer. However, their attempted flight from the Great War was not successful – from China in 1919 La Motte told the *Oakland Tribune*, 'I decided I must somehow altogether get away from it *(World War One)*. But where could I go? China seemed the most likely place. But I ran into the same old war that I thought I had left behind.'[439] La Motte had seen echoes of Europe in Asia, echoes that angered her and that she fleshed out in her book on the opium problem, *Peking Dust*.[440] In that book she argued that the European Great Powers were inveigling China into the war: 'The assurances from Europe, cabled daily to the Chinese press, that the Allies are fighting for liberty, for

439   'Ellen Newbold La Motte', *Oakland Tribune*, April 13, 1919, p.11.
440   Ellen Newbold La Motte, *Peking Dust* (New York: The Century Company, 1919).

justice, for civilization, for the protection of small nations, mean nothing to the Chinese. Such professions leave them cold.'[441]

La Motte came to realise that a major cause of the war in Europe was the continuing scramble for empire and "spheres of influence" in China: 'One thing stands out clearly . . . and that is that the European war had its origin in the Orient. Supremacy in the Orient is the underlying cause of the struggle that is rending Europe in twain. The world does not go to war for little stakes, for trifles. It fights for colossal stakes, worth gambling for.'[442]

The war in Europe aside, even while sojourning in faraway Peking Emily remained a popular topic in the Chicago gossip columns. In February 1917 the 'News of Chicago Society' column in the *Chicago Tribune* reported Emily 'still ransacking curio shops in China' though, apparently, intending to settle back in Chicago upon her return from the Far East.[443]

This talk of curio hunting perhaps makes the pair seem a little frivolous; two financially independent sojourners with little to do in China but shop. But this wasn't the case. Indeed both had early on set themselves against the stereotype of the "Peking Silhouette", coined by the authors Baron Léon Viktorovitch de Hoyer (by day the head of the Peking branch of the old Tsarist Banque Russo-Chinoise) and the French diplomat and comte Damien de Martel in their slightly scandalous comedic novel of Legation Quarter manners, *Silhouettes of Peking*. De Martel and de Hoyer lampooned the "silhouettes" of post-Great War Peking who led privileged and hedonistic lifestyles in the foreign clubs, hotels and racecourse of Peking, yet did no more than touch the surface of Chinese society:

> Peking is a city of officials, slightly formal and perhaps a trifle
> snobbish, but anyway clean-minded and agreeable to frequent. It is
> a casual and temporary agglomeration of people who have seen the
> world, have stayed in Paris and London; passed through Florence and
> Athens, played with politics in Petrograd or with finance in America;
> people who have crossed all the seas, made collections in the East and
> made love in Venice... but it is above everything else, a city that has

441 Ibid, p.27.
442 Ibid, p.201.
443 'News of Chicago Society', *Chicago Tribune*, February 11, 1917, p.vii.

given birth to a special type of human being... the Peking silhouette.[444]

Curio hunting aside, the vapid world of the Legation Quarter social set was not for Ellen and Emily. They were made of more serious stuff. And on this initial China sojourn the two women had found a shared passion – the campaign against opium.

La Motte first wrote about opium in *Peking Dust* and then shortly afterwards once again in her 1919 collection of essays, *Civilization: Tales of the Orient,* specifically in the essays 'Homesick' and 'Canterbury Chimes'.[445]

'Homesick' had first been published in *The Century Magazine*, which began as an Evangelical Christian and nationalistic publication in the nineteenth century, but had gradually moved towards more progressive ideas, embracing civil rights and a mild sort of socialism. 'Homesick' begins with a Chinese man straddling the border of the Shanghai International Settlement and the adjacent Chinese-controlled territory. La Motte makes the point:

> From this you will see that he had been standing with one foot in
> China, where opium traffic was prohibited, where heavy fines were
> attached to opium smoking and to opium buying, where heavy
> jail sentences were imposed upon those who smoked or bought
> opium, while the other foot, planted upon the ground of the Foreign
> Concession, assured him of his absolute freedom to buy opium in any

444   Damien de Martel & Léon de Hoyer, *Silhouettes of Peking* (Peking: China Booksellers, 1926). It should be noted that although published in 1926 the novel was written around 1916 or 1917, shortly before Ellen and Emily arrived in the city.
445   Ellen Newbold La Motte, *Civilization: Tales of the Orient* (New York: George H. Doran, 1919).

quantity he chose, and to smoke himself to a standstill in an opium den licensed under European auspices.[446]

The Chinese man is an opium addict. He is opposed to the foreign concessions on Chinese soil but, craving the drug, finds he must visit them to obtain it. He purchases opium at a 'European influenced' shop and returns to Chinese sovereign soil. La Motte then shows us a European, Lawson, pursuing the proprietor of an illegal gambling den who has crossed out of the Settlement into Chinese territory.[447] He cannot follow as the jurisdictional rules of the concessions do not allow him to arrest the man on the other side of the boundary. La Motte shows readers that in Shanghai, thanks to the concessions and the laws of extraterritoriality, 'Morality appeared arbitrary, determined by geographical lines – a matter of dollars and cents.'[448]

And indeed it comes down to such as Lawson is eventually paid off to leave the gambling den alone and indeed to leave Shanghai and return to England. 'Homesick' appears to be La Motte's first public broadside against the opium trade and foreign involvement, particularly in Shanghai, in selling opium as a narcotic. She repeatedly expressed her dislike for the Shanghai International Settlement and Shanghailanders in general, which was probably a factor in the decision by La Motte and Chadbourne to locate themselves for the majority of their China stay in Peking.

In 'Canterbury Chimes' we are introduced to an English bishop posted to somewhere in Southeast Asia.[449] A young and westernised local man complains to the bishop about the prevalence of the opium trade, but is told that it is '...something that is no concern of mine – nor yours

446 La Motte, *Civilization*, pp.40-41. It should be noted that the 'auspices' of the International Settlement were those established by the so-called Treaty Port Powers and the elected Municipal Council (which at that time included no Chinese members), composed of Europeans, Japanese, various Latin American countries and the United States too.

447 Lawson is described by La Motte as 'a salaried clerk, a court runner, whose duty it was to enforce the laws against gambling in the Settlement.' La Motte, *Civilization*, p.46.

448 Ibid, p.42.

449 La Motte does not name the precise location though they speak English, the bishop later visits the Chinese quarter near the docks, and a Malay kriss is mentioned, so most likely she is thinking of Singapore.

either.'[450] The men argue in a rather didactic style for some pages – the bishop defending both the opium trade and imperialism while the young man concisely lays out the profits and power Britain accrues from the opium trade. The bishop argues that the local population need not buy and smoke opium; the young man counters that it has been imposed on a people not prepared to resist and that, after all, its trade is banned in Britain. The bishop argues that the profits from the opium trade are spent on schools for locals; the young man laughs at this notion: 'You know how freely you provide us with opium, so that we may be docile, easy to manage and exploit.'[451] The bishop accuses the young man of sedition and attacks him physically though later, upon reflection, begins to read up on the opium trade and is disquieted by his government's profiting from it and his church's role in it as a beneficiary of the trade too.

The bishop then receives a letter from England saying that his wayward young nephew has disgraced himself in some way and is being sent to the East to escape his debtors. At the docks in Asia the young man disappears. The bishop hires a private investigator to find him. Later the bishop is summoned to a Chinese opium den by the detective, is shown the establishment's government licence, and the body of an overdosed white man. The bishop is shaken to the core, but it turns out not to be his nephew as he had feared. The bishop returns home, now convinced that the opium trade is a pernicious and vile one. La Motte's point in the story is of course obvious and, it has to be said, rather over-laboured. She uses the interactions between the Englishman and the local to prescriptively hash out the arguments against the British government's involvement in the opium trade in Asia. Clearly, in the time La Motte and Chadbourne had been sojourning in Asia since 1917, they had found their cause.

The Opium Monopoly

The couple settled in Peking in 1916 for a spell and then again in 1919 through 1920. Established in the city, Chadbourne began visiting as many curio stores and markets as possible to build her collection of Chinese antiquities, manuscripts, textiles and books. Simultaneously, having worked out her reactions to her wartime experiences in Europe

450   La Motte, *Civilization*, p.122.
451   La Motte, *Civilization*, p.125.

and the role of European 'Spheres of Influence' in China in *Peking Dust,* and her initial dislike of the foreign involvement in China in all its many dimensions in *Civilization,* La Motte focussed her attention almost entirely on gathering data and anecdotes concerning the opium trade while living in Peking.

In her 1920 study of China's opium problem, *The Opium Monopoly*[452], La Motte, despite being the sole credited author of the book, begins her introduction with, 'We first became interested in the opium traffic during a visit to the Far East in 1916.' Throughout the introduction Ellen continues to refer to 'we', without ever specifically naming anyone. Clearly she means her travelling companion in China, Chadbourne. La Motte claims that prior to visiting Asia both of them had been neophytes on the subject of opium, the opium trade and the history of the Opium Wars. They were introduced to the subject by a young Hindu fellow passenger on the boat from America to Japan. He railed against the British in India for instigating the opium trade (and indeed this real-life encounter may be the model for the young man in her short story 'Canterbury Chimes'). Ellen and Emily were shocked by what they heard and decided to investigate. Their Far East tour was to include Japan, Hong Kong, the Philippines, French Indo-China, Siam (Thailand) and Singapore, as well as China. In all these places they consulted government officials and anyone working in the opium trade and claim to have visited opium "shops", licensed and unlicensed, whenever possible to talk to dealers and users.

ELLEN N. LAMOTTE

Ellen La Motte, London, 1922

452 Ellen Newbold La Motte, *The Opium Monopoly* (New York: Macmillan, 1920).

Ellen and Emily came to the conclusion that opium was intrinsically linked to imperialism, particularly British imperialism. This should not have been particularly shocking and was not exactly a secret, but both Ellen and Emily claimed to have great admiration for Britain and the British due to the Great War and found the levels of Britain's historic and then current involvement in the opium trade both shocking and disappointing. They also claimed that their reason for examining the opium trade in great detail was that they considered it to be a threat to America in terms of drug addiction to morphia stemming from the war and heroin being brought into the country by smugglers.[453]

Throughout their travels the couple were critical of British opium trading in Singapore and Malaya, and the "unequal treaties" extracted from the Qing Dynasty after the Opium Wars that created the Crown Colony of Hong Kong and the treaty ports of China. *The Opium Monopoly* draws together a lot of statistics on the Asia-wide opium trade and links it to British interests in producer states such as Persia (Iran) and India – of course both under British control at the time of La Motte's writing.[454]

Indeed, so outspoken was La Motte that any idea the couple may have had of being entertained in the Legation Quarter was scuppered by her comments to the newspapers in America and Europe. La Motte accused the British of consciously turning their imperial subjects into drug addicts by forcing the drug upon them.[455] La Motte also annoyed the British Legation by asserting that the British Empire used local middlemen – 'a curious crowd of Parsees, Mohammedans, Hindus and Asiatic Jews' – to do the actual selling of the dope. When La Motte told the newspaper columnist Skygac that 'British dignity prefers not to stoop beneath the taking in of profits; it leaves the details of dirty business to dirty hands' she pretty much ensured that no invitation to the British Legation would

---

453   It has to be said that one glaring omission in La Motte's book is that it makes no mention of the vigorous American involvement in the earlier nineteenth-century opium trade.

454   During the First World War the British occupied much of the territory of western Iran and did not fully withdraw until 1921. The British then supported the military coup of February 1921 which saw the Qajar dynasty overthrown and Reza Khan installed as the new prime minister. Eventually he was declared the new monarch in 1925 as Reza Shah, thus establishing the Pahlavi dynasty that lasted until 1979.

455   'The Opium Monopoly', *Courier-Post* (Camden, New Jersey), July 21, 1920, p.16.

ever be forthcoming which, in the opening of the post-Great War period, meant that all doors were pretty much closed to La Motte and Crane.[456]

Campaigner

But they appeared to have cared little for Legation Quarter sensibilities as their campaign against opium was to take them on an extended world tour. By May 1920 Ellen was on a speaking tour of the US east coast, lecturing on the opium issue. In 1922 she decided to stop talking to audiences that invariably agreed with her and took the fight to the belly of the beast – London. She made no bones in the British capital that she considered the continuing opium trade – despite the supposed rules and regulations introduced – criminal. She was ready to counter the arguments of the British opium business. When they told her it was for medicinal purposes, Ellen proved that five tons of opium was more than enough to fulfil the medical needs of the world, yet the British produced 532 tons for local use in British India and a further 781 tons for export. In 1922 the British government's response was: 'the Empire needs the money, a little opium in moderation is not harmful and if Britain didn't carry on the opium trade then somebody else would.' Nobody was much impressed with that defence. 'May she succeed in her fight against the vicious monopoly', cried the *St. Louis Post-Dispatch.*[457]

If La Motte couldn't sway too many minds in England, she did find an argument that worked well in America – British traded opium was finding its way into the United States and creating addicts there. Milton Bonner, the American journalist and scholar of the work of Lafcadio Hearn, after hearing La Motte speak on the pernicious opium trade, wrote, 'Some day Uncle Sam will have to say to John Bull: Look here John, let's talk about that opium monopoly of yours. By reason of your encouragement of the opium industry my sons and daughters are being poisoned by thousands. They are becoming opium, morphine, and heroin addicts.'[458]

If not in Britain, then at least in America La Motte won herself many supporters. Her campaign partly explains the withdrawal of the United

456 'Skygac's Column', *The Toiler* (Cleveland, Ohio), March 26, 1920, p.2.
457 'A Woman's Brave Fight', *St Louis Post-Dispatch*, February 19, 1922, p.14.
458 'American Woman Carries War on Opium to Parliament', *The Central New Jersey Home News* (New Brunswick, New Jersey), May 6, 1922, p.1.

States (and China) from the International Opium Convention that had been established at The Hague in 1912. La Motte had long opposed the wording that 'The contracting Powers shall use their best endeavours to control, or to cause to be controlled, all persons manufacturing, importing, selling, distributing, and exporting morphine, cocaine, and their respective salts, as well as the buildings in which these persons carry such an industry or trade.' She, and others, had been arguing for a more formal prohibitionist approach. She was also a key agitator in the run-up to the 1925 International Opium Convention in Geneva which was to further tighten the rules on opium and narcotics globally, even in the face of British opposition.

Ellen was recognised for this campaigning work in *The Nation* magazine's "honor roll" for 1926 – 'Ellen La Motte, for her struggle against the opium bloc in Geneva.'[459] Though it is Ellen that pops up frequently in the newspapers of the time and in the minutes of the International Opium Convention and then the succeeding meetings of the League's Opium Commission, it was also the case that the conference was also attended by 'Mrs EC Chadbourne of Washington.'[460] Ellen and Emily were together in Geneva.

Back in America Ellen continued to make headway by linking opium smuggling to crime, deaths and addiction. In 1928 she returned from Geneva to America and teamed up with a Republican congresswoman from California's Fourth District, Florence Kahn.[461] They jointly campaigned to support the Laguardia-Wheeler resolution for a congressional investigation into the extent of narcotics use in the United States.[462]

---

459 'American Honor List for 1926 Selected by Nation Magazine', *The Dispatch* (Illinois), January 1, 1927, p.7.

460 'American Women Writers Watch Sessions at Geneva', *The Morning Call* (Paterson, New Jersey), April 20, 1928, p.24.

461 Kahn had been married to a senate representative and took over his seat after his death. She was the fifth woman to serve in Congress, the second from California and the first Jewish woman to hold such office.

462 'Californian Urges Quick House Action', *The San Francisco Examiner*, February 27, 1929, p.7.

A lifetime calling

However, despite successes in London, Geneva and back home in America, Ellen and Emily were unable to find time to return to Peking. Emily particularly had wanted to return to continue her collecting trips and acquisitions. Ellen's relationship to the city had been emotional and visceral as well as political. But it was not to be. Still, their brief sojourns in the aftermath of the Great War had given them a lifelong cause and calling.

After China, Ellen and Emily still appear together, travelling, seemingly still interested in the opium question, giving lectures and interviewing officials concerned with suppressing opium smuggling.

Soon after their return from Peking after their second sojourn, and while in France once again, Emily's portrait was painted by the Paris-based Japanese artist Tsuguharu Foujita. Emily, who was fifty-one at the time in 1922, commissioned Foujita to paint her just as he was becoming a noted portraitist. Being selected by Emily, generally considered to be a woman of taste, as her portraitist of choice was something of a career break for him. Foujita was subsequently to earn many more portrait commissions from wealthy female sojourners in Paris after this initial patronage.

Portrait of Emily Crane Chadbourne by Tsuguharu Foujita

Foujita painted Emily as solemn, seemingly unhappy, a little underweight and perhaps not in the best of health. Foujita's biographer Phyllis Birnbaum has written, 'We will never know whether he traced her solemn expression back to her growing opposition to opium or to a miserable past in her American hometown.'[463] There are overt Chinese elements in Foujita's portrait – Emily wears a vest of golden flowers over a blue dress; the vest is of a Chinese design and is possibly both a souvenir of her recent sojourn in Peking, and perhaps also a portent of her next adventure after Paris. She is wearing green stockings and shoes; what was once a detail in silver leaf on the wall behind Emily has long since oxidised to black. However, it is still a vibrant and colourful portrait, and includes one of Foujita's trademark black cats on the couch with Emily.[464]

Ellen returned to America and bought a house in Stone Ridge, a hamlet in Ulster County, New York State. She was awarded the Lin Tse Hsu Memorial Medal in 1930 by the Nationalist Government of China for her campaigning against the opium trade. The medal bore an engraving of the face of Lin Tse Hsu (Lin Zexu), a Chinese scholar-official of the Qing dynasty best known for his forceful opposition to the opium trade. In the 1930s she attended at least three conventions on the opium trade convened by the League of Nations in Geneva. In 1932 La Motte campaigned hard for the election of Franklin D Roosevelt as president, despite declaring that she had been a lifelong Republican.[465] After World War Two she bought a second home in Georgetown, Washington DC, a once run-down 1860s house she then fixed up. She reportedly had a picture of a rhinoceros on the wall of her living room, the animal she thought best represented her character. Her daily routine was to look after her house plants, spend time talking with friends and play the stock market (apparently with some success).[466]

Emily Crane Chadbourne became almost nomadic, with periodic visits back to Chicago to stay with her brother Richard on Lake Shore Drive, regular appearances in the New York society columns as well as a trip to Spain in the late 1920s and back to Paris to empty her apartment (donating the furnishings to the Chicago Art Institute) before more travel

463 Phyllis Birnbaum, *Glory in a Line: A Life of Foujita – The Artist Caught Between East and West* (New York: Faber & Faber, 2006), p.110.

464 *Portrait of Mrs. Emily Crane Chadbourne*, Tsuguharu Foujita, 1922. Now at the Art Institute of Chicago.

465 'Noted Woman, Lifelong Republican, to Vote for Roosevelt', *Victoria Advocate* (Victoria, Texas), October 31, 1932, p.2.

466 Jane Eads, 'Women in Washington', *The Manhattan Mercury* (Manhattan, Kansas), January 8, 1952, p.4.

in the 1930s – to England, Belgium, France. Indeed, she appears to have been on one long antique-buying trip followed by swift donations of much of her purchasing to Chicago cultural institutions. She donated a collection of two hundred and sixty-eight books on Chinese and Japanese art to the Ryerson and Burnham Libraries at the Chicago Art Institute, along with Elizabethan English, Orleanist French and colonial American furniture; 'a seventeenth-century Persian rug; two hundred and six textile pieces; one hundred and thirty-six items of pottery and glass; thirty-two pieces of jewellery; fifty-one pieces of Gothic ironwork and US$50,000 in cash'.[467] Her giving never stopped either – an Ingres engraving of the painter Henri Fantin-Latour; two hundred Japanese prints; a grant to sustain the Chicago Art Institute's department of decorative arts; as well as Japanese pottery, lanterns and bowls, Persian paintings and ceramics, French lace and Chinese pottery. Not a year seems to have gone by without significant donations from Emily to the Art Institute, and the Depression doesn't seem to have slowed her down much either.

By 1930 Ellen and Emily were in their late fifties but still very much together though, as ever, living in different homes. Still they regularly travelled together. Evelyn Waugh encountered them, along with many other Europeans and Americans, in Addis Ababa attending the coronation of Emperor Ras Tafari – Haile Selassie, King of Abyssinia. Waugh provides a characteristically cutting portrait of the pair:

> Two formidable ladies in knitted suits and topis; though unrelated by blood, long companionship had made them almost indistinguishable, square-jawed, tight-lipped, with hard, discontented eyes. For them the coronation was a profound disappointment. What did it matter that they were witnesses of a unique stage of the interpretation of two cultures? They were out for Vice. They were collecting material, in fact, for a little book on the subject, an African *Mother India*, and every minute devoted to Coptic rituals or displays of horsemanship

467 James O'Donnell Bennett, 'Art Institute Outlook Bright Despite Smoke', *Chicago Tribune*, January 2, 1927, p.5. US$50,000 in 1926 was equivalent to approximately US$1 million in 2019.

was a minute wasted. Prostitution and drug traffic comprised their modest interests, and they were too dense to find evidence of either.[468]

Waugh's description of Ellen and Emily is harsh. They were women interested in politics and current affairs as much as in arts and culture. They were serious – politically committed to causes, particularly the suppression of opium, and intellectual in their approach to life. Waugh would always mock such seriousness and intellectualism. Emily was a lifelong collector of art and *objets;* famously a woman of taste and with the funds to indulge that taste. They were also, it seems, lesbian companions who dressed in masculine clothing *à la* Radclyffe Hall. This lent itself to the kind of mockery seen in Waugh's recollection above (they were in Abyssinia with the League of Nations supporting Haile Selassie against expected Italian fascist incursions). They were dedicated to their political and intellectual pursuits, but they were not all seriousness.

In the mid-1930s Emily bought an historic house in Stone Ridge, close by Ellen's home. It was, the press reported, filled with antique china and paintings, mostly from the Far East and presumably collected during their Peking sojourn. Emily's house was near the former revolutionary tavern run by Sally Tock and, in 1937, she developed a line of cosmetics named after Tock. Her partner in this new venture? Ellen La Motte.[469] It seems the business wasn't a great success, but Emily and Ellen lived in Stone Ridge through to the 1950s, converting the property's barn into a cinema. Emily was awarded the *Légion d'honneur* medal by France in

---

468   Evelyn Waugh, *Remote People* (London: Penguin Modern Classics, 1985), p.48. Waugh was in Abyssinia (Ethiopia) as a correspondent for the (London) *Times*. His dispatches from Africa were first published as *Remote People* by Gerald Duckworth of London in 1931. *Mother India* (1927) was a then well-known polemical book by the right-wing and white supremacist American historian Katherine Mayo, which attacked Indian society, religion and culture. La Motte did write up and publish her impressions of the coronation in Addis Ababa – Ellen Newbold La Motte, 'A Coronation in Abyssinia', *Harper's Magazine*, April 1931. I suspect that Waugh is also referring to Ellen and Emily later in *Remote People* when he recounts that the foreigners in attendance at the coronation were not invited to the traditional *Gebbur*, a celebration given by the emperor for his tribesmen. Waugh notes that nobody from the visiting international press was permitted to attend this event, except a black correspondent representing the syndicate of African-American newspapers in the USA, and 'two resolute ladies.' (Penguin Modern Classics edition, p.70).

469   June Provines, 'Front Views and Profiles', *Chicago Tribune*, July 20, 1937, p.11.

1955. Ellen La Motte died in 1961 aged eighty-eight and Emily followed several years later in St. Louis, Missouri, at Christmas 1964, aged ninety-three.

Emily had not had the chance or thought to change her will since Ellen's death three years previously. As well as bequests to her surviving relatives, her gardener Mr Traphagen and housekeeper Jeanette, and further donations to several art institutes and museums, she left a generous US$425-a-month annuity for life to Ellen.[470] Clearly, had Emily predeceased Ellen, she intended for her "life companion" to be well provided for after she had gone.

---

470   In 2019 money, that would be approximately US$3,500 per month.

Harry Hervey's Peking of the Imagination:
Harry Hervey (1924)

"At sunrise," she says, "we reach Shanghai." [471]

471 The suggested last line of Harry Hervey's 1931 treatment for the movie *Shanghai Express*.

All aboard...

The railway station at Peking, crouching beneath the great Tartar
Wall. Alongside, an express train – an armoured train, with soldiers
slouching in the vestibules and by the train-steps. On the station-
platform, a motley throng, in it several Chinese ladies scurrying and
stumbling along on bound-feet; guards yelling in Chinese. Beyond the
archway of the station: the roadway and the city wall. Suddenly, seen
through the archway, the small camel caravan of a Tartar merchant
heaves into view; stops. When the camels have knelt, the chieftain's
servants gather up boxes and follow their master through the station.
While the caravan is kneeling there, a smart motorcar dashes up,
between the caravan and the station archway – and out of the car, very
dignified and dressed lavishly, steps a barbarically beautiful Manchu
woman, followed by her maid. Immediately coolies seize the baggage.
The Manchu woman moves imperiously through the crowd, looking
neither right nor left. A Chinese officer looks at her and laughs:
"Loquiia!" he says to his companion, meaning, "Courtesan"...[472]

The opening scene of the 1932 movie *Shanghai Express*. However, this
is not from the script by the celebrated Hollywood screenwriter Jules
Furthman, but from the original treatment for the movie written in 1931

---

[472] Hervey, Harry, *Mimeograph copy of "Shanghai Express"*, Joseph Freeman Papers
(Collection Number: 80159), Hoover Institution Archives, Stanford CA – Folder 11.
Incidentally, Hervey had a slight obsession with the word '*Loquiia*' and used it often
and over a long time. In his travelogue of Hong Kong, Hervey obviously seems to
have heard the word, or a similar phrase, and it stuck with him (though I can find no
other uses of it by anyone): 'Of course, a glimpse of the brothels was included in this
excursion. They, like the opium houses, were depressing, tawdry places, opening directly
upon the street, with ornate scrolls on the walls and narrow curtained recesses. In each
was an altar dedicated to the god of pleasure, and the air was rich with the mingled
odours of incense and opium, alive with coiling drifts of blue smoke. The girls, some
with spots of scarlet on their eyelids, wore the usual brocaded jackets and trousers.
Chang explained, in his grandiose manner, that they were called loquiia, and their
duties consisted, among other things, of singing and playing to patrons and filling their
opium pipes.' – Harry Hervey, *Where Strange Gods Call: Pages Out of the East* (London:
Thornton Butterworth Ltd, 1925).

by the far less celebrated novelist, playwright, travel writer, scriptwriter and self-declared "Orientalist" Harry Hervey. Hervey it was who produced the original thirty-three-page movie treatment called *Shanghai Express* that was subsequently acquired by Josef von Sternberg and then given to Jules Furthman to adapt. Despite having worked as a journalist, written novels, travelogues, short stories, stage plays and several film scripts, Harry Hervey was never hired to contribute anything to the final shooting script for *Shanghai Express*. Even though he knew both Shanghai and Peking, Hervey wasn't even invited to the Hollywood set.

The movie, which was the fourth collaboration between the Viennese von Sternberg and his muse, the Berliner Marlene Dietrich, went on to be one of the greatest cinema hits of the Depression, grossing US$3.7 million in 1932 money on its initial run, the highest grossing movie of that year by some considerable margin.[473] At the Fifth Academy Awards, *Shanghai Express* was nominated for Best Picture and Best Director, though it lost out to *Grand Hotel* (based on the book by sometime Peking and Shanghai sojourner Vicki Baum[474]) and Frank Borzage for the now-forgotten movie *Bad Girl*. However, Lee Garmes, the cinematographer on *Shanghai Express*, did get an Oscar. Most people involved did well out of *Shanghai Express*, it seems. Of course von Sternberg and Dietrich did well, as their legendary collaboration triumphed; also the supporting cast of Clive Brook, Anna May Wong and Warner Oland, who all got good reviews; Jules Furthman became one of the most in-demand scriptwriters in Hollywood; and Paramount Pictures made a fortune in the midst of an economic collapse. Only Harry Hervey, the originator of the story, got left out of all the furore and success of *Shanghai Express*. Harry Hervey is the forgotten man in the story of that great movie.

Nevertheless, it's worth remembering Hervey, his China sojourns, and the origins of the tale of a bandit hijacking of a Peking-to-Shanghai train that inspired the story that became *Shanghai Express*.

473 Nobody made more money in 1933 or 1934 until MGM's *Mutiny on the Bounty* in 1935 with Charles Laughton and Clark Gable (US$4.5 million). *Shanghai Express* made over a million dollars more than the second-highest-grossing film of 1932, Eddie Cantor's *The Kid From Spain* for United Artists (US$2.6 million). Incidentally, Cantor's co-star in that movie was the Warsaw-born, but Shanghai-raised, actress Lyda Roberti, who gets her own chapter in *Destination Shanghai*.

474 For more on Baum's Peking sojourn see Chapter 1, *The Rooftop of the Grand Hôtel de Pékin*.

Harry Hervey, author of "Caravans By Night," as he is in every day life and as he looks dressed in the garb of the East. of which he writes.

Where Strange Gods Call…

Harry Hervey was born in November 1900 in Beaumont, Texas. His parents were jobbing hotel managers, moving regularly from establishment to establishment across the south and southwest of the United States. Hervey attended local schools and then, in 1916, the Sewannee Military Academy in Tennessee for three years before a stint at the Georgia Military Academy in Atlanta for a final year's formal education. After school Hervey worked briefly as the elevator boy at the Winecoff Hotel in downtown Atlanta, then briefly as a reporter on *The Atlanta Constitution*, and as a clerk for the Texas Oil Company.[475]

475 Hervey later confessed, after having claimed his experience as a reporter on his résumé for years, that he was only employed at *The Atlanta Constitution* for a grand total of three days.

Wanting desperately to be an author, Hervey had to find time to write after work and on weekends. His first novel, *Caravans By Night, A Romance of India*, was published in 1922 when Hervey was just twenty years old.[476] After *Caravans by Night* Hervey always claimed that he never earned his living any other way than through 'peddling prose'.[477] The novel was generally well-received and Hervey was described as 'the most promising young romancer in the country' by one prominent critic, though the novel was all based on factual research (despite Hervey posing for the newspapers dressed as a maharajah!).[478] He followed this up swiftly with a second novel, *The Black Parrot, A Tale of the Golden Chersonese*, which ranges around Asia from Malaya to Lhasa – again all based on secondary research.[479] Once more, though, it found an enthusiastic readership. The book was abridged and serialised in newspapers across America while the reviewer for the *St. Louis Globe-Democrat* waxed lyrically, '*The Black Parrot* is a dream of liveliness interrupted by a nightmare… I was delighted with the flow of words, the suggestiveness of the pictures, but most of all with the naïve sincerity of its fancifulness.'[480]

Despite later claims that he survived financially solely on his writing, it seems that in actuality Hervey used his parents' travel industry connections to get a job as a cruise director travelling though Asia. It seems that his mother, living in Savannah, also got a job on the ship for the four-month cruise. How good he was as a cruise director is unrecorded, but he certainly seems to have found time to explore Asia, though he never mentions his mum coming along on the trip. Harry and Jane Davis Hervey sailed on January 17, 1924 on the RMS *Laconia*. The *Laconia* had only been built in 1921 and was a British Royal Mail ship that began the first around-the-world cruises, which lasted a hundred and thirty days and called at twenty-two ports. Hervey boarded what was, at the time, one of the world's largest ships. It could accommodate over two

476 Harry Hervey, *Caravans By Night, A Romance of India* (New York: The Century Company, 1922).

477 'Georgia Writers Conference Opens at Candler Library', *The Atlanta Constitution*, June 9, 1948, p.17.

478 'Houston Boy Tells of Work', *The Houston Post*, May 1, 1922, p.1.

479 Harry Hervey, *The Black Parrot, A Tale of the Golden Chersonese* (New York: The Century Company, 1923).

480 WE Matthews, 'Mysterious East Vividly Portrayed in Hervey Novel', *St. Louis Globe-Democrat*, September 22, 1923, p.15.

thousand passengers, although this included the crowded third-class deck from Southampton to New York that brought immigrants to America. For the rest of the round-the-world cruise that deck was closed and the ship carried just four hundred and fifty mostly middle class, Mid-West American, passengers.

Canard R.M.S. Laconia   Tonnage 20.000

Hervey travelled aboard the *Laconia* through Asia for the first six months of 1924, writing as he went. The resultant book, rapidly published that October, *Where Strange Gods Call: Pages From the East* [481], was called 'extraordinary' by the *Chicago Tribune*, which provided potential readers with a good overview of the book:

> "*Where Strange Gods Call*," by Harry Hervey, is something more than one of those green jacketed travel books. It is the spirited chronicle of a romantic young man who goes adventuring all over the east: across the Pacific to Zamboanga in the Philippines, to Japan and China, through the Malay Archipelago that Joseph Conrad wrote about, to India. This is really an extraordinary book in its color and imagery and romance. It is not merely a book of places, but of places and people... Mr. Hervey has put zest and charm into the characters that stray across the pages of "*Where Strange Gods Call*"...[482]

---

481 Harry Hervey, *Where Strange Gods Call: Pages Out of the East* (London: Thornton Butterworth Ltd, 1925).
482 *Chicago Tribune*, October 5, 1924, p.51.

The *Los Angeles Times* also praised the book and spoke to Hervey about his next trip to Asia, this time without mother, but with an unnamed companion. 'We may be gone six months, or six years', Hervey told the paper. He told them he wanted to get to Angkor, the Cambodian jungles, Rangoon, the Shan States, the Himalayas, and finally Tibet. He was planning to write it all up again and call it *Drums at Dusk*.[483]

Hervey was coy about his unnamed companion given the times and the intolerance of gay relationships. But it was the Charleston-born and based editor, author and actor, Carleton A. Hildreth, who was to remain his close companion until Hervey's death in 1951. Together they did return for another trip to Asia, concentrating their stay mostly in French Indo-China, sailing on the Pacific Mail Steamship Company cargo-liner *President Polk* that left from San Francisco for Honolulu, Manila, Saigon, Singapore and Calcutta. Hervey had been hired by *McCall's* magazine, which was impressed with *Where Strange Gods Call,* to write another travelogue. And he did write up the trip for *McCall's* as a serial, which was later published in book form as *Travels in French Indo-China*.[484] While Hervey concentrated on his impressions of France's Asian empire in his writing, he did revisit China on this trip. Previously having seen only southern China, Hong Kong and Macao, this time the couple visited, and sojourned for some weeks, in Peking.

Afterwards, back in America, Hervey stayed inspired by Asia. In 1927 he made his first foray into Hollywood when director Fred Niblo cast the British actor Clive Brook, the Polish-born Gilda Gray and the Chinese-American actress Anna May Wong in *The Devil Dancer*. The silent movie was based on Hervey's 1924 short story *The Young Men Go Down*, which had featured in a prestigious annual American publication, *The Best Short Stories of 1924*.[485] The movie has an exotic Oriental location and a number of Asian actors – among them the Japanese silent movie star Sojin Kamiyama and the Shanghai-born actor James B. Leong, as well as Anna May Wong. Sadly, no print of the movie survives and it is considered "lost".

483 *Los Angeles Times*, December 21, 1924, p.56.
484 Harry Hervey, *Travels in French Indo-China* (London, Thornton Butterworth, 1928).
485 Ed. Edward J. O'Brien, *The Best Short Stories of 1924 and the Yearbook of the American Short Story,* (Boston: Small, Maynard & Co., 1925).

We have to assume Hervey liked the attention and money Hollywood offered as he began writing a number of treatments and story ideas for the studios. A few years after *The Devil Dancer* he hit big with his thirty-three-page treatment for a story he titled *Shanghai Express*.

The Lincheng Outrage!

The idea for *Shanghai Express* had been in Hervey's mind for a while. It is often said that the story of *Shanghai Express* is essentially a retelling of the Guy de Maupassant story of a French prostitute set during the Franco-Prussian War, *Boule de Suif.* First published in 1880, the story is set among the passengers fleeing Rouen aboard a stagecoach. Among the passengers are Boule de Suif (or "Butterball"), a prostitute whose real name is Elisabeth Rousset, and others who constitute a microcosm of French society in the late nineteenth century. Certainly, there are similarities – Boule de Suif to Shanghai Lily; a stagecoach to the *Shanghai Express;* Rouen to Le Havre becomes Peking to Shanghai. But, whatever echoes of de Maupassant are in the story, what really brings *Shanghai Express* alive is the setting of warlord-era China. And that came partially from Hervey's own travels and experiences in China.

When he was in China in 1924, moving between Hong Kong, Macao, Canton and Peking, a recent major news story concerning foreigners in

China that everyone was still talking about was the so-called "Lincheng Outrage!" of May 1923 – invariably with an exclamation mark attached in blood-curdling headlines. Even if Hervey hadn't been in China at the time, he would have been hard-pressed to miss the story of the kidnapping and ransoming of twenty-five foreigners and three hundred Chinese by a thousand-strong army of bandits, led by their twenty-five-year-old "Commander-in-Chief" Swen Miao. The bandits attacked the Tientsin to Pukow Railway[486], derailing the *Blue Express,* the new deluxe fast train that plied the route between Shanghai and Peking. Hervey himself would take the *Blue Express* from Peking to Shanghai in 1925, presumably mulling the idea of both the incident at Lincheng and *Boule de Suif.* When he was interviewed by *The Atlanta Constitution* in 1932 about the inspiration for *Shanghai Express* he elaborated somewhat:

> Once the lure of the Orient gets in the blood there is no resisting the call, says Harry Hervey, writer of the original story. "*Shanghai Express*" was born of a thrilling experience I once had on a trip from Pekin *(sic)* to Shanghai. The Chinese revolution was in full swing and my train was held up by revolutionists, a common occurrence at the time. By adding a few characters and embellishing the drama – there was plenty of it there at the time – I had the story.[487]

It seems that in reality Hervey's train ride was uneventful, but he was right that there were often bandit attacks.

The *Blue Express* was the first all-steel train in Asia; the most modern locomotive in China with an elaborate dining car, bar and viewing platform. Swen Miao and his soldiers kidnapped all the passengers in the early hours of May 6, 1923 near the town of Lincheng close to the Kiangsu-Shantung border (though technically in Hopei province), leading to the whole crisis becoming known as the "Lincheng Outrage". The train was ransacked, all valuables taken and even the mattresses and light bulbs stripped by the bandits as loot. When Hervey was to travel

---

486 Tianjin to Pukou, a station close to Nanjing and, at the time, a connection to services onwards to Shanghai.
487 'Cameo Offers Chinese Film for Two Days', *The Atlanta Constitution*, May 8, 1932, p.7.

on the *Blue Express* a year later there were, so he claimed, still bullet holes from the bandit attack.

Lloyd Lehrbas, an army veteran and journalist with the Shanghai-based *China Press* newspaper travelling on the *Blue Express* to Peking, managed to escape and started filing stories about the incident almost immediately. He gave the impression that Swen Miao's men were the most desperate and depraved bunch of bandits in China. The American advertising entrepreneur in Shanghai, Carl Crow, reading Lehrbas's articles got the impression that Swen Miao was 'a real throat slitting bandit of the sort that splash blood on the pages of fiction and sometimes get into Hollywood.'[488] While not as totally cut-throat as perhaps Lehrbas had reported, as things dragged on several Chinese hostages did die from beatings, several more later expired of hunger and exposure, and a few of the western hostages were beaten up pretty badly too. The veteran China journalist JB Powell, himself a hostage at Lincheng, had to defend himself with his fists on one occasion.[489] Joseph Rothman, a Romanian on a British passport, had been shot dead after refusing to surrender his valuables and provoking his guard by throwing a teapot at the bandit's head during the storming of the train.

JB Powell described Swen Miao as a 'young chap... from a formerly respected family'.[490] It seems that he had once been in the army of Chang Ching-yao, a warlord who had taken control of Beijing briefly in 1920.[491] Returning to his home village he understandably fell out with a local magistrate who had beheaded his father on trumped-up charges while he was away. Wanted, he then took to the hills with a few clan members. His gang grew rapidly following the Yellow River flooding in 1920 and 1921 which ruined many peasant farmers and left them with few career choices but banditry. Swen Miao mostly raided police stations or ambushed armed police detachments to get guns. Disaffected warlord troops fed up with low pay and meagre rations swelled his band's number to approximately a thousand men (though many were effectively part-time, leaving and

488 Carl Crow, *The Chinese Are Like That* (New York: Harper & Bros., 1938), p.313.
489 John B. Powell, *My Twenty-Five Years in China* (New York, Macmillan, 1945).
490 John B. Powell, 'The Bandits' "Golden Eggs" Depart', *Asia*, December 1923.
491 Zhang Jingyao was one of the warlord era's most notorious leaders, feared for his troops' atrocities in Hunan. He was removed from office for his abuses and assassinated in 1933 for working to establish the monarchy of Puyi in Manchuria with Japanese money.

going home to help during harvest season). Swen Miao began to raid rich landowners and morphed into a Robin Hood-type figure for many peasants in the surrounding region. He cleverly developed this myth by naming his gang the Shantung People's Liberation Society and set up a semi-permanent camp on the slopes of Paotzeku Mountain.[492]

Lincheng hits the headlines

In Lincheng the American Red Cross, with Carl Crow as a hastily conscripted negotiator, was trying to free the hostages. Building trust was a slow business; food supplies, blankets and medicines all had to be ferried up the wet and muddy mountain on the backs of porters.

More international headlines were written when it was revealed that one of the female hostages was Lucy Aldrich, the daughter of former governor of Rhode Island Nelson Aldrich and a sister-in-law to John D. Rockefeller Jr. Aldrich was travelling with her companion Miss McFadden and her French maid Mademoiselle Schonberg who were kidnapped along with their mistress. Among the remaining hostages was an assortment of Americans, British, French, Italian and Mexican nationals. Celebrity hostages like Aldrich ensured that the newspapers couldn't get enough of Lincheng. And the daily updates from Shantung province were all feeding into Harry Hervey's vivid imagination – in *Shanghai Express* General Chang's men massacre the Chinese government soldiers guarding the train.

As with the warlord General Chang's hideout in *Shanghai Express*, Swen Miao's Mount Paotzeku camp was remote and involved a ten-day forced march for the captives. The temporary lodgings of Shanghai Lily, "Doc" Harvey, Hui Fei and the others from the *Shanghai Express* are spartan but seemingly luxurious compared to the *Blue Express* hostages, whose accommodation in an old run-down monastery was reportedly flea-ridden. Dysentery and malaria quickly became major problems, with Crow and the Red Cross desperately trying to ferry up medicines with the porters. The hostages were soon hungry, having been fed little but a few cans of tinned sardines that JB Powell had managed to beg from a bandit, some unappetizing dog meat, and a plate of scorpions with

492 Sometimes spelt Paotzuku, or Pao Tse Ku, and now the Baodugu National Forest Park and mountain in Shandong province.

their stings removed that nobody was quite sure how to eat. Hollywood skipped those details.

The *Shanghai Express* captives' ordeal is over relatively quickly. But it took Carl Crow, and his old friend the veteran China Hand Roy Anderson (acting as the official go-between for the Chinese government), six weeks to finally reach a deal with Swen Miao, rescue the surviving Chinese and foreign hostages and take everybody back to Shanghai.[493] According to a rather overblown report in the Shanghai-based *North China Herald* detailing the arrival back in the International Settlement of the foreign hostages (throughout the ordeal it seems the English-language press had not given much thought to the Chinese captives): 'Hats were thrown into the air and men cheered themselves hoarse, while tears streamed down the cheeks of those near and dear.'[494] Of course the final delayed arrival of the *Shanghai Express* at Shanghai Railway Station (Santa Fe Railway Station doubling for Shanghai in the movie) sees General Chang's hostages safe and sound in the International Settlement with little official fanfare.

The Chinese government didn't forget the trouble and embarrassment Swen Miao had caused them in the international press. Six months later, the bandit group were surrounded and outgunned as they had little more than pre-First World War vintage weaponry. Swen Miao himself was shot and wounded in the chaos, eventually captured, and then publicly beheaded while six hundred of his men were machine-gunned on the orders of Shandong's governor.[495] Looking back on the "Lincheng Outrage" Carl Crow was forced to admit that Swen Miao slipped pretty quickly from history: 'He was not a very successful bandit, for he was young and more ambitious than practical; but he might have travelled far after he had gained more experience if he had not been beheaded before he reached the prime of life.'[496]

---

493   For more on the Lincheng Outrage, Crow, Anderson, JB Powell, kidnapping at the time and bandits, see Paul French, *Carl Crow – A Tough Old China Hand: The Life, Times and Adventures of an American in Shanghai* (Hong Kong: Hong Kong University Press, 2006).

494   *North China Herald*, June 16, 1923.

495   Though it was widely reported that this happened, it's not altogether clear that it actually did. These executions were more *pour encourager les autres*. While some of Swen Miao's men certainly were executed, it appears this was largely to encourage the others to join up with the official government militia.

496   Crow, *The Chinese Are Like That*, p.314.

The story of the *Blue Express* remained news internationally for some time afterwards, not least because Lucy Aldrich published her memoirs of the event in the *Atlantic Monthly* and revealed that she had buried her diamonds under a rock during the forced march. Later, a clerk from Standard Oil's Tientsin office had been sent out to Shantung with a map drawn by Lucy to recover the jewels. He apparently successfully located them under the rock.[497]

Back in America after his own travels on the *Blue Express* shortly after the Lincheng Outrage, Harry Harvey knew that Josef von Sternberg was looking for a China-set script. The Austrian director loved exotic locales – French Foreign Legion Morocco, aristocratic Vienna, Imperial

Harry Hervey in China, 1926

Russia and *fin-de-siècle* Spain. Von Sternberg was not to visit China until the mid-1930s, though he had long been fascinated by the country. Of his trio of China films – *Shanghai Express*, *Shanghai Gesture* with Gene Tierney and Victor Mature in 1941, and *Macao* with Jane Russell and Robert Mitchum in 1952 – only *Shanghai Express* was to be entirely from his imagination, guided by Hervey's experiences.[498] And so Harry Hervey took the tale of the Lincheng Outrage in 1923, his own China adventures on the *Blue Express* afterwards, and combined them with Maupassant's

497 Lucy T. Aldrich, 'A Week-End with Chinese Bandits', *Atlantic Monthly*, November 1923, pp.672-686.

498 It is hard to estimate exactly when von Sternberg was in China. His memoirs are annoyingly lacking in specific dates. However he does note that he arrived after Manchuria had been annexed by Japan (i.e. after 1932); when a diplomat called Hungerford B. Howard was an attaché at the American Consulate in Shanghai (mid-1930s); and shortly before the "Bloody Saturday" bombings of mid-August 1937. Josef von Sternberg, *Fun in a Chinese Laundry* (London: Secker & Warburg, 1966), pp.79-84.

Boule de Suif into the treatment for *Shanghai Express*, which he then sent to Josef von Sternberg in Hollywood, who read it and loved it.

Harry Hervey's Shanghai Express

The plot of *Shanghai Express*, as laid out in Hervey's original movie treatment, follows the various characters boarding the southbound express train at Peking Railway Station (correctly identified in the movie by platform signage reading "Peiping") destined for Shanghai. In Hervey's treatment the character that would become Dietrich's Shanghai Lily is an American woman called Laura Mason. In the original treatment Hervey writes: 'She's a well-known "Coaster" (Note: a Coaster is a woman who, although not technically a person of easy virtue, makes her living off men up and down the China coast.)' One of Hervey's characters notes: 'They say the American Marines fire a salute every time she enters the Legation.' Furthman worked this China Coast slang into his script as one of the British soldier's notes:

> *'Shanghai Lily is aboard, the Coaster...'*
> *'What in the name of Confucius is a "Coaster"?'*
> *'A woman who lives by her wits on the China Coast.'*

Laura Mason shares a compartment with the Manchu courtesan Hui Fei (Anna May Wong's character in the movie) who is 'smoking and playing cards with her maid – A-Lu.' Both Henry Chang, a Eurasian merchant from Harbin, and Doctor Carmichael, a travelling physician (who becomes a Reverend in the movie), disapprove of Hui Fei and will not share her carriage. 'I haven't been in this country ten years without being able to recognise a strumpet when I see one,' Carmichael declares. In the movie script Henry Chang, seeing the foreigners alarmed by a Chinese man being dragged off the train by soldiers to an uncertain fate, states rather solemnly: 'You're in China now, where time and life have no value.'

Laura and Hui Fei are also joined by Mrs Haggerty, a Cockney boarding house keeper in Tientsin, who is decidedly less stuck-up in Hervey's treatment than she was to be portrayed (by the American character actress Louise Closser Hale) in the final movie. Also aboard are several British soldiers (Galloway and Kent) departing Peking for Shanghai. With them is Laura's former lover in Peking, Captain Esme Simpson (changed to Captain Donald "Doc" Harvey and played by Clive Brook in the film).

The rest of Hervey's treatment was, more or less, closely followed by Jules Furthman as the plot for the movie. Laura and Esme meet again, but he is unable to forgive her for a trick she played on him five years earlier to gauge his love for her. Her stratagem backfired and he left her despite having kept her photograph in his wristwatch. During the night the train is halted at a Chinese village and the passengers forced off by armed bandits, though they are uniformed and seemingly a little more of an organised warlord army than Swen Miao's casual mercenaries. The passengers are now the prisoners of General Feng, a 'brigand general'. In the movie the Warner Oland character, Henry Chang, is revealed as the general, though in Hervey's treatment they are two separate characters. Still the group are faced with the fact that the bandits demand one of them be executed in return for the death of a Chinese in Shanghai at the hands of the foreign-controlled Municipal Police. A decision must be made.

Through a similar plot twist to Hervey's original treatment the major characters board the train once more and are allowed to proceed to Shanghai. In the film, when the train finally reaches Shanghai safely, Lily offers Harvey her love unconditionally, but demands the same in return. Harvey finally breaks down and embraces her. Hervey's original ending in his treatment is a little less obvious perhaps:

> And now the *Shanghai Express* is on its way again… We see the soldiers Galloway and Kent in their compartment, chatting and smoking complacently, as though nothing has happened… We see Mrs Haggerty in hers. She glances toward the seat where Carmichael sat… and takes a nip of brandy… Henry Chang, smoking a cigar and reading a newspaper… Hui Fei, playing cards with her maid… And, in another compartment, the two lovers, Laura and Esme…
>
> She smiles at him.
>
> "At sunrise," she says, "we reach Shanghai."

Reaching the screen

Shanghai Express eventually premiered in Los Angeles, but with little mention of Harry Hervey. We have to assume that he knew Clive Brook and Anna May Wong from working with them on *The Devil Dancer* five years previously. But there was no great reunion mentioned in the press.

As this was Hollywood there were a few snafus and some bitchy backbiting – Dietrich claimed von Sternberg really did all the cinematography on the movie, and not Lee Garmes who got the Oscar. The Hays Office censors had some issues with the portrayal of a religious man perhaps not setting a great moral example and quibbled some lines about 'white blood' and racial mixing. The Nationalist Chinese government banned the movie from cinemas in China for a time. People pointed out that Chinese extras (one thousand in total, and all recruited in Los Angeles) were heard to be speaking Cantonese (and in some cases Taishanese!) while supposedly in northern China. Old China Hands might have noticed a few gaffes too – the opening scenes of Peking Railway Station that seemed to make it look like a Southeast Asian or Indian train line rather than Peking; Warner Oland in Yellowface; an apparent advert for Guinness stout at Shanghai Railway Station (more Waterloo Station than Shanghai Station in 1932 as the Irish beverage was never exported that far!); the telegram forms are American and not Chinese; they got the price of a First Class ticket from Peking to Shanghai in 1932 slightly wrong ($35 Mex). The pedants had a field day; audiences loved the flick.

The critics too enjoyed themselves. Most liked the movie, though *Vanity Fair* thought the director's gaze lingered on Dietrich's 'legs in silk, and buttocks of lace… of whom he has made a paramount slut.'[499] Ayn Rand (a massive Dietrich fan) loved the movie, specifically for 'The way the wind blows through the fur-piece around Marlene's shoulder when she sits on the back platform of the train!' However, Soviet director Sergei Eisenstein thought *Shanghai Express* a rip-off of a Russian movie.[500]

Looking back some years later, von Sternberg admitted that when he finally did manage to take the *Shanghai Express* from Peking to Shanghai (around 1936), it 'was thoroughly unlike the train I had invented.' It was

---

499   Quoted in Steven Bach, *Marlene Dietrich: Life and Legend* (Minneapolis: University of Minnesota Press; reprint edition, 2011), p.152.
500   Rand and Eisenstein both quoted in Josef von Sternberg, *Fun in a Chinese Laundry*, p.263.

more basic where the movie had the line, 'everything but a Turkish bath' – also the *Blue Express* was never painted in camouflage. However, he claimed that there was a complement of armed soldiers on the train, and that he did get lucky and enjoyed a lengthy delay caused by bandits on the line, which partly vindicated his imaginary Peking to Shanghai train ride.[501]

Star-studded, lauded by the critics, and financially successful as it was, it seems *Shanghai Express* never got the big Hollywood premiere at Grauman's Chinese Theatre (what more suitable elaborate faux-China cinema for an elaborate faux-China movie?), the Klieg lights, the Hollywood paparazzi, the movie star audience. It's not clear why, but von Sternberg wasn't in California; Dietrich was in heated contract discussions with Paramount and not feeling much like doing them any publicity favours; Clive Brook was reported as being on a ship heading towards New York from Southampton; and Harry Hervey?

Indeed von Sternberg rather rewrote history when he later claimed that the film was '…loosely based on a single page by Harry Hervey which featured a hold-up by bandits.'[502] It's worth reiterating that Hervey supplied a thirty-three-page treatment featuring all the characters that appear in the movie with only some name changes, all the major plot points, a full outline of the Dietrich character of Shanghai Lily, and a detailed description of the train itself. It's not quite clear what happened. It doesn't seem that Hervey fell out with either von Sternberg, Furthman or Paramount. Most likely it was just Hollywood forgetting whose original idea the whole thing had been.

A return to Peking

Hervey hung around Hollywood for a while, picking up scripting work on other movies. He worked on the 1932 Claudette Colbert vehicle *The Wiser Sex* and a Tallulah Bankhead movie (with Gary Cooper, Charles Laughton and Cary Grant) called *Devil and the Deep*, as well as a few more not very memorable ones. Later, in 1940, he wrote the story for the Bing Crosby, Bob Hope and Dorothy Lamour franchise movie, *Road to Singapore*. At one point it was reported he was making a thousand

501   Von Sternberg, *Fun in a Chinese Laundry*, pp.263-264.
502   Ibid, p.263.

dollars a week in Hollywood, but he claimed that he had travelling debts and that, anyway, it cost a thousand bucks a week to live in Hollywood. He seemed happier moving between Charleston and Manhattan with his long-term partner Carleton Hildreth. His somewhat sensationalist and titillating tales of Savannah and Charleston life, as well as a few exotic novels set in French Indo-China, found a steady readership. If Harry Hervey is remembered today then it's invariably for his 1939 novel *The Damned Don't Cry* that stirred up some controversy in Savannah for its depiction of the city's underbelly (and is still enjoyed by readers in that part of the world for its raciness), but which *Kirkus* described as:

HARRY HERVEY.

A flamboyant story of decadence in the old South... Zelda, born in the gas-house district, of whores and drunks... strives upward. This is the story of her revenge on the city... but Hervey is too facile, he never quite succeeds in being as hard-boiled as he pretends, and he goes in for some pretty purple writing, and some mystic-romanticism. A sure renter – but not for discriminating readers.[503]

But Harry Hervey never quite forgot Peking. Probably the last piece of work he completed before his death from cancer in 1951, at just fifty-one years of age, was a short story that concerns the city. Hervey had contracted a particularly painful form of cancer some years before which had slowed his literary output and his movements considerably. *On the Wall* was published posthumously by *The Georgia Review* in late 1953.[504] It is

503 Harry Hervey, *The Damned Don't Cry* (New York: The Greystone Press, 1939), *Kirkus Review*, March 23, 1939.
504 Harry Hervey, 'On the Wall', *The Georgia Review*, Vol.7, No.4 (Winter 1953), pp.390-402.

after the Second World War and two old lovers – Steve Bart, one-time adventurer and now hotelier, and Marcia Cleverdon, former "Coaster" now married to a millionaire – meet in an unnamed Far Eastern port city. The old European empires in the east are collapsing; China has 'gone Red'; the city is pockmarked by shrapnel blasts.[505] Bart, still sore more than a decade later for having lost her to a wealthy man, recalls his first meeting with Marcia...

> "I met her in Peiping," he went on without pause; "only then it was called Peking. And the thing to do, in the late afternoon, was to take a stroll on the wall. Remember that little section near the Legation Quarter? – where everybody who was anybody used to ogle each other after sundown? After dark – well, it wasn't exactly *comme il faut*[506], as the French say, to be caught on the wall after dark... That's where I met her, one night.
>
> Spic and span in my full-dress blues and cotton gloves – I was in the Marines then, helping to guard that sacred bit of soil that was the American Embassy; yes, hard-boiled and twenty-three and ready for anything – even something like Marcia. I sized her up right away – one of the embassy bunch out slumming; matter of fact, she'd slipped away from some stuffed-shirt affair at the Dutch Legation. Oh, I knew her type, though I'd never had a close-up before; sure, I knew how to treat a dame like that..."[507]

Hervey is back in a pre-war Peking, indeed back to the days when he sojourned in the city, the 1920s, for it was then that strolling, horse riding or cycling on the wall was most in fashion (and, before 1927, it was a capital with embassies rather than consulates). Sojourners to Peking in the 1920s often recall that for an unmarried couple to go up on the unlit (except by moonlight) wall at night was considered a little risqué. With a marine? Positively louche. Wallis Simpson recalled the wall as a romantic

---

505 From the few clues he gives it can be guessed Hervey is writing about Rangoon/ Yangon.
506 Meaning correct in behaviour or etiquette.
507 Hervey, 'On the Wall'.

spot in her memoirs of Peking.[508] The sometime novelists Damien de Martel (a diplomat by day) and Léon de Hoyer (a businessman), in their 1926 comedy of manners of the city's foreign colony, _Silhouettes of Peking_, note that on warm summer evenings foreign residents of the Legation Quarter went up on to the wall to listen to the orchestra of the Grand Hotel des Wagons-Lits, whose music carried on the light breezes.[509] The wall remained a popular rendezvous with young couples – in the mid-1930s Edgar and Helen Foster Snow, newly moved to Peking from Shanghai, walked hand-in-hand along the wall at sunset.[510] We also see that in Marcia Cleverdon, Hervey is still playing with variations of his "Coaster" character of Laura Mason from his _Shanghai Express_ treatment of nearly twenty years previously.

Naturally Steve and Marcia fall in love. He is getting discharged from the marines and has a job lined up in the China trade with a firm in Tientsin. After hiring a car to go and visit the Summer Palace, the couple return to Peking to find themselves surrounded by an angry mob of Chinese students protesting against foreigners in China after the shooting of some students in the Shanghai International Settlement. Again, Hervey situates us in the 1920s – May 30, 1925 to be precise, and the nationwide protests after the Shanghai Municipal Police opened fire on Chinese protesters, leaving many dead and wounded. Marcia is terrified, feels vulnerable and wants only to get out of China. Steve continues his reminiscence:

> "I was on the wall at the regular time the next night," he said finally. "But I knew she wasn't coming… It wasn't long afterward that I read about her engagement in the _Gazette_.[511] She'd really snagged herself somebody: Gerald Cleverdon, the big _taipan_, the number one catch in China, in all Asia for that matter."

Steve doesn't see Marcia again for over ten years, until that night when she walks into his hotel in another Asian city, in another decade, and

508 Wallis, Duchess of Windsor, _The Heart has its Reasons: The Memoirs of the Duchess of Windsor_ (London: Michael Joseph, 1956).

509 Damien de Martel & Léon de Hoyer, _Silhouettes of Peking_ (Peking: China Booksellers, 1926).

510 Helen Foster Snow, _My China Years: A Memoir_ (New York: Morrow, 1984).

511 Hervey presumably means the English-language _Peking Gazette_.

in another period of turmoil. It's not an unfamiliar trope for Hervey – when Madeline, aka Shanghai Lily (Laura Mason in Hervey's original treatment), boards the *Shanghai Express* and encounters Captain "Doc" Harvey (Captain Esme Simpson in Hervey's treatment) she is a Coaster who is set to marry a wealthy man in Shanghai. The two former lovers have not seen each other for five years since he left her after she tested his intentions and it all backfired. Marcia Cleverdon is essentially just a slightly different form of Laura Mason/Madeline.

Throughout his career Harry Hervey came back again and again to his fascination with and travels through China, and more than once to the Peking of his sojourns and then to the Peking of his imagination. Hervey has been forgotten now; nobody reads his novels or his travelogues; his own scripted films are totally lost or never now shown; his short stories hidden away in obscure literary journals, gathering dust in archives. Cinema audiences and movie fans still love *Shanghai Express,* they still enjoy Dietrich, Brook, Anna May Wong. But rarely if ever does anyone mention that Harry Hervey originally dreamt up that great story.

The Woman Who Created the Wartime Image of China in America:
Martha Sawyers (1941)

SPECIALIST: Martha Sawyers, shown in her New York apartment with one of her paintings, is an acknowledged authority on peoples of the Far East. She paints in New York, but has tracked down her models in their homelands.

"China is Helping Us – Help China!" [512]

---

512 Slogan for United China Relief (UCR), 1941.

"China Shall Have Our Help!"

Martha Sawyers did not sojourn for long in Peking; perhaps she made the shortest visit of anyone considered in this collection. But her brief trip to the city did lead to some excellent illustrations and drawings and, more importantly, some years later led to her firm commitment to China's cause in World War Two. This took the form of her active involvement in United China Relief (UCR), the focal point of American support and fundraising for Nationalist China at that time. Her later artwork for UCR campaigns really redefined positively the way foreign artists in general had portrayed the Chinese people: giving them strength, dignity and agency at a time when the country was in an all-out fight for its very survival.

In the summer of 1941 Martha Sawyers' images of China and the Chinese appeared seemingly everywhere in the United States. It was the year the UCR organisation had been founded in New York. The UCR brought together eight different organisations that had all been working to the same ends under one umbrella. The UCR's goal was to raise the American public's awareness of China's resistance to Japan and to collect funds to directly aid civilians. The images the new combined UCR chose to promote their work were a series of striking full-colour posters that appeared in newspapers, magazines and on billboards nationwide. The images would resonate with the American public and be seared on many people's memories long after the war. The UCR's posters were largely the work of Martha Sawyers.

The first of Sawyers' images to be published was a striking portrait of a Chinese man, lean, stern and strong of jaw, but with his arm in a sling. Alongside him stands a woman, presumably his wife. She displays a weary sadness. Their child, barefoot, is carried on her back. The background indicates a China on fire. The trio are symbolic, at one and the same time, of China's suffering and the millions of people forced to become refugees due to the Japanese invasion. However, the image also displays a sense of courage and resilience, a desire to resist and overcome adversity. The caption reads:

"China Shall Have Our Help!"

The aim of the initial UCR poster was to raise US$5 million to aid China's estimated fifty million refugees displaced after four years of war against the Japanese invasion. It easily surpassed this target.

The board of the UCR, which included such luminaries as First Lady Eleanor Roosevelt, the China-raised author Pearl Buck, and the publisher of *Time*, *Life* and *Fortune* Henry Luce (born in Shandong to missionary parents), had specifically chosen Martha Sawyers as their in-house artist.

Sawyers had built herself a reputation for her detailed portraits of Chinese and Southeast Asian subjects. For Sawyers, the images she was to craft for the UCR became a very personal challenge. Throughout World War Two, Sawyers was to continue to promote the cause of the UCR with many other striking images.

The posters became national icons on billboards along major highways and in full-colour magazine appeals. A Nationalist soldier, his wife with her arm bandaged, and their clench-fisted young daughter, all looked straight out of another poster with the slogan:

"China: First to Fight!"

Yet another poster features Uncle Sam along with a determined Chinese mother and child beside a soldier with a head wound:

"China is Helping Us – Help China!"

And another, a portrait of a young Chinese pilot, fit to be a Hollywood leading man, looks skyward at China's fighter planes…

"China Fights On"

Throughout the war the UCR did use several other artists, perhaps most notably the *Life* magazine illustrator known for his political posters during the New Deal era, James Montgomery Flagg. However, there was a strength to Sawyers' portraits of wartime Chinese that had attracted the board of the UCR and was to resonate with the wider American public. Sawyers' imagery was noticeably free of the pre-war tropes of many other western artists depicting Chinese people – intimations of weakness, backwardness and lassitude. Sawyers' Chinese portraits showed a strong, determined people; handsome men and women; cared-for children, all now suffering the horrors of invasion and war. The artist's wartime China is one of recognisable and, crucially for spreading the cause, relatable people, rather than exoticised caricatures. A strong, proud nation fighting (after December 1941) a common enemy with the United States. A steadfast ally.

Sawyers' posters were to become ubiquitous throughout America during the war. Most importantly, they worked – the UCR raised over US$50 million in donations, and greatly heightened public consciousness of China's struggle. The posters have remained popular as postcards, sold through poster reproduction websites and displayed in exhibitions on wartime propaganda. Yet Martha Sawyers herself, as an artist and as an activist, has been largely forgotten.

Few have ever asked why Sawyers was the UCR's first choice as their in-house artist. What did they see in her? The answer is that her pre-war career had been dedicated to representations of Asia and Asians. And crucially, although she only spent a short time in Peking before the war, it significantly influenced her sympathies towards Nationalist China in its struggle with Japan and the unique aesthetic she chose to represent that struggle to the American people.

A most productive honeymoon

Martha Louise Sawyers was born in 1902 in Cuero, Texas – turkey farm country. Her father worked for the local power company. Martha set out as a young woman to become an artist, encouraged by her parents to show her work. She won a series of local scholarships that allowed her to travel, in 1922, to study drawing, painting and stained-glass techniques at the Art Students League of New York on Manhattan's West 57th Street.

By the mid-1920s she was living in a female-only boarding house on 22nd Street, the Greenwich Village-Chelsea border, filled with rather interesting characters. Martha occupied the first-floor apartment, much of which she had converted into a stained-glass design studio. A floor above her was 81-year-old Virginia Moon, a.k.a. Miss Ginger, a one-time "Southern Belle" from Memphis who claimed to have been a Confederate spy during the American Civil War. Miss Ginger chain-smoked all day and told anyone who'd listen how she had turned down over a dozen proposals of marriage in her long life, gone to Hollywood in its earliest days, and had a semi-successful theatrical career on Broadway. In the evening the whole house became something of a salon, presided over by Miss Ginger and her good friend William Jacob "WJ" Baer, considered by many to be the foremost American miniatures painter. Martha, and the young theatre actress Virginia Warner, Miss Ginger's niece who also lodged in the building, attended the salon regularly.

It was probably at one of Miss Ginger's salons, or perhaps at a painting class at the Art Students League, that Martha met William "Bill" Reusswig (pronounced "rice-wig"). Reusswig was the same age as Martha, from New Jersey, and also attempting to make his name as an artist, selling illustrations to the weekly news magazines. Martha was thinking her future might lie in illustration and painting rather than stained glass, though she was successfully designing for J&R Lamb, America's oldest continuously run decorative arts company.

William Reusswig

Martha and Bill married in 1928. They asked their wedding guests for money to allow them to travel, rather than gifts. Martha told her friends, 'A dollar in the hand is worth more to us than a silver-plated compote dish.'[513] The guests must have provided cash as the newly-weds went on an extended honeymoon to Paris. There they soaked up the Bohemian art scene as part of that legendary American

---

513 Willa Martin, 'Martha Sawyers from Texas Found Herself in the Tropics', *Tampa Bay Times*, March 28, 1944, p.2.

colony that clustered on the Left Bank in the post-Great War decade. A year later, in 1929, they returned home to America broke.

Back in New York, Martha and Bill began living and working at 22 East 72nd Street, painting and drawing like mad to make a living as artists. They needed to sell their work to eat and pay the rent. Martha got paid cash in hand for illustrating Broadway theatre programmes and providing cover art for movie magazines. This meant mixing with the stars occasionally – she was commissioned to draw portraits of the leads in the MGM movie *Grand Hotel* and sketched Greta Garbo, Joan Crawford and Lionel Barrymore. She also began to carve out a reputation for herself with Manhattan galleries, while Bill became a regular paid artist for news magazines such as *Collier's, Cosmopolitan, The Saturday Evening Post* and *Country Gentleman*.

The couple were doing well. They built up their bank account and moved to a large shared apartment and studio at a more prestigious address on East 84th Street. But the New York art scene didn't satisfy them – it was too incestuous; too self-congratulatory. They decided to travel once again and departed for an extended trip to the Far East. Bill Reusswig was able to operate as a sort of prototype "digital nomad". From Southeast Asia, Japan and China he fulfilled commissions and sent illustrations to the burgeoning pulp story magazine market back in America. His work for *Adventure, Argosy, Complete Detective, Detective Tales,* as well as *Wild West Weekly*, ensured the couple could continue to travel. As Bill kept getting paid, Martha was able to concentrate on drawing what she saw as they travelled.

Asia works its magic on Martha

From the start of their prolonged sojourn in Asia it was people that fascinated Martha – and rarely in a primitivist, condescending way. Her portraits invariably alluded to strength and dignity, qualities that would recommend her to the UCR board a decade later. The couple started their sojourn travelling by Dutch cargo steamer to the South Seas, stopping at random ports for freight to be unloaded and new cargoes taken aboard. Martha and Bill went ashore – she to paint the local scene; he to find a post office to send his illustrations back to New York. Martha later told reporters that she had, as a young girl, been inspired by tales of the South Seas and the life of the French artist Paul Gauguin in Tahiti. Martha's early paintings of the South Seas reveal her identifiable strength of character in her portraits but are far from exceptional. They are rather too obviously commercial, postcard-like. It was to be Bali, in the then Dutch East Indies, that would provide her with inspiration.

Sawyers in Bali, 1937

Bali worked its magic on Martha as it had done previously on so many artists in the 1920s and early 1930s – Charlie Chaplin, the Dutch painters Rudolf Bonnet and Arie Smit, the Belgian Adrien-Jean Le Mayeur and, perhaps best remembered for his Bali-inspired paintings, the German artist Walter Spies. Martha and William left their island-hopping tramp steamer at Denpasar and rented a place on the beach. It was basic living conditions – they got sunstroke, had to have three electric fans running constantly all day to overcome the lassitude brought on by the tropical heat, were eaten alive by mosquitoes, and got sick taking too much quinine to avoid malaria. But it was where Martha believed her work finally came alive, the "'turning point" in her artistic career. At night she would journey to the local communities and start drawing the people she met at the markets, in the villages, at the temple dances.

Moving on from Bali, Martha and Bill headed to China. They decided to spend some time in Peking. Bill continued to send his illustrations of the Wild West, gangsters and gangsters' molls back to America while Martha continued sketching local people. Her work in Bali and Peking cemented what became her trademark style of portraiture and her representations of

Northern China and its people presage her later work for the UCR. New York art reviewers at the time described Sawyers' 'draftsman-like quality' and how she imbued her subjects with a 'masculine strength and virility', 'marked by a keen characterisation'. Certainly they were noting, in the language of their times, a style of realism that revealed age, blemishes and beauty similarly while invariably giving her subjects strength and respect. Sawyers may have started her sojourn in Asia admiring Gauguin's Post-Impressionist and Synthetist work in Polynesia, but by Bali, and then Peking, she had forged her own distinctive realist style.[514]

Trapped in Peking

But history caught up with the travelling artists. The couple found themselves in Peking in early July 1937, just as the Japanese attacked and occupied the city. They quickly boarded a train for Shanghai before the Japanese declared martial law which could have stranded them in northern China. In Shanghai the pair managed to board a passenger liner for home. They arrived safely back in New York that autumn. Martha was able to sell many of her South Sea Islands paintings to collectors, while Marie Sterner, a well-known Manhattan gallery owner and strong champion of modern American women artists at the time, exhibited Martha's portraits of Balinese and Chinese subjects. The good reviews of this exhibition, matched by strong public attendance and interest, led to Martha receiving many commissions from the news magazines *Collier's*, *Liberty* and *McCall's* for more drawings and paintings with specifically Asian subjects.

Martha's fortunate escape from occupied Peking to Shanghai and then back to the States had obviously given her a first-hand experience of Japan's invasion of China. And she wanted to do something to help. It seems Martha was involved with the UCR right from the start of its existence in 1941, when it was founded in New York and began raising money. However, many supporters of China, particularly Americans with direct experience of the country, had been doing what they could to

---

514 Synthetism, in art, a method of painting evolved by Gauguin and others in the 1880s to emphasise two-dimensional flat patterns, thus breaking with Impressionist art and theory. The style shows a conscious effort to work less directly from nature and to rely more upon memory.

Former Victorian Making Good

Miss Martha Sawyers, a former resident of Victoria and daughter of Mr. and Mrs. A. B. Sawyers of Cuero, is rapidly gaining fame through the nation as an illustrator. Only last week one of her drawings adorned the cover page of Collier's Magazine. A New York Mirror columnist recently wrote that Martha Sawyer' original drawing of a "Chinese Mother" adorned "The Book of Hope" presented to Mme. Chiang Kai-shek. The book contained the names of 1000 leading American women who had contributed $100 worth of medical supplies to China. Martha Sawyers attended school in Victoria and she and her family are well known to many Victorians.

raise awareness and cash for a number of years already, Martha and Bill included. So-called 'Bowl of Rice Parties', where attendees paid for a four-course meal and then had just a bowl of rice, with the difference going to China charities buying medicines, blankets and humanitarian aid, were popular everywhere from suburban Ladies' Supper Clubs to Hollywood movie star mansions.

So too charity auctions. In 1940 Martha provided an illustration of a Chinese mother to accompany a small book by the author Pearl Buck, then perhaps the best-known American associated with China. Martha knew Buck and had previously provided illustrations for the magazine serialisations of her novels. Buck had formed the Women's Committee of Tribute to China and persuaded one thousand prominent American women to sign the *Book of Hope* and donate US$100 each. The book was then presented to China's ambassador to the United States, Dr Hu Shih, and he in turn passed it on to Soong Mei-ling, Madame Chiang Kai-shek. According to the *San Francisco Examiner*, the US$100,000 raised was spent on medical supplies to be sent to Free China.

In 1941 Sawyers was approached by the new UCR and agreed to donate her work. The images swiftly appeared nationwide to support pledge drives and were also used by China aid groups operating in Canada too. North of the border, radio stations used Sawyers' work to advertise special radio shows aimed at raising awareness of China's struggle and featuring Hollywood stars such as Bob Hope, Loretta Young, Tyrone Power, Anna May Wong and Claudette Colbert.

Martha and Bill settled into a new home with his-and-her studios. Martha's had high ceilings and windows to allow in as much light as possible – her eyesight had never been very good. Bill had a studio upstairs that included a photographic laboratory. They maintained strict working hours and saved hard. Martha took many commissions to make money, including one for *Life* magazine where she provided a series of illustrations of Bengal Lancers, presumably drawn from paintings or her own imagination (perhaps fired by Hollywood and Errol Flynn's movie *The Lives of a Bengal Lancer*).[515] Bill and Martha knew that eventually the war would end and they wanted to have funds to travel once more.

China Sky, *oil on canvas, 1940*

Though she wasn't paid for her UCR work, the posters did bring Martha additional public interest. Throughout the war she had a rolling series of exhibitions of her Asian portraits, mostly up and down the East Coast. She also managed to create a portfolio of portraits of Indian men and women, without ever leaving New York or visiting the sub-continent. She trawled the city's seamens' clubs, universities, few Indian restaurants and student lodging houses to find her subjects. The portraits were exhibited and excited a lot of press interest.

Having paid attention to Martha's profiles of Indian men and women, the United States War Office decided it had plans for the couple – although it wasn't clear that they had understood that Martha had never been to India! They encouraged Martha and Bill to leave their new studio and

---

515 The illustrations accompanied the novel by John Masters, *Nightrunners of Bengal* (New York: The Viking Press, 1951).

accept a joint posting as war artist-correspondents with *Collier's* magazine. *Collier's* arranged for Martha and Bill to fly to India in 1945 to draw their impressions of the Burma-India theatre of operations. Newspaper article after magazine profile had long described Martha as just five feet tall, slight of build, and with thick-lensed spectacles. Yet she was never anything less than intrepid – either in 1920s Paris, travelling through Asia on a shoestring before the war, or as a war artist-correspondent bunking down with the troops. The couple took the opportunity to fly the notorious 'Hump' over the Himalayas with the United States Air Force ferrying supplies into the Free China bases of Yunnan-fu, Cheng-tu and the Nationalists' wartime capital at Chungking.

The travel bug continues to bite

Clearly the travel bug never left the pair. After the war they immediately headed back to China, as well as to Hong Kong, Penang, Singapore, Sumatra, Java and Tokyo. Later they travelled to Istanbul, back to India, up to Nepal and down to Mexico. Back in America, gallery owners were furiously searching for Martha, leaving messages at all her stated ports of call and invariably just missing her as she moved on. Her UCR posters, and the exposure they brought her earlier work from Bali and China, had made her a popular artist with the public. Finally returning from their trip, Martha was able to add to her exhibitions – new portraits of Javanese dancers, Indian Lascar seamen and studies of Japanese life. At times in the years immediately after the war it seems Martha had exhibitions on in half a dozen cities and galleries at once across the USA. Galleries and museums as far afield as New York, Kansas City, Chattanooga, Iowa and Wisconsin claimed to be 'deluged with requests from the public to exhibit Martha Sawyers.'

Clearly having seen her success with the UCR campaign and as a war artist-correspondent, Martha was hired in the aftermath of World War Two by the US Army Recruiting Service. She created two campaign posters for them, notably 'Envoy of Peace', which emphasised the US Army's post-war role in Japan. The poster depicted three Japanese children in national dress conversing with an American corporal in full dress uniform sitting on his kitbag. The whole deliberately Orientalised image was reinforced by one child holding a *janomegasa*-style traditional oil-paper umbrella. As an original full-colour poster it was striking, and still attracted attention when reprinted in countless newspapers in black and white. This was during the last years of the US occupation of Japan, though the poster also appeared just as the United States was becoming embroiled in the Korean Civil War.

The couple went on to work on many book cover illustrations in the 1950s, including an excellent one for the last in JP Marquand's Mr Moto series, *Stopover Tokyo*[516], and a series of crayon and oil portraits for Pearl Buck's later novels. Martha accepted commissions to illustrate the once popular (but now almost totally forgotten) novels of Mona Gardner. Seattle-born Gardner had lived in Hong Kong for over two decades (where Martha and Bill had met her) and, before the war, she had regularly

Self-portrait, 1945

summered in northern Japan. She wrote *Middle Heaven* in 1950, described by one reviewer as 'the Japanese *Good Earth*', comparing it to Pearl Buck's China bestseller of twenty years before. Gardner also wrote *Hong Kong*, a 1958 novel set in the Opium Wars and *The Shanghai Item* set during the war.[517] Bill and Martha also worked on a number of books together – Bill wrote the text, Martha provided the illustrations. Best remembered is *The Illustrated Book About the Far East*, which came out in 1961 aimed at Grade School students and covering everywhere from Siberia, northern China and Tibet down to the Philippines.[518]

Eventually the couple retired to Connecticut and then later moved back to Texas. Bill died in 1978. Martha Sawyers Reusswig died in her San Antonio nursing home in 1986 at 84 years of age. She was a senior member of the American National Watercolor Association and the Illustrators League of New York City. When the newspapers published

516 The specific edition being JP Marquand, *Stopover in Tokyo* (New York: Little, Brown & Co., 1957).

517 Mona Gardner, *Middle Heaven* (New York: Doubleday, 1950); *Hong Kong* (New York: Doubleday, 1958); *The Shanghai Item* (New York: Doubleday, 1959).

518 Martha & William Reusswig-Sawyers, *The Illustrated Book About the Far East* (New York: Grosset & Dunlap, 1961).

her obituaries, every single one recalled her striking posters for the UCR during World War Two: the posters that had been initially inspired by her brief sojourn in Peking.

Drinks with the Foster Snows
of Kuei Chia Chang Hutong:
Edgar & Helen Foster Snow (1936)

*'Peking was like a little old Rome, dominated by dowager hostesses
and an intellectual aristocracy.'* [519]

519   Helen Foster Snow's first impressions of Peking, *My China Years: A Memoir* (New York: Morrow, 1984), p.86.

The Tartar City's "It" Couple

This collection began with dancing under the stars on the rooftop of the Grand Hôtel de Pékin. So, let us end with cocktails at sunset in a beautiful courtyard on a hutong close by the Tartar Wall.

They were the pair of the moment, the "it" couple of the times, as close to a celebrity marriage as the foreign colony of Peking had in 1936. Edgar and Helen Snow (née Foster) were among the best-known foreigners in the city, admired by the more liberal and Bohemian members of the foreign colony for their journalism, chic and *bonhomie*, but equally reviled by plenty of the more sober and conservative Legation Quarter set for their partisan leftist politics.

Today, nearly a century since their sojourn in Peking, Edgar remains by far the best remembered of the couple. The reason for this is largely down to *Red Star Over China,* the book he completed in late 1936 while the Snows were residing in a luxurious courtyard house on a shady hutong in Peking. It is a book that excites emotions in readers still. For many foreigners who have come to China in more recent times it is one of the first books they read on the country. It has remained in print in one way or another in English pretty much constantly since it was published. Due to its flattering portrait of Mao and the communist base at Yanan it has constantly been reprinted in China too – in both English and Chinese editions. *Aidejia Sinuo* is still a name known by many Chinese.

The site of the courtyard house where Edgar and Helen once lived is now commemorated with a large billboard. Edgar is pictured in a writerly pose with a pipe and hunched over his typewriter; Helen is shown in a more formal portrait. Her authorial pen name of "Nym Wales" is mentioned, but she is not shown writing. However, between them are the Chinese and English covers of their best-known books – his *Red Star Over China* and her 1939 book *Inside Red China*. The location – now a decidedly ugly late 1980s/early 1990s budget hotel on Kuei Chia Chang Hutong – is identified as the "Red Star Over China Writing Site". And so the cult of the Snows, particularly Edgar, continues...

Edgar Snow is certainly interesting. But Helen's story is too, and, it can be argued, her writing on China is far better, wider-ranging and more nuanced than it has been given credit for. As a couple they were considered

The author outside the former Snow residence

good company and excellent hosts. They were a team – working together on each other's manuscripts, editing each other, and jointly producing a journal on Chinese politics. But they were also individuals with differing interests and thoughts on the situation in China. Crucially, perhaps, for a couple so noted for being social, not all Edgar's friends were Helen's and not all Helen's were Edgar's. Yet, at their drinks parties on Kuei Chia Chang Hutong in the Tartar City, close by the Fox Tower that loomed over the southeast corner of the city, the different sides of their lives in Peking mixed together.

We can make some generalisations about the Snows in Peking. They were well known to be on the political left; some saw them as serious intellectuals, others as "parlour pinks". It is true that they were as likely to appear in the society pages as on the British Consulate's politically suspect persons list. It's true that they did live a life some might describe as rather high on the hog, but then, thanks to the exchange rate of the mighty

American dollar at the time, the purchasing power parity meant servants and other luxuries were comparatively affordable in Peking; indeed they were relatively wealthy at a time of Depression back in America. To supplement their incomes from publishing and freelance journalism, Edgar taught journalism at Yenching University and Helen worked as a shop mannequin at Helen Burton's The Camel's Bell store at the Grand Hôtel de Pékin, modelling fur coats and silk dresses. Their joint income allowed them to rent the large and luxurious courtyard house a stone's throw from the Legation Quarter, where they hosted regular cocktail parties.

On Kuei Chia Chang Hutong Edgar and Helen were at the centre of an eclectic and interesting circle of friends who gathered at their courtyard for what became an informal salon. They were able to fund their own political journal, eat, drink and dress well, and even keep a racehorse at the Paomachang track four miles outside the city. Though their politics were to the left of most of the American community in Peking, the couple were welcomed at the Paomachang race course, mixed with various American diplomats and the Marine Legation Guard in the city, and regularly used the outdoor swimming pool at the US Legation compound. Their weekend cocktail parties and informal salon were, for those who liked the couple, a hot ticket in town.

Edgar and Helen

Edgar was from Kansas City, had studied journalism at the University of Missouri, moved to New York to work in advertising, and made a little money on the stock market a year before the Wall Street crash. He used his funds (wisely as it turned out, as they would have been wiped out a few months later) to go travelling and, in the summer of 1928, pitched up in Shanghai. The city interested Edgar, and he stayed on in China – a sojourn that was to last thirteen years and make his name famous worldwide.

Helen Foster was born in Utah a year or two after Edgar. Her parents were descendants of Mormon pioneers and, though the family moved around a lot – Chicago, Idaho – they eventually settled in Salt Lake City. Helen's parents didn't think much of a girl getting a higher education although, after some arguments, she was allowed to spend a couple of years at the University of Utah. She then got a job as a secretary with the American Silver Mining Commission where her boss had contacts in Shanghai. Helen had wanted to visit Europe, but China sounded good too and, as with Europe, also had the advantage of not being Salt Lake City. She arrived on the Bund in 1931.

Helen, who was called "Peg" by her friends in China, and Edgar met almost immediately after she arrived. He was at a low point – his mother back in America had died and he had contracted a bad bout of malaria. Helen, who had read his freelance reporting from Shanghai while stuck in Salt Lake City, convinced him to stay. They would both be China correspondents.

Helen Foster Snow

Edgar's career is much better remembered, though they covered the terrible 1931 Yangtze floods and the January 1932 Japanese invasion of Shanghai together. Helen was reporting in her own right for the *Seattle Star*. She'd planned a year in China, but the couple had fallen in love. The foreign correspondent life appealed and Helen was working on a book. Edgar proposed to Helen on her twenty-fifth birthday, but she turned him down, fearing marriage would interfere with her writing. A few months later he tried again and this time she accepted. The couple were married at the American Embassy in Tokyo on Christmas Day 1932.

In 1933 they decided to move to Peking. Edgar was to teach journalism at Yenching University. Helen enrolled in courses at the university – English, philosophy and China studies.[520] Both had begun a political journey to the left after initially being enthusiastic supporters of Chiang Kai-shek and his government. They had become disillusioned with what they saw as the corruption and nepotism of the Nationalist government. At the same time the concerted anti-Japanese attitudes of many of Edgar's Chinese students at Yenching, and Helen's new classmates, had impressed

---

520   Helen was a student with a young Derk Bodde, who later became the renowned Professor of Chinese Studies at the University of Pennsylvania. She also took philosophy with the Rev. Lucius Chapin Porter, who happened to live on Kuei Chia Chang Hutong for many years and may have been how the couple knew of the available property to rent.

them greatly. They were soon to become much more embroiled in the Chinese left. In Peking they were both to move from being reporters and observers to dedicated activists. But they were still, wherever their sympathies lay, outsiders, sojourners, members of the foreign colony, and comparatively privileged.

A shady hutong

Thanks to extremely beneficial exchange rates and cheap local prices for goods and services, the Snows lived very well in Peking compared to the local population and non-Americans in the foreign colony. Things were so advantageous towards those with American dollars and Peking prices so low that Edgar was able to buy Helen a leopard-skin coat for Christmas in 1935.[521]

Helen with Gobi in Peking, 1935

When they'd first arrived in Peking in March 1933 the couple had spent a few weeks in the Grand Hôtel de Pékin on Chang An Chieh, the Avenue of Eternal Peace. This was a not inexpensive, but quite common, first stop for those planning to sojourn in Peking for some time. The hotel was very much the centre of the foreign colony's social life – the *thé dansants*, the rooftop dances in the summer, the popular shops in the lobby such as The Camel's Bell and Mr Vetch's French Bookshop (where Helen said that she loved to pass an afternoon in conversation with anyone who walked in, as just about anyone who did was interesting), not to mention the travel ticket, money changing and banking facilities with American Express and Thomas Cook's. They hadn't been sure that they would like Peking after the frenetic rush and

---

521   For various reasons linked to silver exchange, the US$ was especially strong in China at this time and so Americans with dollar earnings had beneficial exchange rates compared to European currencies and the Japanese yen.

buzz of Shanghai but soon after arriving Helen noted in her diary that Peking 'was like a little old Rome, dominated by dowager hostesses and an intellectual aristocracy.'[522] They decided to stay.

After the Grand Hôtel they rented a newly built western-style house near the Tartar Wall for a while. Then they lived for some time in Haitien, at that time a village outside the city.[523] But, by late 1935, they were in the market for somewhere larger and fancier. At first the Snows rented a very basic courtyard house at No.21 Mei Cha Hutong (Coal Ashes Alley)[524], handily near to Morrison Street for the shops and Helen's job at The Camel's Bell, but with only rudimentary plumbing and electricity and no telephone. Basic, but still quite spacious – a sizeable garden, five rooms and a bathroom for the couple, as well as a further three rooms and a bathroom and kitchen for their servants. Edgar took one room as a library to work in and decorated it with batiks the couple had bought on a trip to Bali. The Snows both began taking daily Chinese lessons from a Mr Huang.

But for the same money they found they could rent a far grander courtyard on a shady hutong, south of Mei Cha Hutong across Chang An Chieh and a mile or so east of the Legation Quarter – Kuei Chia Chang Hutong. The street was better known to foreigners as Armour Factory Alley. This area was technically the Eastern Tartar City, close by the Tartar Wall, almost in the shadow of the Fox Tower, the wall's six-hundred-year-old Ming Dynasty watchtower.[525] It was a short bicycle or rickshaw ride to the amenities of the Legation Quarter – department stores and other shops catering to western tastes – and even closer to the shopping and dining along acacia tree-lined Hatamen and Morrison Streets, just to the north. Hatamen Street offered a variety of treats including a Polish-Jewish bakery, a Russian restaurant called the Royal, a German beer hall

---

522 *My China Years*, p.86.

523 Today Haitien is Haidian, out near the Summer Palace and several universities, including Yenching where Edgar taught and Helen studied. Quite a few students, teachers and academics, especially those in more straitened financial circumstances, chose to live out in Haitien. The area was earmarked for development in the 1950s, and then later in the 1980s was redeveloped again after being identified as a technology zone. It is now home to over two million people.

524 Now Meizha Hutong, truncated from the Snows' days, but still running between Xiaowei Hutong and Chaoyangmen (previously Hatamen Street).

525 Also known as the Dongbienmen.

and restaurant called Hempel's and several Japanese sukiyaki restaurants. Helen could easily cycle to The Camel's Bell at the Grand Hôtel. Quiet, traditional, shady – Kuei Chia Chang had long been popular with foreigners in Peking looking for the hutong experience. Along with Shih-chia Hutong and Nan-chi Tze Hutong (both to the north of Chang An Chieh), Kuei Chia Chang was one of the most desirable hutong addresses in the city.

Kuei Chia Chang ran west into Soochow Hutong (then, as now, a noted food street), which continued through to the edge of the Legation Quarter at Hatamen Street. It was close to the old imperial examination halls and had traditionally been the area where various concerns linked to the Chinese arsenal had been situated in the Ming Dynasty – hence its association with armouries. It later became home to several papermaking factories; small family businesses that had given the warren of lanes around Kuei Chia Chang the name of the Papermakers' District. The hutong was lined with plane trees and had poplar and ginkgo trees within most of the courtyards.

As well as the hutong's location, its fifteen courtyard properties had long proved popular with foreigners. The mostly Chinese owners, keen to secure the higher rents the foreign colony were willing and able to pay, had been quick to realise the potential of the hutong. Traditional windows of thick translucent paper had been replaced with glass; the courtyards fitted out with electric lights, modern Western-style bathrooms and WCs, water boilers, modern plumbing and steam heating. Over the years, luxuries had been added – modern stables for ponies allowing residents of the hutong to take morning canters along the nearby Tartar Wall (twenty feet wide on top), tennis courts and additional structures. The Snows' courtyard had it all – a ginkgo, a tennis court, pony stables and a separate writing hut that Edgar occupied.

Their neighbours were almost exclusively other members of the foreign colony. The American Board of Commissioners for Foreign Missions (ABCFM), or simply the American Board, had leased several adjacent courtyards on the street for many years. The hutong's best-known resident was the former British diplomat and noted Sinologist ETC Werner, who lived in an equally large courtyard with his teenage daughter Pamela and their servants. As Pamela was away at school in Tientsin, Werner had the house mostly to himself. It was a more traditional courtyard than the Snows', though it had electricity and a plumbed-in WC. Werner worked in his library, reputedly the largest private library in Peking. Helen nodded to Werner when she saw him; Edgar appears to have been unaware of him.

What the American missionaries along the hutong thought of the Snows is unknown, but perhaps easy to guess – regular parties, cocktail hour "sundowners", coming home at all times, gramophone music, maybe the occasional voluble row, not to mention their left-wing sympathies.

Throughout the 1920s No.13 Kuei Chia Chang had been the home of William Collins, a British mining engineer and director of the Anglo-French China Corporation that mined mineral deposits in Yunnan province. Collins eventually returned to England and sold the courtyard in 1931 to an acquaintance, Dr ET Nystrom, a wealthy Swedish geologist. Nystrom reputedly knew China's steel and coal reserves to the nearest ton and had used this knowledge to make a fortune. With his money he founded the Nystrom Institute for Scientific Research in the coal-producing town of Taiyuan in Shansi province. Nystrom and his wife lived half the year in Sweden, as she refused to move permanently to Peking.

When Nystrom was in China he spent most of his time at the Peking Club on Rue Marco Polo, or on his own five-hole golf course he'd built nearby at the Jesuit Observatory. The Nystroms found the courtyard too big for them and decided to occupy just a couple of rooms and lease out the majority of the house, tennis court, stables and writer's hut included. They had had all the modern conveniences fitted as well as their own telephone number – "Peking 2670". The Nystrom house was luxurious by any standards in Peking in 1935. It had a long glassed-in conservatory, greenhouses for Nystrom's plant collection, marble bathroom fittings, steam heat and fireplaces too. There was a semi glassed-in pavilion ideal for entertaining if the weather was cold or if it was raining.

This meant that the Snows basically had the run of the entire property. Flush with Chinese dollars, they rented the place immediately. They actually got a good deal considering the size of the place. The fact that the hutong was considered haunted by fox spirits meant few Chinese would rent houses along it. Edgar and Helen got most of the Nystrom courtyard for a very reasonable US$10 a month – the same rent in 1936 as a small Greenwich Village walk-up apartment. The courtyard also came with its own team of servants – a "number one boy" (in reality a relatively elderly man), his assistant, a maid and a chef as well as a gatekeeper and gardener.[526]

Edgar acquired the stout Mongolian pony that he kept stabled out at the Paomachang racecourse. The Swedish explorer Sven Hedin was rather taken with Helen and gave her a lean white Kansu greyhound. She named the dog, that set up camp in an overstuffed armchair Edgar had bought at a jumble sale at the French Legation, "Gobi" (Hedin of course having explored that particular desert extensively).

No.13 Kuei Chia Chang Hutong was the perfect location from which Ed and Peg could launch themselves on Peking's foreign society…

The salon at No.13

Arriving in Peking with their reputations as journalists and as a fashionable couple, Edgar and Helen soon acquired a "set". It was wonderfully eclectic – Sinologists and academics overlapped with journalists and explorers, left-wing activists with visiting movie stars, long-time residents of Peking with temporary sojourners.

No.13 Kuei Chia Chang was quite the residence to entertain in. The high grey walls and red gate led into a stone-flagged front court through a small foyer where guests could leave any baggage, umbrellas, coats and galoshes (Kuei Chia Chang did get muddy when it rained as it wasn't tarmacadamed). Arriving in the second interior courtyard, guests appreciated the coloured lights and Chinese lanterns that had been strung up. Servants, under Edgar's watchful eye and training, would mix cocktails and prepare *hors d'oeuvres*. Guests sat in rattan chairs with little bamboo tables for their drinks amid small orange and lemon trees. They could admire the beds of carefully planted (by the Nystroms' Chinese gardeners) peonies, lilacs, pomegranates and roses set against carefully arranged rock displays with wisteria running up the walls. Adding to the Nystroms' efforts, Helen bought masses of plants, sold by a local hawker for just 25 cents each, to furnish the impressive flower beds. In summer the courtyard's ginkgo tree provided some shade.

---

526   For more on the history of foreigners renting on Kuei Chia Chang and the various properties on the hutong, see Paul French, 'A Most Foreign Hutong: Beijing's Kuei Chia Chang in 1922', *Journal of the Royal Asiatic Society China*, Vol.78, No.1, 2018, p.154.

Helen owned up to choreographing her salon quite deliberately to stimulate the senses. Guests entered though a moon gate, adjacent to which she had planted her most fragrant flowers – jasmine, tuberoses and oleander. Inside, the curtains and chair covers were matched in hand-woven fabrics (all obtained at a discount from Helen Burton at The Camel's Bell, of course) printed with modernist designs to get away from the traditional and rather stuffy "Victorian Peking" style favoured by the Legation Quarter set. Bookcases lined the walls and there were prints by Grant Wood and Thomas Benton, the leading lights of the American Regionalist movement (mostly everyday scenes of the American Midwest). Their work desks cleared, canapés on willow pattern plates and drinks were laid out between silverware vases containing bamboo sprays. Golden straw woven mats lay on the hard earthen floors and, if the sun was particularly hot, large mats of bamboo (known as *pongs* or *pengs*) were hung across the courtyard to provide some additional shade.

By the standards of many of the Peking foreign colony, especially the more exclusive Legation Quarter circles, the Snows' salon at No.13 was not an overly lavish affair. *Hors d'oeuvres* were served, though not necessarily with a full meal (which, invariably in the Legation Quarter, would be multi-course) to follow. Often, after drinks, any remaining guests at No.13 would depart for a local restaurant and more conversation; though if provided, dinner was never considered before 8pm at the earliest. Snacks started with cookies and sandwiches, with coffee or tea for the non-drinkers, and later included toasted cheese (or tofu), red caviar (i.e. from the roe of salmon, trout or cod), stuffed mushroom puffs, small crab canapés, some cold duck meat perhaps, prawns fried in ginger, and small delicious hard-boiled quail's eggs.

Helen took the position that salads were too risky in Peking, though some hosts were known to wash their salad in permanganate of potash, which she considered still too risky.[527] Only fruit that could be peeled was served and then one still had to be careful to ensure the fruit was cut with a clean knife. It was a strict regime but sensible – before marrying Helen, Edgar had suffered both dysentery and malaria in Shanghai. After marrying her and adopting her hygiene rules he never suffered those

---

527 Given that this is more usually a treatment for fungal infections of the foot, impetigo, pemphigus, superficial wounds, dermatitis and tropical ulcers, it is intriguing to imagine what a Peking salad treated in such a way actually tasted like.

unpleasant ailments again (which, when dysentery was severe, could lead to the removal of much of a patient's intestines).

True to her Mormon upbringing Helen was not a drinker of either alcohol or coffee; Edgar drank both copiously. Neither was Helen a smoker; Edgar was. But a good salon must have some alcohol. For drinks, cocktails were the fashion – Peking followed Shanghai in preferring the *stengah* (whisky-soda) to the more tropical gin and tonic, though it would be nice to think that Edgar perhaps mixed up some Gloom Chasers, the preferred cocktail of Harold Acton's *Peonies and Ponies*.[528] Imported spirits, though, such as Scotch, were expensive. Edgar developed a taste for the local *baijiu* (which Helen also used as an accelerant to light the fires in winter), and cheap Russian vodka mixed with canned grapefruit juice to take the gasoline-like edge off. All cocktails would be chilled in ice, but nobody would be silly enough to actually put an ice cube in their drink if they wanted to avoid hepatitis or worse. The Legation Quarter consular socials, or the Peking Club, might have been able to afford and be able to get sufficient amounts of champagne, but the Snows and their set usually settled for perfectly good Asti Spumante. The couple regularly visited a French monastery in the Western Hills, which Helen Burton knew about, that made their own liqueurs. Helen would cheekily decant these into more expensively branded, yet empty, bottles of crème de menthe or Cointreau, claiming nobody could ever tell the difference.[529]

Do please mingle…

And then there were the guests… the most important element of any salon.

Journalists were of course a major component, including the Peking-based foreign correspondents, especially the infamous workaholic Francis McCracken ("Mac") Fisher of the United Press. Mac had been stationed in the city since March 1935 after completing a bachelor's degree in journalism at Yenching. Fisher (originally from Pittsburgh), as well as

---

528 The Gloom Chaser – take a generous measure of Grand Marnier, the same of triple sec, slightly less of lemon juice, a dash or two of grenadine, shake or stir as preferred, add ice (if not in a hepatitis zone!) and serve. It was all the rage in Peking in 1937.

529 *My China Years*, pp.95-97.

another regular guest, James D. White of the Associated Press, had both previously spent time at the Missouri University journalism school, as had Edgar.

Roving *Daily News* journalist John Gunther and his journalist wife Frances Fineman, who like Helen with Edgar worked closely with her husband, stayed with the Snows when passing through Peking and beginning their research for the Asia volume of Gunther's popular *Inside* series.[530] Wang Haisheng, aka "Newsreel Wong", called when visiting from his base in Shanghai and, in 1936, added some Hollywood glamour to Kuei Chia Chang when he brought along his friend, the Chinese-American movie star Anna May Wong, whose visit to China he was filming.

The left-leaning journalist James Bertram, a New Zealander and former Rhodes scholar, was in Peking busy writing for the *Times*, *The Manchester Guardian* and the *New Statesman* while also studying Chinese at Yenching. Bertram was one of the couple's most regular guests and closest friends during their Peking sojourn. He often brought along his Yenching roommate, Wang Ju-mei, who later changed his name to Huang Hua, rose up the ranks of the Communist Party and became one of the PRC's longest-serving foreign ministers[531]. In his memoirs Bertram wrote that 'Meeting the Snows was for me the real turning point in my discovery of modern China'. The couple had introduced Bertram to many of the star leftists in Peking and China at the time, including the more usually Shanghai-based Soong Ching-ling (Madame Sun Yat-sen), the Indusco founder Rewi Alley, the seemingly omnipresent Agnes Smedley and the author Lu Xun, all of whom were occasional guests at No.13 Kuei Chia Chang when in Peking.[532]

But eclectic also meant Sinologist friends and these included Herrlee Creel, a brilliant young Sinologist studying at the Harvard-Yenching Institute who was briefly part of the Snows' salon before he left Peking to become a professor of Chinese at the University of Chicago. Another

530 Gunther wrote more than half a dozen *Inside* books – on Europe, Latin America, Africa, USA and Russia, as well as *Inside Asia*, published in 1939.

531 Excepting only Zhou Enlai.

532 James Munro Bertram, *Capes of China Slide Away: A Memoir of Peace and War 1910-1980* (Auckland: Auckland University Press, 1993), p.95.

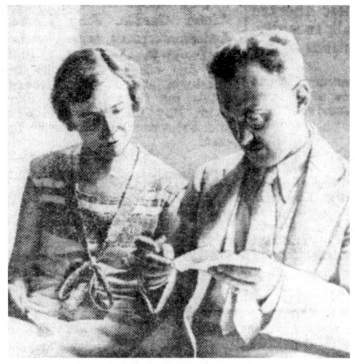

The Lattimores, 1934

regular was John K. Fairbank, known as "The King", and his new wife Wilma, as well as Owen and Eleanor Lattimore.

Fairbank had studied Chinese at Oxford as a Rhodes scholar and then moved to China to study at Tsinghua University. Fairbank's wife Wilma was herself a scholar of Chinese art. The Fairbanks moved in quite high Chinese circles and were good friends with the American-trained architect Liang Sicheng, the son of the famous reforming politician of the Qing Dynasty, Liang Qichao. The American-born Sinologist and Mongolist Owen Lattimore had been raised in Tientsin where his parents taught English at a local university. In 1936 he was editing *Pacific Affairs*, the journal published by the Institute of Pacific Relations. Snow, who shared many political opinions with Lattimore, was to clear the way for him to visit the communists in Yanan in 1937. His wife, Eleanor Holgate Lattimore, had developed a deep interest in Central Asia after the newly married couple journeyed across the region on their honeymoon in 1926: a honeymoon that had got off to a slightly rocky start as somehow the couple's plans to meet had got confused and Eleanor ended up travelling alone by horse-drawn sled for four hundred miles to rendezvous with Owen.[533]

Another Sinologically-inclined occasional guest who might seem a surprising regular was Teilhard de Chardin, the brilliant and iconoclastic French Jesuit palaeontologist-philosopher who challenged church orthodoxy with his social-ethical application of evolutionary theory. De Chardin had been involved in the archaeological dig that revealed the Peking Man at Choukoutien near Peking. He had somewhat communistic leanings for a Jesuit. Helen thought him quite the most handsome man in Peking – an opinion shared by many women in the foreign colony.[534] The couple met de Chardin early on in their Peking sojourn and became firm friends, joining him on long walks along the Tartar Wall from the Chienmen Gate to the Fox Tower, exercising her dog Gobi and debating philosophy. It was a political relationship too – the Snows and de Chardin collected around fifty Chinese woodcuts by various left-wing Chinese artists which they sent to the Galerie Billiet in Paris for what Helen claimed was the first exhibition of left-wing Chinese modernist art in Europe.[535]

Although the Snows' politics were viewed as rather extreme by many in the American community, the couple did have friends in the diplomatic corps and the official US representatives in China. Helen was very good friends with Robert Ward, the American consul in Tientsin since his appointment in 1935. He was regularly in Peking on official business and able to pop in for a drink. John S. Service had been born in Sichuan to missionary parents and attended the Shanghai American School. The American foreign service appreciated his knowledge of western Chinese dialects, recruited him and sent him to the US Consulate in Yunnan-fu. After two years in Yunnan he was then sent to Peking for further language training where he met the Snows and regularly attended their salon. Like Lattimore, Service was later to be a victim of McCarthy in the post-war "Red Scares".

533 A journey and honeymoon she describes in Eleanor Holgate Lattimore, *Turkestan Reunion* (New York: John Day, 1934).

534 The American sculptor and Peking sojourner Lucile Swan, who also made the Peking Man skull moulds, fell hopelessly in love with de Chardin at a Peking dinner party – hopeless because despite his radical politics he maintained his vow of celibacy.

535 *My China Years*, p.114.

Primary among the Snows' friends who held official positions was Evans F. Carlson, who had first been posted as a United States marine to Shanghai between 1927 and 1929. In the early thirties Carlson had been a student of Chinese and adjutant of the US Marine Legation Guard in Peking. Then, in 1937, he received his third posting to China, once again to Peking to continue his language studies, as well as being tasked as America's military observer with Chinese forces. He was living in Peking with his wife, Estelle. They met the Snows at a picnic given by Helen Burton in her Western Hills weekend temple. Carlson had read an early draft of *Red Star Over China* and, though the Carlsons shared little common ideological ground with the Snows, they became firm friends and enjoyed arguing the toss over Chinese politics. Estelle and Helen became particularly close. As with Owen Lattimore, Edgar was instrumental in getting permission for Carlson to travel to Yanan to meet Mao, Zhou Enlai and the Chinese communists.[536]

Alongside the more liberal elements of the local diplomatic corps, certain leftist foreign correspondents and the Sinology community, the Snows often invited fellow Peking sojourner friends from literary backgrounds, including the author and Mr Moto creator JP Marquand with his new partner Adelaide Hooker.[537]

Pearl Buck, whose novel *The Good Earth* had won the Pulitzer Prize in 1932, was probably the western woman most associated with China in the wider public's mind. If the English aesthete Harold Acton, living in Peking at the time, was to be believed then Buck was a prize guest. Acton notes in his *roman à clef* of the 1930s Peking foreign colony, *Peonies and Ponies,* that among the Legation Quarter set, 'laborious conversations invariably commenced with Pearl Buck, since all at least had read *The Good*

---

536 As a side note it was Carlson, as a lieutenant colonel in World War Two in command of the Second Marine Raider Battalion (partly modelled on the communist organisational units he had seen in Yanan), who coined the term "Gung Ho!" as a Marine Corps battle cry. The slogan comes from the Chinese *gong he*, roughly meaning "work together" though is, technically, an Americanism that is derived from Chinese. Carlson got the term originally from Rewi Alley and his Chinese Industrial Cooperatives and technical training schools, nicknamed Gung Ho. Carlson first met Alley at a cocktail party at No.13 Kuei Chia Chang.

537 For More on Marquand and Hooker see the previous chapter, 'Finding Love and Mr. Moto in Peiping'.

Earth...'[538] Buck was accompanied by her new husband, Richard Walsh, whose John Day publishing house and *Asia* magazine were print outlets for the Snows – Helen wrote a number of articles on Chinese modern art for him.[539] Opinion of Buck swings with changing ideas and politics. Helen thought her important, as 'It was primarily through her novelist's mind that the West, especially America, got its picture of China.' Later the Communists banned her for having 'vilified the Chinese people.' Helen described her as 'large and matronly', though with 'a lovely voice and blue green, sea-changing eyes.'[540]

Edgar would also sometimes invite his students from the journalism faculty at Yenching to join the party, along with some friendly staff. Ran Sailer, who spent thirty years teaching psychology at Yenching, was sympathetic to the communists and was a help to the Snows when they first arrived in the city. Harry Price taught economics and sociology and often invited the Snows to his courtyard house. Peking-born Hsiao Chien (Xiao Qian), then in his early twenties, had started out as an English major but switched to studying journalism under Snow at Yenching. He graduated in June 1936 and later claimed that the techniques he learnt from Snow at Yenching stayed with him throughout his reporting life. He was to travel to Cambridge University for post-graduate study and became a lecturer at University College, London, before returning to work on the Shanghai edition of the Hong Kong newspaper, *Ta Kung Pao*. After the initial Japanese invasion of China he took a trip up the vital Burma Road.[541] He then returned to England and reported from London during World War Two and the Blitz for *Ta Kung Pao* as the only Chinese foreign correspondent in the British capital during the bombing.[542]

538 Harold Acton, *Peonies and Ponies* (London: Chatto & Windus, 1941), p.131.
539 They married in 1935, the same day Pearl divorced her first husband, the American expert in Chinese agriculture, John Lossing Buck, in Reno, Nevada.
540 *My China Years*, p.115.
541 Hsiao Chien's experiences on the Burma Road would become the basis for the wartime propaganda novel written and illustrated by fellow London-based Chinese writer and artist, Chiang Yee – *The Men of the Burma Road* (London: Methuen, 1942).
542 See, Hsiao Chien (Xiao Qian), *Traveller Without a Map* (London: Hutchison, 1990).

A few who were hard to classify as one group or another were regulars: for instance, the aforementioned Swedish explorer Sven Hedin.[543] One of Helen's closest friends was Janet Fitch Sewall, part of a large missionary family that first left Ohio for China in 1874. Janet had, according to Helen, 'big blue eyes, fair skin and blond hair' and attracted many suitors, though she lived a quite frugal life with her husband and just two servants. She worked as an artist and designer and was an expert on motifs in Chinese art.[544]

And finally, LC Arlington, who was a special guest at the salon and a man both the Snows loved to listen to.[545] Arlington had seen service in the Qing navy, was an expert on Chinese drama and was also one of the most knowledgeable men on the city of Peking itself, having written (with William Lewisohn) *In Search of Old Peking*, that had been published in 1935 by Helen's good friend the bookseller Henri Vetch.[546]

LC Arlington

With a mixed group of people all in the courtyard in the shade of the ginkgo tree and later under the twinkling fairy lights, cocktails in hand, cigarettes lit, servants circulating with trays of *hors d'oeuvres*, what conversations must have been had at No.13 Kuei Chia Chang?

543 This was obviously a couple of years before Hedin became notoriously pro-Nazi and had regular access to many senior Nazis as well as Hitler, which rather destroyed his reputation and put him into social and scientific isolation in post-war Stockholm.

544 Janet Fitch Sewall's memoirs are called *Foreign Devils: Reminiscences of a China Missionary Daughter, 1909-1935* (San Francisco: Chinese Materials Center, 1981).

545 To avoid repetition, I simply point the reader to the chapter 'The Peiping World of Peonies and Ponies', which contains more details on Arlington's varied and interesting life and work in Peking.

546 Arlington's memoir is *Through the Dragon's Eyes: Fifty Years' Experiences of a Foreigner in the Chinese Government Service* (London: Constable, 1931). His study of Chinese drama is *The Chinese Drama from the Earliest Times Until Today* (Shanghai: Kelly & Walsh, 1930) and his great study of the city is LC Arlington & W. Lewisohn, *In Search of Old Peking* (Peiping: French Bookstore, 1935).

When the party stopped

Eventually the Snows would decide to move on from Peking. Edgar was spending time with the communists in Yenan; Helen visited Manchuria and stayed in Dairen, Mukden and ventured into Japanese-occupied Korea as well as covering Chiang Kai-shek's kidnapping in Sian. Helen also then visited northwest China and the communists too.

Back in Peking by January 1937 they were already nervous. Edgar was finishing the manuscript of *Red Star Over China*. Helen was editing the chapters before they were sent off to the publisher. Already Edgar had got wind of the fact that the Nationalist government was not happy about what they thought he was going to publish about the communists. Edgar knew that they were definitely not going to like the book. He was nervous of the more fascistic elements of the Guomindang, the Blue Shirts – some of whom practised martial arts near Kuei Chia Chang at the foot of the Fox Tower.

When the Snows' neighbour Pamela Werner was brutally murdered, and her mutilated body dumped at the Fox Tower in early January 1937, Edgar feared that the killers might have been targeting Helen to get at him. Helen worried about that too – both Pamela and Helen were slim, blonde and about the same height. The couple had been out on the night of the murder at a party at the home of one of Edgar's colleagues at Yenching. Still, they were nervous and Edgar insisted on hiring four extra guards armed with large broadswords to man the front gate of No.13. Helen was questioned by the police. They thought the idea of a potential assassination plausible. It was a bad start to the year.

The situation with the Japanese got steadily worse. In early July, Japanese provocations intensified to firefights and skirmishes, and eventually the Japanese moved to open confrontation. When Peking finally fell, the city was declared the seat of the Provisional Government of the Republic of China – a collaborationist puppet institution that would have been laughable if it wasn't so brutal. The long wait for the Japanese to move was over and Peking was occupied. The lights went out, food queues lengthened, inflation spiralled, the arrests and disappearances intensified. Day after day, the Japanese military poured into the city through the Chienmen Gate – tanks first, followed by infantry marching in columns of four. They took over the hotels as well as large houses and courtyard residences abandoned by Peking's intellectual class and foreigners, who had mostly fled.

Helen arrived back in Peking from an extended reporting trip in October 1937. She checked into the German Hospital with amoebic dysentery and found her room adorned with pictures of Hitler. Helen packed up the couple's belongings at No.13 Kuei Chia Chang and in November 1937 took the train to Tientsin and then the Butterfield and Swire ferry to Shanghai, where Edgar was waiting for her. The days of the Kuei Chia Chang salon of the Foster-Snows was over. Edgar and Helen's Peking sojourn was over. The Peking they had briefly known was almost over too.

Appendix

Placenames, old and new

Peking roads

Old	New
Canal Street	Zhengyi Road
Chang An Chieh	Changan Street
Chienmen Street	Qianmen East Street
Hatamen Street	Chongwenmen Street
Legation Street	Dong Jiangmi Xiang
Rue Marco Polo	Taijichang Street
Rue Meu	Zhengyi East Road
Morrison Street	Wangfujing
Thieves' Market	Hong Qiao, or the Red Bridge, Market
Wangfuting	Wangfujing

Cities and towns

Old	New
Amoy	Xiamen
Canton	Guangzhou
Chefoo	Yantai
Cheng-tu	Chengdu
Choukoutien	Zhoukoudian
Chungking	Chongqing
Dairen	Dalian
Foochow	Fujian
Hangchow	Hangzhou
Hsinking	Changchun
Ichang	Yichang
Kalgan	Zhangjiakou
Kongmoon	Jiangmen
Manchouli	Manzhouli
Mokanshan	Moganshan
Mukden	Shenyang
Nanking	Nanjing

Nankow	Juyong
Ningpo	Ningbo
Pakhoi	Beihai
Port Arthur	Lushun
Port Edward	Weihai City
Pukow	Pukou
Sian	Xian
Samshui	Sanshui
Suanhwafu	Xuanhua
Tientsin	Tianjin
Tsingtao	Qingdao
Weihaiwei	Weihai
Wenchow	Wenzhou
Wuchow	Wuzhou
Yenan	Yanan
Yunnan-fu	Kunming

Provinces

Old	New
Chekiang	Zhejiang
Chihli	Zhili (now Hebei)
Hopei	Hebei
Kansu	Gansu
Kiangsu	Jiangsu
Kwangtung	Guangdong
Ninghsia	Ningxia
Shansi	Shanxi
Shantung	Shandong
Sinkiang	Xinjiang

Acknowledgements

Thanks to all those people I've talked old Peking with over the years: Paul Bevan, Robert Bickers, Julia Boyd, Douglas Clark, Patrizia van Daalen, Ambassador Extraordinary and Plenipotentiary of the Russian Federation to the People's Republic of China Andrey Denisov, Peter Goff, Fred Greguras, Simon Rom Gjeroe, Anya Goncharova, Jiang Wen, Jeremiah Jenne, Sarah Keenlyside, Ned Kelly, Katya Knyazeva, Ed Lanfranco, Melinda Liu, Jeffrey Long, Thomas O'Malley, Michael Meyer, Lars Ulrich Thum, Ying Wei and Frances Wood.

Wallis Simpson's time in China has long interested me – mostly because of what everyone thinks they know about Wallis, her life, and her adventures in China – ninety-nine per cent of which is completely and utterly wrong. I still have plans to set that particular record straight sometime soon. Wallis's biographer Anne Sebba was a wealth of information on all aspects of the Duchess of Windsor's life and was kind enough to share her in-depth research and thoughts with me. My thanks to Sarah Keenlyside of Bespoke Beijing as well as the management and staff of the Nuo Hotel Beijing, which now occupies the original Grand Hôtel de Pékin that Wallis knew, for facilitating several stays at the old Grand Hôtel. The original part of what is now the Beijing Hotel complex that Wallis would have known is now the Nuo (a.k.a. the charmingly named Block B). The Stalinist-inspired part of the hotel to the west (Block C) was added in 1954; the hotel on the corner of Wangfujing that resembles a public housing project (Block D) was added in 1974. The creation of this uninspiring piece of architecture necessitated the sad demolition of the original red-brick 1915 wing. Who the hell knows what happened to the non-existent Block A? Block B has been added too at the rear with a sort of shopping mall-cum-hotel and false ceilings throughout. The famous rooftop is now permanently closed and forgotten. But there are some nice touches – some interior windows and the main staircase (though spoiled at higher levels by false ceilings) remain, which make it worth a visit.

An anonymous bookseller at the excellent Elliott Bay Book Company in Seattle first found me a copy of Curzio Malaparte's *The Kremlin Ball*.

Despite Malaparte's often unpleasant politics and associations on both the left and the right I had long been a fan of his two war reportage books, *Kaput* and *Skin*. When Malaparte mentioned Karakhan he excited my interest.

Peking Takedown developed out of research and writing done for a commissioned narrative-drama for BBC Radio 3, *Peking Noir*. My thanks to Sarah Wooley who wrote the dramatic scenes for that production and to Sasha Yevtushenko for pushing so hard to get that show made and then producing it. Professor Robert Bickers of Bristol University was kind enough to share his knowledge of Peter Lawless with me while Chinamarine.org were kind enough to allow me use of their photographs of Dewolfe Schatzel.

Two great Shanghai historians, Tess Johnston and Patrick Cranley, helped me track down Denton Welch's teenage home at the Rivers Court Apartments. Thanks to Shanghailander photographer Graham Keelaghan for photographing the remaining buildings for me so assiduously. Rachel Rapaport and Julie Chun at the Royal Asiatic Society in Shanghai kindly invited me to talk about Denton Welch in 2019, which gave me an excuse to look at his time in Shanghai and Peking in greater detail.

'Peking is Like Paris' was originally published in the Journal of the Royal Asiatic Society (China) as '"Peking is Like Paris" – Isamu Noguchi and his Encounter with Peking's Avant-Garde Milieu in 1930', Vol.76, No.1, 2016. That article was itself an extended version of a lecture I gave entitled "Peking 1930" at The Noguchi Museum, Long Island City, New York in October 2013 to coincide with the museum's 2013/2014 exhibition, 'Isamu Noguchi and Qi Baishi: Beijing 1930'. I must thank the editor of that edition of the RAS China Journal, Lindsay Shen, and Dakin Hart, Senior Curator at the Noguchi Museum. Since writing the original article I have discovered some more details on the amazing life of Nadine Hwang, some of which have been added to this chapter. For some of those details my thanks go to the Archivo China España.

Edmund Backhouse's best biographer Derek Sandhaus was kind enough to talk through his last days with me, and to share his copy of Hoeppli's postscript to *Décadence Mandchoue*. Jeremiah Jenne helped me locate Backhouse's former Peking addresses. My thanks also to Jean-Louis Bussiere for information on his father.

I found the time to research more on Eugen and Helma Ott's time in Peking after being commissioned to review Owen Matthews's biography of Richard Sorge for the *South China Morning Post* in Hong Kong. My thanks to Adam Wright for commissioning that review, and to Adam Cathcart of Leeds University for pointing me in the direction of more information on Dr Walter Fuchs.

I have long loved Harold Acton's *Peonies and Ponies*. Frances Wood, the Sinologue, author and former curator of Chinese collections at the British Library until 2013, shared with me her ideas about who Acton based his characters on; as did Julia Boyd, the author of *A Dance with the Dragon: The Vanished World of Peking's Foreign Colony*. I also very much enjoyed talking about the Peking aesthetes with the historian Jeremiah Jenne at the now gone and sorely missed Beijing Bookworm, and then again courtesy of Sarah Keenlyside and Sam Braybon at Bespoke Beijing. Jeremiah's article for the *Los Angeles Review of Books China Channel* entitled 'The Peking Aesthetes' is a good summation of our conversations on Acton, Parsons, Kates, Blofeld et al. My thanks to Jeffrey Long of Long Bros. books in Seattle and to Peggy Hartzell for additional details on Thomas Handforth.

Olga Fischer-Togo proved extremely elusive. However, I am extremely grateful to Mátyás Mervay who offered me his own research on Olga during World War One that answered a number of queries about her true nationality (or nationalities). His paper, *A Research on the Austro-Hungarian Prisoners of War in China During World War One*, Master's (M.A.) Thesis (in Chinese), Nankai University, 2017, was also useful.

Dr Anne Witchard of the University of Westminster first introduced me to Ellen Newbold La Motte. Then the independent publisher Camphor Press in Taiwan republished the rather hard-to-get *Peking Dust* as an e-book. That meant that I was able to include comments by La Motte in my Penguin China Special, *Betrayal in Paris: How the Treaty of Versailles Led to China's Long Revolution* (2016), that was part of Penguin China's collection of short books related to China's involvement in World War One. The wonderful Heywood Hill bookshop in Mayfair tracked down the Evelyn Waugh essays for me.

Megan Walsh Gerard kindly found time to visit the Georgia Historical Society Archives in Savannah to search for forgotten Harry Hervey movie treatments when I was too far away and couldn't come up with a good excuse to go to Georgia. Also, Hervey's principal biographer Harlan Greene, author of *The Dead Don't Cry – They Just Disappear: The Life and Works of Harry Hervey*, kindly encouraged me to make further explorations into Harry's Asian sojourns. My wider interest in von Sternberg's movies stems from childhood TV watching. However, I must thank Tammy Lai-Ming Ho, a founding co-editor at Hong Kong's *Cha: An Asian Literary Journal*, who encouraged me to write about von Sternberg. My article, 'Mayhem in Macao: Josef von Sternberg's Fantastical Macao of the Mind', is available in the Macao Special Issue of *Cha* online (Issue 43, April 2019).

My essay on Martha Sawyers and her husband Bill Reusswig first appeared in a slightly different form in the *South China Morning Post* weekend magazine. My thanks to Dave Besseling for commissioning and editing, and Antony Dickson for sourcing images.

Research modern China and there is no getting away from Edgar Snow. But it's always been Helen that interested me more – her journalism, books and autobiography were all better than his. She slipped back into my research by becoming a character in my book *Midnight in Peking* as she was interviewed by one of the detectives investigating the murder of the Snows' neighbour Pamela Werner in early 1937. I should note that the American actress Elyse Ribbons, who played Helen in a thirty-hour Chinese TV production of *Red Star Over China*, has done a lot of work on Helen, including Helen and Edgar's relationship, and was good enough to talk to me about her insights for the *Los Angeles Review of Books* in 2016 – 'Being Helen Foster Snow: a Q&A with Elyse Ribbons'.

And finally, thanks to Anne Witchard for reading, editing and commenting on all these pieces as diligently as she did previously for *Destination Shanghai*, to Pete Spurrier of Blacksmith Books for publishing *Destination Shanghai* and now *Destination Peking*, and to Cara Wilson for the cover design.

Paul French
Email – paul@chinarhyming.com
Blog – www.chinarhyming.com
Twitter - @chinarhyming
Instagram – OldShanghaiPaul
WeChat – paul_french

Image credits

p.33. Laurence Sickman, Nelson-Atkins Museum of Art Archives, Kansas City, MO

p.35 & 208. Carl van Vechten, Library of Congress, Washington DC

p.36. Frank Dorn Papers, Hoover Institution, Stanford, CA

p.36. *The Philadelphia Enquirer*, August 30, 1936

p.42. *Corriere Della Sera*

p.47. Louis Fischer, *The Soviets in World Affairs*, 1930

p.54. Nikolay Petrov, *SovetskoePhoto* (Soviet Photo), 1928

p.57. American Legation Gateway, 1901, Crown copyright

p.59. *New York Times*, 1906

p.62, 254 & 256, 259 & 260. Library of Congress, Washington DC

p.63. Crown copyright

p.65 *Boston Daily Globe*, October 29, 1902

p.68. Originally by Sir Robert Hart, 1900 (courtesy of Jeremiah Jenne)

p.75. Robert Byron Papers, Yale University, New Haven, CT

p.80, 86, 205, 210. New York University (Florence)

p.91 & 109. courtesy of Chinamarine.org

p.92. *Honolulu Advertiser*, October 1, 1939

p.107. *Honolulu Star Bulletin*, October 26, 1938

p.108. Billie Love Historical Collection, Historical Photographs of China, University of Bristol

p.110. *Oakland Tribune*, October 6, 1960

p.113. self-portrait, courtesy of National Portrait Gallery, London

p.118. Walter Stoneman bromide print, courtesy of National Portrait Gallery, London

p.124. Rockefeller Archive Center, China Medical Board, Inc. records, Sleepy Hollow, NY

p.128. John David Zumbrun (est. 1915), Historical Photographs of China, University of Bristol

p.131. Berenice Abbott: Isamu Noguchi with *Glad Day*, c.1930, The Noguchi Museum, NYC

p.134. Christie's Hong Kong

p.135. portrait by Zheng Jingkang, *China Photography*, June 1978

p.139. courtesy of Tong Bingxue

p.140. *Pacific Islands Monthly*, 1938

p.141. *Portada de Estampa*, 1929, courtesy of *Archivo China España*

p.146. courtesy of The Noguchi Museum, NYC

p.151. courtesy of The London Library

p.152. *The New China Review*, vol.1, no.5, 1919

p.159. *Boston Globe*, April 1977

p.165 & 244. courtesy of Museum of the City of New York

pp. 174-175 & 213-214. The Lucy Monroe Calhoun Family Photographs of China, David M. Rubenstein Rare Book & Manuscript Library at Duke University, Durham, NC

p.176. *The Democrat and Chronicle* (Rochester, NY), March 29, 1931

p.180. Hooker – *The Brooklyn Citizen*, February 26, 1937; Marquand – *The Orlando Sentinel*, July 17, 1960

p.183. Arno von Moyzischewitz, 1933, Berlin Document Centre Files

p.186. The *Hawaii Times* Photo Archives Foundation, 1938

p.187, 190 & 197. Bundesarchiv Bild (Federal German Archives)

p.199. courtesy of Jeremiah Jenne

p.201. *The Boston Globe*, April 12, 1949

p.202. *Honolulu Star-Bulletin*, November 2, 1945

p.207. courtesy of Jeffrey Long, Long Brothers Fine & Rare Books, Seattle, Wash.

p.220. Vincent Starrett, *Born in a Bookshop*, (University of Oklahoma Press, 1965)

p.226. Ann Phipps Collection, Historical Photographs of China, University of Bristol

p.242. title page, *My Trip from China, via Siberia to Europe: Including Experiences in a Siberian Prison* (Tientsin: Tientsin Press, 1923)

p.243. *The Brooklyn Daily Eagle*, August 10, 1931

p.251. *The Kingsport Times* (TN), January 19, 1930

p.257. Lilian May Miller passport photo, Library of Congress, Washington DC

p.263. *Daily News* (NY), June 17, 1934

p.268. *The Evening Sun* (Baltimore, MD), February 9, 1934

p.271. *The Indianapolis Star*, March 9, 1934

p.275. *Daily News* (NY), June 4, 1934

p.277. *Daily News* (NY), June 11, 1934

p.281. *Evening Star* (Washington DC), April 19, 1931

p.285. *Chicago Tribune*, August 20, 1908

p.287. *Palladium-Item* (Richmond, VA), November 30, 1920

p.291. *The Central New Jersey Home News*(New Brunswick, NJ), May 6, 1922

p.295. Artists Rights Society (ARS), NYC

p.302. *The Houston Post*, May 1, 1922

p.313. courtesy of The Carlton Hildreth and Harry Hervey Papers, Georgia Historical Society, Savannah, GA

p.318. *The Atlanta Constitution*, May 10, 1939

p.321. *The Atlanta Constitution*, September 17, 1941

p.323. *The Philadelphia Enquirer*, March 19, 1944

p.332. *The Weekly Advocate* (Victoria, TX), October 13, 1940

p.336. Cuero Heritage Museum (TX)

p.339. courtesy of the Helen Foster Snow Papers at Brigham Young University (Provo, UT), Perry Special Collections, Harold B. Lee Library

p.341. courtesy of Sarah Keenlyside

p.352. *Daily News* (NY), August 26, 1934

p.356. Reproduced from LC Arlington, *Through the Dragon's Eyes* (London: Constable, 1931)

p.21, 25, 32, 33 (Sitwell), 41, 44, 79, 82, 129, 136 (x2), 147, 162, 166, 222, 232, 252, 283, 301, 308, 325, 326, 328, 330, 333, 334, 343, 344. public domain

p.22, 27, 29, 31, 49, 69, 70, 96, 99, 122, 217, 245, 288, 306. author's collection

front cover photo: camel train arriving at Peking postcard, author's collection

back cover postcard: Peking Railway Station postcard, author's collection

Also by Paul French:

From the bestselling author of
MIDNIGHT IN PEKING

PAUL FRENCH

DESTINATION
SHANGHAI

"Shanghai, in Mr French, has its
champion storyteller."
- THE ECONOMIST -

DESTINATION SHANGHAI
ISBN 978-988-77927-5-8
US$17.95 / £13.99

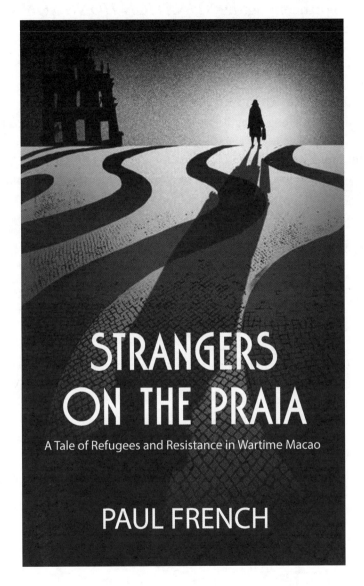

STRANGERS
ON THE PRAIA

A Tale of Refugees and Resistance in Wartime Macao

PAUL FRENCH

STRANGERS ON THE PRAIA
ISBN 978-988-79638-9-9
US$9.95 / £7.99

Forthcoming: *DESTINATION HONG KONG*

by PAUL FRENCH

Including:

A Night in a Hong Kong Bordello – Aleko Lilius, Madame Pompadour & La Belle Marie (1930)

Miss Hong Kong Goes to Hollywood – Judy Dan (1952)

A Flying Visit from Sydney's Mr Bigs – Len McPherson & Stan Smith (1966)

A Kowloon Boy who Recreated the Orient in Hollywood – Louis Vincenot (1935)

The Victorian Madams of Hong Kong – Bridget Montague & Maria Roza (1873)

Hemingway's Hotel Room – Martha Gellhorn & Ernest Hemingway (1941)

The Painted Veil in Court – The Lanes, Mr Fletcher & Somerset Maugham (1925)

A Sunday Afternoon in Hong Kong – Eunice Tietjins (1917)

Smuggling Opium from Hong Kong to Los Angeles – Tong Get Wing (1935)

A Free Frenchman in Hong Kong – Roderick Egal (1940)

Two Writers Have Dinner – Eileen Chang & JP Marquand (1955)

His Wicked, Wicked Hong Kong Ways – Errol Flynn (1932)

Bound for the Movies, Destined for Murder – Wendy Barrie & Frank Jenkins (1936)